CRIMSON AND GOLD

Luton Modern School, Luton High School for Girls
and Luton Technical School

UBI SEMEN IBI MESSIS

Anne Allsopp

Anne Allsopp

THE LUTON MODERN SCHOOL FOR GIRLS & BOYS
VOLUME TWO

The
Book
Castle

Dedication

This book is dedicated to Mary Woods who was a student at the School while it was still in the huts. She was Head Girl when the School moved into the new building and took part in the Opening Day celebrations.
After studying at University, she returned to the School as a member of Staff.
She later became a Headmistress in Shaftesbury.

First published September 2004
by
The Book Castle
12 Church Street
Dunstable
Bedfordshire LU5 4RU

ISBN 1 903747 55 4

Printed by Antony Rowe Ltd, Chippenham, Wiltshire

Contents

Chapters prior to 1919 contain material by Anne Allsopp and James Dyer

Foreword

by Sam Whitbread, Esq, JP,
Lord Lieutenant of Bedfordshire

The Luton Modern Schools opened a hundred years ago in Park Square, in a 'curious-looking building … of a temporary character' in the words of *The Bedfordshire Times and Independent.* Four years later a new, purpose-built school was opened, also in Park Square.

Two leading figures in local education were present at both opening ceremonies. One was Rowland Prothero (later Lord Ernle), Chairman of the Higher Education Sub-Committee of the County Council, becoming Chairman of Governors of the new School. The other was my grandfather, Samuel Howard Whitbread, formerly Member of Parliament for South Bedfordshire and, by 1908, Member for South Huntingdonshire, while at the same time being Chairman of the County Council's Education Committee from its formation in 1903 until his retirement in 1928.

The first school (the Luton Secondary School and Technical Institution) was opened by Mrs Wernher of Luton Hoo (her husband Harold did not succeed to the Baronetcy until 1905) and the aim of the school was to provide secondary education for boys and girls from the age of twelve upwards. The curriculum for the four-year general course included English, Geography, History, French, German, Mathematics and Physics, as well as domestic hygiene, botany, drawing and needlework. In the final two years, book-keeping, shorthand 'and other specialised commercial subjects' would be added.

In his address, Rowland Protheroe emphasised the co-operation between the County and Borough Authorities. 'Luton has taxed itself for the school maintenance to the limits which the law allows; the County has responded to the appeal with conspicuous generosity.' He described the ages of twelve to sixteen as 'the most critical period of our existence' and urged parents to make every effort to find the fees of £6 a year 'including all extras', accepting that 'the wages that the boys and girls might earn are a temptation.'

The new Luton Modern School, opened in 1908 just across Park Square, could accommodate twice as many pupils as its predecessor. The opening ceremony was performed by the Duke of Bedford, Chairman of Bedfordshire County Council, whose wife, Duchess Mary, had been a Governor of the School from its foundation. He said that the school provided 'a fresh and striking proof of that spirit of cordial co-operation for the general good, which animated the County Council and showed that Bedfordshire could unite to promote the welfare of every class.'

In proposing a vote of thanks to the Duke, Howard Whitbread highlighted the difference in Higher Education provision between Bedford and Luton. 'In Bedford there existed venerable, well-tried and efficient institutions for the promotion of higher education; in Luton they had to fend for themselves. Yet it is characteristic of Luton that it was always entering into friendly and vigorous competition with Bedford in order to show that it was the more vigorous portion of the county.'

Do we detect in these words a hint of the divisions between Luton and the rest of the County which emerge from time to time, even in our own day?

In any event it is right and proper that the centenary of the Luton Modern Schools should be marked by the publication of this comprehensive history and I can think of no more suitable authors than Dr Dyer and Dr Allsopp.

Sam Whitbread, Southill, 2004

Preface

The idea for this book took root many years ago when it became clear that, apart from newspaper reports about significant occasions, very little has ever been written about the life of Luton High School for Girls and the Grammar School for Boys. It seemed sensible, therefore, to produce a record for what would have been their centenary in 2004. Until 1919, the School was co-educational and the first chapters of the two companion volumes are therefore, very similar and include the combined work of both authors.

Similarities there may have been, but there are essential differences in the way in which the books have had to be presented. The first of these concerns the amount of material available. The boys' School, unlike the girls', was blessed in having a considerable amount of detailed information which has been collected and saved over the years. The other important difference is the way in which the lives of boys and girls have been viewed. At the beginning of the twentieth century, boys were set to follow careers but girls' lives were seen to be primarily domestic. By the time the Schools closed, perceptions were changing but 'equality' was still largely an aspiration rather than a reality. Consequently, the two books are dissimilar in both content and format. However, they really do need to be read together to get a wider picture. For example, the Dramatic Societies of the two Schools put on some splendid productions which have been described in much more detail in the book on the Grammar School.

The aim of this book has been to capture the atmosphere of the times in as accurate an historical framework as possible. Memory plays tricks and recollections of schooldays are often focused on personal experiences and not on the larger picture. It would have been tedious to record every little detail, so generalizations have sometimes had to be made. It is important to acknowledge the contribution of Patricia Gillespie (Evans) who allowed her complete set of the *Sheaf* magazines to be used. Without them, the task would have been almost impossible.

When former pupils of the Technical School heard about the research they began to share their memories and it became clear that their story also needed to be told. There is a dearth of material about the Technical School and not even a complete set of the *Shell* magazines was forthcoming. Therefore, much of the research about the Technical School has depended on personal recollections. Three former members of staff have been invaluable in this respect. Not only have they willingly given me a great deal of information but they have also had to endure my repeated questioning. To Mr Roy Ellis, Mr Ivan Jones and Mr Ralph Whalley I offer my very sincere thanks.

Acknowledgements

This book has depended on the goodwill of many different people.

Particular thanks are due to all those who have helped to gather material for this book. The main credit has to be given to Patricia Gillespie who allowed her complete collection of the *Sheaf* magazines to be used. Her husband, John, has also given me considerable help. We have taken the liberty of printing material which was originally published in the *Sheaf* in the belief that the original writers, having agreed to be 'published' once, will be happy to be published again. A great deal of material has disappeared but some records remained at the old High School building, now known as Denbigh High School. Thanks are due to the Governors of Denbigh High School (DH) who decided to transfer all their archive material to Luton Museum and Art Gallery for safe keeping. Even though most of the records have been removed, the site manager and the caretaker have continued to be on the lookout for anything which might be tucked away in some quiet corner.

I want to thank the following:

James Dyer. He has been very generous in sharing his expertise and I have enjoyed working with him in this joint project.

Elizabeth Adey, keeper of historical records at Luton Museum and Art Gallery LMAG (LM). As always, she has willingly helped in whatever way she can.

Chris Grabham, also from the Luton Museum and Art Gallery, has made a number of photographs available, while John Buckledee, editor of the *Luton News*, (LN) gave permission for these to be published. Mr Bob Norman has helped with some of the photographic material.

Mrs Elen Curran, Librarian at the North London Collegiate School (NLCS) sent information about the time when the School was evacuated to Luton.

Mrs Y. Bevan, Headteacher, and past and present members of the staff at Denbigh High School.

In November 2000, Mrs Kathy Green, organized a reunion to celebrate the 70th anniversary of the School building. She gathered together material for an exhibition and then made the collection available for this research.

Many thanks are due to the considerable numbers of former staff and pupils who have responded to my requests to write, e-mail or phone with their recollections. I do thank them most warmly. Those who have not been quoted verbatim in this book did not help in vain because all their reminiscences and anecdotes have combined to give me a feeling for the School which I would not otherwise have had. Those who wrote specific contributions include: Paula Allsopp, Jeannette Ayton, Denise Barber, Moira Burness, Margaret Currie, Molly Fardell, Helen Gething, Patricia Gillespie, Danae Johnston, Shirley Jones, Valerie Kilner, Rita Lewis, Margaret Lincoln, Maureen MacGlashan, Jennifer Moody, Jean Munn, Janice Rimbault, Leonard Rising, Margaret Rowley, Sally Siddons, Anne Simkins, Frances Smith and Lesley Southgate. I also wish to thank all those who have lent photographs; these are acknowledged beside the captions.

I am grateful to friends I see regularly who have had to endure my ceaseless questioning, particularly Rosamund Hayward (Lane), Betty McKean (Hickman) and Joan Moulsley (Day). Joan Moulsley read the early drafts of my chapters and I owe her special thanks. My husband, Basil, also read the book in its early stages; he has always supported me and has never complained about my time-consuming wanderings and writing. I am, as ever, indebted to my son, David, and his save-the-day computer skills. I will forever be grateful to Emeritus Professor Richard Aldrich who taught me all I know about historical research.

There were others who answered my telephone queries. They often phoned around themselves and came back with a network of contacts. I especially thank Fay Weighall and Mary Wilson. It is impossible to record everybody's name; many have been acknowledged in the text but there are others whose help has been invaluable.

Former members of staff have also given assistance. This was particularly appreciated when we attempted to compile a list of staff over the years. There is no complete record and the provisional list was sent around in the hope that gaps could be filled. The assistance of these members of staff is especially appreciated: Patricia Gillespie, Gwendoline Gribble, Christina Scott and Mary Woods.

When it came to researching the history of the Technical School, there was an even greater problem with a lack of written evidence. There were miscellaneous papers which surfaced at the Luton Museum and Art Gallery and Bedfordshire and Luton Archive and Record Service and some dissertations have survived. A considerable amount of material was collected by Barry Dymock of the Old Students' Association and deposited at the Library of Luton University. Alan Bullimore, from the University Library, has willingly accessed these for research.

Three former members of staff, Roy Ellis, Ivan Jones and Ralph Whalley, have given invaluable help in an attempt to reconstruct the atmosphere of the Junior Technical School. Former pupils, including Paddy Norman and Walter Rainbow, have supplied useful material, while Lois Counter and Peter Goodwin contributed interesting reminiscences.

These are but a few of the people who have helped in the production of this book. I thank them all.

Aerial view of the Modern School, dominated by the College of Technology (now Luton University), prior to its demolition in 1959. St Mary's Church beyond. (LN-LMC)

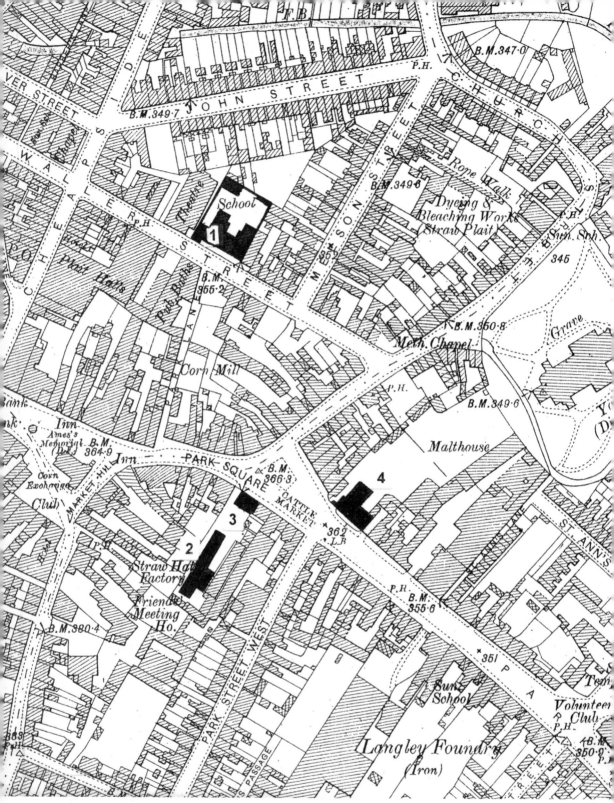

Section of Ordnance Survey map of 1901, showing the position of 1) Higher Grade School, Waller Street; 2) Luton Secondary School 1904-08 in Vyse old hat factory; 3) School Office and Headmaster's Study; 4) The White House.

Chapter One

Boys and Girls:
the Mixed School 1904–1908

I was waiting for my train on Stroud Railway Station, which is dominated by the tall chimney of the local brewery, and I could smell the unmistakable odour of hot malt. It was then that I experienced a curious sinking feeling in my stomach, and my mind went back to 1904.

My first day at School at the Luton Secondary School, a *new* school, housed in an *old* disused hat factory, a gaunt brick building in Park Square, some hundred yards from the street and almost adjacent to Green's Brewery. Having suddenly been transferred from a Board School, I attended prayers conducted by the Head, in cap and gown, and supported by a small staff, also similarly attired. Overawed somewhat by this display of academic splendour, and feeling a little home-sick, (and possibly school-sick, too) I was in no way comforted by the sickening pungent smell from Mr Green's malt, which permeated the whole neighbourhood, and that crowded the room.

It is authoritatively stated that the sense of smell is the most evocative of memory, and I well believe that this is so, for over a span of 56 years I could recall vividly my first day in that strange school.   [C.C. Bennett (1904–09)]

Luton in 1904 bore very little resemblance to the town we know today. It was a prosperous, somewhat grubby, little market town with a population in the region of 36,000. Most of its wealth came from the manufacture of hats, its labour force dominated by women. Local businessmen, aware of the dangers of basing an economy on one industry alone, and of the presence of a surplus of unemployed male workers, invited other manufacturers to the town. Among the companies which responded were Hayward Tylers, Laportes, the CWS Cocoa Factory, Vauxhall Motors, George Kent Ltd. and the Skefko Ball Bearing Company. The running of Luton was mainly in the hands of the business and professional classes, although the Crawley and Wernher families, of Stockwood and Luton Hoo respectively, showed a real interest in the welfare of the town.

From the seventeenth century, education in Luton was only available to a small number of boys and girls. Cornelius Bigland and Roger Gillingham both left bequests for the schooling of poor children from Luton, though there is no evidence that a school actually existed there. By 1706, the *Episcopal Visitations Returns* for Luton record 'a free-schole within the parish, the endowment of which is about £15 a year.' In 1709 is added 'John Swonell Master. About 50 boys.' By 1717, we are informed of 'One publick school. About 70 children well taught in it, and well Instructed in the principles of the Christian Religion, and duly attend the Service of the Church of England' and three years later, 'about 39 Boys taught therein.' John Richards in 1731 and Thomas Long in 1736 left further generous endowments for the education and apprenticing of Luton boys.

Luton had no long-established Grammar School, or things might have been different. In a will made in 1537, John Norrys of Luton left £29 to his brother Edward with the proviso that, if Edward died before the will was proven, '30 shillings is to be used for his burial, and the remaining £18 10s is to be used to build a house for a grammar school, the house to be near the church, and the parish to decide where it shall be set.' Sadly for Luton's children, Edward did not die and the school was never built!

With the introduction of Forster's Education Act of 1870, all children in Luton, as well as those in the neighbouring villages and hamlets, who had come from a labouring or working class background, had the right to elementary education. Even so, although Luton made attendance compulsory in 1874, it was still possible for a boy or girl to leave school before reaching the statutory leaving age. To do this, they only needed to apply for a Labour Certificate, which could be gained either by passing an examination or by attaining at least 250 attendances each year for five years (increased to 350 in 1900). Luton provided elementary education in some eight denominational schools and also in the nine schools set up after 1874 by the Luton School Board. There was little doubt that most children brought up in the elementary system were likely to spend the rest of their lives in it.

It was not considered appropriate for the children from the professional classes or the sons and daughters of hat factory owners or managers to attend the local elementary schools. A few might take the train each day to one of the Bedford public schools, but the majority were more likely to be enrolled locally in private schools. For boys, there was some choice: Norton House School (or College) in Havelock Road with the adjacent facilities of Bell's Close and People's Park, Grosvenor College in Rothesay Road, St Gregory's School in Down's Road, St John's College off New

Bedford Road or the larger Dunstable Grammar School founded in 1886. Girls could attend St Dominic's Convent School in Rothesay Road, described as 'a Boarding School for the daughters of Gentlemen', Luton High School in Cardiff Road (not the one described in this book) or travel to Moreton House in Dunstable, established since 1864.

It was accepted that some boys needed business skills and many of them had been able to take commercial subjects in classes held under the auspices of the County Technical Instruction Committee. It was also recognized that, in order to keep the schools running, there was a need to train teachers under the old pupil-teacher system. Luton's attitude to education was essentially utilitarian and, for most children, a basic education in the 3Rs was all that was expected.

Although elementary schooling was available for every child, secondary education was only accessible to a few in the Public and Private Schools, which were 'locked, bolted and barred' against any but wealthy parents, and a few endowed Grammar Schools. These often granted scholarships to elementary school pupils, but they were but a drop in the ocean. Many local authorities started Higher Grade Schools like the one in Waller Street, Luton, which offered boys a wider curriculum. It was highly regarded in the town, but was, strictly speaking, illegal because it was funded with money specifically allocated by the government for elementary education. There were several unsuccessful attempts to set up a Higher Grade School for girls from more 'respectable' families but, on the whole, the education of girls in Luton was confined to the traditional 'female' 4Cs: cookery, clothing, church and children.

Government Provision

In 1902 came the Balfour Act. Under the terms of this Act, the overall responsibility for education was transferred to the County Councils. Luton, however, was large enough to be a Part III authority. This meant that the Town Council was allowed to keep control over the elementary schools but Bedfordshire County Council became responsible for rural schools and secondary education. The wider concept of secondary education was familiar to the people of Bedford, who had enjoyed the benefits of the Harpur Trust, but was new to Lutonians. The Bedfordshire Education Committee and Luton Town Council lost no time in preparing plans to open a combined Day Secondary School and Technical Institution for Luton and the south of the County in September 1904. This was to provide secondary education for boys and girls during the day and technical classes for older students in the evenings. The setting up and running of the school was to be funded by Government Grants, School Fees and a one penny rate to be raised each year by the Luton Town Council.

For some years, evening classes had been successfully conducted in Luton under the direction of the Technical Instruction Committee. In future, they would be co-ordinated into a definite Institution under the direction of a Principal, who would also be the Headmaster of the Secondary School. The joint Institution would be managed by a body of Governors constituted as follows:

Elected by the Bedfordshire County Council:
Her Grace the Duchess of Bedford
A.J. Hucklesby Esq. Hat Manufacturer, JP, Mayor (5 times)
W.T. Lye Esq. Plait Dyer, JP
R.E. Prothero, Esq. MVO, (Chairman) Chairman, Higher Education Committee
R.Richmond Esq. Pharmacist, JP, (from Leighton Buzzard)
H.O. Williams Esq. Builders' Merchant, Brickmaker, JP, Mayor

Elected by the Luton Town Council:
E.Oakley Esq. Hat Manufacturer, JP, Mayor (3 times)
A.A. Oakley Esq. Provision Merchant, Mayor
C.H. Osborne Esq. Hat Manufacturer, Mayor
J.H. Staddon Esq. Hat Manufacturer, JP, Mayor
G. Warren Esq. (Vice-chairman) Hat Manufacturer, JP, Mayor
A. Wilkinson Esq. Architect, Mayor

Co-opted
W.R. Hawson Esq. Banker
Miss Amy Walmsley Principal, Bedford Training College
Mrs Alice Wernher (later Lady Wernher, then Lady Ludlow)

The school in Luton was to be a mixed one; this was not an ideological decision but one of convenience. 'It was always intended to have separate schools as soon as circumstances warranted them, but the project was delayed by the First World War, after which a separate school for girls was provided.' The official prospectus claimed that 'the education [to be] offered was for both professional and commercial life and [would] prepare the way for a University and Higher Technical Education and also for prospective teachers.' The local Chamber of Commerce welcomed 'the desirability of Luton lads [not lasses!] receiving a special training for commercial life' but, as was to be expected in the early days of the twentieth century, there seems to have been some resistance towards giving girls a better education, especially in a town where they were likely to become a life-long part of the local hat industry. This was demonstrated by a piece in the 1905 *Luton Year Book* entitled *Are College Girls Marrying Girls?* which pointed out that only 22 per cent of college girls marry after graduation, compared with 80 per cent of non-college girls who marry and have children.

Setting up the School

For its first four years, the school was housed in a temporary building which stood back from the western side of Park Square and had formerly been a straw hat warehouse run by Messrs. Vyse and Sons. £600 was spent on renovations which allowed for three classrooms, with a laboratory on the ground floor and an assembly room 57ft long and an Art and Mechanical Drawing room 60ft long on the floor above. The adjoining Brewery yard served as a playground. The Headmaster's study and school office were housed in an old cottage which stood on the frontage of the factory site, some distance from the school itself and facing onto Park Square (it subsequently served for a time as the United Omnibus Company's Office).

Three rooms on the ground floor were used for Woodwork instruction. The stairs in one of these led up to the stationery sales office and the Head's room which overlooked the street. It can be imagined what noise the Head had to endure from hammers and saws inexpertly wielded by potential craftsmen. Bicycle sheds were provided at the back of the school. It seems that, in 1904, all these buildings were owned by Mr Joseph W. Green, the brewer, who later demolished some of them in order to extend his Brewery. He negotiated a rent of £80 a year while also subscribing £100 towards the initial cost of establishing the school. Mr Green's business was also on Park Square and the earliest scholars remembered that their 'senses of hearing and smell' were deafened and tortured by the buzzing and odour which emanated from the Brewery next door.

A major consideration was the appointment of a suitable staff, and in particular a strong Headmaster or Principal. Local expectations probably favoured H.C. Middle from the Higher Grade School (a non-graduate) or J.H. Hargreaves from the Pupil Teacher Centre, but the Governors looked further afield and chose T.A.E. Sanderson. Thomas Arthur Edwin Sanderson, aged 36, was born at Litlington near Royston, Hertfordshire, where his father was the Vicar of St Katherine's Church. The family moved to Hampshire when he was four. He was educated at the City of London School from which he obtained a Beaufoy Leaving Exhibition and Major Mathematical Scholarship at Trinity College, Cambridge. He graduated in 1890 with a 1st Class degree in Mathematics. He achieved high marks, earning the distinction of being 21st Wrangler (a person placed in the first class of the mathematical tripos). Before coming to Luton Mr Sanderson had done a certain amount of coaching at military establishments including Sandhurst. Perhaps the innumerable forms that were a feature of his organization were the result of the time he spent at these. More probably, they were the signs of a neat and orderly mind.

Mr Sanderson has described the events leading up to his appointment.

Early in the summer of 1904 appeared an advertisement stating that the Bedfordshire County Council was about to open in Luton a Secondary School for girls and boys. I decided to apply for the Head Mastership. At that time I was on the staff of Bath College, a school run by a private company on public school lines.

For various reasons I did not apply till the last moment. When called for interview illness in my family made it desirable that I should not leave Bath before it was absolutely necessary. So I took a night train to London, arriving in Luton about breakfast time. Making my way through damp streets to the George Hotel I formed the impression that Luton was rather like the suburbs of Manchester. At the hotel, having asked for a room in which to change, I was shown to No. 13 – a bad omen. Many of the other candidates wore frock coats with silk hats; I had a boater, which in a straw hat town may have been one of the reasons why I was selected.

Of the ten or twelve candidates interviewed in the morning, three of us were asked to return after lunch: Mr R.S. Haydon, Mr C.C.H. Walker and myself.

The afternoon proceedings were short, and after being offered the post I was asked whether I had any special remarks to make. I replied that I hoped no school rules would be made except such as could be strictly enforced. This remark seemed to make little impression on the committee, but perhaps accounts for the fact that later on I was sometimes regarded as an ultra-strict disciplinarian.

Ronald Phillips, who joined the staff in 1927, said that 'in his earlier years, to his pupils Sanderson was a formidable figure with a striking head, a fierce dark moustache, a fresh complexion and wavy hair, but later he shaved off his moustache and assumed a more benevolent aspect.' F.M. Edwards spoke of 'his piercing eye, which could make a boy feel extremely 'small', also a powerful voice which could make the rafters ring.' Another of his first pupils, C.C. Bennett wrote, 'The Head, 'Puggy' Sanderson, was rather a terrifying figure and a strict disciplinarian. I cannot remember anyone being caned – it was not necessary. His dominating personality was quite sufficient to tame the wildest spirits.' Among the tributes paid to him on his retirement in 1933 was 'his complete impartiality … he never harried the delinquent with a nagging tongue, nor pursued the clever boy with fulsome praise.' His devotion to the School was well known: 'it is common knowledge that even during the holidays he was to be found at his post and, somehow, it seemed natural to find him there.' He was also remembered for 'a certain sternness that has sometimes led to his being misunderstood.' Sanderson admitted that he found running a mixed school very difficult and it seems that his empathy lay more with the boys than the girls. He recalled that one of his greatest reliefs was the opening of the Girls' School – 'not that the pupils gave any trouble, but I found a male staff far easier to deal with than a mixed one.'

During the summer of 1904, staff were appointed whose services would be divided between the Day and Evening classes at the Headmaster's discretion. Sanderson observed, 'This arrangement led to many difficulties, for when members were not actually teaching they could not be expected to remain on the premises and so no evening duties outside the classroom could be insisted upon. After the first year, the day and evening work were separated and the staff were treated as full-time teachers in the day school, with extra pay for any evening work they did.' Apart from Messrs Edmunds, May and Otter, who had been instructors under the Technical Instruction Committee, the staff all appear to have been appointed from out-of-town, since none of the names is familiar from the time of the Luton School Board.

Principal:	T.A.E. Sanderson MA (Maths)	Salary £300 p.a.
Senior Assistant:	E.W. Edmunds MA, B.Sc. (Classics, Science)	£200 p.a.
Assistants:	J. Bygott (English, Maths, Geography)	
	Clara S. Gardner LL.A (History, English, French, German)	
	J.B. Hoblyn ARCS (Chemistry, Physics)	
	C. Wesley Hutchinson BA (General Subjects)	
	W.E. Llewellyn (Modern Languages)	
	Frederick F. May ARCA (Art and Design)	
	Miss R.E. Moylan (French, English)	
	William Otter (Manual Instruction i.e. Handicraft)	

Admissions

An advertisement was placed in *The Luton News* on 1st September 1904 which informed its readers that:

The **Luton Secondary Day School**
will open for the First Term on
Wednesday, September 14th, 1904.
Boys and girls who desire to become
pupils at the above school
must pass an entrance examination.
Fees £1 10s 0d per term.
A Second Admission Examination will be held
on Saturday, 17th September, 1904.
Full Particulars and Entrance Forms may be obtained
of the Headmaster, at the School, or of the Undersigned.
Special Contract Tickets at reduced rates
are Issued by the Railway Companies
to Scholars journeying daily to the School.
FRANK SPOONER
Director of Education,
Shire Hall, Bedford

The *Prospectus* for the new school included these rules:

- No pupil could be admitted below the age of ten and none could stay beyond the age of 18 without special permission.
- Day pupils must live with parents, guardians or near relations or at a house approved by the governors.
- No pupil was to be admitted unless of good character and sufficient health, and who had been found fit for admission in an examination under the direction of the Headmaster. (Health certificates were introduced in 1907).
- Preference was to be given to children who resided within the Borough of Luton and the County of Bedford.
- Examinations were to be held three times a year in December, April and September. Dates to be advised in the local newspaper.
- Compulsory examinations in Arithmetic, Dictation, Composition, Reading, English Grammar, Geography or History.
- Optional examinations in Elementary French, Elementary Science and Elementary Mathematics.
- Fees – £1 10s 0d per term, Stationery and textbooks to be supplied by the authority but paid for by the scholars, as were fees for games.
- Free scholarships. These were held for two years and were renewable for the remainder of the course subject to good conduct and satisfactory progress.
- A Report concerning the pupils' progress and conduct was to be sent to parents or guardians at the close of each term.

The fees were prohibitive for the ordinary working classes but a whole new world was about to open up for children who passed the examination for free places, although the money had to be refunded if the pupil left within two years. 25 per cent of these places were offered by the Governors to Luton children in the school's first year and Bedfordshire made County Scholarships available for out-of-town children. The first scholarships were awarded to:

> R.J. Aldred; C.C. Bennett; G.L. Bond; Nellie Breed; F. Buckingham;
> Edith Fensome; G.W. Fensome; L.T. Few; Eveline Fletcher;
> Mabel Hawkes; J. Hunt; Leila King; A.E. Perry; Hilda Pilkington;
> A.T. Reeve; Marion Robinson; F.R. Simpson; W.C. Waldock;
> A.T. Wheeler; E.C. Wright.

From December 1906, all scholarships awarded by the Governors included free books and stationery, and this applied retrospectively to the scholarships already operating. In 1908, the Board of Education insisted that all fee paying Secondary Schools must provide a proportion of free places. This was usually about 25 per cent of the total pupils on roll. Failure to comply could lead to substantial cuts in grants.

Bedfordshire responded by introducing Junior County Scholarships in 1908. Over the years, money was also made available from certain local charities, notably Chew's, Bigland's and Richard's. The Bigland, Long and Gillingham trusts were combined in 1915 to provide Secondary School Exhibitions, Technical Exhibitions, University Exhibitions or maintenance allowances for 'necessitous boys and girls resident in the Borough of Luton, who have attended public elementary schools for at least the last two years.' These were still being awarded in 1966 when the Schools became the Sixth Form College. In 1918, the Bedfordshire County Council began to give Leaving Scholarships for further education based on a set examination, school records and a personal interview. These covered tuition fees and a contribution towards maintenance.

G. Rodell was a scholar at St Matthew's Day School in 1907. Hearing that two of his friends at Hitchin Road School were going in for the Secondary School entrance examination, he obtained the necessary forms and got his Headmaster, Mr G.N. Barton to sign them. He passed with sufficient marks for a free scholarship.

At the time of his retirement from Luton Grammar School in 1964, Dr John G. Dony wrote:

> The School was started when I was five years old, and in its early days it was intended mainly for those who were financially better off rather than those who might benefit from a higher education. As a child I was resigned to the fact that I could not go to the School, but got a little consolation in doing the homework for some of those who did. I was lucky as the school to which I went was not cursed with the homework abomination. Looking back, I feel that it is probably the strangest feature of my life that I taught for so long (23 years) in the school that I was unable to attend, and as I leave it the first impression of my childhood remains, namely that there are scores of boys in the school who would be better educated elsewhere and as many boys in the town who could well replace them.

There is some evidence to show that the elementary school Headteachers were biased towards which of their pupils they entered for the entrance examinations, favouring, as Dr Dony said, those from the relatively better off homes, rather than poorer children with good brains. As late as 1919, A.J. Mander, Head of Old Bedford Road School, chose half a dozen of the better class boys to sit for the Modern School Entrance Examination. These did not include Fred Dyer and Frank Potts who believed that they could do better. Together, they went to the Modern School and talked with a friendly teacher who gave them application forms. These were filled in and, in due course, they both took the exam and passed. Fred's father said he could attend if he wanted, but thought he would do better with an apprenticeship. Other relatives also urged him to get apprenticed, and so he did. Frank was also talked into an apprenticeship. For Fred, it was a mistake that he regretted for the rest of his life.

Although Mander knew that the two boys had passed, he never acknowledged the fact to either of them.

The First Students

The early Admission Books make interesting reading. According to these, 47 boys and 38 girls were admitted to the school in September 1904 and many names familiar in the history of Luton can be recognized. It would take up too much space to name them all but, as a token, the names of the first three on the list (all scholarship holders) are included here.

1. Arthur Edward Perry, 30 Victoria Street, Luton.
   Previous School: Waller Street
2. George William Fensome, 41 Waller Street, Luton
   Previous School: Waller Street
3. Nellie Breed, School House, Stopsley
   Previous School: Stopsley (Her father was C.H. Breed, the Headmaster)

Waller Street Higher Grade School was well represented, 27 of the first 85 pupils having been educated there. Other Luton elementary schools sent children, and boys and girls also came from Leighton Buzzard, Eggington and Dunstable (all conveniently close to the Great Northern Railway line). Private schools lost a few pupils but it looks as though parents were hesitant at first. However, once the new school had proved its worth, the trickle became a flood and some of the private schools went out of business. Even Waller Street began to feel the impact on its older pupils.

The Admission Books give 'father's occupation'. As has been noted, few of the ordinary men in the street could afford the fees, so it is not surprising that occupations listed are teaching, clerical posts, managers, farmers, ministers of religion, retail, etc. Owners and managers of hat factories took top place; this was only to be expected in a town where the manufacture of hats was the main source of wealth. This situation had altered only slightly by 1960 when a sociological survey of class 4A at Luton Grammar School, carried out by David H. Kennett, indicated that the only real change showed many fathers employed on the managerial staff of Vauxhall Motors replacing the declining hat industry's senior executives.

Students had to travel from all over Luton and south Bedfordshire. When places were available, students also came from north Hertfordshire. There were two convenient rail links: one was the Great Northern Railway from Leighton Buzzard, through Dunstable, to Luton and Welwyn. The other, the London, Midland and Scottish line, followed the present Thameslink route. F.M. Edwards travelled:

…twelve miles daily to and from school. The train left Flitwick station at 7.40am. School was reached at 8.15am, long before the playgrounds became crowded. The morning train was always crowded with young men and women employed in the straw hat trade; on one occasion twenty-three souls were crushed together in our compartment, normally seating ten.

Only once in four years did I miss the train. Cycling some twelve miles against a stiffish head-wind, I arrived in time for morning prayers, but unfortunately some two minutes late. Some five days later I received the white card summons to attend the headmaster's study at once. After much ranting and threats of expulsion, I was advised of dire penalties if ever it occurred again.

Lessons ended at 4.20pm and my train left at 4.47pm, giving me ample time to collect goods – ironmongery, hardware or grocery items for my parents who ran a country store. They found my school journeys most convenient in giving customers prompt service.

Trains were very fast in those days and they were very punctual. We often covered the home journey in thirteen minutes. This could not be bettered by modern engines.

The railway companies made deals concerning fares, but they were not always so accommodating in response to requests to change their timetables. On the contrary, after the first two years the school hours were changed from 9 a.m. – 12.40p.m. and 2p.m. – 4.30p.m. to 9a.m. – 12.20p.m. and 2p.m. – 4.15p.m. to make life easier for the pupils who travelled by train, particularly those from Leighton Buzzard. In 1908, trams were introduced; they ran from their depot in Park Street to Dunstable Road, New Bedford Road, High Town Road and Hitchin Road up to Round Green. No doubt some families could afford the £7 or £8 for a bicycle, but many children would certainly have walked to school.

'Feeling rather like David Copperfield', Rex Clayton made his first journey to the new Luton Secondary School in a village carrier's van. It was a cold January morning in 1908. The journey from Markyate, four miles of hilly country and over flinty roads, took over an hour. A few minutes before 9 a.m. I was put down on Park Square to make my lonely way into the converted hat factory which for ten terms had housed my predecessors. After a week or two I was allowed to cycle to and from school.

About that time Luton's new tram system came into service. We boys who cycled to school were longing to ride in those shiny tram-lines. We learned our lesson the first morning.

Luton Secondary School Opens

On Tuesday, 13th September 1904, members of the Bedfordshire County Council, Luton Town Council and numerous Civic and Religious dignitaries met for an inaugural ceremony at the Luton Corn Exchange, which was performed by Mrs Julius Wernher, later Lady Ludlow.

It was not until a week later, on Monday, 19th September, 1904, that 'Luton Secondary School met for the first time in a room, the bareness of whose walls was solely relieved by an engraving of G.F. Watt's *Sir Galahad*, most kindly presented by Miss Walmsley (Governor).' There were 85 children present, 46 boys and 39 girls.

> From the opening morning, – when groups of excited girls and boys assembled on Park Square and discussed the possibilities of the new life on which they were about to enter – to the end of the school year, when those same scholars listened with excitement, mingled with awe, to the reading of the form lists, our first year at the school was one long round of novelty and pleasure. Firstly, we had the delight of criticising the mistresses and masters, and it is only fair to add that our criticism – though quite impartial and candid, as all schoolgirl and schoolboy criticism is – was decidedly favourable. The same cannot be said of the school building, I fear. [E.B.]
>
> It was, I think, surprisingly well adapted, bearing in mind the original function of the place. There were four or five classrooms, a good chemistry laboratory, a large Art room, and a cloakroom [toilet] so well equipped that I was filled with wonder, after having experienced the contraptions which then graced the streets of Luton. [C.C.B.]
>
> We were initiated into the mysteries of many new and interesting subjects. We learnt of angles and parallel lines; made the acquaintance of the mysterious x; were delighted with the truly wonderful results we were soon able to obtain in the chemical laboratory (results as marvellous to our instructor as to ourselves, one would imagine!), and were soon deep in the study of Specific Gravity, and of Weights and Forces.
>
> The Art Room was the scene of our first drill lesson, though afterwards we were promoted to the dignity of the Plait Hall. [E.B.]

Games were at first held on a field in Crescent Road belonging to Model Farm, lent by Mr John Facer, father of one of the first pupils, H.H. Facer. Unfortunately, the field was soon required for building. The pupils were then invited to subscribe to a voluntary games fund which enabled them to hire a meadow belonging to Faunch's Farm, on the east side of Old Bedford Road almost opposite Wardown House (Museum). During the summer of 1906, the Governors purchased a plot of land in Dunstable Road, together with some buildings, from the Wesley Guild, for use as a playing field. This land was sold in 1909 to Beech Hill School. At that time, the town ended near Waldeck Road and there were three miles of open country between Luton and Dunstable.

Miss Jane Macfarlane joined the staff in 1907 to teach German and French. She later recalled:

> …the pungent, but not unpleasant, smell of hops from Green's Brewery, the Headmaster's Study and the Common Staff-room. There was, of course, a 'sick room', and I have a vivid recollection of looking after a casualty, and stretching the girl out upon a hard form – the only thing upon which she could lie down.
>
> We formed a Hockey Team among the girls and entertained our first visiting team to tea in the Woodwork Room, perched precariously upon stools and benches. We enjoyed ourselves tremendously. The boys played football, but had no teas as far as I can remember.

There was little attempt to establish a school uniform in the early days. Sanderson said that during his years in office he 'always aimed at avoiding window-dressing and at keeping the essential expenses of pupils as light as possible, for in the early years pupils often came from homes that were far from affluent. Except for a school cap there were no restrictions about dress.' Even so, when the first whole school photograph was taken in 1908, there was a definite uniformity in the boys' and girls' clothes, seen again in the celebration of King George V's coronation photographs of 1911. By the time Edith Webb started at the school in 1917, something more was expected of girls: 'The uniform consisted of a navy-blue gym-slip with braid girdle, white or cream blouse, navy-blue bloomers with linings and a straw boater complete with band, embroidered with the school badge. Other items requested were indoor shoes, shoe bag and a dictionary and a satchel.'

When the boys' and girls' schools separated in 1919, both schools had adopted distinctive uniforms, of which more will be said later.

The Curriculum and Relevant Examinations

From the beginning, it was hoped that all pupils would take the General Course, which, the prospectus stated, should last for four years. In the first two years all the pupils worked together and the subjects offered were: English, Geography, History, German, French, Mathematics, Higher Arithmetic, Geometry, Chemistry (theoretical and practical), Physics (theoretical and practical), Domestic Hygiene, Botany, Drawing, Manual Training and Needlework. During the next two years, some degree of specialization was permitted and pupils were allowed to choose two subjects from the following: Book-keeping, Shorthand and specialized Commercial subjects, Higher Mathematics and Advanced Science.

After four years, pupils could take the London University Matriculation Examination or the Junior Certificate of the London Chamber of Commerce. In July 1907, the first 30 pupils were put in for the Cambridge Local Junior Examination and 29 gained certificates. These were the school's first public examinations. A few pupils went on to do the Cambridge Local Senior exams. Matriculation was an important step up the academic ladder. It was originally intended to be a qualification for a degree course but became more and more used as a school-leaving exam and could be demanded by employers. Most issues of *The Luton Modern School Magazine* meticulously listed the name of everyone who passed these examinations. So keen was the Headmaster to record pupils' progress and to ensure their academic success, that tests were rigorously held at the end of each week. Those who failed to reach the required standard were severely chastised, and persistent offenders were threatened with expulsion.

Unfortunately, many of the people of Luton were out of tune with the concept of secondary education and successive Headteachers attempted to persuade parents to keep their children at school rather than let them leave early to take up some form of employment. Later, agreements had to be signed and fines were imposed on parents who allowed their children to leave. This was a serious problem and concerned the Education Committees, the Governors and the Staff throughout the life of the Schools.

It appears that German was the first foreign language to be taught. An article in the school magazine noted how the subject both interested and appalled the pupils. 'How we struggled with the unfamiliar guttural sounds, and sighed in despair as we made the acquaintance of 'das kleine Madchen, Anna' and 'der gute Knabe, Karl'.' French came onto the curriculum in the second year and then the pupils struggled 'to produce French vowels correctly … faces underwent various contortions until the shape of the mouth was considered passable.' By 1909, there was a demand for Latin and pupils began to struggle with the complexities of its grammar:

> O genie of the Grammar Land,
> Take thy pupils now in hand,
> Lead us to thy dread abode.
> Teach us now the rules of prose,
> And verbs that govern every clause,
> Make us understand.
>
> [Balbus]

At the end of the First World War, with anti-German feelings running high, and following the recommendations of a Board of Education report, the Governors declared:

That, as from the Autumn Term, 1918, French shall be the first foreign language taken in the Luton Modern School', and 'That for a second foreign language the pupil shall have the choice of German or Latin but, as a general rule, a second language cannot be taken before entering Form III, and only then on showing aptitude for languages, and providing the pupil is remaining at school for at least a further two years.

Readers will notice that religious education is also omitted from the school syllabus, and remained so until 1920, by which time the Boys' and Girls' schools had separated. When challenged, Sanderson replied

> I am not in favour of introducing Scripture teaching, because I am very much afraid of introducing hypocrisy. My experience of the instruction in boys' schools is that it has done more harm than good. There is the fact that some who are teaching it are not doing so from conviction, but simply because they are more or less compelled. Then I think Luton is a more ethical place than others, and there is a stronger sectarian feeling in Luton than in many other places.

At the Girls' Modern School in 1920, Miss Sheldon held different views, stating that she was strongly in favour of some Biblical teaching. At present, the children could be given no such knowledge, but it should be available to them if it could be given without dissension. She knew of no other girls' secondary school where instruction on the words of the Bible was not given, but personal feelings must not run away with the teacher. She knew where it was taught by people of various denominations, but all were most careful not to show their feelings, and it would have been dishonest to do so. Following a lengthy debate, the Joint Governors decreed that religious education should be introduced into both schools from September 1920.

In the early days, drill, which was traditionally thought to improve discipline, was on the timetable. There was no particular place for teaching this. If the weather was fine it might be in the Brewery yard, but classes could also find themselves in the Art Room, the Plait Hall or the Corn Exchange. On rare occasions, space was even found in the Town Hall (this was the one which was burnt down in 1919).

> It mattered little to us pupils in which building it was held. Either involved a few minutes' walk which was eagerly looked forward to. Then these public buildings were not so secluded as the Town Hall; little surprises inevitably occurred. Once in the Town Hall the girls were considerably startled to see a man emerge from a small recess in one of the corners. It was afterwards discovered that he had been attending the clock; but at the time, he was regarded as a most mysterious person, and naturally our nerves, and consequently the steadiness of our drill, suffered from such paralysing shocks.

The children had no objection, as the few minutes extra walk meant shorter lessons. One prepared for [drill] by 'simply removing the coat, and possibly even the waistcoat, in the case of the more enthusiastic.' 'Weird and wonderful garments' were fashioned in Needlework classes and 'many a test tube and beaker were smashed in the Laboratory.' In the Art Room 'drawing lessons seldom occurred without many distractions. Desks would suddenly tilt, pots of water would be accidentally upset, and sometimes singing lessons were conducted on the other side of a curtain.'

From these accounts and from the reminiscences of Edith Webb and other pupils, it appears that behaviour was not always exemplary. Apart from the usual writing out of lines, punishments included detention and suspension. C.C. Bennett noted that the School 'was co-educational, and we got on well with the girls. We had two or three women teachers with whom we did not get on quite so well … I recall my embarrassment and anger on being ordered by one of them to brush my hair before coming to class.'

Starting a tradition

Sanderson noted that 'one of the main advantages of starting a new school was the absence of tradition. I was able to introduce my own fads such as weekly examinations, one-way traffic, and so on, without treading on the heels of precedent.' Rowland E. Prothero, Chairman of the Bedfordshire Higher Education Committee and of the School Governors, who was later described as 'the father of this great school', explained the part he played in this by giving the school its badge and its motto.

> The badge consists of three ears of corn loosely bound together. I meant it to connect this new foundation with an ancient monastic establishment in the neighbourhood, which had been conspicuous for keeping alight the lamp of learning during the Dark Ages. In the fine parish church of St Mary's in Luton is the tomb of one of the abbots of St Albans, Abbot John of Wheathampstead. From this monument are taken the ears of corn which were his canting arms. But monastic institutions were unpopular in Luton, and the ears of corn, with their stalks might have been unacceptable, if they had not also represented the material of the straw-plaiting industry on which the commercial prosperity of the town had been founded. The motto links together badge and school, by the reward which awaits the labour alike of sower and teacher. Without a sowing, neither soil nor mind will yield harvest. This is tensely expressed in the Latin motto: *Ubi semen, ibi messis* (Where the seed, there shall the harvest be).

Since Prothero wrote this, it has been shown that the arms in the church are not those of Abbot John of Wheathampstead but are in fact those of William of

Wallingford, Abbot of St Albans from 1476 to 1492.

At first the words *Luton Secondary School* were written below the badge but, in 1908, these were removed and the motto took their place. This idea of sowing seed and reaping a harvest became a recurring theme in the ethos of the school. However, academic success was not to be the only harvest; the school was expected to produce good citizens who would always place public duty before private interests and should encourage real sportsmen and women who would always play the game. These were certainly high ideals and they well suited the spirit of the age.

Ronald Phillips wrote that:

> Among the many features of Mr Sanderson's administration one or two may be noted here. He instituted the unusual system of weekly examinations, whose chief merit was that it eliminated the end-of-term rush for the masters and the end-of-term inactivity among the boys. Another feature, which also eased the burdens of the teaching staff, was the system of coded reports, which made it possible for a master to do the whole of his reports in one period. Noteworthy too was his absence record system whereby a check was kept every period upon attendance. This proved so effective and easy to work that it still [1960] remains in place.

The efforts to establish a successful school were appreciated by His Majesty's Inspectors, Mr Westaway and Miss Crosby. After the first inspection in 1906, they congratulated Sanderson on the excellence of much of the work. They also took up the idea of building a tradition and hoped the pupils would develop their 'social instincts' by sharing in the corporate life of the school.

Two of the pupils who joined the new school when it opened in 1904 were Fred Buckingham and Dora Middle, daughter of the Higher Grade School Headmaster. Although the school entered no pupils for public examinations in 1906, the year that they left, they were to become the first old boy and girl of the school to obtain degrees. He gained a B.Sc. in engineering at London University in 1913 and she a BA in 1914. Essie Keating, who left three years later in 1909, went on to University College, Reading, where she also gained a BA in 1914. Lucy Stafford joined the school from 1906 until 1912 and followed Essie to University College, Reading, to obtain her BA. A.T. Reeve, the school's first Royal Scholar, was awarded the Forbes Medal for Botany at the Royal College of Science in 1913. He was placed first in the First Class in the Botany Division at the examination for the Associateship of the College. In 1911, Nellie Breed and Margereta Harris were awarded Teachers' Certificates from Homerton College, Cambridge. Ethel Janes and Constance Breed emulated them in 1913. Frank Milner Leighton (1906–14) was the first pupil to be awarded an Open Scholarship to Selwyn College, Cambridge, worth £40 per annum, and later, in 1913, an Open Scholarship worth £60 to Trinity Hall, Cambridge. He obtained a First in Chemistry after five years' war service, followed by a B.Sc. at London University. C.J. Nixon was awarded a Mitchell Scholarship (value £40) at the City and Guilds Technical College, Finsbury, in 1914. The following year, Dorothy Currie and A.E. Perry received BA degrees from London University.

The School's temporary buildings in the hat factory were overcrowded and inconvenient, and work began on a new building in Park Square. On 6th April 1908, just a month before the new School was due to open, the old School was burgled. The Headmaster's office had been closed for the night soon after the evening classes finished. The Caretaker, Mr T. Hooker, locked up the premises and made his way home. In the meantime, the burglar, who clearly knew the layout of the building intimately, hid himself in the Woodwork rooms below. He then let himself into the Headmaster's room, without tampering with the lock. He rifled the drawers of the Head and his Clerk, taking money and stamps, and he then broke into the Stationery Office. Having acquired about £4.9s (£4.45), including 30s (£1.50) collected by the pupils for the Bute Hospital Fund, he slipped the catch of the front door, let himself into the street, and closed the door behind him.

Chapter Two

The New Building
1908–1919

The school had rapidly outgrown the temporary premises. Back in 1903, the Bedfordshire County Council had obtained a mortgage for a new building on the eastern side of Park Square, some fifty yards from its junction with Church Street, on what is now the Luton University frontage. This had been the site of 'Park Square House' or 'The White House' as it was more commonly known, with its extensive garden backing onto St Mary's churchyard. It was purchased from the old established local brewing family, the Burrs, whose Brewery adjoined it to the south. The County Council invited architects to submit outline design proposals for the new school. Some 200 were submitted, but only six were chosen to compete for the contract. The trade magazine *The Builder* criticized the Council for limiting the competition, asserting that the best interests of the Bedfordshire public were not being served. A minority of Councillors agreed and some architects complained, to no avail. The architects Spalding and Spalding were chosen, and they produced plans for a three-storey building, designed to accommodate 300 pupils. During the day, this would house the Secondary boys and girls and, in the evening, the Technical students. In 1938, after all the Secondary children had moved either to Alexandra Avenue or to Bradgers Hill, the Technical pupils remained in Park Square. Only a chestnut tree survived from the old 'White House' garden, and stood in the new playground, providing shade and conkers for a generation of pupils, until it was unceremoniously uprooted in 1936 to make way for engineering workshops.

The formal opening of the new school was by Herbrand, 11th Duke of Bedford, on Friday, 1st May 1908. He was accompanied by Mary, Duchess of Bedford, who had been a Governor of the school from its inception. The ceremony was described at length in *The Luton News* for 7th May 1908:

> The buildings have been erected by the Bedfordshire County Council, under whose jurisdiction in all matters of higher education Luton remains and in whose control the school is vested. No better indication of the fact that the new school is a county institution could be needed, perhaps, than the presence at the opening ceremony of representatives from all parts of the county.
>
> The large central hall of the new building (measuring 64 feet by 36 feet) provides seating for some hundreds of people, but it was not large enough to seat all who had obtained invitations to the ceremony and, when the Duke of Bedford, attended by representatives of the County Council, the Borough and the School Governors, stepped on to the platform prepared to hand over the keys to the Governors, the two circular galleries, in addition to the body of the hall, were crowded. His Grace took the chair, and was supported by the Mayor (Councillor Harry Arnold), Mr S. Howard Whitbread MP (chairman of the Beds Education Committee), Mr Rowland Prothero (chairman of the School Governors), Councillor George Warren JP, Mr W.W. Marks (clerk of the Beds County Council), Mr T.A.E. Sanderson MA (Headmaster) and Mr Frank Spooner BA (secretary to the Governors).

The newspaper recorded the names of more than a hundred special guests, which included Bedfordshire and Luton councillors, local dignitaries, clergy, headteachers and representatives of the architects and contractors (Messrs. A. Lewin and Son of Kettering). The scholars and teaching staff filled the galleries. After a brief speech, the Duke of Bedford declared the building open and handed the key to Mr Prothero 'in the confident expectation that the Governors would administer the School, on behalf of the County Council, with energy and with success to the very great profit and advantage of the inhabitants of the southern portion of the county.'

In reply, Rowland Prothero observed that:

> …they had spent some four years in temporary premises. Those four years had not been wasted. They had gathered around them a staff of teachers who were second to none, even in Bedfordshire, which was famous for its educational establishments. The organising power and directing ability of the Headmaster and the zeal and enthusiasm of his assistants had laid the foundations firmly for their future advance.

Prothero explained to the pupils that it was within their power to 'create an atmosphere in which nothing mean, cowardly, despicable, nothing that could not bear the light of day should thrive or find existence.' He hoped that they would remember the school with gratitude 'for the strength and firmness it had given to

Luton Modern School, Park Square. (A.C. Jordan)

their moral character.' He told the parents that giving their children a sound education was the 'best commercial investment' they could make and he pleaded with employers to give the young people a chance to develop their talents, to become better sons and daughters, husbands and wives, fathers and mothers, citizens 'of no mean city' and custodians 'of a mighty Empire'.

Councillor George Warren noted that this was a high day, something some of them had been dreaming about for a number of years, and now their dreams had been realized.

> He was glad it had been pointed out that the institution was erected not only for Luton but for South Beds. There seemed to be an idea the Modern School was intended specifically for Luton, but that was not so. Facilities had been provided for scholars to come in from the villages and towns outside Luton. He hoped it would be well understood that they did not desire in the least to injure the

excellent work that was being done at the Dunstable Grammar School under Mr Thring …

After the opening ceremony the principal guests were entertained at the Town Hall by the Governors of the School. Slaters, the well-known caterers of Park Square, were entrusted with the arrangements, and the manner in which they carried them through reflected upon them the greatest credit. The entrance hall was very prettily decorated, and, in the Council Chamber, the effective arrangement of a buffet along the whole length of the Chamber, and the placing of charmingly decorated tea tables about the room, gave it a very inviting appearance. The Duke of Bedford and a large number of out-of-town visitors enjoyed the dainty spread.

The New Building Described

From *The Luton News* 7th May 1908:

A large number of the guests took advantage of the opportunity given to all to inspect the buildings, and on every hand expressions of admiration were heard. The great central hall, which stands in the heart of the Park Square block, and covers quite half the ground floor, was greatly admired. Few members failed to ascend to the first and second balconies which surround the hall, and from those eminencies gained a bird's-eye view of the animated scene below. The splendid lighting of the hall also called for much comment. Daylight pours in through glass in the slopes and in the ends of the roof, and yet further streams of light filter in through the glass doors and partitions that shut off the class-rooms from the central hall.

Great interest was also taken in the class-rooms which surround the central hall. A full description of these may be interesting. In the front of the building, on the ground floor, are the physical laboratories, the physical lecture room, and a class-room. To the rear are also three class-rooms of similar type, two of which may be thrown into one by opening double, sound-proof sliding doors. On the floor above, the arrangement of class-rooms is almost identical, but the rooms open on to a spacious balcony instead of on to the floor of the central hall. Similarly, on the next floor, there are six class-rooms. Four of them, however, are for special purposes. Two of the three overlooking Park Street are fitted with a chemical laboratory and a chemical lecture-room. The laboratory is fitted with a heavy concrete floor, and is fitted with benches for chemical experiments. Two of these three class-rooms, which overlook the rear playgrounds, and have a north-easterly aspect, have been fitted especially as art rooms.

Without exception the class-rooms throughout the building are splendidly lighted by extensive windows. But, in this respect, the art rooms have been very specially favoured. Massive plate-glass windows provide the maximum of north-easterly light – the light most favourable to art class work – and ensure a minimum of shadow.

Experts, who were certainly well represented amongst the visitors, were struck mostly by the fact that everything has not been sacrificed to provide a school of well-lighted class-rooms. In a truly extraordinary manner, every inch of space has been utilised, and the Headmaster, the male and female teachers, the stationery and general office staff, and the caretaker, are all provided with suitable rooms for their special purposes. There are also separate boys' and girls' entrances, leading from Park Street by lengthy corridors to washing-rooms, cloak-rooms and lavatories.

To illustrate the Headmaster's methodical attention to detail in the new school, every class-room has been fitted with a bell, attached electrically to the school clock, which will ring automatically at the beginning and end of every lesson.

Much attention was also given to the playgrounds, at the rear of the main block of buildings, in which a manual block has also been erected. [Later, affectionately known as the Ark.] This block consists of four rooms – two on the upper floor for cookery and needlework, and two on the ground floor for woodwork. The upper rooms are only accessible from the girls' side of the building by an asphalted, covered way. Similarly, the woodwork rooms can only be approached from the boys' side.'

By 1933, the ground-floor of the 'Ark' had been relegated to hold the school's entire stock of text-books with, above, a mixture of class-room, museum, library and secondary dining-room.

At the end of 1908, the insurance for the new building and its fittings was set at £8,000, with the movable furniture, books, maps and utensils etc. insured for £2,000. The premium for the £10,000 was £7.10s.0d (£7.50) per annum.

The Headmaster summed the new building up succinctly when he observed that 'it was designed for use rather than beauty, and proved a great boon after our temporary home which had by that time become inconveniently crowded.'

The children moved over from the old temporary building on the opposite side of Park Square on the following Monday, 4th May 1908, and it is recorded that, on that opening day, every one of the 170 pupils on the books was present. The report in *The Luton News* added 'the children all wore the regulation head-gear, the girls in their wide-brimmed 'boaters', each trimmed with a black band and badge, looking very smart. The boys, all wearing dark caps and badges, also looked much smarter than in the old days, when any kind of tweed cap might be seen. Most of the girls also wore cream blouses and red scarves ornamented with the school crest. Parents present at the opening ceremony on Friday probably noticed the effectiveness of this costume.'

Staff

Over the years, staff came and went. Some stayed for a short while but others were there long enough to make their mark and to become part of the history of the School. Of the original staff, the Headmaster, Thomas W.E. Sanderson (1904–33), Mr Frederick F. May (1904–36) and Mr William Otter (1904–33) stayed for the longest time. Mr Otter came out of retirement from 1941–44 to help during the wartime staff shortage. Also from the original staff, Mr John B. Hoblyn, Head of Sciences, left in 1915 to become chief chemist for Vauxhall Motors.

Edith Webb, who joined the School in 1917, has written a colourful description of the staff as she knew them.

> Since it was wartime, the staff had been very much depleted and places were filled by rather unusual characters. Geography was taught by an Irish clergyman, M.W. Thompson, nicknamed 'The Parson', whose temper was very uncertain and who constantly threatened 'to put you down in the book' [detention]. 'Granny Wheeler' was a little old lady who crept around. [Miss E.S. Wheeler was at the school for two months during 1917.] In their classes discipline was very lax – a favourite trick of the boys was to make pellets of blotting paper dipped in the ink wells and to catapult them onto the ceiling from the end of a ruler. Other members of staff were of sterner stuff. 'Ma' Bell [Miss C.B. Bell] taught Geometry. She wore a green velvet dress, had flaming red hair and a temper to match. Mr E.J. Taylor taught German. He was red-haired also and had a violent temper. I heard much later that he 'came into money' and was taken to school in a chauffeur-driven Rolls Royce! Miss C.K. Thomas [languages] was a diminutive Welsh woman – a strict disciplinarian who had even the tallest boy under her thumb. Freddie May taught art and was invariably dressed in ginger-coloured Harris tweed. Miss C.D. Rose took gym in the hall. The equipment consisted of a few balls, bean bags and benches. Needlework and cookery classes taught by Miss H.G. Forsaith were held in a small building in the playground known as the 'Ark'.

Looking back in 1954, T.A.E. Sanderson wrote in *The Bedfordshire Magazine*:

> What I owe to the staff would take too much space to describe in detail, but I must mention Mr Hoblyn who was responsible for our early scholarship successes, and Mr Forbes who was able to imbue his colleagues with a co-operative spirit which before his time [1908] was sometimes conspicuously absent. I was lucky too in the chairmen under whom I worked. First Lord Ernle [R.E. Prothero], whose principle was that the man at the wheel should be interfered with as little as possible; then Mr H.O. Williams, who always consulted me before each Governors' meeting; and lastly Mr Harry Arnold, who never gave me any trouble

Staff of the Modern School 1908. Standing: F.F. May (Art), Miss E. Webb, Mr W. Otter (Woodwork), Mr G.J.Denbigh (Science), Miss J. Macfarlane, Mr J. Bygott (English, Mathematics), Miss E. St S. Poulton. Seated: J.B. Hoblyn (Science), Miss C.S. Gardner (Senior Mistress), T.A.E. Sanderson (Headmaster), E.W. Edmunds (Senior Master), A. Kirsch (French,German). *(LMC)*

at all. Then there was H.M.Inspector Mr F.W. Westaway whose visits I always cordially welcomed. Discussions with him usually ended with one of us converting the other to his point of view; in the rare cases where we failed to agree he would always leave the final decision to me, saying that I knew more about local conditions than he did. Last, but by no means least, I must mention my secretary, Mr H.J. Jeffs, who came to me straight from school and served me faithfully for some 25 years. No hours were too long for him, no tasks too exacting. I owe him more than I can say.

Charles Wareham added a postscript: 'No one ever got to see Mr Sanderson without passing John Jeffs' scrutiny!' Mention should perhaps be made at this point of Mr Andrews, the School caretaker, and Skylark, his deaf and dumb assistant. The latter's

Emporium was the broom-and-bucket shed by the rear entrance to the boys' cloakroom. Another early caretaker was Mr Hooker, known to everyone as 'Policeman'.

The staff of the Modern School were naturally concerned about their salaries. In 1913, certain members of staff had attended a meeting with the Governors in order to appeal for a rise. Mr Edmunds spoke on their behalf. He reminded them of the importance of the School to the life of the town and claimed that the standard of work done there was as high, and measured by average was probably higher, as that done at the Bedford Modern (where some masters were said to earn more than £250 p.a.). Edmunds then went on to ask them to recognize the dignity of the teaching profession and the high standard of personal life and character which was expected of them, pointing out that the next generation would reap the benefit of their 'high character' and 'expert knowledge'.

The following salary scales will not make happy reading for women in the twenty first century, but unequal pay for teachers was par for the course until the middle of the twentieth century.

		Minimum	Maximum
1908			
Men	graduates	£150 x £5	£180
	non-graduates	£120 x £5	£150
Women	graduates	£120 x £5	£150
	non-graduates	£100 x £5	£125
1914			
Men		£150 x £10	£200
Women		£120 x £10	£160
1917			
Men			£220
Men with special responsibilities			£280
Women			£180
1918			
Men		£200 x £10	£360
Women		£160 x £10	£300

(These amounts included special War bonuses)

Teachers in Training

At the beginning of the twentieth century, the pupil teacher system was still the main route taken by girls and boys who wished to become teachers. The first step was to become a monitor in an elementary school. Those who were judged to be competent could then be apprenticed as pupil teachers. This meant that they would have to teach for up to 25 hours a week, but were also to receive tuition themselves. From 1897, instruction was provided at the Pupil Teacher Centre in Waller Street, Luton, at first under Mr T.E. Margerison MA and, from 1899, Mr J.H. Hargreaves. At the conclusion of their apprenticeships, pupil teachers could become uncertificated teachers or, if they had obtained the Queen's (or King's) Certificate, progress to a Training College.

One of the criticisms of the pupil teacher system was that boys and girls received all their instruction within the elementary school system and then went on to work in that same system. Critics claimed that a secondary education would produce a better class of teacher and everything began to change when secondary education was provided. The first effect was that monitors were admitted to the secondary school on half fees; in 1904, three boys and 11 girls were allowed this concession. A concession it may have been, but parents whose children had been earning ten shillings a week as monitors, were now faced with the need to feed and clothe them as well as finding fees. Nellie Breed, whose father was Headmaster at Stopsley and had himself come up through the pupil teacher system, was one of the first pupils to benefit, and passed her London matriculation in July 1908.

In 1908, the Bedfordshire Education Committee complied with government legislation and began the student teacher scheme. Instead of trainee teachers coming through the elementary system, they had to come from secondary schools. Maybe this was an improvement in some respects, but the door was firmly slammed in the faces of girls and boys who were unable to go to the secondary school for whatever reason. From 1908, Luton Modern School was involved with this scheme. Pupils who committed themselves to teacher training became Bursars. This meant that they received grants during their last year at school and then began their training as student teachers under the auspices of the Bedfordshire County Council.

In July 1908, the Pupil Teacher Centre in Luton was closed. During the 11 years of its existence, the Waller Street Centre had taken 200 students, of whom 168 were known to be teaching, including 44 who had also had College training.

Sports and Games

Recalling the opening years of the School, Mr Sanderson observed: 'the school curriculum made no provision for games: they were not even mentioned. This did not trouble me. I held, and still hold the opinion that games and classroom work should be quite distinct, and in no circumstances should the former be allowed to interfere with the latter.' Later he claimed that this was a mistake and looked forward to a time when games would form an integral part of the school curriculum, where everyone would be obliged to take part unless they had an exemption on medical grounds. In a retrospective article written 20 years after his retirement, he seems to have reverted to his original opinion. He noted that 'soccer was started, mainly because the father of one of our boys, Mr Facer, was kind enough to lend us a field for the purpose.' In spite of Sanderson's misgivings, games, which were played on Wednesdays and Saturdays, soon became an established part of school life. They were compulsory on Wednesday afternoons (officially designated a half-holiday) but not on Saturdays unless you were part of a school team. Ronald Phillips has recorded that, on Sports Day, the Head was keenly interested in the timing of the various events and did not approve if the programme was not completed in its allotted span. With the other out-of-school activities he had little sympathy, so that during his regime very few clubs or societies existed.

Playing Fields

As already mentioned, the School's first official playing field was, from 1906, at Beech Hill (Dunstable Road) but, in 1908, Sir Julius Wernher of Luton Hoo provided a site, on favourable terms, off Trapp's Lane (now Cutenhoe Road) in West

Modern School boys and girls (left and centre) gather for the Coronation celebrations in Luton Hoo Park, 22nd June 1911. All are wearing straw boaters and hats specially provided for the occasion. *(A.E. Bodsworth)*

Hill Road. This was to be the School's recognized Sports Ground until 1922, when Lady Wernher gave the land to the Borough of Luton as a Park, in memory of her son, Alexander Pigott Wernher, of the 1st Welsh Guards, who was killed in action in 1916. Games at Trapp's Lane (West Hill) 'made steady, if slow, progress. Tennis courts were laid; and a cricket pitch was levelled; and for several years we were able to engage a cricket professional for the summer months.'

Drill instructors were appointed for the first time in September 1910, Miss C. Howland for the girls, and Major J.H. Plummer for the boys. Previously, exercises had been superintended by various members of the teaching staff. The First World War upset the sports programme for several reasons. The masters who took the keenest interest in games were the first to enlist: Drill Instructor J.H. Plummer, Mr J.M. Forbes and Mr Ernest I. Barrow who was killed in France in 1916. Sergeant Major C. Kitchener was appointed Drill Instructor from 1917–18 on the grounds that, since he had been a machine-gunner during the War, he would be better able to control the boys. He had to wear a uniform, and his duties included discipline in the playground and supervision of cleaners and caretakers.

LEFT Modern School girls doing Drill in the School yard. *(LN/LM)*

Speaking at Speech Day in March 1919, Mr Sanderson observed:

> In 1914 the military took possession of our field for trench-digging, and of the hut which served as a cricket pavilion. This hut came to an untimely end, being mysteriously burned to the ground one Saturday evening. The President of the Board of Agriculture was appealing to the Country to increase food-production, so a portion of the field was ploughed and planted with potatoes. Many of the boys did good work, first in erecting a fence, and later in trenching a part of the ground. The venture didn't appeal to them quite as forcibly as I could have wished, but we succeeded in lifting some five or six tons of potatoes; enough to supply the school kitchen for a year and leave a considerable quantity for disposal. Thus for a time games have been practically in abeyance. Moreover the restricted train-service necessitated the abandoning of the mid-week half-holiday; and this alone did much to dampen athletic enthusiasm.

After the War there was no man on the staff officially responsible for boys' drill, physical training or games until the appointment of Mr H.H. Horseman in 1924. The girls were not affected, Miss D.C. Rose being responsible for their sporting activities from 1912 to 1919.

School Houses

From 1913, the boys were divided into four Houses for inter-house sports; these were somewhat innocuously named Bees (yellow), Grasshoppers (green), Hornets (brown) and Wasps (red). How these names were chosen remains a mystery. C. Wynne Parry, writing in 1954, quoted 'one popular theory', that during a discussion on naming the Houses, one Governor said: 'My name begins with a B; let's call one house the Bees.' Upon this the other Houses are said to have received their names by analogy. 'Such stories are usually apocryphal. There may be more in the unflattering theory that someone, believing that schoolboys are unpleasant creatures, found the names of hostile creatures to suit them', though one can hardly call grasshoppers hostile! The girls had three Houses for hockey, named after birds: Pelicans (purple), Eaglets (green) and Ravens (orange).

Football

The School opened its doors in September 1904 and, before the end of October, had formed its first football club. Difficulties were swept aside: a school without a football team was somewhat anomalous, a character and reputation had to be made, and on a precious but diminutive piece of ground in Crescent Road the boys set about their task. How long, they wondered, would it take to match themselves against the older schools in the district?

In 1906–7, the move to the sports ground at Beech Hill, with the luxury of a small pavilion, gave the team a new impetus. This became evident in 1907–8 with the best season to date. More boys began to take part, perhaps helped by the first official School jerseys: blue with red and gold collars and cuffs. There were inter-house games and, in time, the School teams were able to organize matches against Crescent Football Club, Dagmar House School at Hatfield, Dunstable Grammar School, Hitchin Grammar School, St Albans Grammar School, Westbourne Club, Vauxhall Juniors and other clubs.

In September 1908, the School moved to the new ground in West Hill and there was ample room for expansion. A Form Competition was introduced and a School 'league' formed in which almost every boy in the School took part.

Although there were many boys keen to play, it appears that there were not always enough enthusiastic supporters, judging from this appeal from Frank Facer in the School Magazine in 1913.

> It is not the boys who play who are at fault; because who can deny that the play is generally full of enthusiasm? But where are the supporters? Why, even at the last match there were not half a dozen boys down at the pitch; and again at the Hitchin match there were, in fact, more masters than boys looking on … Now, this is not the state of affairs which should exist, and I think it is quite time the lower school should rally and help the School to obtain as good a name on the sports-field as it holds for school-work.

The War was to have a devastating effect on the School's football. Someone signing himself 'Passiton' wrote a scathing article for the *School Magazine*.

> The Art of football at School has disappeared since the War began. Matches arranged at School have been played only amongst the 'Inner Circle' …
>
> Come Moderns, buck up, let us have the old fighting spirit back again. Nowadays boys have done nothing but slack. And what is the alternative use a fellow wishes to make of his time? Getting on a bike armed with a muslin net, and catching 'bugs'! Is this a true picture of a Modern boy? I fear that it is, and it makes the outlook for school games, such as cricket and football, a very gloomy one. Come, it is not too late; let us turn into the old and proper paths, and, above all, learn to put 'the School' before our own miserable selves.

One cannot help but sympathize with those hundreds of bug-hunters who, throughout the School's existence, found kicking a bladder of air around for an hour, an utterly futile and mind numbing exercise!

Cricket

The beginnings of school cricket were fraught with difficulties. The lads were all 'new boys' and the first task was to find out who could play. In many cases, theirs was not always cricket of the orthodox style! A major difficulty was to get equipment and to find a ground. The first season in 1905 consisted mostly of practice on the Moor with the aid of a few stumps and borrowed bats. Surprisingly, by the end of the summer, they had developed into a very fair side. The next year they were able to play at Faunch's Farm in Old Bedford Road with better equipment. The lads put in hours of hard labour to get the pitch into good condition, and benefited from the coaching of Messrs. E.W. Edmunds, J.B. Hoblyn and C.W. Hutchinson. The team was well assorted with fast and slow bowlers, sloggers and stone wallers, and all madly keen on their cricket. Actual matches were few, their main opponents being Bury Park Club and Dagmar House School at Hatfield.

Cricket was soon taken very seriously and, prior to the First World War, the services of a professional coach were made available. Accounts in the *School Magazine* give blow-by-blow records of matches and there are detailed lists of batting averages. The masters were also keen and played in their own team against the boys. Although the school had a cricket pitch at Trapp's Lane (West Hill) until about 1920 and, from 1925, at Chaul End, they quite often played home matches on the better prepared upper sports ground at Wardown Park. During the wet summer of 1912, they had net practice for the first time, with extra evening coaching. Also, that season, the Chairman of the School Governors, Mr Prothero, invited the team to his home beside the Ouse at Oakley to play cricket against his village team, and enjoy an afternoon of boating, swimming and refreshments in a beautiful garden.

By 1916, the war was having an adverse effect on the cricket season. The team had no professional coach and the boys had to do the best they could for themselves with help and advice from the masters. It was observed that 'as a whole the boys are small in size and possess little knowledge of the finer points of the game. However, there is no lack of energy and enthusiasm, and many of the house matches have proved extremely exciting.'

As well as house matches, the boys played against Forman's Cricket Club, Hitchin Grammar School, Luton Town Cricket Club, St Albans Grammar School and the Old Boys.

Hockey

Not to be outdone, the girls played hockey although, if the accounts in the school magazine are to be believed, the standard of play in the early days was not high. There were matches between the three Houses: Pelicans, Eaglets and Ravens. An article in the school magazine pokes gentle fun at these 'hockey birds', although it is reassuring to see that the piece was written by 'two pelicans' and not by any of the boys.

The most striking feature of the hockey bird is the exceeding rarity of the male specimens, and this remote part of the globe has failed to produce a single one. This doubtless, accounts for the irrepressible loquacity which invariably attends their social debates and migrations … It is perhaps surprising that creatures possessed of such superb intellectual powers should, every half-holiday, become entirely oblivious to everything except the ecstasy of pursuing a white speck over a surface of muddy ground. What a waste of energy it is! And what lack of common sense it shows. Maybe these creatures will one day wake up and resume a more natural mode of pleasure. Personally we think it will be an exceedingly long time.

Some of the girls who were keen hockey birds were Lucy and Pamela Stafford and Winifred and Dorothy Burley. Matches were played against Old Girls and also Hitchin Girls' Grammar School, Kent's, Moreton House in Dunstable, Stockwood Ladies, St Helena's from Harpenden and Stopsley School. A memorable game in which the School team lost 5–0 to Hitchin Girls' Grammar School was played on 1st April 1914 and was reported, in verse, in the *Luton Modern School Magazine*.

Did dainty oread or woodland fay
    Dance with more lightness in elysian glades
Than leapt with hope, that sunny April day.
    Eleven Luton maids?

But lo! There came, like blasts of biting North,
    Eleven grisly dragons, breathing fire;
The Knights of Markyate let his caitiffs forth
    For conflict grim and dire.

Sad was the slaughter when the cudgels fell!
    Sad was the doom of those fair maids to see!
Five goals to nil! – who won, I dare not tell –
    So, ask the Referee!

        [Y.Z.]

Athletics

Sports Days tended to be held on Wednesday or Saturday; sometimes the boys' and girls' sports were held on the same day but, as more and more events were introduced, different days were often selected.

The first detailed record of the Modern School Boys' Sports days was 3rd May 1913, at which Frank Facer won the Senior Championship Medal by winning the 100 yards, 440 yards and long jump. He came second equal in the mile:

Five started in this event and ran in very close order until the last lap; then on rounding the dip every one made a fine spurt and in a splendid race home Lacey stayed longest and won by three yards, while the proverbial hair separated the next three. Seamark ran very pluckily and was not far behind. (Time: 6 min. 14 sec.)

The full programme of events that year consisted of: 100 yards, 220 yards, 440 yards, one mile, high jump, long jump, obstacle race, Old Boys' race, slow bicycle race (50 yards), throwing the cricket ball, House relay and House tug-of-war.

The Girls' Sports had been held the previous week after heavy rain had made the field very damp. Jumping proved somewhat difficult and dangerous, and a small pool of water on the track had caused several girls to come to grief. The choice of events for the girls was less strenuous than for the boys: 440 yards, egg and spoon race, high and long jump, hockey driving, potato race, slow bicycle race and three-legged race.

Better weather the following year allowed the Boys' and Girls' Sports to be run on the same day. W.F. Summerbee was the Senior Boys' Champion, and for the second year running, Dorothy Burley the Girls' Champion.

The boys' obstacle race provided much amusement; the custard supplied with the apples proving rather too burnt for most of the competitors and seemed to be the most difficult obstacle; indeed the first arrival at these choice dishes could not make up his mind to partake thereof for quite a considerable time. Winner: H.S. Rentell.

Cross-Country Running

Cross-Country at the Modern School is first recorded in 1914, when it was still know as a 'Paper Chase'. Readers may recall the famous paper chases featured in *Tom Brown's Schooldays* and *The Railway Children*. Two boys, the 'hares', run a course known only to themselves, scattering scraps of torn paper at intervals to mark their route. After a short time, a pack of boys, the 'hounds', follow in pursuit and endeavour to catch the hares before they can return to base. On 21st January 1914, Rex Clayton and Frank Facer were chosen as hares and wrote in the *School Magazine*.

We decided upon a circular track, and took our followers between eight and nine miles. We crossed Stockwood Park both on our outward and homeward journeys, and the sprint through the 'Lawn' home was perhaps the most enjoyable part of our run. We arrived home in good time, about half an hour before the first hound – Mr E.I. Barrow.

One rather amusing incident occurred, when about two miles on our way, we were crossing a ploughed field and were running direct towards a spinney. As we approached the latter, we ran across a farmer and his son, who were spending the afternoon in their hut pigeon shooting. Naturally enough, the farmer was most indignant at our sudden appearance together with the disappearance of his feathered friends. He commanded us to retreat, which of course would have been disastrous for us and the chase. We entreated him to let us pass, but he was insistent, whereupon we struck off at right angles, and left our 'friend' busily picking up our trail – (a somewhat tedious task, as the trail somehow seemed thicker than usual at that spot) – he no doubt knew that no sooner had his sport begun again, than the hounds would put in an appearance. His efforts however did not prevent Mr Barrow and his pack from paying him a visit; and intending to pay us out, he unfortunately, (although fortunately for us), sent them off in an opposite direction to the way we had gone. Had it not been for this, no doubt the chase would have been a closer one.

The School Magazine

A number of references have already been made to the *School Magazine*, which provides unique material for a history of the establishment. The first issue, called somewhat unimaginatively, *Luton Modern School Magazine*, appeared in December 1912, in a red paper cover, which incorporated the crest with the motto *Ubi semen, ibi messis* and a list of its contents. It then appeared half-yearly, cost sixpence, and was approximately A5 in size. There were advertisements for local firms on the other three cover sides, W. Lacey & Son for clothing, H. White for boots and shoes and S. Farmer and Co for music. The Editor's name is not given, though it is reasonable to assume that it was E.W. Edmunds, the Senior Assistant and English Master. Printed locally by W.F. Bunker, it was initially published termly, but in order to save paper, no editions were published in 1918, 1921 and 1922.

The aim of the Magazine, as defined in the first issue, was 'to be a record of the life and doings of the school from year to year, so that every pupil shall have a souvenir of his or her school life, which shall be pleasant to look at in after years.' The earlier issues made somewhat confusing reading in that the first two or three pages were devoted each time to the 'history' of the years before the first publication i.e. 1904–1911. It didn't get sorted out until 1919. Every issue contained brief accounts of each year's progress, the names of new and leaving staff, scholarship winners and other important items of news. Articles and poems were written by members of staff or pupils, but it is not always possible to identify contributors as initials were used instead of full names and some were anonymous. When names do appear, girls are given their Christian names, but boys receive only a surname and initials. There is a general impression that more articles were the work of boys than girls.

Articles were often rather long and carefully written. School games and societies are well reported, especially the activities of the Literary and Scientific Society (from 1926). During the First World War, military matters were prominent; in themselves providing a powerful social history of the war. There is a strong flavour of patriotism which tends to evaporate in the later years. C. Wynne Parry, reflecting on the magazines in 1978, noticed 'a marked preference for prose rather than poetry.' Some of the poetry was, interestingly enough, translation from French poets: *Le Temps a laissé son manteau* by Charles d'Orléans, Villon's *Les Chansons d'Antan*, some Gautier and Hugo's *Extase*. Parry noted that 'this fondness for translation returns briefly in the 1940s with, this time, some odes by Horace.' An article from 1917 on caring for teeth reflects the initiatives which were being introduced into schools to monitor aspects of children's health. Copies of every issue were deposited in Luton Central Library.

Throughout the Magazine's history there seem to have been problems with its marketing and a malaise amongst its intended readers. An Editorial written in March 1913 lamented that

> …too many pupils are slow in realising their duty to the school. They take little or no interest in the games; they take as much interest in the school magazine. They say it is not worth sixpence! No argument will ever convince such boys or girls that patriotism is one of the highest of human traits; but those who cannot confess to a feeling of loyalty to their school now will never know the larger patriotism of the citizen in after-years.

That was written only a few months before the outbreak of the First World War, when thirty-six boys and three masters would make the ultimate sacrifice.

When the girls moved to Alexandra Avenue, they created their own Magazine, the *Sheaf* and, in due course, the Junior Technical pupils produced the *Shell*.

Some Administrative Matters

The School received its second Inspection on the 1st, 2nd and 3rd November 1910. This was the first inspection in the new building and was conducted by Mr F. Spencer, Mr F.W. Westaway and Mrs M. Withiel, all of whom seem to have been suitably impressed by what they saw.

By 1912, the number of children on the School Roll stood at 297, compared with 85 pupils in 1904 and 207 in 1908. Numbers were rising rapidly and Sanderson anticipated that there would be more than 300 children within the next two years. It was clear that further accommodation would be urgently needed. With this in mind, in 1913, the Governors, through the County Council, entered into negotiations with Luton Suburban Estates to purchase ten acres of land in Alexandra Avenue (named after Queen Alexandra) and plans were prepared for a new School for girls. The outbreak of the First World War brought progress to a standstill and delayed any move until 1919.

Numbers of pupils on roll each September:

Year	Boys	Girls	Total
1904	46	39	85
1905	46	67	113
1906	53	61	114
1907	76	70	146
1908	121	86	207
1909	149	88	237
1910	147	96	243
1911	149	127	276
1912	161	136	297
1913	189	145	334
1914	197	153	350
1915	204	148	352
1916	223	158	381
1917	208	176	384
1918	209	181	390
1919	265		

Most years, more boys than girls joined the School. By 1919, the school population of Luton was 7,791, of whom 555 were receiving a secondary education and, of those, 474 were in the two Modern Schools.

For the first time since the Modern School was opened, a system of Monitors was introduced in the Spring of 1915. This was chiefly due to the fact that Major J.H. Plummer, the Drill Instructor, had enlisted and was no longer available to maintain discipline. Six boys and seven girls were chosen for the task. Mr J.E. Anderson, writing the *School Magazine*, commented that 'there is much to be said of the value of putting boys in control of boys; the old saying, "set a thief to catch a thief", applies very well in this instance.' At first the Monitors had little power, their duties being mainly confined to traffic control in the Hall and on the staircases. Later, they were allowed to give impositions for insubordination. The system was deemed a success and, in 1916, a further three girls and seven boys were promoted. Sadly, one of the boys, David McL. Johnston caught a chill and died of pneumonia on 22nd December 1916. After the girls had moved to Alexandra Avenue in 1919, both schools replaced Monitors with Prefects and chose a Head Prefect each year. The Prep Form wrote: 'The prefects swank. Thompson says that his father says all prefects are the same. Thompson says his father was Head prefect in his school. Perhaps he was and perhaps he wasn't. Anyway, his father says we will be just as bad when we are prefects.'

Discipline in the School seems to have been very strict, largely maintained by the strong personalities of the Headmaster and his staff. An imposition or after-school detention seems to have been a suitable deterrent for most pupils, coupled, if very serious, with the threat of a visit to the Head's study for a lecture. There is little indication of the use of corporal punishment. Impositions usually consisted of writing a hundred lines or conjugating French verbs.

Social Life

Concerts and entertainments featured early in the School's life. To celebrate George V's Coronation, on Thursday, 22nd June 1911, children from all over Luton processed to Luton Hoo, where pupils of the Modern School performed scenes from *A Midsummer Night's Dream* on a temporary stage set-up amongst the trees in the Park. Unfortunately few records exist of this and other performances, and it is not until the publication of the first *Luton Modern School Magazine* in 1912 that we get any comprehensive details.

A series of annual winter concerts began in 1911, of which the second, held in the School Hall on Saturday 16th November 1912, was described at length by Alice Knight.

> For some time prior to the 16th November, we had been delighted during evening preparation by the practising on the piano, by songs and violin solos, by the jingle of tambourines and the tripping of country dancers on the hall platform … At last the great day arrived … The galleries around the Central Hall were festooned with banners bearing the School badge, and the platform was also tastefully decorated. By 6.30 p.m. the Hall was packed and our masters were still flitting about in their university caps and gowns when the first item, *The Dance of the Demons*, a pianoforte duet by F.M. Leighton and A.L. Matthew, was announced.
>
> Miss C.S. Gardner accompanied two German songs sung by a number of boys and girls. It is hoped that these songs showed the visitors that German is not the harsh and unmusical language most English people think it to be. The first was *Das Ringlein* and the second a German carol, *Stille Nacht*, which brought visions of Christmastide and thoughts of holidays into the minds of those who understood it. The tambourine dance, *Lurline*, which followed, performed by five girls, was the liveliest item on our programme … and according to the remarks heard on every side it was thoroughly appreciated.
>
> A scene from Sheridan's *The Rivals* was next presented to us. It was rather a short scene – in fact too short for most of us, who would fain have seen the great duel enacted. Frank Leighton as Bob Acres and Rex Clayton as Sir Lucius O'Trigger, both acted their parts extremely well. Clayton looked a born fighter of duels and appeared most threatening when pointing the pistol at Bob Acres.

At this point the Headmaster made a short speech, as did Mr Prothero, the Chairman of the Governors, while Mrs Prothero distributed examination certificates. After more songs and dancing and a further scene from *The Rivals*, in which

> Pamela Stafford, as Lydia Languish, proved stubbornly loyal to the love of her own choosing. Her bosom friend Julia was acted by Marthe Schefer. Gwendolen Amos as Mrs Malaprop was exceedingly good; her 'malapropisms' evoked much laughter. Frank Facer as Sir Anthony Absolute looked an ideal country squire. We shuddered to think of the drastic methods he would employ to force his daughter – if he had one – to comply with his wishes. The National Anthem brought to an end the best concert which has yet been held in the School.

The following year, 1912, the concert was performed twice to some 600 visitors. After a musical introduction, Hilda West

> …very demurely and with a pretty accent recited one of La Fontaine's fables. The puzzled appearance of some of the younger scholars, as they vainly endeavoured to gather the drift of this piece would have formed a fine study for the camera. The 'pièce de résistance' took the shape of a German play by eight boys and girls in Ia. It was not only the easy way and fluency of speaking German that was noticed in *Grossvaterchen und Grossmutterchen*, but also the very natural manner of acting. It was worth a long wait on the gallery to see Barbara Slatter and C.A. Mowse dressed in their antiquated costumes; and Mowse's fall over the chair, to the great harm of his 'churchwarden', was received with loud applause and laughter.

Mr W.W. Marks, Clerk to the Bedfordshire County Council, was Guest of Honour on that occasion. After he had distributed the prizes, an all-girl cast performed scenes from *As You Like It*.

> From the outbreak of War in 1914 all annual concerts ceased. My memory of these is that the girls looked extremely becoming in their white dresses and red ribbon sashes. Juniors were generally perched on the top galleries at the school and had difficulty in hearing the words of the performers. [F.M. Edwards (1912–16)]

It is, perhaps, remarkable that in a co-educational school very little is heard of schoolboy and schoolgirl romance. But it was there, F.M. Edwards again:

> During my second year I fell madly in love with a certain young maiden (not in my class). My lessons must have suffered a good deal from lack of concentration. Every day I was happy if only I caught one glimpse of her as we changed

classrooms. She was younger than I. Even now as I write I can picture that figure in neat school dress, carrying her books with handkerchief in hand, and dark curled locks. I wonder if life has been kind to her or otherwise. Her school number was 572. At this time I was very shy and sensitive.

The Modern School gave boys the opportunity to attend the Secondary Schoolboys' Camp which was held under canvas each year on the Isle of Wight. The site, according to 'M.S.' writing in the School Magazine for July 1915,

> ... leaves nothing to be desired. The ground at the top of a cliff is level and affords good pitches for football, cricket, hockey and squash-racquets. One of the greatest attractions is the bathing, generally held five times a day. I strongly advise those who can to take bicycles because the roads are good, and excellent rides may be had to Sandown, where noted ices and American iced-stone-ginger may be obtained. When you arrive the bicycle is also a great aid in finding a passably smooth place on which to sleep at night: the rule is "first arrive, first choose" and there you have a great advantage over those who have to walk.

The previous summer, G.B. Walkerly had described how the campers had watched the preparations for War, observing crowds of sailors congregating around Portsmouth, where 'two wicked-looking destroyers were coaling.' They watched soldiers digging trenches around a fort near Sandown:

> ... dashing about with a machine-gun, placing it here, pushing it there, and then digging furiously until they had their gun nicely commanding the bay.
>
> One evening, a friend and I were coming back to camp, and suddenly, "Halt! Who comes there?" and we saw the glint of a bayonet. As we answered correctly, we were allowed to proceed, but only to be challenged twice more in about twenty yards.
>
> Every day mine-layers were to be seen in the bay, and sometimes torpedo-boats would plough across, but no Germans appeared.
>
> At night searchlights would come peeping over the hills from Portsmouth, and wander along the coast, while many a sentry strained his eyes for the Germans who never came.

Another activity during the First World War was the Holiday Competition which was organized because 'doubtless many find that they have a good deal of time to spare during the summer holidays.' Members of the Staff offered book prizes. In 1916, the categories for Senior Pupils in Forms V, IV, IIIa, b and c were:

1. A sketch of a tea-table (ready laid) or a landscape, in pencil, pen or colour.

2. An original story or poem.
3. (a) *For Boys only:* The wooden part of a Tangent Galvanometer. A model can be seen in Room 17, on application to Mr Denbigh.
(b) *For Girls only:* A collection of wild flowers, stating their names and where found. All specimens must have been collected during the summer holidays.

The categories for Junior Forms 1a, b, c, d; Pa, b. were:

1. A landscape in pencil, pen, or colour.
2. A description of any entertainment at which the competitor was present.
3. (a) *For Boys only:* A jig-saw puzzle.
(b) *For Girls only:* A holland workbag of original design, size 16in. x 12in. when finished; or: A doll's hat or bonnet made and trimmed by the competitor.

During the Christmas holiday the tasks were similar but boys could make a 'burette stand' or a piece of fretwork, while the girls might grow daffodil bulbs. The written task for the Juniors was to expand the following story and also choose a suitable title. 'A lion casts hungry eyes upon a donkey. A cock, standing by, sets up a vigorous crowing; the lion is startled and runs away. The donkey pursues the lion, and is devoured.'

Chapter Three

Social Responsibility
1914–1919

When War was declared on 4th August 1914, a surge of patriotism swept through Britain, engulfing everyone from the youngest children to the oldest citizens. It was to have a profound effect on all those connected with Luton Modern School who were, at that time, enjoying their summer holidays.

One of those was Edith Webb who had taught French and German at the School from 1907 to 1911. Writing to the *Luton Modern School Magazine* in December 1914, she described how she had left a quiet England on 29th July 1914, bound for a Modern Languages Course at Kaiserslautern in the Rhineland-Palatinate. She found Brussels crowded with troops and, on arrival in Germany, discovered her fellow students – mostly English and French – in a state of agitation, uncertain whether they should return home. With several others, she left Kaiserslautern for Metz, where they found thousands of Germans assembling. All trains had been commandeered for the transport of troops. The students were forced to stay in the town and on 5th August, at breakfast, heard that Great Britain had declared war on Germany. They were obliged to register at the Police Station, their rooms were searched for bombs and weapons, and they were not allowed to leave the town. At the end of August, Edith and two companions attempted to escape. Obtaining passports from the American Consul in Manheim, they boarded a boat that sailed down the Rhine as far as Worms, where

> … the steamer was boarded by two officials who examined our papers and refused
> to allow us to proceed. We were obliged to descend into their little boat and landed
> near Worms Bridge. Two soldiers with fixed bayonets were summoned, and off we

had to march in single file, one soldier in front and the other bringing up the rear. We were shut up in a room on the bridge to await the arrival of the police. A detective arrived and escorted us through the town to a most beautiful building, which we entered through a door marked 'Criminal Department' and we found ourselves in the Headquarters of the Police. We were interviewed by the chief … and after two days were conducted back to Kaiserslautern by our friend the detective.

On Saturday 19th September, the party were told that they had permission to return to England, but must wait for a Military pass which would arrive almost immediately. It eventually arrived in 8th October. They started home next day, reaching England nine days later, after numerous minor adventures.

As soon as War was declared, troops were called up and billeted in schools across southern England. The Modern School was no exception and was occupied until mid-September. The building was left in a filthy and damaged state and it was some days before the children could be re-admitted. There was considerable delay before the School eventually received £99.17s.3d (£99.86) in compensation.

The Editor of the *School Magazine* wrote passionately in the December issue congratulating the first fifty Old Lutonians who had hastened to respond to their country's call:

> … the sacrifice which they make, and the danger they incur, are great; but the honour and the privilege are great also. It is rare for an Englishman to have such an opportunity of striking a blow in a cause so just, and so necessary to the welfare of the world.
>
> Our enemy … has shown himself an unscrupulous and brutal soldier, as well as arrogant and grasping in his international dealings. The German name will be associated for ever with deeds as foul and atrocious as the worst in modern history: the violation of treaties; the devastation of Belgium and the massacre of the civilian population; the barbarous outrages at Louvain, Termonde, Senlis and Rheims; the wholesale looting of private residences; the submarine attacks on hospital ships; the strewing of mines in neutral waters – these are but a few items that the civilised world has against Germany.
>
> We shall not, as our Prime Minister has said, sheathe our sword until Germany is compelled, by the only process she can understand, to recognize her duties. Our part in this very necessary task is an important one, and we hope to hear of still more Old Lutonians joining in it.

To so many boys, in the first few months, the War was a great adventure, and they faced the future with eager anticipation.

We saw Lieut. Frank Facer, looking fit and well, bowling along on a brand new N.U.T. motor-bike. He pulled up and informed us that he had that very morning made his first official flight in an aeroplane. Facer was always a first class man on the football field and if his flying is anything like his football was, he ought to be able to show the Huns a few tricks.

We are sorry to hear that Cpl. W.H. Wooding had a nasty fall from his motor-bike. It appears that he was riding in the neighbourhood of the Suez Canal, when the ground suddenly caved in and Wooding went with it, breaking the frame of his bicycle and experiencing a severe shaking. We hope there are no permanent injuries.

The Board of Education made it clear to all teachers that in the eyes of the Army Council, teaching was a public service and, therefore, grounds for *not* enlisting. In spite of this, at least six members of staff felt compelled to join the Old Boys at the front, possibly encouraged by one of the girls, Doris Garside, who wrote this verse for the *School Magazine*.

O'er England's shores is cast again
A Cloud of strife and war:
Yet not of war for greed, for gain,
But justice to restore.
Your duty and your country call:
Why tarry then, I pray?
Why let your comrades for you fall,
Whilst you at home do stay?

One of the first masters to rush to the Colours in August 1914 was Ernest I. Barrow B.Sc. who had taught Mathematics and Science at the School since September 1911. He had entered enthusiastically into school life, taking part in concerts, chairing debates and playing for the staff football team. When he left to join the Army, he told Sanderson to do what he thought best with his post, but the County Council decided to hold it open and paid him a salary of £80 to supplement his Army pay. He fought with the 2nd East Lancashire Regiment, becoming a Lieutenant.

The *School Magazine* for May 1915 has a piece written by Barrow and called *The Life of a Recruit* in which he describes, with some humour, his Army training.

We have learnt very thoroughly, and some of us at our cost, that the old adage – "an army fights on its stomach" – is true in more senses than one. To be running and then fall flat, with lightning celerity, while burdened with rifle and pack, needs practice if it is to be done without a severe shaking up.

One unhappy sight, after a shower of rain, was to be seen scampering madly up a hillside, with a rifle in one hand and a greatcoat in the other. On the word of command to drop, the coat went down first, then the rifle, and lastly the man on top of the coat.

We know (some of us) what it is to be on night guard, with the rain coming down in sheets, wet through to the skin, with mud over the boot tops, and ½ of a mile of delightfully slippery mud, traversed by deep trenches, to plough through on the way to and from the guard-hut.

Later he wrote:

I was slightly wounded the other day, but it is nothing to worry about. A piece of shell casing hit me on the chest. It was considerate enough to hit me flat side on, which was lucky for me. As it was, it knocked me head over heels, raised an enormous bump, and broke a rib. I refused to go into hospital and am still "carrying-on". Apart from this little dent in the frame-work I am very fit.

Rex Clayton wrote in the 1959 issue of *The Lutonian*:

Mr Barrow, a young Manchester graduate who was as full of mischief as any boy and incidentally was most popular with us all, was left alone in the staff room for the last period on a Friday afternoon where, unseen, he could remove an electric light bulb and put a piece of metal across the terminals, blowing the main fuse, and plunging the whole school into darkness. This continued for the whole of one winter. Boys were suspected but the culprit was never discovered. Knowing Mr Barrow as well as I did, I can imagine how he would enjoy doing it and never being suspected. It was the same enjoyment of living dangerously that caused him to lose his life in the First World War.

Lt. Barrow died during the Battle of the Somme on 23rd October 1916. He was 27 years old. Two other former members of staff also died during the War. Captain Thomas Huffington MA, who taught History and Languages from 1913 to 1914, died of wounds on the Somme on 8th February 1917, aged 24. James H.R. Lendrum became a Chaplain 4th Class attached to the 8th Battalion, Kings Own (Royal Lancaster Regt.). He had taught Languages and Mathematics at the School from 1910 to 1912. He died near Bienvillers in the Pas de Calais on 22nd August 1918, aged 31.

Two of our masters were killed, one a particularly handsome young man, with features like an Adonis. He was extremely popular with the whole school, and I believe caused many heart flutterings among the senior girls. The other was the most easy-going of any of the school's masters though he rose to the commissioned rank of Captain. Such was the passing of Isaac Barrow and Thomas Huffington.

[F.M. Edwards]

Three teachers who fought and survived the war were J.M. Forbes, Connaught Rangers, (3rd Batt.); H.W. Gilbert, 3/1st East Anglian Division, Signal Company, R.E. (in other words a dispatch rider!); and A. Jordan, Royal Engineers. G.J. Denbigh was rejected for Active Service so volunteered for chemical work and was sent by the Ministry to Brotherton's in Leeds, manufacturing picric acid.

The first Old Lutonian to die during the War was Private Ernest Allin of the 24th County of London (Queen's) Regiment. Allin attended the Modern School between 1907 and 1909. He left to become a technician apprentice at the Vauxhall and West Hydraulic Engineering Company. 'He worked hard and was a regular student at Evening Classes. His ready wit and unfailing good humour made him a general favourite; he was an indispensable singer at the Old Lutonian entertainments.' He was badly wounded at Béthune by a stray bullet while leaving the trenches to draw the day's rations, and died two days later on 1st May 1915. A characteristically cheery letter from him had been published in the *School Magazine* the previous December.

> Many of you will agree that Old Lutonians who enlisted, did so for the one outstanding reason that His Majesty's Army would not and could not be complete without some O.L.s in its wake. Those of us in the Queen's Own Rifles have, since joining, found that it was not merely for the meagre 7/- [35p] a week that they became soldiers, but absolutely for the honour of being able to serve their Country.
>
> What tales we'll have to relate when we return to our one and only Luton.

Private Frank Rimmer joined the School with a free place in September 1906, and left in 1909, after which he worked in the straw trade. He served in the 5th Battalion, the Bedfordshire Regiment and 'died in the terrible charge in which the Regiment received their fire-baptism' after landing at Gallipoli on 16th August 1915, aged 21.

> Captain Cumberland called for two volunteers to scout, previous to the advance on 15th August which proved so fatal to the battalion. Frank Rimmer and a friend went and had an exciting time, as the bullets were flying thickly around. When they got back the battalion stormed the hill in fine style. Frank Rimmer ran on ahead with the leaders. That was the last that was seen of him. His body was found near that of Lieut. Brighten – he lies buried with him in 'Lone Tree' valley.

A fellow Old Lutonian, Private Harry Berry, aged 21, died on the same day and in the same campaign. At the Modern School from September 1906 for less than a year, he was on the staff of *The Luton News*.

Arthur D. Gladwin had been in Horton War Hospital in Epsom for three months with gunshot wounds in the hip, from which he happily recovered. He wrote to the *School Magazine* in March 1917 to say:

> Whilst in France last Summer, I met Second Lieut. Arthur Howarth, who was a close friend of mine at the 'LMS', and we had many happy talks of school days. I saw poor Hawarth last a few days before his death, and managed afterwards to secure a button from his tunic – a token of remembrance which I shall always treasure. He was a fearless, gallant soldier, and met his death whilst operating his machine gun in an exposed position with an utter disregard of danger.

Arthur Howarth served in the 16th Battalion, The King's (Liverpool Regiment), attached to the Machine Gun Corps (Inf.) and died near Laventie in the Pas de Calais on 19th July 1916, aged 20.

Sergeant F.G. Harmer was the first Old Lutonian to receive the Military Medal and happily survive the War. Lance Corporal John Hayden Healey was not so lucky. He died in Belgium on 17th July 1918, aged 29, and was awarded the Military Medal for outstanding bravery. Lieutenant Sidney Charles Squires received the Belgian Croix de Guerre. He had rallied his battalion when it was pushed back on Vimy Ridge, and had taken them 'over the top' again. He was later accidentally killed on 28th October 1918. 'Whilst his spirit is among us, we have something to live for and something to hope for'. Sergeant H.C. Hunt, attached to a fighting squadron in France, was awarded the Distinguished Flying Medal for bringing down nine German aircraft and one observation balloon. On one occasion he brought down three machines in one patrol.

In all, 39 old boys and staff lost their lives as a result of the War; 34 in the Army, three in the Royal Flying Corps and two in the Navy.

Edith Webb described her joy on 11th November 1918 when she saw the Town Crier, Charlie Irons, on the top of St Mary's Church tower, ringing his bell and declaring that the Armistice had been signed. In 1930, a poem to recall the occasion, written by a teacher, H. Hugh Watson, was published in the *School Magazine*.

> Twelve years have passed since that November day,
> When sick of carnage, strife and clash of steel,
> Hardly believing war would ever cease,
> We heard the bells ring out a joyful peal.
> The end had come, now men had ceased to slay
> Their fellow-creatures, and at last was peace.

Comrades, whose merry laugh once rang out clear,
Though Death, with icy hand, was ever nigh,
No longer do you tread this earth below,
But your brave souls, will never, never die.
Smile down on us, who toil and struggle here,
Until we reach the goal, that one day we shall know.

At Speech Day on 24th March 1919, Mr Sanderson listed the contribution which boys from the Modern School had made to the War effort:

More than 250 have been serving in the various branches of HM Forces; and of this number at least 40 were awarded Commissions, many of them after a period of service in the ranks. According to our present information the highest positions were gained by Captain P.G. Horsler, Captain F.M. Leighton, Captain R.E. Oakley, Captain BA. Smart and Major C.G. Hyde.

Foreign Distinctions
The Belgian Croix de Guerre S.C. Squires.
The French Croix de Guerre B.A. Smart

British Distinctions
Mentioned in Despatches F.F. Biggs (2), T. Dickson, E.F. Foster (2), H.W. Gilbert, C.E. Hayward, C.G. Hyde (2), R.E. Otter, W. Sharp (2), W.J. Twidell (2), A.G. White.
Meritorious Service Medal A. Gilder, W. Sharp, W.J. Twidell.
Military Medal H.W. Child, C. Farr, E.F. Foster, G.F. Harmer, J.H. Healey.
Military Cross W.W. Brown, P.G. Horsler, F.M. Leighton, R.E. Oakley.
Distinguished Flying Medal H.C. Hunt.
Distinguished Service Order with a bar – B.A. Smart.

Cadets and Guides

In May 1918, with the War in its final phase, it was somewhat belatedly decided to form a School Cadet Corps. At the instigation of Cllr. W.J. Primett, and with prompt and generous donations from 18 Governors and friends, an Establishment Fund amounting to over £120 was soon forthcoming. Initially, 71 boys mustered each Saturday for drill and parades, led by Sergeant-Major C. Kitchen and Sergeant Sanders. Mr W.H. Ovenell, the classics master, took charge of the Corps until

January 1919 when Lieut. H.H. Watson joined the school staff and was made Commanding Officer.

Early in the summer term the Corps received an issue of rifles, belts, etc. which gave the boys a chance to drill with arms, as well as keeping equipment clean. Messrs. Day of St Albans supplied caps free of charge, but it wasn't until the middle of December that khaki uniforms became available. A secure room in the Church Street premises was used as an armoury.

It is worth noting that not all the School Governors were in favour of the formation of the Cadet Corps. Henry Latchmore was a prominent Quaker and member of a well-known local banking family who found difficulty in accepting most objectives of the Corps. He would have liked to see the boys and girls interested in such subjects as the League of Nations, international courts of arbitration for the settlement of disputes by peaceful means instead of by the sword, and the gradual elimination of militarism for human relationships. Having felt unable to subscribe to the establishment of the Corps, he offered instead to fund, for at least three years, essays on the subject of dealing with international disputes.

With the formation of the Cadet Corps, the girls were naturally not willing to be outdone and, during the Autumn term 1918, the School formed its own Girl guide Company composed of members from Form IIIb upwards. The first company consisted of 17 girls under the command of Miss Lewin, Miss Netherwood, Miss Forsaith and Miss Sugden who were all 2nd Class Guides themselves. Meetings were held every Thursday and, by the end of November, they had recruited a full complement of 32 members. The new recruits were from the lower forms and were soon training for their 2nd Class and Proficiency badges.

During the summer term 1919, the girls held a field day.

> A grass meadow below Bluebell Woods was the headquarters for the day, and we arrived there about 11 a.m. on Saturday. Signalling was the first event, when several of the girls showed good progress. The afternoon was spent in following the trail through the woods; most of the Guides then made their way back to headquarters for tea. A little later those left behind also returned in triumph with two kettles full of hot tea; we were very pleased with the successful camp fire – lit with only one match – and felt we deserved the tea. (Perhaps it was as well Miss Forsaith was not there to criticise the method we used to make the tea.) Message carrying was the next affair, and then after a few round games we struck camp and returned home.

Before leaving the Cadets and Guides, it is worth quoting from an account of Speech Day in 1919.

On the evening of the 28th March, the girls and boys gathered in the Great Hall of the School and, headed by the Girl Guides, marched down to the Winter Assembly Hall, the Cadet Corps, commanded by Lieut. Watson, bringing up the rear …

The majority of the girls in the hall wore becoming white frocks contrasting effectively with the dark blue uniforms and red ties of the Girl Guides, who sat in a body near the platform. Opposite the Guides were seen the boys of the Cadet Corps, whose khaki uniforms helped to introduce a military touch to the proceedings and perhaps reminded many of the great War which had just ended, and of those who had gone forth to return no more.

Social Conscience

Boys and girls at the School were encouraged to support charities each year. One of the earliest was for the maintenance of the 'Modern School Cot' at the Bute Hospital in Dunstable Road. It had been in use almost continually since 1910 and, in December 1916, was occupied by a little girl who called herself 'Topsy Lily' who had had an operation on her neck. The parents of each little patient who occupied the bed paid half-a-crown (12½p) a week, although the cost was nearer £1. The rest of the cost was paid for from the School Fund which raised about £50 each year. From time to time, pupils were encouraged to visit the child in the cot.

In 1919, Mr Sanderson was able to report that the money collected by the School towards a variety of charities since 1907 came to £388. Of that sum, about £150 was allocated to the Bute Hospital, nearly the same amount to the children's Home and most of the balance being expended in purchasing materials for the girls to work up for the benefit of those suffering through the War. In all, 1,253 garments and other useful articles were made and distributed to various hospitals and other institutions; without counting 500 hospital bags sent in response to Lady Smith Dorrien's appeal. Special collections were held during the First World War for the Over-Seas Club £1.9s.10d (£1.50), Belgian Relief Fund £25, Blinded Soldiers' Children's Fund of the National Institute for the Blind £112.13s.11d (£112.70), Dr Barnardo's Homes £45.7s.0d (£45.35). A letter from the Director of Dr Barnardo's to the Headmaster said 'It may interest you to know that it was by far the largest result from any School visited last term'.

In November 1916, a War Savings Association was formed. Pupils were able to buy coupons which could be exchanged for War Savings Certificates. Friends, relatives and former students were included in the scheme and, by Februrary 1917, there were 145 members who had bought a total of 288 certificates. By 1919, a total of £2,000 had been put into War Savings. After the War, the School continued to give generously and, between 1925 and 1930 almost £500 was collected for local charities. At Christmas 1930, £37.8s (£37.40) was raised to help the dependants of those who lost their lives in the R101 airship disaster.

One interesting project was the support of Mr J. Foster Stackhouse's British Antarctic Expedition which left England in August 1914. Its aim was to explore that part of Antarctica lying between King Edward VII Land and Graham Land. It was pointed out that the cost of a tent was £21, a sledge cost £12.12s (£12.60), a cooking stove £10.10s (£10.50), a dog £7.7s (£7.35), a sleeping bag £6.6s (£6.30) and a pair of fur mittens £5.5s (£5.25). The School collected £8.8s (£8.40) and it was decided that the money should be used to buy a dog. A girl in the Fourth Form suggested that the dog should be called Lumo, made up from the first syllables of 'Luton' and 'Modern'. One pupil wrote a letter of advice to the dog, which appeared in the April 1914 issue of the Modern School Magazine:

> Before you set foot upon your expedition to the Antarctic Regions, I should like to offer you a word of advice. We have adopted you into our ever-increasing family: we have given you your name; you have now to prove that you are worthy of such a distinction. Remember that you are working for the Honour of the School, my boy. When the sledge is too heavily laden, when the weather is at its worst, and when food is reduced below the minimum, remember that we in England are thinking of you. Then pluck up your spirits, fight with renewed strength, and never give up hope.
>
> But if you die worsted in the struggle, then die like a hero, and prove to all the world that we Lutonians are game to the end.
>
> On the other hand, if you return, although the world may not notice you, we shall give you a welcome, and your name shall go down to posterity in the annals of the School.
>
> So here's good luck to you, old fellow, from
>
> A Sister Lutonian

Sadly, there are no further references to Lumo in the *School Magazine*, and his fate remains unknown.

Future Success

How can success be defined? It would not be possible to trace the life of everybody who went to the School, and who is to say that one life is worth more that another? Sanderson himself expressed similar thoughts at the first post-War Speech Day on 28th March 1919.

> There is some danger of mistaking for the true harvest such visible signs of progress as Examination successes, Athletic distinctions and promising careers. These will be useful indications that the crop is making healthy growth, but they must not be confused with the real harvest. This will ripen slowly and gradually. We ourselves

must not expect to be the reapers. We must be content if we catch occasional glimpses of the ripening corn. It will indeed be a harvest which requires no reaping, though its fruits will be enjoyed by future generations:– A harvest of good citizens who will always place Public Duty before private interests; of real sportsmen who will always play the game; of men who will swear unto their neighbours and disappoint them not even though it be to their own hindrance.

So, in order to enlarge on the history of the School, and with apologies to the many who have been omitted, we will note the successes of just a representative few during Sanderson's headship.

With the opening of Luton Modern School in 1904, ordinary boys and girls in Luton had, for the first time, been given a realistic chance to take advantage of a college education, and the School was rightly proud of pupils who succeeded in the academic world. It does appear that more attention was paid to boys but Sanderson said that, although there were always more boys entered for examinations than girls, the girls more than held their own. Their results compared very favourably, and in the summer term 1919, six pupils sat their London Matriculation and passed, and only one of them was a boy. Some of the first pupils to achieve university status or to have trained as teachers have already been noted in chapter one.

Modern students are sometimes criticized for enjoying a social life instead of concentrating on their studies. Perhaps things have not changed all that much if this article from the School Magazine (1917) is to be believed.

> Miss Euphemia Makeaway was neither slack nor foolish, though ignorant people called her the former, and superior people the latter. When she went to College she felt no particularly strong inward prompting to study Science, but fate and her father decreed that she should. It was characteristic that her interests were many and varied, and that she was a good all-round sort of girl. She soon came to feel that college is an organised Society for Suppression of Work among the Studious, strongly supported by the powers that be. She made up her mind to work hard, but as a very pronounced social being she was prone to leave the highways of Science for the byways of College life. Physics had no chance against an interesting lecture; dancing tempted her from mechanics; concerts made inroads on her botany; the charms of chemistry were set aside at the bidding of the imperious 'Reeve of the Guild'; her neighbours were always brewing cocoa and inviting her to talk; debates also and socials had to be thought on; were there not also games to be played, meetings to attend, and a hundred other things to be got through.

There were other interesting careers: Alec H. Squires (1907–10) was a student at the Guildhall School of Music. He wrote a hymn tune called 'Lutonian' which was used in the School. Harry Berry (1906–1907) was on the staff of *The Luton News*, Charles

Barnard (1911–14) became an articled chartered accountant to Mr Bernard T. Crew of George Street West, Luton. Henry P. Dunkley (1907–10) and W.A. Gething (1908–12) took exams for entry into the Civil Service.

W.A. Gething was at the School with Blanche Burgoyne, whom he married. Their daughter, Joan, attended the High School (1936–40) and son, Phillip, the Modern School from 1939–46. Phillip's wife, Helen Slater, attended the High School, and both her parents, Wallace Slater and Doris Edwards, were pupils of Luton Modern School.

In an age of Empire, it is not surprising that several ex-pupils sought adventure overseas, Canada being particularly popular. Walter W. Brown (1907–11) wrote:

> Taking things all round Canada has been very good to me and has taught me that all the education in the world is absolutely no use without sound common sense. I've worked real hard both with my hands and head ever since I arrived here: my experiences have been varied and I already feel amply repaid for the sacrifice I made in leaving my home and friends.
>
> Canada is a grand country for a worker but no good for a shirker … I have been Farmer, Cook's Assistant, Marble Worker, Labourer and Boiler Attendant and now I am a soldier with a Maple Leaf for my emblem.

There were also sacrifices to be made as this obituary of Charles Johnson Wing (1906–08) who went in 1911 to take up farming explains.

> He was still engaged in farming at Fort Qu'Appelle when he was stricken with what proved to be a fatal illness, appendicitis. To be cut off in the springtime of youth, far way from all his relatives, renders the circumstances peculiarly sad, and we offer our deepest sympathy to his parents, brothers and sisters, in their bereavement.

Douglas M. Christian from St Albans (1904–08) went to Canada in 1910, served for a time on the Staff of the Toronto *Globe* and then became 'editor of an enterprising newspaper in Redcliff, Alberta'. A.E. Rackham 'took a farm in Manitoba'. A lengthy, anonymous article in the 1916 issue of the *School Magazine* paints a poetic picture of winter in Newfoundland, which can be very cold and bleak.

> By January the Frost King has set his seal upon the land, the Storm Fiend wheels in mad career, and snow lies piled upon snow. The usual marks are no longer visible, and the sleigh tracks cross by the shortest routes, passing over frozen lakes and sometimes topping what was not long since a fence or a green-leafed hedge. Safe beneath her fleecy mantle Nature sleeps, till the voice of Spring again calls to

her in leaping streams, freed from its frost-forged fetters, and in the awakened life of the woods, and then the silent earth once more resumes her robes of green.

But if wild Nature sleeps the winter out, human nature is very much alive. To the fishermen and their families, living in the lonely outposts scattered along Newfoundland's far-flung shores, winter is the season of enjoyment. Social pleasures, out and indoor amusements, games shooting, hunting, trapping – these, and many other recreations are freely and enthusiastically indulged in. Dancing is a favourite winter amusement. To the music of flute, or fife, fiddle or even Jew's harp, the lads and lassies dance for hours with a whole-hearted vigour and honest enjoyment not obtainable, perhaps, in fashionable ballrooms. It does not seem to matter to these people at what hour of the night or morning they disperse. Guests will drive or walk long distances in the crisp frosty air, with light hearts and sometimes lighter pockets, for these meeting are often held for some charitable purpose.

In 1928, Edgar Elvey wrote from Cottesloe in West Australia in favour of emigration.

> After six years in Victoria, we have moved to West Australia. Trade has been very good in the Eastern States in the past few years. The number of motor cars owned by people is amazing. Owing to people over-spending and buying luxuries on the hire-purchase system, money was tightened up by the banks. Last season the wheat crop was bad, which was reflected in the city, and the result is a great slump.
>
> The Government of West Australia helps land settlers and emigrants better than the Governments of the Eastern States. At the present time huge areas of land are being thrown open for selection. The settlers are aided by a grant, a few hundred pounds capital being sufficient to start with.

Although the colonies probably attracted most of the pioneers, many chose other lands. Basil M. Joyce (1910–12) wrote from Bahia in Brazil, whilst another letter was received from a former scholar (unnamed) living in Pakhoi, China in 1917.

> I suppose you want to know what our home is like? We are well off for physical comforts and can boast of having electric light. All around the house is a large veranda; the servants' quarters and our kitchen are outside. We have four servants, viz., a cook, his wife, and two coolies. The cook's wife washes and mends all the clothes, one coolie looks after the house, and the other tends the garden.
>
> We used to use tinned milk, but can obtain fresh butter from Hong Kong …
>
> One of the drawbacks to life out here is the flies. No matter how one tries to keep them out of the house they seem to get into the rooms in thousands, and this in spite of having sieve-like doors and windows.

The Old Lutonians' Club

A strong community spirit soon grew up amongst the old boys and girls of the School. On the evening of Saturday, 23rd March 1912, about 150 old pupils attended the inaugural meeting of the Old Lutonians' Club, which was held in the school hall, at the invitation of Mr Sanderson. 'Prompt to time the Head took the chair, supported by Messrs. Edmunds, Denbigh, Jordan, May and Otter, whilst Miss Macfarlane and Miss Poulton welcomed the old girls and kept them in order'.

Six months later, on 28th September 1912, the First Annual Meeting was held, with Mr Edmunds in the chair. He outlined the hopes of the organizers as to the Club's aims. It was proposed that meetings would be held during the winter months which would afford valuable opportunities for socializing and the exchange of ideas amongst old pupils resident in the town. It was believed that the new *School Magazine*, being launched that winter, would keep Old Lutonians in distant countries in touch with their friends at home, as well as providing an opportunity for literary expression. Mr Sanderson was unanimously elected the Club's Chairman, G.L.Bond its first Secretary and Mr Edmunds the Treasurer. A Committee of eight ladies and seven men were also elected. The evening ended with a musical programme arranged by C.C. Bennett, which was to set a precedent for innumerable future meetings.

Almost immediately the old boys formed a Football Section of the club, but the old girls were somewhat slower in getting a Hockey Section going. 'We hope that age does not yet bar the way' observed an unidentified writer in the *Magazine* for 1912! It didn't, and soon they were playing against the school teams. Tennis and Cricket sections were formed the following year, and membership was marked by the conspicuous appearance on the streets of Luton of coloured hatbands and ties.

The Club became a focus of the old pupils' social life for many years to come. The School Magazine also served its purpose and we owe it a great deal, for without the wealth of material contained within its pages, this book would have been much more difficult to write.

The pattern of the Club meetings was set in the first two or three years. Whist Drives were an immediate success with as many as 70 members taking part. Christmas Parties became an annual event, and tended to bring in new members. The first, on 28th December 1912, was a great and enjoyable occasion.

> In spite of rough weather, dark muddy roads, and in many cases inconvenient train services, at about half-past six the hall contained at least one hundred former pupils, many of whom had travelled some distance. Several members of the school staff were present and the Headmaster presided over the gathering.
>
> All shyness and reserve that some of the old boys might perhaps have felt at once more meeting their old school-girl acquaintances, who to them seemed to

have undergone some strange metamorphoses since those by-gone days, was soon overcome. In a short time even the most timid were walking bravely towards old boys and girls whom they perhaps had not seen for years and were soon asking all kinds of questions in a most unconventional manner.

Interspersed between intervals for conversing with friends, were games and charades, a musical entertainment, refreshments, further games, dances and competitions. Before leaving 'all the members clasped hands and sang several verses of Auld Lang Syne with but little consideration for tone, yet with a vast amount of good feeling'.

The Old Lutonians' Club was certainly very active. At first, lectures and concerts were held fortnightly. In March 1913, Fred Buckingham, the first Old Lutonian to gain his B.Sc. lectured on *The Problem of Flight*. Pointing out that knowledge of bird flight must be applied to the solution of artificial dynamic flight, he spoke 'of balloons of the present day, giving us a classification of modern dirigibles, a branch of aviation as yet in its infancy' and using many blackboard sketches, the full theory of how an aeroplane 'lifts and drifts' 'till our poor benighted heads buzzed, and we gaped in bewildered wonderment'.

The Debating Society proved very popular. The subjects chosen are interesting because they indicate that, while some things have changed in the last hundred years, there are others which have remained much the same. *Has science or art benefited the world most? Capital punishment should be abolished* and *Vivisection* were all debated. In support of the last, R.E. Oakley pointed out the scientific benefits while Christine Roberts called for its discontinuance on the grounds of cruelty. Those who supported vivisection as 'a means to a beneficent end' won the day. A fortnight later, the majority of members were in favour of *The Nationalisation of the Railways*. All these topics are relevant today but the subject for March 1914 *Should women engage in Commercial pursuits?* is much more contentious and would be quite unacceptable. Lizzie Forsyth stated that it was necessary for a large proportion of girls to support themselves, but W.H. Wooding, in reply, said 'that business on the whole spoils a girl, it makes her deficient and coarse, and these are not the sort of girls men want to marry'.

With the outbreak of War, many old boys enlisted, and the old girls rallied to the cause, meeting on Tuesday and Friday evenings in the School Needlework room to make warm clothing for the children in the town who were in distress, and also to make such items as warm gloves, scarves and caps for the troops.

Members who could not immediately join the Forces formed the Old Lutonians Rifle Club 'to prepare themselves in some way so as to volunteer later on'. The Hon, Sec. of the Luton and District Rifle Club offered the Club special facilities and the Headmaster guaranteed the fee for affiliation. Forty members joined and firing practice commenced three days later on the Winter Range, which was situated behind the Royal Hotel in Mill Street.

The *School Magazine* devoted a number of pages to news from Old Lutonians, and soon it began to report marriages between members, such as that of the Club's first Hon. Secretary, G.L. Bond, to Committee member, Miss Hilda Morsley in 1915. This was a trend which continued throughout the life of the School and which earned a humorous comment from Peter C. Vigor (an ex-Waller Street Higher Grade School pupil) in his book *Memories are Made of This*.

> Luton Modern School boys had a wider field for girl friends but a narrower marriage choice. They could have affairs with elementary school girls, Modern School girls [after 1919] – always assuming that the headmistress did not know about it – and girls from the Convent. If marriage was their aim only the more refined type of girl was eligible according to their parents. This adolescent discrimination caused jealousy and snobbery and was one of the reasons why Waller Street became the scene of many a mêlée rivalling those between the Montagues and the Capulets. We had no rapiers or bright swords, and had to resort to cap-snatching and satchel swinging (a deadly enough weapon if it contained a wooden pencil case) or, in season, snowball throwing.

By this time, the epithet 'Rhubarb and Custard' had become a common cry of abuse directed at any Modern School boy or girl displaying an élite red or yellow scarf or other distinguishing mark, by the non-secondary youth of Luton.

The Old Lutonians' Club nominally represented the old boys and girls of both the Modern School for Boys and the Modern School for Girls until 1934. However, in the summer of 1921, after the girls had moved to their own School in Alexandra Avenue, they formed their own Association.

> Park Square is filled with ghosts, friendly, happy ghosts for the most part. It was half-filled in those early days with girls too, some of whose liveliness still lingers in the memory. Then the girls went to 'another place' and the school lost much of its savour, for with the girls went Polly Poulton, one of the finest characters that ever graced the teaching profession [Miss E. St S. Poulton]. I do not know whether the Old Girls remember Polly, but some of the Old Boys do, for to her and her help we owe much, and the world was the poorer when she passed on.
>
> [Arthur B. Allen]

Chapter Four

The Legendary Elysium
1919–1930

After the First World War, the Governors of Luton Modern School had, once again, to address the problem of overcrowding. A ten acre field in Alexandra Avenue had been purchased in 1913 and it was decided that huts, which had been used by the Canadian Army at the Duke of Bedford's Camp in Ampthill Park, should be bought and set up as temporary accommodation, but another eleven years were to pass by before a new building was completed. The plans were, as they had been in 1913, to move the girls to the new location as a first step with the boys following later. It was also intended that the boys should be allowed to use the school field. However, all the plans to accommodate boys were shelved and the Alexandra Avenue site became and remained a school for girls.

The first quotation for the cost of moving the huts was £3,457 but this was revised to £2,840 when it was decided to leave out the brick foundations. Building work included levelling and draining, lighting, heating and fencing and provision was made for classrooms, a hall, a laboratory and office facilities. Some furniture was moved from the school in Park Square, but funding had to be found for extra furnishings, equipment and stationery. Probably the most important decision of all was the appointment of suitable staff, in particular the selection of a competent headmistress.

LEFT Map of Luton and surroundings, specially prepared for the New Industries Committee of the Town Council and The Luton Chamber of Commerce and published by *The Luton News*. It dates from 1921 and was produced by Franklin and Deacon, Architects and Surveyors. (*LM*)

Aerial view of the Huts n.d.
Alexandra Avenue does not continue beyond the Huts. There are allotments between the School
and Marlborough Avenue. George Kent Ltd. and Commer Cars are in the foreground and the
British Gelatine Works is in the background. (*J. Dyer*)

Secondary Education for Girls

In order to understand the implications behind such an appointment, it is necessary to take a brief look at the subject of secondary education for girls from a national point of view. Historically, girls and women have been seen as subordinate and 'relative' members of society with no real right to an independent existence. Their main goal in life was considered to be marriage. Even after the 1870 Forster Education Act ensured that elementary education should be available for all children, the over-riding presence of needlework and domestic subjects in the curriculum reminded girls that their most important role in life was that of a wife and mother. Girls from the middle classes may have received a more refined type of education but that again was intended to qualify them for a respectable marriage. Most men shrank from the 'disgrace' of having an educated wife.

There were other reasons why it was thought inadvisable to educate girls, one being the belief that women would suffer from some kind of brain fever if they studied too hard. Another firmly-held idea was that females of the species were endowed with a limited amount of strength and that, if they used this strength to develop their intellectual powers, there would not be enough left to produce children for the good of the country and the Empire.

However, from the middle of the nineteenth century, a movement grew up which, slowly but successfully, fought for the provision of secondary and higher education for girls. There is no evidence to suggest that there were any women in Luton who were visionaries in the educational field nor, in spite of their economic influence within the hat trade, did they seem to have had much interest in political power.

In fact, it was probably the work of the pioneer educationalist, Frances Mary Buss, which had the most influence on the establishment of the Luton Modern School for Girls. In 1850, Miss Buss founded the North London Collegiate School for Ladies. This became the prototype of all the girls' high schools which were set up throughout the country and, indeed, the 'North London' is still one of the leading girls' schools in the country.

Miss Buss did not believe that good teaching came automatically and encouraged all her teaching staff to study to improve their skills. She introduced a wide curriculum which included not only academic subjects but also a healthy approach to physical education. Her students were among the first to be entered for the Cambridge Local Examinations when, at last, the University relented and agreed to open them to girls. A considerable number of North London Collegiate School girls went on to benefit from a university education.

The fame of the North London Collegiate School spread and staff who had trained and taught under Miss Buss were appointed to headships themselves. In this way a network of similar schools grew up around the country and, in 1919, the influence of Frances Mary Buss began to make itself felt in Luton in the form of Helen K. Sheldon who, almost certainly, shared the same belief in this pioneering approach to the education of girls.

The historical background was acknowledged in a talk on *Ambitions* which a Mrs Woods gave to the girls in 1926. She began by saying that

> girls had at last gained the right of having as good an education as their brothers. Having gained the right, the girls must show that they appreciated it, and the only way they could do so was to set themselves a very high standard in work and conduct. They might not reach the standard they set, but at least they could do their best. Then, when school was left behind, the girls would find that they could acquit themselves well in the new life opening out before them.

Helen Kate Sheldon

There were five applicants for the headship of Luton Modern School for Girls, three of whom were interviewed: Miss E. Edwards MA from the Girls' Grammar School in Bradford, Miss F.M. Jackson, senior assistant at the school in Park Square and Miss Helen K. Sheldon from King Edward VI Grammar School in Handsworth. It was unanimously agreed that Miss Sheldon should be appointed; her salary was to be £400, rising by increments of £50 to £500 per annum.

Miss Sheldon was born in 1882 at Chigwell, Essex, and educated at Great Yarmouth High School and the Royal Holloway College, London (1902–1905) where she obtained Oxford Final Honours – School of English Language and Literature. In 1940 she recalled how she had first come to Luton not realising at the time 'how much I should love this town' and promised that she would try to give it 'the best gift it could have, a good School'.

Nobody who ever had anything to do with Miss Sheldon will ever forget her. She was a lady with the vision and steely determination to provide the town with a school such as it had never had before – or since. Sir Frederick Mander recalled that during her twenty-eight years of service she had made it one of the finest in the country. She never lost her sense of vocation and, when she retired, Sir John Burgoyne, a former Mayor, said that 'Miss Sheldon came to Luton in 1919, and accepted responsibility for fostering the highest graces of our young womanhood; for giving to our people cultural aspirations beyond and above the provisions of compulsory standards of education; for moulding a reputation – character – and not least, a tradition'.

The magazines of the girls' school were entitled the *Sheaf,* a name which picked up on the theme of a 'harvest of good citizens'. They have over the years published articles which describe Miss Sheldon's character quite colourfully. One of these was written by Miss Harris, History Mistress 1929–1946.

Helen K. Sheldon c.1940.

My first meeting with her was in a railway carriage when she was returning to the Royal Holloway College as a Third year, and I was 'going up' for the first time. I cannot remember what she looked like, but I am sure that she put a formidable hockey stick on the rack, for she was a member of the Second Eleven.

About four years later, on a September Saturday morning, I opened the door of my lodgings to greet a thin-faced, brown-haired girl with a bicycle – Miss Sheldon come to ask me to tea. I had just joined King Edward's Grammar School to which she had belonged for three years. After that we became friends, and, later on, shared rooms for ten years, until she left Birmingham for Luton.

Now what was Miss Sheldon like in those pre-Luton days? For some years she played hockey twice on Saturday, and you can imagine with what spirit and energy. Then a long illness curbed her activity without diminishing her interest in games. She continued to play netball with zest and to score numerous goals as a quite brilliant shooter.

Most members of the High School, or, at all events, most Old Girls, will not be surprised to hear that, perhaps our happiest joint memories are of dramatic performances and of the preparation for them: for example, scenes from *A Midsummer Night's Dream*, *Iphigena in Tauris* and a Pageant of English History. Among her other roles, Miss Sheldon played Elizabeth in *Pride and Prejudice*.

Members of Staff

Five assistant teachers from the mixed school in Park Square were transferred to the girls' school but Miss Jackson, who was one of the unsuccessful applicants for the headship, stayed with the boys. Six new members of staff were appointed on a temporary basis but, if their work proved satisfactory, they were to be given a permanent post.

New staff

Miss B.L. Bracey		
(BA Birmingham)	Geography and History	£170
Miss H.G. Budge		
(ACTC Board of Education,		
Teacher Artists' Certificate,		
Royal Drawing Society,		
Bronze Medallist Association of Art)	Art	£200
Miss A. Cooper		
(BA Birmingham)	Mathematics and Latin	£180
Miss M.A. Newton		
(BSc London)	Science	£200
Miss P. Peacey		
(1st class, Board of Education Diploma)	Domestic Science	£150
Miss P.L. Rickards		
(BA Hons in French, London		
B és L. Paris)	French and History	£210

Transferred from the Mixed School

Miss V.M. Barnes		
(BA London)	French	£170
Miss J. Macfarlane		
(Cambridge Higher Local and		
residence abroad)	German	£220
Miss M.M. Netherwood (1917–18)		
(BA Birmingham)		£170
Miss A.L. Price (1918–19)		
BA London,		
Honours in English and French)		£200
Miss C.K. Thomas (1913–14)		
(BA Victoria)		£220

Awaiting appointment

| Miss D.C. Rose | Drill Mistress | £6 per half day per term |

Miss Macfarlane – to be considered as Second Mistress

To be advertised

Post of full-time Singing Mistress, capable of assisting in certain ordinary school subjects.

Mrs Mitchell was the first school secretary and, in 1920, Mrs Richardson 'came as a young bride' to work in the kitchen. Mr D. Clark, the first caretaker unfortunately died in 1921. In 1930 Miss Sheldon and the editorial committee on the *Sheaf* wrote that 'Clark was a wonderful man, and did so much for the school in its early days, that those of us, who knew him, do not want him to be forgotten'. Perhaps this book will help to fulfil that wish. Mr Clark was replaced by Mr W. Mandley. He was ably assisted by his fox-terrier, Scamp, who became the focus of a great deal of attention and the subject of several articles in the school magazine.

> Scamp by name and Scamp by nature,
> Chasing cats and bits of paper,
> Always there, wet, cold or hot,
> When goes the gong, he's on the spot.
>
> [Joan Mason]

Edith Webb remembered that:

> There were some excellent members of staff. Miss Bracey was responsible for Geography and History and took classes out of school to study local history or make maps of Wardown Park … Miss Macnab was an outstanding teacher of English while Miss Graham, the French mistress, was successful in getting most of her pupils through the School Certificate Examination. Miss Rose gradually built up the equipment for PE while her friend Miss Macfarlane taught German and cooled hands with Eau de Cologne in summer.

Miss Bracey was an interesting lady. She was brought up on the Cadbury Estate in Bournville, joined the staff in 1919 and, after working for two terms, was appointed to the permanent staff in March 1920. In 1921 she was given leave for one year, without salary, to attend a Geography course. Instead she went to Vienna and undertook voluntary work with the Friends (Quakers) War Victims Relief Committee, becoming a 'considerable figure in the Society'.

The governors were not best pleased with her change of plan and gave her the option of resigning or having her engagement terminated. She chose to resign and stayed in Europe for many years to work and to help refugees. She spent 21 years in the international service of the Society of Friends, 'for 13 of which, she was Directing Secretary of the Friends Committee for Refugees and Aliens, and its predecessor, the German Emergency Committee'. After the Second World War she was appointed to 'head up a small department of the German section of the Foreign Office' and, in 1951–2, held a similar appointment with the American High Commission in Germany. In 1942 she was awarded the OBE.

Administration

The School was administered by the Bedfordshire County Council Education Committee who, in turn, had to conform to rules and regulations set out by the Board of Education. On a lower level, the School was run by the Governors but any major decisions had to be approved by the Board of Education.

Prospectus of Girls School
- The aim of the school was to provide for girls from the age of 10 to 18 a sound general Education, which shall fit them for the needs of professional and commercial life, and which shall form a step in the passage from the Public Elementary Schools to the Universities or to the Higher Technical Institutions.
- That she shall remain in regular attendance as a pupil until the end of the School Year in which she attains the age of 16 years, unless the written permission of the School Governors for earlier withdrawal is obtained.
  That in the event of her leaving prior to that time without such consent [parents] will pay to the Governors on demand such sum as they may determine, but in no case exceeding a sum of £5.
- It is most desirable that girls should join in September rather than at any other time; and they should never (unless quite unavoidably) leave at any time other than at the end of a School Year, i.e. in July.
- At the annual examination for admission in September a certain number of Free Places are offered for competition. This examination is usually held about May or June, the exact date being advertised in the local newspapers. The subjects of examination are English (Spelling, Grammar and Composition), and Arithmetic, special attention being paid to handwriting and general neatness.
- The Preparatory Course, which should be commenced at the earliest possible age, includes instruction in English (Reading, Grammar, and Composition); English History; Geography; Arithmetic and Algebra; Practical Geometry; Nature Study, or Elementary Science; Drawing; Needlework; Singing; Drill. (In 1919, girls were able to enter the school from the age of 9.)

- The General Course, which should be commenced at the age of 11, covers 5 years. It includes instruction in English (Grammar, Composition and Literature); History; Geography; French; Latin or German; Mathematics; Theoretical and Practical Science; Drawing; Needlework; Cookery; Singing; Drill.
- At the end of the General Course whole Forms are entered for Cambridge Senior Local Examinations, for which no fees are charged.
- A certain amount of specialisation will be allowed after the General Course is completed, and the Senior Local Examination is 'passed'. Girls may then be recommended to give particular attention to subjects bearing more directly on their future careers.
- Parents are requested … to inform the Headmistress if [homework] habitually [occupies] more than the appointed time. This time should be about forty minutes each evening for those in the preparatory classes, increasing to about 2 hours for those at the top of the School.
- Fees will be £2 per term payable before term commences. This sum includes the supply of all necessary books, stationery &c. It also includes membership of the Games Club. (Fees to be paid at the office of the Boys' School in Park Square not later than the day preceding that on which term commences).
- The School is open from 9 a.m. to 12.20 p.m. each morning; and from 2 p.m. to 3.30 p.m. each afternoon except on Saturday, which is a whole holiday. Girls should arrive 10 minutes before School opens.
- Dinners and teas are provided for those pupils who come from a distance. Particulars as to charges may be obtained on application.
- Organised games are arranged for Saturday mornings, and it is hoped that parents will assist in securing regular attendance.
- Girls wishing to join the Girl Guides may obtain particulars at the School Office.
- No girl may be absent, except when unwell, without the previously-obtained permission of the Headmistress … Leave will not be granted for purposes of mere pleasure.
- At the beginning of term each girl must bring the prescribed form of Health-certificate duly completed.
- When journeying to and from School, and when taking part in any School function, girls must wear the recognised School cap or School hat. The recognised hat is a plain white 'boater' with black ribbon and School badge. Badges (price 1/6 – 7½p) may be obtained at the School Office.
- Each girl must be provided with a suitable bag for carrying books to and from School. The School authorities provide bags to contain drill shoes and other shoes for use in School; each girl must purchase one of these (price 1/6) at the School Office.

Regulations regarding Dress

General

- The hair must be worn plaited or tied back so that it cannot fall over the ears or shoulders.
- Ribbons must be navy-blue or black.
- Indoor shoes must be provided for use in School.
- Jewellery must not be worn.
- Money must in no circumstances be left in desk or cloak room. Every girl must therefore be provided with a pocket.

Drill dress

- For drill, physical exercises and games every girl must wear a tunic with a blouse, or jersey, and knickers. The tunic and knickers must be made of navy-blue material; serge is most suitable for general use, but drill or alpaca may be substituted for the summer. The blouse should be made of white or navy-blue material suitable for washing; the jersey should be either white or navy-blue.
- The tunic, which requires two widths of serge, must be pleated into a small yoke, with straps passing over the shoulders; it should be of such length as to just clear the ground when the wearer kneels upright; it must be made without velvet or other ornament. The tunic easily slips over the head, and the shoulder straps are then fastened. It should be worn with a loose girdle made of navy-blue braid. In no case should any form of stiff corset be used.
- The knickers, with their detachable washing lining, should replace all petticoats. They should not be too ample, and must not be visible below the tunic. They are warmer than petticoats and allow greater freedom of movement. Plain black stockings and shoes should be worn.
- For the tunic some 2 to 2½ yards of serge are usually required, and for the knickers about 1½ to 2 yards.
- For drill and for certain games special shoes must be worn.
- NB For general use in School, all girls are urged to wear the drill dress specified above, or a navy-blue skirt and a white or navy-blue blouse.
- Girls who are unable to return home for dinner are not allowed, without special permission, to leave the premises during the interval. Those who do not take the School Dinner may bring their dinners with them. Leave will be given, at the request of the parents, for girls to dine at private houses in the town, but not at restaurants.
- All hats, caps, overcoats, cloaks, shoes, note-books or other articles must be clearly marked with the School number of the owner.

Between 1919 and 1925 the amount charged for fees varied. When the school opened they were £6 a year but were raised the following year to £9. For a while they went up to 15 guineas (£15.75) but were reduced in 1925 to £12 per annum with a reduction of 25% if there were two or more girls at the school. Free places were offered to girls who had passed the relevant examinations.

There was considerable difficulty, as there had been in the mixed school, in persuading parents to keep their daughters at school until they were 16. Girls who left before this were not considered to have benefited from the course and there was also the problem that they may well have deprived other girls of the opportunity to receive secondary education. Parents were fined, usually £5, and, from May 1922, they were asked to sign an undertaking to abide by this rule. Interestingly one family was spared the fine because the girl's mother had signed the form in her father's absence.

The two departments of the Modern School worked different hours. Boys stayed until 4.15 every afternoon but lessons for girls finished at 3.30 p.m. Girls had a five-day week with games on Saturdays while boys had classes every day from Monday to Saturday and organized games on Wednesday and Saturday afternoons.

One of the duties of the School Governors was the task of balancing the accounts. On 9th May 1929, the *Luton News* published their estimated budget.

> The sum of £5,625 was estimated for salaries at the Girls' School last year (1928) and £5,655 spent, so the committee thought it only safe to estimate for £6,200. Fuel, light, water and cleaning required £500, as in the previous year; clerical assistance £160; rates and taxes £110; repairs and renewals £100; books, stationery and apparatus £380; and the Games Club £150, the total being £8,380. The grant from the Board of Education was put down at £500, and that from the Town Council at £950. School Fees were estimated at £2,600 and they were asking the County Council for £3,700, which was £450 more than last year. That would leave them with a balance of £252 in hand.

Opening Ceremony

The school in the huts was opened on 30th September 1919 by the then MP for Luton, Mr Cecil Harmsworth, before a representative audience of parents, girls, Ministers of Religion, local Head teachers, Town and County Councillors, members of the Luton and Bedfordshire Education Committees, the Chamber of Commerce, the Old Lutonians (20 tickets for Old Girls) and the WEA. Elma May described the excitement of the day in the very first edition of the *Sheaf*.

> A memorable day – when two hundred and nine girls all brimful of excitement assembled in the playground at the School in Park Square, and later filed into the galleries round the hall … all wearing the terribly uncomfortable regulation 'boater'. What ill-suppressed excitement – what whispering – what conjectures …

then a sudden hush, followed by a burst of clapping as Mr Harmsworth, the Headmaster, T.A.E. Sanderson, Miss Sheldon, the new Headmistress, and the Governors came on the platform …

During the speeches our one thought was: how we wish they would finish. What did we care just then about the value of education, or the contrast between the modern method of teaching geography and the 'an island is a piece of land surrounded by water' which was taught 'when I was a boy'? We wanted to dash off to inspect our new School.

But all speeches, however wearisome to the young, must end, and so did these, and at last we were free. How we envied our parents getting into the trams and riding in state from one School to the other, while we had to walk! However, we arrived almost as soon as they did, and pressed as closely as we could to the wooden door, now a memory, where Mr Harmsworth turned the silver key which was to unlock a treasure trove richer than any of us then imagined.

The following day, school began in earnest but there were many difficulties to overcome, especially since both the miners and the railway workers were staging strikes, with the result that much of the necessary equipment had failed to arrive. The paint was dry in only half the cloakroom and there were not enough pegs to go round. The hall was not finished, nor was there any accommodation for the girls who stayed to dinner – not even a chair; each girl sat on the floor and held her lunch in her lap while one cracked cup which Miss Rose had 'thoughtfully provided', was passed round. But, as Miss Macfarlane remarked, for Miss Sheldon difficulties existed merely to be overcome.

The Huts – a legendary Elysium

We can do no better than let some of the staff and girls who spent time in the huts tell their own story. While the obvious shortcomings are mentioned, the overall picture suggests that they looked back on those days with genuine pleasure.

Miss Macfarlane, the first Senior Mistress of the School (1919–1939):
The other day I came across some 'Snaps' that I had taken a long time ago, and in a flash I was back in 'the huts' sitting in an 'outside form-room' with door flung wide open. The song of the lark arose above the practising of German vowel sounds, and as heads bent over exercise books, I could see green grass and a field of waving corn. For the sake of those who do not know what is meant by an 'outside form-room' let me explain briefly the layout of the huts.

A wide corridor led up the centre, with form-rooms opening from it on either side. Through each of these 'inside rooms' you passed into an 'outside room' – much to be desired in summer, but not quite so pleasant in winter, for when the

Pictures reprinted from *Town and Country News* for 23rd July 1926.
ABOVE On the School field. BELOW A Classroom.

wind blew hard, it seemed to come through every crack in the wooden walls and sometimes even put out the one stove that heated each form-room.

At the top of the corridor was the hall, running across the width of the four classrooms. This, of course, had to be used not only for Prayers, but also for Gym, for singing lessons and in the end for a form-room. As it was the only room in which there was any clear space at all, you can imagine the competition for it for rehearsals when a play was being produced. As the years went by, the roof began to leak rather badly, and what would you damsels of a later age say to doing your School Certificate examination with buckets and pails set about to catch the raindrops as they fell? Perhaps you would prefer the years when the sun blazed down on the corrugated roof, and the floor had to be watered to prevent the temperature from rising up to 100°.

Such was the inside of our school. Now what of the outside? Not a seat anywhere, nowhere to sit except on the steps of the outside form-rooms; no tennis courts, no netball court, and only a rough hockey ground! … The netball 'court' was just a cinder patch … Cricket and rounders were played on a piece of waste ground where the houses now stand in Alexandra Avenue. The road up the Avenue, by the way, was not made up for a few years, so you ploughed your way to school through thick mud when it rained, counting yourself lucky if you arrived without losing a shoe or a rubber boot.

Pictures reprinted from *Town and Country News* for 23rd July 1926.
ABOVE A Cookery Class OPPOSITE The Library

Mrs Tattershall Dodd (née Breakell), History Mistress 1921–1928:
The road soon petered out into cornfields and from the sixth Form windows, one often watched horses and plough move slowly in silhouette against a winter sky. One solitary tram trundled up from the town to Wardown Park.

Mary Mitchell (1919–1926):
The fields with their long stubborn grass and uneven surfaces must have been the despair of Miss Rose [games mistress] in the early days. Yet we loved them, for there were found larks' nests, over which we mounted fierce guard, and poppies which strayed in from the neighbouring cornfields.

Hilda Hoyle (1919–1926):
The long corridor, its concrete floor then bare of the coconut matting which stretched endlessly up it in later years, the bare rooms and barer pitch-pine walls, the coke stoves which sometimes 'drew' and sometimes didn't, but always gave out fumes … the incredibly black clinkers around the huts, where we played netball and made enormous holes in the knees of our black woollen stockings, and had to ink over the place to 'keep it dark' … the open fields in front of the School where we watched the rabbits play.

Pictures reprinted from *Town and Country News* for 23rd July 1926.
ABOVE Gymnastics in the School Hall. OPPOSITE The Laboratory

Miss M. Macnab (1920–1953):

Another problem was posed by the rats. These intelligent creatures, driven from their slum dwelling in the disappearing wheat-fields, quickly realised that the kindly authorities had provided excellent alternative accommodation underneath the floors of the Huts – dry, safe, comfortable. Moreover, there were fragments of broken biscuits and crumbs, dropped by girls during Break, while an occasional bold and skilful raid into the kitchen pantry produced goodies galore. The rats hardly ever appeared during day-light, though on a few occasions, in wintry weather, I have seen a rat walk up the vertical wall of a neighbouring hut, in an attempt to find some water in the frozen gutter above. Rat-catchers lost their ferrets, if these were introduced under the floors. Rat-poison produced only smelly remains, which Mr Mandley, the caretaker, had to disinter, armed with spade and bucket, from under the floor-boards. The ultimate answer, as Dick Whittington could have told us, lay in cats. So for several years, we had a family of cats, usually ten in number, and marmalade in colour.

Another excitement I remember was when an Old Girls' Social was disrupted by a group of evil-minded young men from a rival Establishment. They introduced some kind of tear-gas through the outside ventilators of the Hall, and the assembly broke up, with coughs, and streaming eyes. But within a few days,

Miss Sheldon, with her detective ability, had found the identity of the malefactors. What happened to them I do not know; they were probably shot at dawn in Park Square.

[Now, could these have been from our brother school, we ask ourselves?]

Mrs C. Mitchell, first Secretary (1919–1929):
The office was of very small dimensions, it just held a small typewriting table which had to do service for all office work, and two chairs, one for myself, another for visitors (for this room was the waiting-room-cum-office in those days) and also in one corner, a school desk for the use of the Sixth Form in study periods. Shelves and pigeon holes around two sides and a telephone in the corner provided the rest of the furniture. It always seemed impossible to squeeze in another thing ... I had a pleasant view of the Park and the adjoining countryside from the small window ... I became a firm favourite with the old railway-carthorse who used to turn his head and put his nose to the window for a piece of sugar on all his visits to the School.

His Majesty's Inspectors' Report 1925
The staff and girls have stamped a refinement on the school ... The school inside is as pleasing as it is possible. The outside is a very different matter.

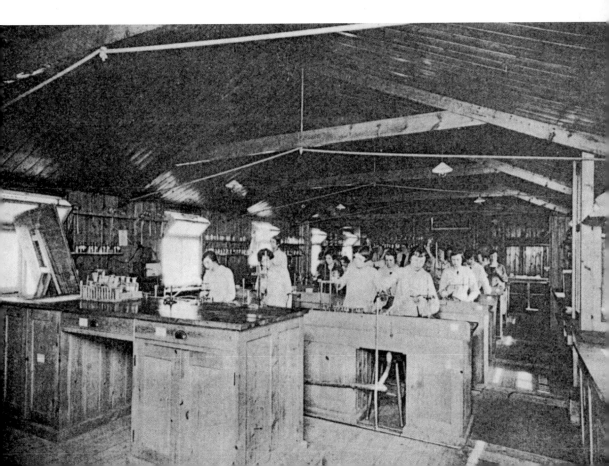

There are a couple of anecdotes about strange happenings in the hut days. One concerns a robbery which took place. Rumour had it that Miss Sheldon had been on the premises at the time and had, alas, been killed. While the girls were sitting and weighing up the situation, Miss Sheldon herself appeared, much to their consternation. Miss Sheldon wrote some time later that it is not everyone who has had the experience of being presumed dead. On another occasion, a former member of staff is said to have turned up at the School one dinner-hour intent on shooting Miss Sheldon. There is some evidence to suggest that this may have been a true story!

Miss Sheldon may have had the ability to overcome difficulties but she was fully aware of the inadequacy of the huts and fearful lest they should become regarded as permanent. In March 1921, she sent a letter to the Chairman of the Governors appealing for more space and another double hut was provided.

> Dear Sir,
> I am approaching you … to ask you to give me the opportunity of bringing before the Governors the question of lack of accommodation and facilities in the Girls' School.
> The temporary building, which is supposed to hold 250 girls, would find even that number A STRAIN ON ITS CAPACITY.

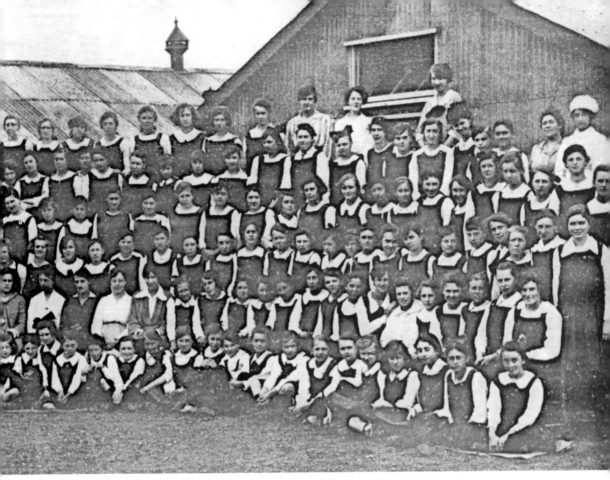

One of the first group photographs c.1920. (*The Old Lutonian*)

But with 260 in the school the difficulties are manifold. We are at times, even now, obliged to make use of my room, the staff-room, and even the store-room, and corridor for classes …

This lack of accommodation is trying now, but the situation will be more acute with the beginning of the new school year in September. Even taking into account that some 40 girls may leave in July, and this is putting the number fairly high, I cannot by any possible arrangement of the girls left, and I have gone carefully into the matter, make room for more than one form, and of these 20 must be free-placers. That leaves about 10 places at the outside for fee-paying scholars. This speaks for itself. With one and the same breath we urge parents to give their children the benefits of secondary education, and deny them the privilege.

A Broad Look at the Curriculum

The official curriculum was based on the Government's Regulations for Secondary Schools but there were also a number of extra-curricular activities. Not unexpectedly, there was a bias towards Arts as opposed to Sciences and, in accordance with the spirit of the age, Needlework and Cookery were included. In the early years of the twentieth century, commercial subjects were considered to be for boys but, by 1930, classes had been introduced at the Girls' School. On the whole, the focus seems to have been academic and it is probably true to say that, under the headship of Miss Sheldon, girls who were gifted academically received the most attention.

English

English Grammar was an important examination subject but Literature and Drama played a very significant role in the life of the school, probably because Miss Sheldon had been an English student herself. According to this observation in Peter Vigor's book, she was successful in passing on her enthusiasm:

> Against all the odds, I once dated a High School girl, being conditioned for a middle-class life by Miss Helen K. Sheldon, a strict disciplinarian, and after a meeting or two, my date repeated these lines of Shelley to me:
>
> > *The fountains mingle with the rivers*
> > *And the river with the ocean,*
> > *The winds of Heaven mix for ever*
> > *With a sweet emotion …*
>
> At the time I wondered what she was babbling about; now I marvel at the type of literature then available to well brought-up young ladies.

The Literary Society

This was started in 1922 and was originally called the Literary, Historical and Debating Society. It was open to girls in the V and VI forms and the sessions included dramatic readings, lectures, performances and discussions both by members and visitors. By the end of the decade there were around 100 members. Among the lectures given were: *Aristophanes – the Athenian Gilbert*, *Twentieth Century Poetry*, *Fools and Clowns in Shakespeare*, *Greek Drama* and *Highways and Byeways of Literature*. In 1928, Arthur Childs talked about *Flight and the Flying Machine* and delighted the girls when he suggested that 'flying would be the mode of travelling in a very few years'.

The following year Mr T.W. Bagshawe, the Arctic explorer, gave a lantern lecture on *A Year amongst Whales and Penguins*. The whole School was invited because this was the first time that a lantern lecture had ever been given in the School. Mr Bagshawe (1931) was the founder and Honorary Director of Luton Museum. Another speaker was the Revd. J.W. Woodhouse who talked about *Sir H.M. Stanley, the African explorer*. The report noted that the 'lecture cast a new light on the ever-absorbing topic of the African problem'.

Topics for discussion and debate included *Novels – good or bad*, *It is justifiable to keep animals in captivity* and *The end justifies the means*. The last two were rejected by a large majority.

In 1928, the Poetry Society offered a Prize of a Luchessi bust of Tennyson for the best Anthology of Original Poems from any School. Luton Modern School for Girls sent a collection which won the competition. It received this accolade: 'the verse subscribed … has a generally higher standard than that of any other School'. Individual book prizes were also given to two girls: Joyce Patterson for *Sleeping Beauty* (best poem in the elder open class) and Joan Childs, commended for *Autumn in Buconnoc*.

Sleeping Beauty

Hush! she is sleeping among the red roses,
 We must not wake her – oh hush! do not speak.
Only the wind where our Princess reposes
 Gently caresses her eyes and her cheek.

Come, we must leave her, the fairies are creeping
 Softly around her and kissing her brow;
Safely they'll guard her while she lies there sleeping;
 – Only the Prince may awaken her now.

Soon he will come with the day's silver dawning,
 To kiss her slim hands and to bid her arise;
Swiftly he'll come with a new golden morning;
 – Only Prince Michael may open her eyes.

Leave her alone where the birches are shaking,
 Leave her asleep with the shy frightened deer,
Come, come away now the moon is awaking;
 – Only Prince Michael may venture so near.

         [Joyce Patterson]

Reading Circle

This group met for an hour after school on Wednesday afternoons and was open to girls from IIIA downwards. It seems that this was a particular love of Miss Easton's; she remarked that 'it sometimes seems almost incredible that so many children can sit so remarkably still and listen so attentively for one whole hour after School – and the hard floor seems to be rather an attraction than otherwise, for the greater part of the audience chooses it in preference to the desks provided'. Among the books read were: *Jeremy and Hamlet, Pollyanna, The Drummer's Coat* and *The Secret Garden*.

There was also a Reading Circle for the VI Form, inaugurated by Miss Easton, and it appears that this may have been held in the homes of members of staff, since it was remarked that the girls had 'to thank [Miss Easton] for many very interesting evenings – and teas'. Miss Macfarlane and Miss Graham also invited girls to spend evenings with them. Books chosen by this group were outside the English syllabus and included *Ipheginia*, *The Lady with the Lamp*, *Trojan Women* and works by Keats, Shelley and Tennyson.

Library

The Governors realized one of Miss Sheldon's dearest dreams by allowing her an initial £100 plus £25 a year to establish a Library. Apparently Mr Sheldon, her father, was despatched to Foyles' bookshop to get a good deal on her behalf. To add to the collection, girls were invited to donate a book when they left and many 'responded generously'. Some of the better off girls no doubt did this willingly but it must have been somewhat of a burden for the girls from poorer homes.

The Library had oak chairs and gate-legged tables and the windows were 'gaily curtained in chintz'. There were blue rugs on the floor where the girls were welcome to sit. Books could not be taken home but there were 'library periods' when they were free to look around and read a book of their choice.

> Here in the oaken Library, I can see the hills,
> And a long, pale, slender finger of amethyst cloud
> Curling down across the sky like mist across the moon,
> And the air is warm and drowsy with the humid breath of noon.
>
> Tennyson and Molière and Hardy on the shelf,
> Hakluyt, Ruskin, and a score of others, bound in green,
> I could sit and read day-long with Kipling by my side,
> Read till sunset floods the room with hues of eventide.
>
> [From a poem by Joan M. Childs]

Languages

Languages were well taught and several former students won university places to study French and German. Certainly Miss Graham was reported by His Majesty's Inspectors (1925) to be so good that 'if she shows signs of leaving you ought to increase her salary or steal her boots'. Latin was needed to gain admission to at least some universities but caused more than a little heartache (1926):

> Latin is one of those things which are most tantalizing. Accusatives and infinitives, ablative absolutes, direct and indirect commands and questions, and verbs, active and passive, indicative and subjunctive all sounded very exciting to me until I tried to fathom its depths. How the Latins ever spoke such a complicated language is solely beyond my understanding! Before I write one verb, I have to think what

> conjugation – what voice – what mood – what tense, and then what person, then
> before I can write one noun I have to think what declension – what gender – what
> case, and what number.
>
> [B. Headey]

Visits to Europe were arranged by members of staff, some of whom had spent time abroad. In 1925, Miss Macfarlane and Miss Rose took 16 girls on a trip to Paris and Fontainbleu and, in 1928, there was a trip to Bruges, Zeebrugge, Ypres and Brussels with Miss Graham and Mrs Mitchell. In 1930, Miss Graham organized a week's holiday in Paris. The *Sheaf* magazines do not mention any visits to Germany but do record an outing to Cambridge in 1930 to see a German play *Die Journalisten* acted by students of the various Cambridge Colleges. Another link with the Continent was established in the sending of Christmas parcels to French children at Le Transloy who had suffered badly as a result of the First World War. One reply from a headmaster said 'Nous sommes touchés de cette marque de sympathie qui nous montre l'intérêt que vous voulez bien témoigner à nos deux pauvres petites écoles, encore bien déshéritées sept ans après la guerre'.

French Club (Cercle Français)
In 1924, the French Club was formed; in the early days it was open to V & VI Formers and Old Girls. The purpose was to encourage reading, discussion and the use of the language in informal ways. Examples of activities were: readings from Sea Poetry, *Le Médecin Malgré Lui* and *L'Homme qui Epousa une Femme Muette*. On one occasion, a French tea was organized for younger girls with games, songs and competitions and another session was devoted to Charades.

Mathematics and Science
An Inspectors' Report (1925) claimed that there was a good deal of weakness in these subjects. This was not because of bad teaching but because most girls had been admitted at the age of 12 which only allowed for a four instead of a five year course. Fortunately the starting age was falling so prospects were brighter. Articles on Mathematics in the *Sheaf* reflect a spirit of frustration rather than enthusiasm. One describes what appears to be some kind of nightmare.

> I went out of the house and seeing the cross-roads, I began to think that the
> vertically opposite lines were equal. I reached the tramway lines which were
> running in parallel lines which will only meet at infinity and seeing where two of
> these crossed, I began to prove that the alternate angles were equal etc.
>
> [R. Scott]

Another writer questions the value of Geometry.

Surely Pythagoras never intended that everyone must first be equipped with his famous theorem before going into the world! Yet nearly everybody on leaving their student days behind them can say that there has been an attempt (at least) to teach them that the square on the hypotenuse of a right angled triangle equals the sum of the squares on the other two sides.   [A.G. Baldock]

Probably in an attempt to stir up some interest, Miss Cooper organized a Mathematical Tea for Form V. Cakes were arranged in triangles and parallelograms, bunches of rulers took the place of flowers and familiar games were given a mathematical bias.

Science Club
Science seems to have been more popular. In 1925, fifty girls joined the newly formed Science Club which featured talks by members, staff and visitors as well as outings. Examples of talks were: *Bees, Geology, Sir Isaac Newton, The Colour of Animals* and *What we owe to Lister*. Illustrated talks (with lantern slides) were becoming popular and topics chosen were *Electrolux Refrigerators* and *Pictures in the Pyrenees*; the latter was thrown open to the rest of the School. A lively debate, carried by one vote, was held on the subject *A training in Science is a better preparation for life than a training in Arts*.

Visits were made to places like Kew Gardens, Laporte's Chemical Works, Lilley Hoo and the Pegsdon Hills where as many as one hundred different flower specimens were collected on one day. A Nature Club for Forms II & III was started to cultivate an interest in natural objects and girls were taken to explore Wardown.

Science Competitions
Everyone could enter for the Science Competitions and points gained were counted towards the annual number of house points. There were many categories to choose from: collections of wild flowers, pressed flowers and leaves, drawings, exhibits of scientific interest, growing plants and photographs.

Religious Instruction
In the early twentieth century, there was a legacy of disagreement over the place of religion in education in Luton as in the rest of the country. Denominational schools were free to promote their particular beliefs but schools which were administered by local authorities had to concentrate on undenominational instruction based on the Bible. Miss Sheldon was in favour of Bible teaching and School Assemblies would certainly have upheld a Christian point of view.

In 1926, a Miss Gray came to talk about the Scripture Union which aimed to make every girl and boy better acquainted with the Bible. Members were expected to read a certain portion of the Scriptures every day 'for they must remember that the spiritual side of their life should be developed as well as the physical and mental sides'. Many girls did join and a Luton Modern School section of the League was formed. Another activity was a holiday competition essay, promoted by the Vicar of Luton, on *The Teachings of the Sermon on the Mount as applied to Modern Day Life.*

History and Geography

The first *Sheaf* magazines do not provide a great deal of information about these subjects but we do know that field work was undertaken from the early days. Also there must surely have been an active and competent History department, as Joan Stalker, who entered the School in 1921, was able to go on to Liverpool University to study the subject.

Teaching Methods

Judged by today's standards, teaching methods were probably formal and mechanical, a point of view which this piece from the *Sheaf* (1925) seems to support. Apparently Miss Sheldon did not use her censor's pen here, so maybe she was sympathetic towards its sentiments.

> The greatest drawback of modern education is Note-taking. This fashionable vice has slowly but surely wormed its way into the system of 'higher' education ... In a very short time the vice gains a complete hold. Note-taking and listening to lectures become simply a reflex action, without the suspicion of a thought being given to the process ...
>
> We are living in an age now in which learning has ceased to be a joy. We are becoming machines and, as a result, examinations are becoming rapidly tests in brute memory, instead of methods of discovering the type of mind of the examinee. [E. Lambert]

Homework was obligatory and parents were asked to inform the School if girls took more than the stipulated time. It may be true, as it was in later years, that girls were consistently economical with the truth in this respect. There were also Assignment plans for every Form; everyone was expected to complete the Minimum plan but the idea was that girls should willingly move on to the Maximum plan and eventually take delight in working on their own.

> Miss Sheldon never tires of hammering away at both parents and girls on the subject of home work. This was her practical advice to parents:
>
> Do not bring up your girls to feel that after 3.30 they have no responsibility to their home or to their school. Bring them up to be willing to work hard at something, otherwise they have no preparation for womanhood. How can you expect girls who have been brought up to think that the day's work ends, or should

end, at tea-time, and that after that time neither school nor home should demand anything of them, to be good wives and mothers?

During the year one or two fathers have mentioned that a workman has a shorter day than have some school girls. I would answer that schoolgirls have a much shorter day than their mothers. The wife and the mother belong to no Trade Union.   [*Luton News* 6th December 1925]

Art

Even in the days when education for girls was viewed with suspicion, Art was considered to be a respectable subject and it seems to have been popular at the Modern School. Although there was an official Art Mistress, other members of staff contributed to the general appreciation of Art.

There was an Art Club. At first it was open to girls from the Lower IV and upwards but, from 1925, the whole school could attend. Practical work included enamelling, gesso (plaster of Paris or whiting mixed with glue), pendants, leatherwork, linoleum cuts, pottery (sometimes fired at Farnham potteries) and woodwork. Girls made passepartout pictures and painted boxes to sell at the School Fête. There was also a weekly sketching trip to Wardown Park. Talks were given on *Architecture, Colour Reproduction, Egyptian, French* and *Italian Art, English Miniature Painters, Pre-Raphaelites, Sculpture, The Florentine School, Water Colour Painting* and *Whistler*.

Regular Arts and Crafts Competitions

As with the other competitions, marks were added to the annual number of house points. Categories included design, dressed dolls, handwriting, imaginative, models, object and plant drawing, paper work and raffia work. After the 1927 Competition, there were some harsh words in the *Sheaf*.

It seems extraordinary that in a town like Luton the girls should show so little originality or aptitude in the actual choice and production of handwork. It is always possible to ask advice, and we do feel, particularly in the case of the younger girls, that this has not been done, as is shown by the fact that there has been a superabundance of articles, such as black satin cushion covers (already shop made) and small mats!

Music

Music usually meant Singing although some musical appreciation was introduced. Practices were held after school on separate days for the Junior and Senior Choirs and repertoires were built up for special occasions such as Fêtes and Prizegivings. Choirs were also entered for the Bedfordshire Eisteddfods. Another group, the Lyric Club, started in 1925, made a study of light opera.

Songs sung by the Junior Choir for the Speech Day in 1929 were:
Traditional: *Amid the New Mown Hay* and *The Skye Boat Song*
Two 'Modern': *Shadow March* and *Sea Horses*
The Senior Choir's programme consisted 'entirely of modern songs':
It was a Lover (a setting by Vaughan Williams)
Orpheus with his Lute
O Springtime, I Greet Thee
The Lark's Grave
Grasmere Carol
Very often songs were sung in French or German as, for example, at the 1927 Speech Day.
Monsieur le Coucon veut se marier
Quand Trois Poules vont au Champ
Liebchen ade
Herbei o ihr Gläubigen

Gymnastics

When Miss Rose was appointed to the staff of the Girls' School, she was described as the Drill Mistress. In fact, the old kind of regimented Drill was on its way out and was being replaced by Swedish Drill which was designed to train the body as carefully as the mind. In their Report (1925) the Inspectors expressed concern that the School had no gymnasium and also pointed out that there was a need for 'really good provision for physical exercises with simple apparatus of the Swedish type'. Miss Rose reported that, in the early days, the School

had to fight against every possible disadvantage. The field was hardly in a condition to be used at all for the first two seasons, but good use was made of the 'clinker' playground where netball was played with much enthusiasm; and also the rough ground outside the School gates where most exciting games of cricket took place. We also tried to begin tennis, using the pathway as a net. We owe our present courts largely to the enthusiastic energy and devotion of our first caretaker, Clark.

The Inspectors' Report (1925) went further saying that

the field is a disgrace to any Secondary School. However permanent or otherwise the buildings are going to be, the field will be permanent. It seems to us that the governors should make up their minds as soon as possible where the new buildings are to be placed and on some other part of the field they should institute as soon as possible levelling, draining and mowing operations.

The poor state of the field meant that it was very difficult to build up teams which could practise systematically and work together. What practice there was probably took place before school on weekdays and on Saturdays. Sometimes other sites were used, Wardown for example, and matches were frequently 'played away' where conditions were better. Audrey Fyson, editor of the *Sheaf* in 1927 wrote: 'although my fingers are exceedingly inky after this somewhat lengthy editorial, I really must mention one particular thing before I close – THE HARD COURT IS NEARLY FINISHED'.

Cricket and Rounders

Cricket was played, sometimes at the School and sometimes at Wardown Park, and, for a time, there was a special cricket coach. Rounders for Juniors began around 1929 and was also played at Wardown. As with the other games, a lot of eagerness was shown but a great deal of practice was needed.

Hockey

It appears that the standard of play was not high. However, by 1927, Miss Rose was able to report improvements and said that 'with hard practice and combined effort, there is now promise of a really good team'. She also pointed out that there was 'a growing comprehension of the fact that systematic training and daily practice are indispensable for anyone who wishes to become a really good player'. In the 1928–29 season, determined efforts were made and groups of girls were taught how to dribble, drive, stop the ball, roll in and so on. Hockey matches were played against Bedford Modern School, the Cedars School at Leighton Buzzard, Hitchin Girls' Grammar School, St Christopher's School Letchworth and also against the Staff and Old Girls.

Netball

The standard of netball was higher and, in 1920–21, the School accepted an invitation to join the South Midlands Netball League. According to Miss Rose, playing against other schools gave the girls 'finesse' whereas their play had previously displayed 'more noise than technique'. Matches were played between houses and against local Elementary Schools. The School team also met teams from Bedford High and Modern Schools, the Cedars School at Leighton Buzzard, the High School Wellingborough, the High School Warwick, Hitchin Grammar School for Girls, Kettering High School, Northampton Girls' School, Parkfields School Derby and St Albans High School. Girls who had played two thirds of these matches could 'bind their blazers'.

Tennis

In 1925, the Inspectors reported that there were two second rate tennis courts and two 'other rate' tennis courts. The general standard of play was certainly hindered by the lack of facilities although practice was possible on the grass courts at Wardown Park. Matches were played against Bedford Modern School, the Cedars School at Leighton Buzzard, Chiltern Tennis Club, Hitchin Girls' Grammar School and the Staff. In 1929, two girls were sent to represent the School in the Inter-School Tournament at Harpenden.

Games Colours

In order to win School Colours, girls had to attend all the team practices throughout the season unless they were absent or ill. They also had to be especially recommended three times for outstandingly good play in matches, by the Games Captain in consultation with the Games Mistress concerned, and sanctioned by the Headmistress. Colours had to be re-won each year but, if a girl had not won her Colours after having been three years in the first team, she could no longer be a member of that team. House colours were presented to girls who attended practices regularly, playing well in matches (in at least three out of four) and whose conduct was of a high standard, not only on the field, but at all times.

Swimming Club

This popular after-school activity took place at the Waller Street Baths. Girls were taught to swim, to improve their style and to dive. Non-swimmers were asked to sew a piece of white tape onto each shoulder of their bathing costumes and had to demonstrate that they were able swim two lengths of the pool before these could be removed. Swimming Sports which featured speed races, high diving, duck diving and obstacle races were held for the honour of winning the Payne Shield.

Sports Days

Sports Days became an annual feature, on a Saturday if one was free, but, if not, on a weekday afternoon. It was also a social occasion when visitors, including governors, came to watch. The programme for the 1924 Sports notes that tea was served during the afternoon under the direction of Miss Macfarlane, and Miss Graham had a lemonade and biscuit stall for competitors. In the run up to the opening of the new school, it became difficult to find enough clear space for the races but there was some compensation in that one of the new brick bicycle sheds made a very acceptable canteen.

The Bicycle Sheds. (1963 *Sheaf*)

The Hoyle Cup went to the winner of the 100yds flat race and the Tress Cup to the high jump champion while individual silver and bronze medals were awarded. Other individual events were: the long jump, netball shooting, and obstacle races. There was also a flat race for Old Girls. House teams competed in 'beanbag', 'through the tape', passing a netball under legs and leapfrog. In 1926, a 200yds race was run and, in 1930, there was one for fathers. Team games included the wheelbarrow and 'Hobble and Bunny' and the obstacle race involved eating a currant bun and then blowing up a balloon until it burst.

The several ages of school life

All this School's a stage,
And all the schoolgirls in it merely players.
All have their exits and their entrances,
And one girl in her time plays many parts,
Her acts forming several ages. At first
The infant, with freckly face and snubby nose,
Her hair strained back into a tiny plait,
Afraid of mistresses, prefects, everyone –
Terrified to do wrong, lest justice great
Should fall upon her inoffensive ears.
And then when in the Middle School she goes,
No longer is she righteous, fearing rules,
Her hair, perchance by now is also bobbed.
And then when Upper School is sometime reached
She feels herself important, and aspires
To be received into the sacred and
Revered order of prefecthood, when
With shingled head, or hair in telephones,
She marches up the hall, 'Stop speaking there!
You know as well as I that there's to be
No speaking here!' And then last scene of all,
Which ends this strange and varied history,
Is when she leaves, bidding sad goodbye
To dearest friends, – and mistresses too.
With flowing eyes, vowing to write to all.
Her vacant office taken by another,
Who in this history has acted too.

[Edna Worboys]

Lectures, Recitals and Visits

The regular curriculum of the School was enriched by lectures given by members of staff and visiting speakers. Educational trips were organized. There were also 'Ten Minute' mini-lessons given by form mistresses on subjects, like First Aid, which were thought to be important but which could not be fitted into the regular timetable. This was much too short a time and sometimes the talks were left unfinished.

Lectures

These were intended to open doors onto the wider world and, as befits the spirit of the age, there seems to have been a bias towards an understanding of the Empire. Captain Marriott spoke on *The British Empire brought to Mind.* He showed slides of the Empire Marketing Board and encouraged the girls to make sure that they always bought 'Empire Goods'. Miss Philippa Bridges, the first woman to journey across Australia, described how she made the trip by boat, train, camel, mail van and motor-car. Another talk, by Captain Mansfield, was entitled *With the mounted police in Canada* and after Mr Hind-Smith's talk about *Dr Barnardo's Homes*, the girls were invited to collect money to provide a tea-party for 50 children who were being sent to Canada as 'little immigrants'.

In 1930 Mr Whelan, who had already addressed both boys and girls at the Park Square School, came to speak about the *League of Nations* which had been founded in 1920. As well as explaining the aims of the League, he listed the French names of associated countries which 'entailed a fair knowledge of Geography'. Mr Whelan also explained that, although the League had immense power and influence, Russia and the United States remained 'outside its domain'.

Some of the talks, like the one given by Professor W. Mark Webb had a modern ring. He used lantern slides and explained how naturalists get rid of pests which would injure the fruit, by transporting other insects which are their natural enemies. In 1924, a Mr Mongiardino set up a wireless in the hall. Mr Day (from the music shop?) came with another 'modern invention', the gramophone, to support a talk which Miss Fuller gave for the Beethoven Centenary. Afterwards Mr Day told the girls about 'the new methods of recording, which enable records to be made while actual concerts are going on. He told us how the volume of sound can be increased or decreased at will, and so can be made suitable for ordinary records'.

Recitals

Miss Sheldon, ever a keen supporter of things theatrical, organized several Recitals. In 1924, Mr Macready spoke about actors and the 'true appreciation of Shakespeare'. Then he delighted the School with scenes from several Shakespeare plays. Mr Runnels-Moss came on more than one occasion. In March 1926, the School was 'in a keen state of excitement' because he was to perform scenes from Scott's *Ivanhoe.*

He made the characters come alive: 'the cringing Isaac, the proud Rebecca, the courteous Ivanhoe and the burly Front de Bœux'. Mr Runnels-Moss said that he aimed to keep his hearers from limiting their choice of literature to the 'penny dreadful' and its companions. He came back later in the year to give a Recital based on Charles Dickens' *A Tale of Two Cities* and kept 'his large audience enthralled'.

Visits

Education was moving outside the walls of school buildings and the Modern School followed the trend. In June 1924, eight charabancs took the girls to Wembley to see the British Empire Exhibition where displays about the countries were on view. The Canadian section displayed rugged rocks over which a small mountain torrent crashed on its way to the real river and there were tall slim Canadians in scarlet tunics. India was the 'land of the temple bells and scented moghra trees'. At the Burma stand the girls exclaimed 'Oh, those rubies, that ivory!' and in Hong Kong they noted the weird odour of burning perfume, beautiful inlaid tables and delicately painted china. Australia was described as a land of little fields of real corn and luscious grapes where rosy apples hung on trees.

In June 1926, Form IVA went to a Fête at Harpenden primarily to watch *Twelfth Night*. Most of them met in Park Square and cycled along the Lower Harpenden Road; apart from one puncture, there were no mishaps. There were other things to see and do, such as buying from Elizabethan pedlars and watching folk dancing. The same month Form IIA went to London Zoo by charabanc with their Form Mistress, Miss Easton.

Employment opportunities for women in the early twentieth century were not as wide as they are now but working in telegraph offices and post offices were some of the earliest acceptable occupations. Possibly with this in mind, 20 girls, mainly from the Lower VI, visited Luton telephone exchange in 1929. They were 'impressed by the facility and apparent ease with which the operators manipulated their instruments and some were allowed to listen in while calls were put through to London'.

Examinations and Scholarships

In the early days of the Mixed School in Park Square, pupils took the Cambridge Local Junior and Senior examinations. Apparently this system was confusing and, in 1911, a Government Committee was asked to sort out the 'tangle of competing examinations'. As a result, new examinations were introduced in 1917. The first of these was the School Certificate which was taken at around the age of 16. Candidates were required to pass in five or more subjects, including at least one from each of three groups: English, languages and science and mathematics. There was a fourth group which included music and manual subjects but this was not obligatory. If a sufficiently high standard was reached in the School Certificate examination 'matriculation exemption', a qualification accepted by some universities and sought after by many employers, could be obtained. The Higher School Certificate was taken two years later after a more specialized course of study. The School Certificate and Higher School Certificate examination system lasted until 1950.

Examination terror is nothing new and the girls at the Modern School experienced their share of it.

> Tucked away in the farthest corner of the world is a green dragon; an ugly little fellow, with baleful yellow eyes, and a sharp stinging tail. He is small and shrivelled looking but he soon fills out and swells to a quite formidable size … about three weeks before the fatal day, he steals from his corner, sneaks up Alexandra Avenue, underneath the front door of LMS, up the corridor, hidden by coconut matting and when I am not looking he worms his way onto my shoulder … When I go to bed he squats upon my pillow and laughs at me … In the Examination room which is his very Heaven, he squats on the back of my neck. He laughs at my clammy hands, at my weak knees, at my fuddled brain, and he chuckles with glee as he reads the impossible questions …   [Gertrude Mitchell]

Scholarships

A University or a College education was still, to a large extent, élitist and usually depended on the ability of families to pay for tuition and maintenance. However, there were some scholarships available for the high flyers. Bedfordshire County Council offered annual Leaving Scholarships, one for boys and one for girls, to pupils who were in need of financial help. Candidates had to be bona fide residents in Bedfordshire, must have attended the Modern School for at least three years, have passed the required examinations and satisfied the Governors in an interview. From 1920, the Government gave a limited number of State Scholarships and local charities, such as the Bigland, Richard and Long or Chew's Foundations, could be asked for financial assistance. In 1928, it was reported that Barbara Slatter had gained a Laura Spelman Rockefeller Memorial Fellowship of 1,800 dollars a year, plus travelling expenses and tuition fees. The Bursary system for aspiring teachers was still in place.

The first girl from the High School to be given a State Scholarship was Hilda Hoyle (1927). There were many more who followed in her footsteps but, unfortunately, their names have not been consistently recorded in the *Sheaf*.

Edith Smith was an outstanding scholar and was helped in her academic career from several sources. She was given a Governors' Exhibition and a Senior Exhibition from the Chew's Foundation (Dunstable). She won an Open Scholarship in French and German (£50 a year for three years) at the Royal Holloway College. (This, the first such award for the School, was greeted with considerable euphoria by the staff and girls.) She received a scholarship from the Drapers' Company, a Driver Scholarship for French at the Royal Holloway College and, while at University, won the Christie Prize for a French essay. This is an impressive list but this kind of success was only open to the few.

Within the School system, there were Form prizes, Subject prizes and prizes for passing the Cambridge School Certificate, Higher School Certificate, London Intermediate Science Examination and London Matriculation Examination. School Honours were given for academic achievement combined with good conduct and, from 1929, good deportment was recognized by the presentation of special multicoloured girdles. School Games Colours went to individuals but everyone worked together throughout the year for the House Trophies.

These were all presented at Annual Speech Days, held at the Boys' School in Park Square. They were very much social occasions with full coverage in the local press and in the *Sheaf* magazine. Governors, friends and parents were invited, Miss Sheldon read her Report and an eminent visitor gave a speech. Presents and bouquets were presented and there was a concert with songs and recitations, culminating in the singing of the School Song.

Magazines

During the first few years of the School's life, the girls had to contribute to a Form Magazine. The work was closely scrutinized by Miss Sheldon and, in early 1924, she decreed that the standard of the articles was high enough for a School Magazine, called the *Sheaf*, to be published. These Magazines have been invaluable in the preparation of this book, particularly since the School Logbooks have, for some reason, disappeared. Not only does the *Sheaf* give information about the school itself but also provides us with a fascinating glimpse into life in the outside world.

There are interesting accounts by girls who had lived in other countries like Aden, China and India. Then there was the talk given by Miss Sorabji, an Indian educationalist who tried to explain the differences between life in England and life in India in the early twentieth century. She described a different land from the modern multi-cultural one we now know, saying that, whereas England had 'one race, one language, and one religion, and is regarded as a Christian country', India had forty different races, a hundred different languages, and many different religions.

The magazine gives us an interesting insight into three events which affected Luton in 1926. In May came the General Strike when there were no trains and workers were given priority on the buses. A girl from Lower VA described how she and her friends managed to get to school.

Morning after morning we came to School on bicycles, meeting with many adventures. One morning we met a herd of cattle and walked behind them for at least half a mile because every time we tried to pass, the wretched creatures strayed into the road and their drover, unsympathetic man, just laughed at our predicament and made no attempt to help us. [M. Lovell]

Jubilee celebrations to recognize the granting, in 1876, of Municipal Borough status to the town, took place on June 30th 1926. Just after one o'clock in the afternoon the girls from the Modern School marched down Alexandra Avenue to join the children from the other schools. They watched the procession and then

the Piper led all the school children into Pope's Meadow for tea. All the schools in Luton were arranged in the meadow, and it was no small task to distribute bread and butter, buns and cakes, to say nothing of trying to avoid tripping over hundreds of legs in a valiant endeavour to pour scalding tea into 'wobbly' cups! [Gertrude Mitchell and Rhoda Scott]

After tea there were other exciting activities including dancing girls at the Sports Ground and a Swimming Gala at Wardown Lake.

Then, on 17th November 1926, there was a visit by the Prince of Wales. Eight girls were invited by the Mayor to represent the school at the Football Ground where the Prince of Wales presented Colours and Silver Drums to the 2nd Battalion of the Bedfordshire and Hertfordshire Regiment.

This was a simple, but very impressive ceremony, and one which occurs very rarely. We all felt a little sad when the Old Colours were slowly marched off the field, to the tune of 'Auld Land Syne'; but this sadness was soon banished when the gaily coloured flags, and shining silver drums appeared! … a very historic and interesting ceremony was brought to a finish. [Ella Jack]

Another article in the *Sheaf* entitled *Travelling on a Country Bus* demonstrates that criticism of the younger generation is nothing new.

The other day, two old ladies were reclining exactly opposite to me, and the persistent wagging of their huge bonnets hid their faces from my view, but their voices were raised in shocked disapproval of the 'modern generation'.

'I don't know what the world is coming to my dear,' the first one whined, 'first they learn to dance and cut off all their beautiful hair. Then they go gallivanting about the streets like men on these ridiculous motor-bikes. I'm sure I live in fear of my life. My young niece Carrie used to be a lovely girl but she's as bad as the others now.' [Ruby Pateman]

Starting a Tradition

During the years in the huts, the pattern was set for life in the School, as generations of girls would come to know it – and remember it, usually with gratitude and often with affection. In 1924, Miss Sheldon asked:

> Are we setting our standard high enough, our standard that should always be just beyond our reach, so that it is only when we are on tiptoe that we can touch it with our finger-tips? I wonder if we are?
>
> Are we forming our Tradition of the right ingredients? What should these ingredients be? Let us consider – First of all, I think we must put that greatest of all virtues 'Charity', or to use the word easier to understand, 'Love', for since none of us can give of our very best unless we love a thing, therefore we must love our School. And with love let us put its twin-brother unselfishness, for we can only 'forget' *ourselves* for those we love, therefore we must be unselfish for our School.
>
> These, I think, are the two chief ingredients and comprise in them the rest, but I want just to mention three others: – A cheerful spirit, for grumbling never has done, and never will do any good to anyone, least of all to the person who practises it – the power of imagination to illumine the dull things, the 'hack-work' of life; and last, but by no means least, the power to see the other person's point of view, always a difficult thing, perhaps the most difficult thing of all.

Rules

Formal rules were set out in the official prospectus, but there were those other rules! Many former pupils have contributed reminiscences to the preparation of this book and their dominant memories are, without a doubt, those rules. Miss Sheldon started as she meant to go on and the rules were firmly established by the time Edith Smith wrote this piece for the second edition of the *Sheaf.*

> Thou shalt not talk in the corridor.
> Thou shalt change thy shoes night and morning.
> Thou shalt keep silent in the train.
> Thou shalt walk in a seemly manner in the street.
> Thou shalt put thy dinner ticket in the box before nine o'clock.
> Thou shalt not have a maximum star unless thou first passest the minimum.
> Thou shalt consume thy dinner, yea, unto the uttermost particle.
>
> More could be added to Edith Smith's list:
> Thou shalt not eat in the street. (Stories have come in of girls having to stand up in front of the school in Assembly because they had been 'seen' to eat in the street.)

Thou shalt not walk more than two abreast.

Thou shalt cycle alone, never beside thy friend.

Thou shalt never, never talk to a boy.

Even girls from the North London Collegiate School, which shared the School buildings at the outbreak of the Second World War, fell foul of these rules. They were especially aghast because their school had a more relaxed regime.

Miss Macnab, a former member of staff, recalled that rules were in general strictly obeyed. 'If they were not, instant, and often public, restitution followed.' For one period at least, a bad offender was compelled to wear a black ribbon of shame on the sleeve of her blouse. She went on to say that 'Today (1976) most of Miss Sheldon's regulations would arouse storms of anger from staff, parents, and girls. It is difficult to decide where discipline ends, and tyranny begins, or where modern laxity must be stopped, before all good standards of decency and of learning are irretrievably lost.'

These strictures ensured that there was a guarded atmosphere in the School, as this piece from the *Sheaf* (1929) demonstrates.

The most prominent sound in the cloakroom on a wet day is drip! drip! as the rain runs off sou'westers, mackintoshes and hats alike in miserable little streams, making puddles on the floor. 'Will you help me off with my Wellington?' says someone in a whisper, but alas! that tiny whisper has been heard by a prefect lurking round the corner, and she pounces on her quailing victim, as does an eagle on its prey. 'Report yourself to your Form Mistress and write out a page of your best handwriting, and bring it to me tomorrow morning,' she snaps. (I have noticed that wet days do not always improve a prefect's temper). Meanwhile the offending Wellington has been conveyed with unnecessary force and gusto on to the rack, but this does not improve matters, for the writing must still be done.

The *Sheaf* carried a lament from another girl who transgressed.

A mistress caught me eating sweets,

Whilst other girls were doing 'prep'.

Her wrath was great, her eye was fierce,

And heavy was her step.

She took me to her study then,

And though I wept and cried full sore,

She gave me lines, without a doubt,

Full twenty score.

[Part of a poem by Barbara Smith]

Other punishments, handed out over the years, have been recalled. One girl had to learn Gray's *Elegy* for failing to deliver her dinner ticket on time. Then there were the trips to fetch pink tape, if hair fell below the regulation collar line. A girl who permed her hair was told to 'wash it out'. Some, like Gladys Gardner, seem to have accepted their punishment with stoicism. She wrote that 'it is truly said that schooldays are the best time of your life; whether in the detention room or on the playing field, every moment is enjoyed'. Others tried putting on a bright face, like the girl who wrote 'Amen' at the bottom of her lines. The response from the teacher involved was apoplectic. Members of staff have been very discreet but it has been suggested that there might, just might, have been rules for them as well!

Several other traditions were set up in the early days but it is not clear just when they were instigated or when they ended and generalizations have had to be made. In the 1928 *Sheaf* there is a mention of pasting specimens into books. Were these the dated, signed and beautifully written texts which concluded with the words: 'this is a specimen of my best handwriting' and which were intended to be the yardstick by which every subsequent page would be judged? Work which was particularly neat or of a high standard was awarded a 'Show' and could be handed to Miss Sheldon for her signature of approval. At the other end of the scale came a 'Rejection'. A high

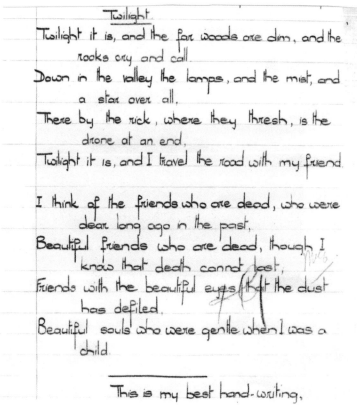

A Handwriting Specimen, 1934.

standard of neatness and cleanliness was also demanded in the classrooms and the regular end of term vinegar and polish routine was in place by 1934.

> There is something about a stationery cupboard that is extremely fascinating. The neatly-piled packets of exercise books, some of them with torn tops which shew a gleaming blue cover, the stacks of foolscap, not a sheet out of place, the little clusters of rulers and set-squares – how very clean they all look! … It really does seem a pity to spoil their tidiness with ugly ink marks. Yet new paper has a very good influence, for who would willingly write atrociously on the very first page? Even those unfortunate people who do not write well, naturally feel some impulse to work miracles by suddenly writing beautifully. After the first one or two, alas, ink-blots, and lack of time, cause good resolutions to disappear.   [M.E. Woods]

Girls from the School were easily identified by their hats which *had* to be worn. These hats became a bone of contention over the years and all manner of ways were found to challenge authority by wearing them high, low, pushed up or pulled down. Hats became the focus of attention from children in the town, especially boys, during the snowballing season.

The Seven Stages of Hat. (1958 *Sheaf*)

It seems as though girls from the School developed a recognizable character. In 1925, the Government Inspectors remarked that the girls had 'stamped a refinement' on the School and Mr E. Whitaker, the first headmaster of Denbigh High School (1967), said that they 'had a character of their own'. Then there was the particular style of handwriting which identified former pupils for years to come. This was similar but not exactly like the one designed by Marion Richardson. Another mark of identification was probably the ruling that girls had to shout 'Hurrah' and never, never 'Hurray' when called upon to shout 'three cheers'.

The School inherited the motto 'Ubi Semen, Ibi Messis' (where the seed is, there shall the harvest be) but they very much made it their own and the theme was taken up in the School Song written by Miss Whelan in 1925. Apparently, if one looks closely, the House mottoes can also be found.

Let us 'ere our day be ended,
Sing a happy song,
Of the stories long remembered,
Of the records as we wrote them,
And the triumphs as we made them,
Of the School.

Let us tell again the memory,
In our happy song,
Of the roads we trod together,
And the wonders that we found there,
Where the ways of learning lead you
To the stars.

May the lesson still be cherished,
In our happy song,
Each for all in courage steadfast,
One in hope, in work unwearied,
Hearts uplifted, hands most willing,
This the seed.

While we think on things accomplished,
Let us sing our song,
For the seed then sown shall ripen,
Till the harvest must be gathered,
And we too shall come rejoicing
With our sheaves.

Miss Sheldon concentrated her ideals into a tradition and, from 1933, every girl was given a card with the tradition printed on it. This had to be kept underneath the lid of her desk and, provided that a girl's conduct had been satisfactory, the Headmistress signed the card each term. This practice seems to have been suspended in 1956.

Our school tradition

of

unselfishness,

honesty

and

hard work

has been worthily gained.

Let us pass it on unsoiled.

In January 1930, the name of the School was changed from Luton Modern School for Girls to Luton High School for Girls. This was no doubt an indication that the School identified itself with the other Girls' High Schools around the country which aspired to the principles of Frances Mary Buss.

Houses

During the first term, the School was divided into five Houses, each named after a famous woman and each having its own colour, motto and badge or button. The fact that the houses were named after women might seem to be obvious but, in fact, other girls' schools were still being offered masculine rôle models. Twenty-one years later, Ella King recalled that the girls were told to choose well as the Houses 'would last as long as the School lasted. It was a great responsibility.' The style of the House buttons seems to have changed over the years; the first were handmade from silk and 'a sorry sight' some of them were. They were abandoned in favour of enamelled badges which had to be worn as a 'necessary passport' to House Meetings. The House colours were also changed slightly over the years.

The Houses were always in competition with each other, probably to provide motivation for extra-curricular activities. Philanthropy was actively encouraged and each House looked for a charity which had some connection with the achievements of its patroness.

The following quotation is taken from a Fry House Report but it obviously refers to the kind of attitude expected from all individual House members: 'we firmly hope that every girl now realizes that as a member of her House she is not a separate individual but part of a body, and that whatever she achieves or does not achieve affects the House as a whole, whether it be in work or in play'.

Working for the honour of your House was an ever-present concern and points were won for a variety of activities from Games to Arts and Crafts. The highest accolade was the House Shield which was presented on Speech Day. However, there were also lesser trophies.

The Bateson Cup	Sports
The Barnes Cup	Tennis
Netball Cup	
Jack Cup	Hockey
Payne Shield	Swimming
Gardening Shield	
Lovett Shield	Arts and Crafts

Boadicea

This is the Latin form of Boudicca, who was the Queen of the Iceni around the middle of the first century AD. She incited a rebellion against the Romans and attacked Colchester, Verulamium and London before the Roman army retaliated.

The House colours were blue and cream or white.

Motto: Non Sibi Sed Patriae – Not for ourselves but for our country.

The House Shield. (*Cleaned and repaired by John Gillespie. Photograph by Bob Norman*)

In 1927, the girls of Boadicea House collected clothing for the Luton Guild of Service, a local charity which worked for poor and destitute children in the town. However, their main charity was Dr Barnardo's and special attention was paid to the Howard Home in Bedford. One gift to the Home was a picture of St Christopher but there were regular treats for the children at Christmas and Easter.

As their contribution to the new School building, girls in Boadicea House gave a concert to raise funds for pictures.

Darling

Grace Darling (1815–1842) was the daughter of a lighthouse keeper on the Farne Islands, off Northumberland. She became famous after she and her father rowed through a storm to rescue nine people from the wreck of the *Forfarshire*.

The house colours were blue and silver.

Motto: Immersabalis – Unsinkable.

In the early days, the House adopted a small school in Le Transloy, France. Then the girls decided to send woollen garments, reading material and gramophone records to the Ipswich Headquarters of the Missions to Seamen for the use of the sailors in lighthouses and lightships. When that charity closed down (c.1929), the official charity of the House became the Royal National Lifeboat Institution.

In 1930, the girls gave an entertainment, a burlesque called *The Three Wonders*, the proceeds from which were spent on pictures for the new School building.

Fry

Elizabeth Fry (1780–1845) came from a leading Quaker family and worked, among other things, to improve the lives of women in prison.

The colours, at first, were purple and grey, later red and grey.

Motto: Non Nobis Solum Nati Sumus – We were not born for ourselves alone.

In 1926, a letter was sent to Bedford Gaol asking what the members could do to help. The reply stated that there was a need for socks and shirts. So, for six months, the girls raised money, sewed shirts and knitted socks to send to the prisoners. In 1927, it was decided to help the Luton Police Court Mission. Both of these were appropriate charities to mark the work of Elizabeth Fry but they seem to have been abandoned in favour of the National Society for the Prevention of Cruelty to Children. The girls sent garments and toys to the NSPCC's distribution centre known as 'Mother Hubbard's Cupboard'. They also sent money to Victory House, the headquarters of NSPCC. Money was collected for the League of Pity, the Junior section of NSPCC.

The Fry gift to the new School was a glass-covered model of the old School made by Mollie Chick. Money for this was raised at a fruit and sweet sale.

Keller

Helen Keller (1880–1968) became blind and deaf after an illness at the age of 19 months but, with the help of a dedicated companion, she learned to talk and became a campaigner for the welfare of the blind.

The house colours were green and gold.

Motto: Per Ardua ad Alta – Through hardship to the heights.

(It was suggested by Canon Baker at the 1929 Speech Day, that the translation could be 'Through the army huts to the High School'.)

Keller House chose to help the blind in Luton by making collections, selling flags and providing tea and entertainments. In 1929, they sent a letter to Helen Keller, signed by Miss Sheldon and translated into Braille. To their delight, they received 'a beautiful photograph of Miss Helen Keller with a message written by herself, saying how pleased she was to hear of our House, and sending us her greeting.' The photograph was framed and displayed with much pride as the Keller House was the only one whose Patroness was still living.

The girls entered into a sweet-making activity to buy vases for the new School.

Nightingale

Florence Nightingale (1820–1910) is considered by some to be the founder of nursing as a profession and is particularly remembered for her work during the Crimean War.

The house colours were flame and black.

Motto: Sursum Corda – Lift up your Hearts.

The girls from Nightingale House helped hospitals by collecting silver paper but they particularly took to their hearts the children from a Children's Home, probably the one in Beech Hill. They sent toys, books and clothes, sent seasonal gifts and money to send the children on a trip to the Zoo. In 1928, the juniors, helped by the seniors, made a 'Nightingale Villa' which 'any doll family might be proud to possess'. On completion it was sent to the Children's Home. In 1929, they played Father Christmas to the Beech Hill Homes and took clockwork toys, books and dolls: two

presents for every boy and girl all labelled with their names and wrapped in gay paper, together with several boxes of crackers. These were placed in two large decorated tubs which were taken down to the Homes by the House Committee. The following year, they sent balloons, presents and two Christmas trees. The House Captain, dressed as Father Christmas, distributed the presents. They were equally generous at Easter 1930 when they took yellow chickens (supplied by Keller House) and enough Easter eggs for the children to have 16 each.

The House contributed framed brass rubbings for the new School, paid for by an entertainment which consisted of a Chamber of Horrors and a Picture Gallery.

Social Life and Social Conscience

The ethos dictated that the School was a community in which everyone should be actively involved. As an extension of this, the School was seen as a part of the wider world to which everyone had a duty. One of the most delightful expressions of caring and sharing was the sending of flowers to children in deprived parts of London. This started in the Spring of 1921, when the younger girls sent wild flowers to Gravel Lane LCC School, Houndsditch, a school in the midst of tenements and

Portion of a photograph of the whole school c. 1926. Staff (l–r) Miss M. Breakell (partly hidden), —, —, —, Miss Pratt, Miss Whelan, —, Miss Macfarlane, Miss Sheldon, Miss Rose, —, Miss Dowdall, Miss E. Breakell, Miss Macnab, Miss Easton, —, —. [Rosomond Hayward]

warehouses, and far from any park or open space. Such appreciative letters were received that Miss Sheldon decided that the project should be broadened to involve the whole School.

Every year, on or around Empire Day (May 24th), masses of flowers were brought to school and placed in basins of water. Then there was the huge task of packing them and labelling the boxes ready for despatch to London by passenger train. It would appear that this was an efficient service, for the flowers usually arrived in good condition. In 1929, 65 boxes were sent.

Excerpts from 'thank you letters' were printed in the *Sheaf*. Some London children 'had never experienced the joys and delights of the countryside'. The flowers 'brought real sunshine into a very dingy school and neighbourhood and raised anew a little curiosity as to what the country is really like and a longing to make its acquaintance'. The children of Stepney did not know about buttercups. Some schools allowed children to share their delight with their parents by allowing them to take bunches home. It was the sweet scent of the wild flowers which especially entranced some of the little ones. One little girl 'was lucky and had a large piece of lilac' and another had a bunch of lilies of the valley. She said: 'They did smell so sweet that I was smelling them all the way home'.

The flowers were not just sent to girls' schools; the headmaster of Barlby Road LCC Boys' School wrote (1926) on behalf of his 300 boys saying 'May every such action realise the reward it deserves, that it has brought sunshine and happiness, joy and new wonder into the hearts of many dull blunted and monotonous little humans'.

Empire Day

Now all the flags are hanging out,
And guide and ranger, cub and scout,
Salute the British flag.

The girls wear daisy chains and crowns,
Excitement reigns in all the towns,
For it is Empire Day.

Our girls collect all sorts of flowers,
In spite of rain, or hail or showers,
They bring them all along.

Then these are sent away to cheer,
The poor slum children whom we hear
Have never seen the flowers.

This is our gift to Empire Day,
To make poor children blithe and gay
To show they're not forgot.

[Constance Craddock]

Plays

Miss Sheldon took a particular delight in dramatic performances. In 1927, she produced *Robin Hood* by Alfred Noyes which

Persons of the Drama.

Robin, Earl of Huntingdon, known as "Robin Hood"			N. Watson
Little John	Outlaws, and followers		R. Scott
Friar Tuck	of Robin Hood		W. Cray
Will Scarlet			H. Stewart
Much, the Miller's Son			B. Smith
Prince John			E. Breakell
King Richard, Cœur de Lion			E. Jack
Blondel, King Richard's Minstrel			S. Pardy
Thorn Whisper, King of the Forest Sprites			M. Eade
Fern Whisper, Queen of the Forest Sprites			J. Phillips
Bramble Scratch, a Sprite			E. Joyce
The Sheriff of Nottingham			M. Thorn
Deputy Sheriff			N. Burditt
Fitzwalter, Father of Marian			F. Backshall
Shadow-of-a-Leaf, a Fool			R. Bate
Arthur Plantagenet, Nephew to John			E. Michie
Elinor, Sister to King Richard and Prince John			D. Easton
Marian Fitzwalter, known as Maid Marian, betrothed to Robin Hood			B. Headey
Jenny, Maid to Marian			F. Harling
Widow Scarlet, Mother of Will Scarlet			R. Clark
Prioress of Kirklee			H. Hoyle
Novice			B. Mills
A Serf			A. Rhaidr-Jones
A Beadle			D. Swales
A Blind Man			H. Graham
First Old Man			M. Bovey
First Woman			N. King
Second Woman			V. Horne

Cast of *Robin Hood* by Alfred Noyes, performed in June 1927.
The rest of the School made up a supporting cast of serfs, children, townsfolk, courtiers, pages, outlaws, mercenaries, nuns and sprites.

brought honour to the School, not merely because the performances went off well, and because people praised us, but because all sections of the School worked together, in a happy and friendly spirit, in an endeavour to produce *well* something really worth doing. I am a very optimistic person. I feel that most things, however difficult they may be, can be done if the spirit of enthusiasm and of hard work is strong enough, and the School has proved me in this case to be right, to an extent that has astonished even me myself – and I should like to thank all those who took part, whether as principal characters, or as one of a crowd, or as curtain-pullers or as waitresses, for making my 'task' such an enviable and happy one. I have stage-managed many performances, I have enjoyed every one – but never one more than *Robin Hood.* [Helen K. Sheldon]

Thackeray's *Rose and the Ring* was performed by the staff in 1929. The School 'seethed with an excitement unequalled since the memorable days of *Robin Hood* … it seemed as if the whole school was going to swoon with joy'. The staff rehearsed after School having 'carefully peered into each formroom, and behind each pillar to make quite sure that no spying girls were secreted there'. On the day, everyone looked to see who was 'hiding behind a large false nose, or whose true person was hidden by an orange wig and a large magenta rose; not even brown curly moustaches or furrowed brows … kept us from eventually penetrating all disguises … And think what an extra 'spice' it adds to a lesson to imagine one's self being taught by a witch, a blushing bride, a lion, a cruel king, a dashing hero, a petulant princess or – a door knocker.' The proceeds from this play went to the Prefects' (red) Blazer Fund.

Open Days and Fêtes and Parties

Parents and friends were invited to Open Days when the girls' practical work would be on display. There were demonstrations of drill and performances of singing and plays. Refreshments were provided. Fêtes were held on Saturday afternoons and, in 1925, 'girls sang the Fête open'. Attractions included an Aunt Sally, a Bran Tub and a Chamber of Horrors. There were displays of Gymnastics and Old English Dances.

Then there were the School parties: lower, middle and upper. They were held after School, starting at 4 p.m. to give the girls a chance to change into fancy dress, and went on until 6.30 p.m. or even 9.30 p.m. for older girls. According to the Reports in the *Sheaf*, they were very jolly occasions and almost invariably, 'the best ever'. However, they had a serious side: Miss Sheldon would graciously agree to greet everyone and, to conclude, there were the School Song, cheers for the headmistress, prefects and staff and the National Anthem.

Food was laid on and there were bonbons (crackers). Games included Charades, Farmyards, Musical Cushions, Nuts in May, Singing Proverbs and Musical Chairs, which Miss Sheldon won without fail. However, dancing seems to have been the most popular activity with Excuse-me Waltzes, Foxtrots, Sir Roger de Coverley, Spot

Dances, and Balloon Dances. In these, the girls had balloons tied to their ankles and the 'gentlemen' had to burst them. Apparently the most popular of all was the Paul Jones.

> A stranger, hearing that the LMS for Girls is the model school for work decided to visit it to see for himself. One Friday evening, forgetting that school ended at 3.30, he entered the precincts. As he walked up the curiously deserted corridors, weird sounds greeted him – laughter, singing and the music of a piano. Then with eyebrows lifted in surprise he peeped through the Hall doors to see – ah, what did he see? The Hall, that hive of hard work, desecrated by coloured streamers, crinkly lamp-shades, deck-chairs and gay cushions, and the over-worked (?) pupils fox-trotting round the room to the music of *Side by Side*.   [E. Meakin]

From 1930, all Sixth Formers were expected to attend monthly teas. Miss Harris, Miss Macfarlane and Miss Sheldon attended them all and the rest of the staff came, two at a time, in alphabetical order. These were apparently 'hilarious gatherings' with games and competitions. It was hoped that they would continue as long as the High School continued but that hope was not realized.

Old Girls

Social life in Luton in the early twentieth century was simpler and more straightforward than it is in the twenty-first century. One could visit the Baths in Waller Street (which doubled as a ballroom in winter), the Carnegie Library, the Grand Theatre and the Palace Cinema and there were sporting facilities at Wardown Park. However, many leisure activities were based on clubs and organizations, in particular those affiliated to the different Churches. A social club, the *Old Lutonians*, had been set up by former pupils from the Mixed School and the idea of a similar group for Modern School girls obviously appealed. On 1st June 1921, the Old Girls' Society was inaugurated.

Miss Sheldon was to be President and the Committee consisted of two mistresses, three Old Girls and one girl still attending the school. At first girls from the VI Form were allowed to join to provide continuity but, once the Society was up and running, this link seems to have stopped. Old Girls who had attended the Mixed School could become members if they made a personal application to Miss Sheldon.

It was proposed that there should be one meeting a term. The subscription was to be two shillings (10p) but this was raised to three shillings (15p) in 1924. At first the brooch of the Society was a bar, with the badge of the School but without the motto, but, in 1924, a special badge was designed. In 1930, the cost of the badge was 6s.9d (34p). With Miss Sheldon's permission, Old Girls were allowed to wear a school blazer but they had to stitch a strip of gold braid across the top of the pocket.

A blazer badge could be bought from Messrs Alexander & Son, also with Miss Sheldon's permission. In 1924, the number of members was around 100 but, by 1926, it had increased to 144.

The second meeting which was held on 22nd February 1922 was devoted to a piano recital by Mr Augustus Lowe but this was not well supported and the decision was made that, in future, meetings should be half educational and half social. In the warm weather cricket or tennis were played but, at other times, there was dancing or games. Dances were sometimes held at the Corn Exchange and, on occasions, the Press came to take photographs. The Old Girls, having been well trained in the ethos of the School, expected to give their time and money to good causes. They raised funds at a handkerchief stall at the School Fête and, when the new School building was ready, they were asked to contribute towards the £50 needed for stage curtains.

Old Girls wrote articles for the *Sheaf* and sent letters to the School to describe their new lives. There were contributions from girls at Universities, Colleges, Hospitals and other training establishments. There was also news of engagements and marriages. Former members of staff were not forgotten; some moved to other posts but, in an age when the marriage bar hindered the employment of married women teachers, several of them forsook the academic for a domestic way of life.

The last meeting to be held before the demolition of the huts, took place on 18th June 1930 when 230 Old Girls and former members of staff met for a formal meal, prepared by Miss Wolverson. This was intended to be a celebration of the very happy times they had enjoyed in their 'legendary Elysium'. There were flowers from the School garden, ice creams from the 'Wall's man' and toasts to the present girls and staff, the School, Miss Sheldon and the King. Not surprisingly, this was a time of nostalgia. Girls who had lived in the huts seem to have formed a particular bond and, in their opinion, nobody who joined the school after the huts were demolished ever achieved the same status. These were special times which would never return.

> They were not very comfortable those old days … but they had their joys. One could flick a fountain pen on the floor … mistresses could pin up any number of notices on the walls. Never again would mice nest in the piano, or larks by the door, never again would the eyes of bored school girls be rejoiced with the sight of acres of waving corn outside the class room window. There would be some losses when we moved, if many gains.

Looking Back and Looking Ahead

Before you open the wide door of strife –
Stand steady and pause for a while –
Behind you is the youth of life,
In front the endless mile.

Did you play the game as you should have done,
When you felt so strange and new?
Did you aim for the goal of 'won,'
Or fall with the hopeless few?

Were you just the girl you might have been
When the pulse of youth was high?
Were you a friend when faults were seen,
And sneers made you wish to die?

Then you sang for the last a song of sheaves,
With three hundred voices clear,
Your heart was stirred for those you leave,
And your eye blurred with a tear.

Your thoughts were rising to high spheres of love,
As you sang that glorious song –
School seemed like a dream from above,
As you followed its way along.

You sang through the mist of a thousand days,
Then you saw the sudden bend –
But you knew school would steer your ways
Right through, to life's great end.

[W. Read]

Photograph of the 1930 Building, as used on the cover of the *Sheaf*.

Chapter Five

The Promised Land
1930–1939

At the Modern School Speech Day in 1919, The Rt. Hon. H.A.L. Fisher, President of the Board of Education, sent a message to the people responsible for planning a new school building for the Modern School. He said:

> Don't stint your imagination. Be ambitious! ... If you plan largely and upon a great scale, with some magnificence, then you will find that your reward will not be slow to come. These buildings, ladies and gentlemen, ought to be planned for perpetuity. A school in a modern city in England ought to be planned and built and conceived in the same spirit in which the Gothic Cathedrals in the middle ages were planned and conceived. They should be made as beautiful and attractive as possible, they should be in a sense the cathedrals of the mind of the whole community. You should get the best architects, you should have artists to adorn them, and you should spare no expense.

In 1927, plans for a new building to be erected in Alexandra Avenue were sent to the Board of Education and received general approval. The Chairman of the Governors, Alderman H.O. Williams, gathered that the only thing the Board was likely to find fault with was the expenditure and, if it became necessary to leave anything out, it would be the gymnasium. The Chairman declared that, in his opinion, this would be 'a great pity and a piece of folly'. The Governors hoped that the Board would be 'larger-hearted in the expenditure of other people's money, and when the time came would see the reasonableness of what was wanted'. Had it materialized, the proposed gymnasium, together with changing room, lavatories and drying rooms would have been housed in a separate building overlooking the playing fields and would have been connected to the main building by covered ways on either side of the hall.

Messrs Brown and Parrott, local architects, were chosen to design this 'cathedral of the mind' and Mr S.C. Parrott LRIBA apparently took a great personal interest in the project. The contract price was £50,000 and the building was intended to accommodate 500 girls. The building was E-shaped with potential for an extension to one side. Fifteen of the sixteen form rooms were situated to receive the morning sun and, consequently, avoid the heat of the afternoon. There were laboratories, two art rooms, a library, a prefects' room, a small greenhouse and a 'domestic' area with a kitchen and dining room. The Board of Education did not approve the building of the separate block for gymnastics and the dining area had to double as a gymnasium. A series of arches was built to allow cooking smells to evaporate.

The floors in the corridors and cloakrooms were terrazzo – reconstituted marble – and those in the classrooms and hall were made with wood from the Philippines. Experts have said that this wood could not be obtained today and that the hall floor is still a 'floor to be treasured'. At the back of the hall was a gallery with a clock set into the panelling, a gift from Mrs Carruthers, one of the Governors. At the front was a stage, with curtains, and the School was also the proud possessor of a grand piano. Donated pictures were exhibited in the corridors and every girl contributed to a frieze, depicting the history of the School, which was displayed in the Entrance Hall. The front of the building, where the huts had been situated, was suitably planted and sown with grass. A caretaker's cottage was built beside the Argyle Avenue entrance.

The *Luton News* described the official opening which took place on 5th November 1930. The building was declared open by the Duchess of Atholl, DBE, MP, former Parliamentary Secretary to the Board of Education, who opened the door with a golden key. It is said that, unfortunately, this part of the ceremony did not run smoothly, either because the key became stuck in the lock or because the front door was bolted from the inside. Miss Sheldon somehow managed to salvage the situation and, in due course, all the guests were able to make a dignified entrance. The ceremonial key is now at Blair Castle.

In her speech, the Duchess reminded the girls that a secondary school was the most usual form of avenue to college and university, 'a place in which they had to have a good long school life'. This became a recurring theme, for girls were still being tempted to leave school before they were sixteen by the prospect of employment. Secondary education, said the Duchess, was not something to 'nibble at' but was a 'very square solid meal' to dig into and digest. Quoting Plato, she said that education 'is not filling the mind with knowledge, but turning the eye of the soul towards the light'.

The plans for the new building also included an up-grade of the field. By Whitsun 1931, six hard courts had been completed, at a cost of £1,354, and the

25 October 2000

Cathy Green
Denbigh High School
Fax 0944 1582 483 937

Dear Cathy,

Thank you for asking me, through Edna MacKay at Blair Castle, to write this letter; I was delighted to learn of my association with the school through its having been opened by Duchess Kitty in 1930, and to know that the ceremonial key is kept at the Castle.

Being the next duchess of Atholl after a gap of 36 years has a special meaning for me as far as Denbigh High School is concerned and I hope that we may maintain our association.

I would appreciate it if you will convey to all present at the School's 70th anniversary celebrations, my congratulations and very best wishes for the future.

Yours most sincerely,

Peggy.

Duchess of Atholl

Copy of a letter written by Peggy, Duchess of Atholl, October 2000.

following Spring a new hockey pitch was ready. Miss Sheldon was not satisfied, however, and set about raising money for the next project, a swimming pool. Each girl was expected to make five shillings (25p) before September 1931 to prove that the School had used its own initiative before asking others for help. Miss Sheldon set out a list of 'wants':

1. Employment of any suitable kind (we are willing to do anything within reason to *earn* money in our spare time).

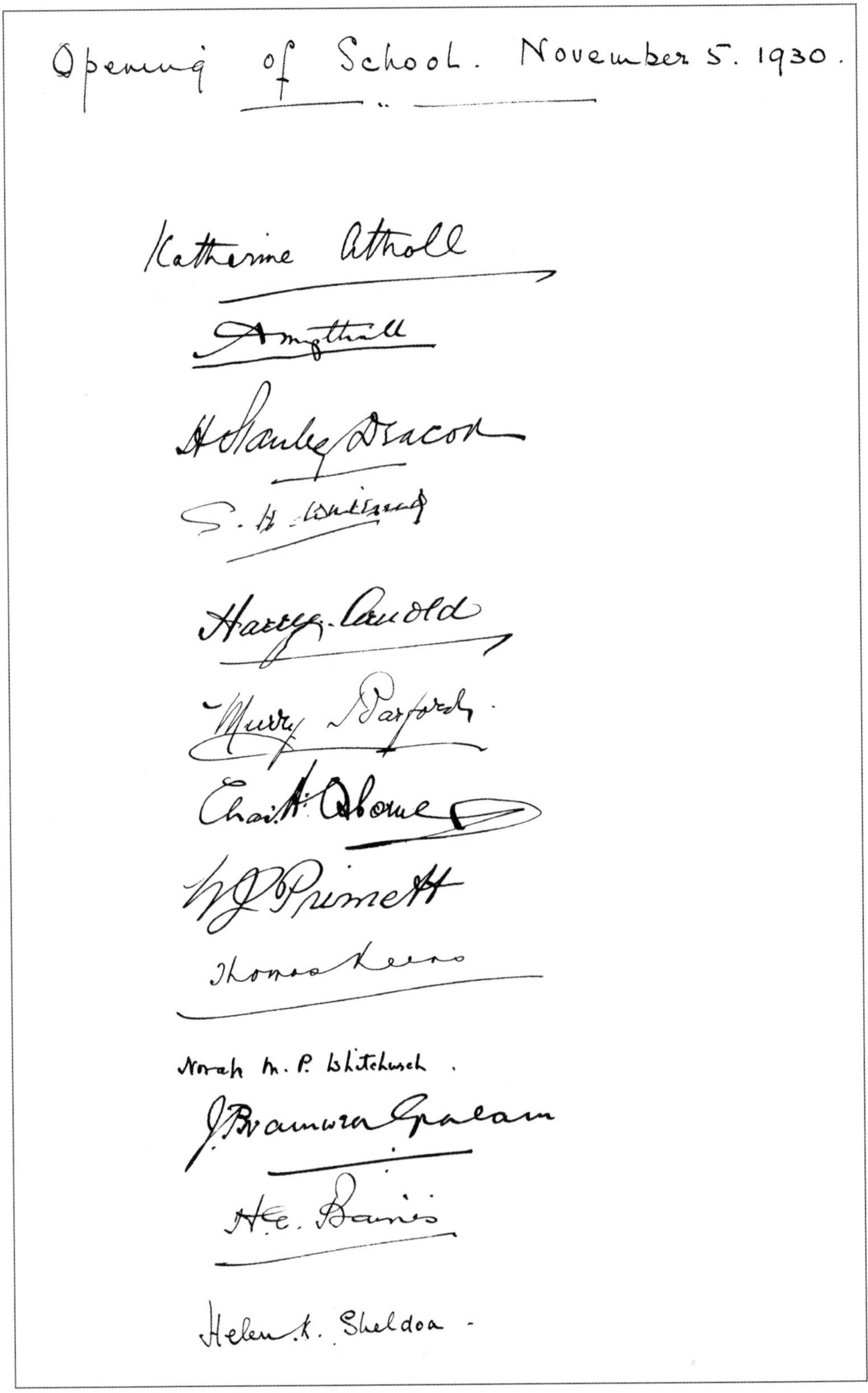

Opening of School. November 5. 1930.

Katharine Atholl

Ampthill

H. Stanley Deacon

S. H. Whitney

Harry Arnold

Murry Naysorth

Chas A. Osborne

W.J. Primett

Thomas Keens

Norah M. P. Whitehurst .

J. Bramwen Graham

H.E. Davis

Helen A. Sheldon -

2. Story books in good condition.
3. Anything suitable for a 'White Elephant' Stall.
4. Anything suitable for a 'Bran Tub' (small things).
5. Offers of help of any kind (e.g. Private Whist Drives, Sales, Concerts, etc.).
6. Gifts of any kind for sale.
7. Donations.

> One goes to school at nine, but instead of the usual comments about lessons and games, it is, 'Oh, and how much have you got towards your five shillings?' and 'I'm making jug covers, a shilling [5p] a time' …
>
> I see that someone has applied for a bunch of honeysuckle, and will pay sixpence [2½p] for it …
>
> At bedtime, I sink into a restless slumber … then as dawn breaks, and the birds begin to twitter in the garden outside, the great idea comes. In that garden of ours, grow dozens of lavender bushes. I will make lavender bags, and sell them to all and sundry. Cheered at the thought, I turn over and fall asleep. I have my idea.
>
> [L. Bowler]

> Three-pence [1p] for polishing the drawing-room surround, a penny for cleaning Daddy's boots, so now I have four shillings and eight-pence [23p] to earn …
>
> I am sure that by the time every girl has obtained her share of money, every home will be almost perfect.
>
> [Joan Bateson]

By June 26th 1931, £22 had been collected and money raising went ahead in earnest. Different Forms organized their own activities: a netball tournament, a sweet stall, an entertainment, a social and so on. The School Fête (1932) realized £168 and, by the summer of 1933, the grand total had reached £870. Other schemes put forward by Miss Sheldon were Life Membership and Season Tickets; holders being allowed to use the Baths at stipulated times, after school and on Saturdays. The pool was completed and formally opened on 14th June 1934 by Lord Ampthill.

> 'To travel hopefully' is said to be 'better than to arrive'. If you think that that is always so, go, guided by the sounds of splashing, to the corner of the Junior entrance. There ask the gaily capped heads that swim bodiless on the surface of the water, what they feel about it all. Probably they will say:
> Three cheers for Miss Sheldon who thought of the Bath!

LEFT The official opening of the new building 5th November 1930. Signatures from the Visitors' Book include: Katherine, Duchess of Atholl, DBE, MP; Lord Ampthill, Chairman of Beds County Council; Alderman Murry Barford, Mayor of Luton; H.E. Baines, County Director of Education.

(DH)

> Three cheers for Mr Parrott who made it!
> Three cheers for Lord Ampthill who opened the Bath!
> Three cheers for Miss Rose and Miss De la Mare who are helping us to use it!
>
> [D.M. Harris]

The pool, which had cost about £1,100, was being well used but fund raising continued in order to find the extra £600 needed for a filtration plant. A year later, this aim was achieved and Miss Harris could add to her previous observations: 'And so to bed! The great day [of the Fête] is over; the Filtration Plant paid for, and we can sleep the sleep of those who, like the Village Blacksmith (with necessary adaptation), "Look the whole world in the face for they owe not any man"'.

> For the first two or three weeks this season [1935] we recalled the comparatively dirty and uninspiring water that we thought so lovely all last season, but since then our conditions have altered … we now splash in clean, clear water to the gentle hum of the filtration plant behind the boxes, and the gurgling of the cool incoming water at the shallow end.
>
> [M. De la Mare]

The School now had a beautiful new building but the problem of shortage of space had still not been solved. In 1935, a School Inspection noted that

Combined Speech Day and official opening of the Annexe, 8th June 1938. (*LN*)

The building is a good one, but is now inadequate in several respects for the numbers attending … The most obvious need is for a gymnasium and changing room, the present arrangement whereby the dining-room is used for gymnastics being quite unsatisfactory; if no new neighbouring school is to be erected [for example, in Dunstable] two gymnasia will be required. The Science accommodation is quite inadequate; at least one full size laboratory or a lecture room and small advanced laboratory are required. The Library and Geography room are much too small. The cloak rooms require considerable extension, and storage space generally is lacking.

'There is never enough room' became a recurring theme and, in June 1938, a new wing to house the ever-increasing numbers was formally opened by County Alderman V.E. Goodman. There were three classrooms, each accommodating 35 girls, a gymnasium, cloakroom, a medical inspection room, a new junior library, offices and store rooms. The gymnasium was much admired; it had changing rooms, showers and equipment for all kinds of activities. Along the outside of the building was a balcony which overlooked the forecourt and terracing for spectators was laid beside the pool.

LEFT Swimming Sports 24th July 1935. (*LN*)

Official Opening of the Annexe 8th June 1938. (*LN*)

Libraries were always high on Miss Sheldon's list of priorities and the School now had two. The new Junior Library was light and airy with cream walls, blue curtains and fittings made from polished Austrian oak. The junior art mistress, Miss Oldham, decorated the wide frieze with sketches depicting some of the School's activities and a Library Committee, consisting of 12 girls, provided flowers and kept the room in good order.

> There was yet just such a feeling of 'family' and of affection as we used to have in those early days in our Huts when we were only a 'handful' as it were. If we can keep alive among us that feeling of being all joined in 'one', then our School will never have anything to fear, but can proceed from strength to strength.
>
> [Miss Sheldon, referring to the opening of the Annexe]

The very size and atmosphere of the School presented problems for some new girls, particularly those who came from small village schools or who were the only ones from their elementary schools to have passed the entrance examination. Another difficulty which some of them faced was the long and time-consuming journey which they had to make, often on public transport.

Staff

In 1935, there were 25 full-time members of staff; this gave a ratio of one Mistress to 25 girls. Some of these were new appointments but a strong group of long-serving teachers began to establish themselves. It is interesting to note that Old Girls were beginning to return as members of the Staff. The first was Edith Smith (1928) and, ten years later, Mary Woods joined the School. Over the years, many more were to follow in their footsteps.

Miss H.K. Sheldon (1919)

Miss Sheldon continued to attach a great deal of importance to 'health, energy, and the development of character and personality'. She had set her standards high and used her considerable literary skills at every opportunity to rally staff and pupils to share her philosophies and ideals. Her outlook was always positive and no difficulties were allowed to stand in her way.

> We are nearing the close of another School Year – 1937–1938 – the nineteenth year of our history. I think that when we look back, it will stand out as a year of Sunshine and of Shadow – and I put Sunshine first, as I think that that is what will remain most vivid – for the Shadows melt into the Sunshine and are lost in it.

Miss J. Macfarlane (1919)

When Miss Macfarlane left in the summer of 1939, Miss Sheldon wrote:

> To me, her going will leave a very great gap, for she has been a loving friend, and a most loyal colleague for all the years that I have been in Luton – almost twenty. I felt that she would be so when I first saw her, and what I felt then has always been true.
>
> And to our School, she stands for something very big. She has set a standard of dignity and of responsibility as a Second Mistress; of vigour and energy both as a teacher and as a member of staff; and of generosity, kindness and reliability as a friend.
>
> She has been a 'rock' in helping to set a standard and a tradition for our Girls' School in Luton, and only those of us – very few now – who were here in the very first year know what that has meant.
>
> The name of Jane Macfarlane will, I hope, stand enshrined in the annals of our School, as it will always stand in the hearts of those of us who have known her here; and not in our hearts only, but in the hearts of all those countless boys and girls who know her, loved her and admired her in the Modern School in Park Square in those many years before September 1919.
>
> 'Mac' was very dear to them, as she is and always will be to us; we shall miss

her dreadfully, for it just feels as if a piece of the School is being broken-off. We wish her happiness in her retirement, and hope that she will often come back to see us.

Miss D.C. Rose (1919)

Miss Rose taught drill and also had the thankless job of supervising the girls as they tried to master games on the untamed cornfield. After her retirement, she went to live with Miss Macfarlane in a rural retreat in Warwickshire.

> And the fruit! Does it make your mouth water when I tell you that Miss Rose and I gathered quite a hundred and fifty pounds of raspberries? Then came the plums. Then the damsons, and when the gales blew in September and in October we were almost literally knee-deep in pears and in apples. Stewed apples, baked apples, apple charlotte, apple jelly, and apple pulp, all helped to get rid of this overwhelming surplus.
>
> [J. Macfarlane]

Miss D.M. Easton (1920)

Miss Easton started at the School in 1920 and became Deputy Headmistress after Miss Macfarlane left. She will be remembered by generations of girls for her wonderful story telling at the after-school reading group. When she died, in December 1945 while still a member of staff, Miss Sheldon spoke about her qualities as a teacher and also her practical skills.

> Few people can have had a greater gift of arousing enthusiasm in their pupils and for inspiring them to question, to think, to work. She had a perfect genius for designing and cutting out costumes for plays, literally by the hundred, and perhaps she enjoyed more than anything else our dramatic performances.

Miss H. Graham (1920)

Miss Sheldon recorded her appreciation of Miss Graham who retired in 1937:

> Miss Graham joined us in September 1920, at the beginning of our second year, and from the very first moment that she became a member of our school, she has given unsparingly of herself in every way. She found our French a weak struggling little plant, and she has turned it into a flourishing tree, whose roots are set fast in the good soil of fine learning and of fine traditions, and whose ever-spreading branches are laden with the fruit and the flowers of high endeavour and of great achievement.

Edith Smith added that 'we cannot count the times that we have blessed Miss Graham's Lemonade Stall on sweltering Sports' Days and other open-air occasions'.

Miss C.A. Dowdall (1929)

Miss Dowdall joined the staff in the days of the huts and retired in 1959 'after a gracious reign of thirty-four years over the Mathematics Department'. She was described as wise and generous, an 'elder statesman' and an 'inspiration and tranquil breath of vision invaluable to us all'.

Miss Laurie G.C. Fuller (1926)

Miss Fuller joined the staff in 1926 and remained head of the Music department until 1963. She tried hard to teach generations of reluctant girls to master the tonic sol-fa and succeeded in teaching them a repertoire of national songs and lieder. Under her guidance, the choirs were able to reach high standards. She was said to be 'another of those skilled and generous givers to whom we all owe so much' and her dramatic gifts were demonstrated in 'many diverse roles from the Snow Queen to dowager duchesses'.

Miss D.M. Harris (1929)

Miss Harris, who taught History, had been a friend of Miss Sheldon's before they came to Luton. Miss Sheldon wrote of her high standards and humble spirit, which were 'of lasting value to us all'. She was frequently called upon to write reports for the *Sheaf* and was recognized as a gifted poetess.

> Not only for the glorious things of Earth
> The Sun, the Moon, the softly dappled sky
> The Spring's sweet hope; the Harvest's thankful Mirth,
> Do I lift up my heart to Thee on high!

Miss V. Ling (1932)

Miss Ling came to teach Mathematics in 1932 but, over the years, became Head of the Lower School and then Deputy Head. She was always a popular member of staff.

Miss M. Macnab (1920)

Miss Macnab (who wore pince-nez) was an inspired teacher of English. Her 'knowledge of written English both past and contemporary is both encyclopaedic and discriminating – her capacity to run a context to earth was proverbial! Her feeling for the good word and simple style has helped many a woolly thinker to hammer out a lucid phrase.' She was also a gifted pianist. When she retired, she, together with Miss Wesley, collected information about Old Girls for the *Sheaf.*

Miss E.M. Smewing (1927)

As well as teaching Chemistry, Miss Smewing was very active in School charity work and, during the War, helped to run the School Company of Service.

Miss C. Stableford (1930)

Miss Stableford came in 1930 as a French teacher but became better known for her commitment to the Church. As Head of the Divinity Department she instigated the Christmas Festival of Nine Lessons and Carols and the Festival of the Passion at Easter time.

Miss K. Stephenson (1928)

Miss Stephenson taught Mathematics and also enjoyed country-dancing, singing and dramatics. In the school plays which Miss Sheldon produced, she always had a prominent part 'usually as a man, because of her noble voice and bearing.'

Miss A.W. Wesley (1929)

Miss Wesley came to teach Geography but became Deputy Head when Mrs Evans became headmistress. Mrs Evans said that 'it was no easy task to succeed such a great headmistress as Miss Sheldon, and without Miss Wesley's unfailing support, her quiet wisdom and her unswerving courage, I realise just how impossible it would have been'. A quotation from the *Sheaf* refers to her 'quiet strength and tranquillity'. Miss Wesley was also remembered for her delightful singing voice.

Miss M.E. Wolverson (1928)

Miss Wolverson taught Domestic Subjects and was called upon to provide refreshments for special functions. Her catering skills were described as 'an eighth art'. During the war, she encouraged girls to produce garments for the war effort. Apparently she was always good for a 'what I have done this week' sort of chat, during needlework lessons.

Administration

All schools were regularly inspected by His Majesty's Inspectors. One such Inspection was held at the High School between 29th October and 1st November 1935.

> At the end of October we were told by Miss Sheldon to appear very neat and tidy the following week as she was expecting some visitors, but she did not say that they were Inspectors …
>
> Everyday, until Friday morning these 'mysterious' men and women were continually entering the form-room, but as they were so nice and friendly, nobody minded their presence. [Margaret Thorne]

At the time of this Inspection, there were 606 pupils and figures from the previous academic school year show that 68.1% of girls came from Luton, 24.3% from the

County and 7.4% from Hertfordshire. One girl lived in Buckinghamshire. Annual tuition fees were £12 for local girls, £32 for girls from Hertfordshire and for girls from other counties, £20. On top of the fees, the cost of hiring books was 15 shillings [75p] a year.

The School worked against a background of changing educational ideas. Luton schools, apart from the High and Modern Schools, were known as 'elementary schools'. The *Hadow Report* (1926) proposed that schools for children up to the age of 11 should become known as 'primary' schools and that education for all children above 11 years of age should become 'secondary'. These new secondary schools would offer different types of education to children with differing abilities and needs. These ideas took almost 20 years to come to fruition and, meanwhile, the High and Modern Schools and, from 1937, the Technical School, remained the only secondary schools in Luton.

From the time the School was opened in 1904, 25 per cent of places were offered free to children who had passed well in the entrance examination. However, in 1933, and as a result of stringent national economies, the scheme was revised and 'free places' became 'special places' which were means tested. Local Authorities were told to draw up scales based on parents' earnings and only families on very low incomes were excused the fees altogether. The standard fees of £12 per annum were reduced by 25% for subsequent members of the same family.

> The happiest day of my life was when I heard that I had passed the High School Entrance Examination … I waked to find my friend and a long envelope waiting for me. In the envelope was a paper on which were the names of the girls who had passed the High School Entrance Examination. Where was my name? I could not find it for a minute and then – yes, there it was. My friend's name was there, too. How glad we were, we could hardly wait until the term began. When we arrived it was even better than our wildest imagination. [Jean Mason]

The matter of finance has been mentioned frequently. There were, without any doubt, many girls who would dearly have loved to attend the School but whose parents, even with financial help, could not afford the uniform and the extra commitments. Special places were awarded on the basis of the family income for the previous year and, if this fell before the new school term began, the offer had to be declined. Another difficulty was that there were parents who did not see the value of education, particularly for girls. As a result of these anomalies, there must have been many girls in the elementary schools who could have easily out-performed some of the girls who were privileged to attend the High School. The economic situation which encouraged girls from the High School to leave before the recognized age of sixteen, continued to haunt the School and the Education Committee.

BEDFORDSHIRE SECONDARY SCHOOLS.

Examination for Special Places.

WEDNESDAY, 25th MAY, 1938. 9.30—10.30

ARITHMETIC.

1. Find the value of
   253 + 20906 + 1032 + 11 + 7618

2. Divide 2985617 by 293

3. Multiply 3 tons 12 cwts. 2 qrs. 9 lbs. by 17.

4. Find the total cost of
   $1\frac{1}{2}$ doz. eggs at $2\frac{1}{4}$d. each.
   $2\frac{3}{4}$ lbs. of butter at 1/8 per lb.
   3 gallons of milk at $7\frac{1}{2}$d. per quart.
   $\frac{1}{2}$-pint of cream at 5/6 per quart.

5. Find the value of
   (*i*) $2\frac{2}{3} + \frac{11}{15} - 1\frac{1}{5}$.
   (*ii*) $(5\frac{1}{4} - 1\frac{1}{12}) \div \frac{1}{2}$.

6. At a concert $\frac{1}{5}$ of the seats were sold at 2/- each, $\frac{1}{2}$ at 1/- each, $\frac{1}{4}$ at 6d. each, and the remainder, numbering 40, at 3d. each.
   Find (*a*) the number of seats of each kind.
   (*b*) total amount of money taken at concert.

7. The cost of supplying a school of 750 children with stationery for a year is £84 7s. 6d. What will be the cost of supplying a school of 375 children?

8. A motorist sets out with 5 gallons of petrol in his tank. He travels for 50 miles and then stops for lunch. After lunch he travels for two hours at a speed of 30 miles per hour, and reaches the end of his journey with $1\frac{7}{8}$ gallons of petrol in his tank. How many miles does the car travel for each gallon of petrol used?

9. A bridge cannot support a load of more than 6 tons. A lorry weighs 2 tons 4 cwt. when it is empty; a sack of cement weighs 14 lbs. and the lorry driver weighs 12 stones. How many sacks of cement can be taken over the bridge in the lorry without exceeding the maximum weight?

[*Turn over*

BEDFORDSHIRE SECONDARY SCHOOLS.

Examination for Special Places.

WEDNESDAY, MAY 25th, 1938. 2.15—3.15.

ENGLISH I.

1. Rewrite in correct English:
   (*a*) I do not like those sort of bicycles.
   (*b*) Walking down the street yesterday my purse was stolen.
   (*c*) She gave the largest half of the cake to George.
   (*d*) The Duke with many of his officers were at the Ball that night.
   (*e*) She wears her hair like her sister does.
   (*f*) He has never forgiven me refusing to help him.
   (*g*) My train didn't ought to have arrived while 9.15.

2. By adding syllables turn the following nouns into adjectives:
   (for example, hope—hopeful, hopeless).
   brother, courage, girl, scorn, wealth, comfort.

3. Rewrite the following, putting in all the necessary stops, inverted commas, etc.:
   But what good came of it at last
   Quoth little Peterkin
   Why that I cannot tell said he
   But twas a famous victory

4. Describe (using one sentence for each):
   traffic lights, a kangaroo, an insult, a pillar box, coal.

5. Write a composition (20 or 30 lines) on ONE of the following:
   (*a*) Imagine that you were one of a small party from your School spending a day in London. Describe exactly what you did.
   (*b*) Write a short fairy story, introducing an imprisoned princess, a wicked uncle, and a magic ring.
   (*c*) Write a reply to a letter from an imaginary uncle in Australia, who is shortly coming home, and asks, "What is the old place like?"

Examination for Special Places 25th May 1938. (*LM*)

> It is clear that the desire is not to pay anything for education for girls, because there is so much employment for girls in Luton at the age of 14. This has been the case for years in Luton. Many parents who have accepted in the past free places, have done so because it meant no payment, and have then broken the agreement soon after the age of 14 has been reached. The Head Mistress says the parents who have accepted special places really want education for their children, but are willing to make little sacrifice. [H.S. Deacon, Chairman of BEC, addressing a meeting of the Committee at Bedford on 24th November 1933.]

Certainly there were inequalities in the system and it is timely to acknowledge the sacrifices which were made by ordinary, working-class families who did struggle to meet the financial demands.

Health

Local Education Authorities had become responsible for monitoring the health of children in their care. At the High School, medical examinations were carried out at 12 and 15 years of age and at other times if necessary. Eye and dental treatment were provided at low cost.

> Consternation reigned throughout the school, for what was described as 'a wonderful opportunity' was to be ours. A dentist was coming to the school, and every girl's teeth had either to be inspected and attended to by the school dentist or by a private dentist …
>
> Before the dentist came to the School, I had always had the impression that school dentists were horrible fiends, who pulled heaps of teeth out, for the fun of the thing. I had never thought of them as human beings, who themselves perchance dislike other dentists, as does our School dentist, and who carry on a most interesting conversation, all the time they are attending to your teeth, and who ask questions, when one's mouth is fixed open, when they know perfectly well one cannot answer, except by a grunt.
>
> Thus, I was agreeably surprised, and do now sincerely agree with Miss Sheldon, when she terms it ' a wonderful opportunity'. [Margaret Impey]

At the beginning of every term, girls had to bring a Health Certificate declaring that they had not been in contact with anyone infected by chicken pox, diphtheria, enteric fever, German measles, measles, mumps, ringworm etc, scarlet fever, scarletina, smallpox or whooping cough during the previous three weeks. No Health Certificate – no admittance – non-negotiable. Girls were sent straight back home to fetch the vital document.

There were schemes to fund milk and free meals for children and, in 1934, the Government joined with the Milk Marketing Board to supply milk at reduced rates, namely ½d instead of a 1d a bottle (240p to the £). On the request form was a picture of a bottle of milk and, on the label, were Fanny Fat and Susie Sugar for energy, Minnie Mineral for purifying the blood and Peter Protein for flesh and muscle. An article in the *Sheaf* (1937) described a rush to sell biscuits at Break and expeditions to the kitchen to see if there were any bottles of milk left over.

School discipline continued to be strictly observed although detentions were abolished. By 1932, names of Form Captains were being listed in the *Sheaf*. There were Senior Prefects, 'A' Prefects, 'B' Prefects and Sub-Prefects. In 1938/39 the colour of the Prefects' blazers was changed from scarlet to harvest-gold apparently because children attending the Junior Technical School had red blazers as part of their uniform.

Organization and Curriculum

Organization

The school assembled each morning for Prayers. At some stage the excellent idea of playing a movement from a symphony or concerto was introduced with the result that everyone left the School with a rich fund of musical memories. After Prayers girls returned to their rooms to discuss form business or to listen to the general Ten Minute Talks. There were set hymns and readings on House and Form meeting days which were alternate Tuesdays. One of the best remembered Bible readings must be

> Finally, brethren, whatsoever things are true, whatsoever things are honest, whatsoever things are just, whatsoever things are pure, whatsoever things are lovely, whatsoever things are of good report; if there be any virtue, and if there be any praise, think on these things. [Philippians ch.4 v.8]

Most memorable of all were probably the beginning and end of term services. Terms began with *Lord behold us with thy blessing* and ended with *Lord dismiss us* which brought tears to many an eye. Then there was *We plough the fields and scatter the good seed on the land* which related very well to the School motto, followed by the School Song and the National Anthem.

> Let thy father-hand be shielding
> All who here shall meet no more,
> May their seed-time past be yielding
> Year by year a richer store
> Those returning
> Make more faithful than before.

The School Library contained about one thousand English books. There were also books to support Arts and Crafts, Geography, History, Languages and Science. No one teacher was in charge of the Library but subject Mistresses looked after different sections. Periodicals were available in a special news room devoted to current issues and the chief History mistress displayed summaries of the important news of each day. There was also a Fiction Library.

An assignment scheme took the place of homework. Proposed subjects for home reading or writing and independent research were set out at the beginning of term. The only compulsory homework involved learning by heart and 'chorus work'.

> Homework is almost entirely voluntary and is permitted as a privilege; the punishment for bad work is to be prohibited from doing homework. There can be no doubt of the success of these unconventional methods, but a price has to be paid

and it is clear that some subjects of the curriculum suffer from the shortened time given to teaching.   [HMI Report]

Curriculum

The Report of His Majesty's Inspectors (1935) gave an outline of the School curriculum. It also provided an outside assessment of the standards reached and noted that results in the School Certificate examinations had shown 'very rapid improvement since the School moved into its present building'.

All the 'customary subjects' were taught but choices had to be made at certain levels, for example, between Physics, Domestic Science, Latin and German. In the last two years, Chemistry could be taken instead of Geography and Scripture while Art and History could be given up in favour of extra work in other subjects. Subjects considered to be 'very good' were English, French and Music. Art, German, Latin, Physical Training and Scripture were 'good' while History was 'good but narrow in scope'. Geography, Mathematics and Science were handicapped by insufficient time.

In 1919 the School had made application to the Board of Education for permission to start a course in Modern Studies (general studies). At the same time, the Boys' School had asked for permission to run advanced courses in Science and Mathematics – a sad reflection on the different ways in which the education of boys and girls was perceived. It is not clear when the subject was introduced but, by 1931, girls were taking Modern Studies as a subject for Higher School Certificate.

At a time when the idea of Domestic Science as a compulsory subject was being debated against a background of belief that a girl's role in life was primarily domestic, it was recorded that there were two teachers in the Housecraft Department. One was responsible for Needlework and the other supervised school dinners, Cookery, Laundrywork, Housewifery and simple Hygiene.

Why is there such a hideous gap between Richard Coeur de Lion and rissoles, or between pressing flowers for the science competition and pressing handkerchiefs for one's husband? … Who would have thought that I should remember with envy those white-aproned forms lined up outside the kitchen while I passed in the self-righteous file of 'second language' section? How glad I was that the local gas company donated me a cookery book to supplement my sparse knowledge of the inevitable 'hash' …

Would Drake, I thought, have had so much stomach for a fight without the sixteenth century equivalent of eggs and bacon, or would the Elizabethans in general have 'ruffled' quite so bravely without the careful mixing of the starch?

[O.G.]

Commercial

> Miss S[heldon] drew attention to the introduction of a 'Vocational' Form in the school. In this, girls who were above the agreement age, or who had obtained a good School Certificate at the age of 15, and whose parents did not wish them to go on to a higher examination, could have a year's course in business subjects. There was no excuse now for girls to leave before the agreement had been complete, to attend commercial schools, as the school could give them what they wanted. The vocational course had been introduced solely at the request of parents, who felt that Luton needed such a course in its girls' school. It was up to the parents to prove that they appreciated its introduction and wished it to remain in the school organisation, by allowing their girls to take the course.
>
> [*Luton News* 1927]

Mention had been made of secretarial classes while the School was in the huts but, when the girls moved into the new building, a Commercial Sixth Form was set up under Miss W. Cooper. There were six typewriters (not enough) and practice was done to musical rhythms. Royal Society of Arts examinations were taken and there were also School Commercial Certificates. At the 1933 Speech Day, successes in Typewriting, Shorthand, Book-keeping and Geography were rewarded. In 1934, four girls had reached speeds of 80 words a minute in Pitman's speed tests and one had won a Pitman's medal. When Miss Cooper left, in 1935, Miss Sheldon remarked that 'many girls now in offices in Luton owe their methodical ways and their knowledge of signs and symbols' to her.

The 1935 Inspection stated that there were 29 girls taking a one-year course in Commercial Subjects while, at the same time, continuing their general education. Of these, 28 were hoping to take French studies in RSA examinations and a number of girls were continuing to study German. The curriculum also covered English, Music, Physical Training and Speech Training as well as five periods a week of Book-keeping, seven and a half of Shorthand, four of Typewriting and three and a half of Arithmetic.

Physical Activities

Until 1938, Gymnastics were limited by the need to move furniture around in the dining area but the School could now boast properly laid out hockey pitches and hard courts. Practices were held before school, during the dinner hour, after school and on Saturdays. There were tournaments for individual honours, for example in tennis, and there were also House competitions and inter-School matches against schools as far away as Leicester. Although the School had most contact with other secondary schools, a team did play against a Luton Elementary Schools' VII in 1933. Individual records were broken and some girls gained places in County teams. Luton

High School was fortunate in having a good relationship with the pioneer, Miss Margaret Stansfeld, at the Bedford Physical Training College in Bedford.

Hockey

Apparently there was little enthusiasm for hockey, even after the new pitches became available. The few girls who were keen were in the minority and it was difficult to field second teams or find suitable reserves. In 1931, Miss Marjorie Pollard, a famous international player, came to lecture and show a film. She demonstrated with a hockey stick and a white woolly ball, explaining all the important strokes and pointing out common faults. The Games teachers persisted in trying to encourage the girls and there does seem to have been an improvement by 1939 when it was reported that girls were turning up for early morning workouts and 'a spirit of real keenness' was apparent at the dinner hour practices.

Netball

Girls from the High School seemed to favour netball and their teams were very successful. In 1931, they won the Shield of the South Midlands School Netball League by beating Bedford High School in the Finals. Miss Sheldon showed her approval and delight by declaring a day's holiday. This success also meant that the girls in the team were invited to the Midlands Netball Association tournament at Bournville, where they were 'royally entertained' by Messrs. Cadbury and tied for second place with Birmingham University in the B section. The South Midlands Shield was won in 1934 and 1935.

> Netball is a game which can be developed into a fine art by those players who not only work their bodies but who use their brains as well to work out various changes of position and to anticipate where they will be needed for a pass, and so on. The teams have shown a marked improvement during the season in such fundamental things as catching and throwing a netball, which to a spectator looks easy enough, but which in fact requires much thought and care.
>
> [Games Report 1937 by D.C.R. and J.M.S.]

Gymnastics

Annual competitions included work on the bars, balancing and somersaults. Miss Stansfeld gave a shield for the Juniors. Another, donated in memory of Freda Currant, a well-loved former pupil who had died in a climbing accident, was presented to the winner of the Middle and Senior competition. Miss Stansfeld allowed members of her staff to adjudicate and the advice given usually mentioned being 'light on the feet'. On one occasion Miss Adams remarked to the Upper and Middle School that weight should not go into the floor but girls should practise coming 'off the floor'. She said much the same to the Juniors, observing that Forms 'often resembled small herds of elephants instead of the light-footed deer in the Park!'

Sports

Tunics were discarded on Sports Day and each girl wore a square label to indicate which House she was in. There were the usual flat races, as well as visitors' and fathers' races, and other competitions included high jump, long jump, throwing the cricket ball and, later, hurdling. Individual medals were awarded but all the points gained went to the annual total in the House competitions. Sports Days were always at the mercy of the weather but, in 1932, the event had to be postponed for another reason, namely that too many girls were suffering from the after-effects of vaccinations and were unfit to run.

Swimming

Swimming became ever more popular after the School had its own pool. In the short season, girls learnt a variety of skills, from how to breathe correctly to diving and Life Saving. In 1938 four girls were selected to swim for the County. The pool was open, apparently without supervision, in the evenings and on Saturdays for existing and former students.

Tennis

A match between the Staff and Girls on 28th May 1931, won by the Staff, marked the opening of the new courts. According to the annual Reports in the magazine, there was a lot of enthusiasm but most girls were reluctant to put their names forward for tournaments. The county coach gave lessons and advice was offered in the *Sheaf.*

> Footwork; you must MOVE about the court, never stand still.
>
> Keep your eye on the ball; make yourself watch until your racket hits it.
>
> When on the courts practise strokes for ten minutes before starting to play.
>
> Try to place your returns in such a way that your opponent never knows where to expect the next ball.
>
> Improve your service until it becomes a weapon of attack; make up your mind always to win your service game.
>
> Be 'on your toes'.

Another piece of advice was to watch good playing, if and when there was an opportunity. That poses no problem these days when the Wimbledon tournament can be seen on television screens in most homes, but this was another age! The new shorts-dresses, specially designed in 1936 for the team, were well received and, in warm weather, tunics were discarded and ankle socks replaced stockings.

Dancing

Miss Flecknoe, a dancing teacher, came to give classes after school hours and trained girls to give displays. At one performance, the Senior girls did a fire dance; they wore flimsy flame-coloured dresses and 'twirled pieces of smoke-coloured material to give the effect of smoke'. Then they did a dance of all nations, 'dressed to represent a certain European country'. The Middle classes danced an Elizabethan Minuet. Miss Flecknoe also taught slimming classes – exercises, not dieting.

> We are all ready to endure this for the sake of graceful forms. Much to our delight, Miss Flecknoe is teaching us the Charleston which, we are told, will be popular this year in the modern ball-room; also the tango, rumba, and variations in the valse and foxtrot.

In 1938, the High School became one of only a few in the country which tried an Open-evening experiment. The idea proved popular although some girls who lived in the country found it impossible to get back to School. Unfortunately the problems which came with the outbreak of war brought an end to the experiment.

> On Wednesday evenings there was to be no homework, but the school was going to be opened from 5.30 p.m. to 7.30 p.m., during which time we might go back to do all the things we couldn't find time for in school hours. Girls who did Chemistry could do a little Biology and those who took a second language could do Cookery. Some of the mistresses were very kindly taking First Aid classes, two of the Seniors were going to teach ballroom dancing in the Hall, Miss Fuller was giving music talks; the Gymnasium, the Libraries and the Art rooms were going to be open the whole evening. There were to be discussions, debates and Shakespeare readings too. Miss Sheldon then went on to say that she wished the Seniors and Juniors to mix so that we might all be a united band, which was not always possible in school hours. The Prefects and the Sub-prefects were at their own suggestion discarding their badges of office … Biscuits and lemonade were to be sold.
>
> [Jean Buckingham]

Societies

The School societies were similar to those which had been set up while the School was in the huts. Formal lessons occupied six periods a day and then, from 3.30 until 4.30 each afternoon, girls could attend these various clubs and societies while others could, with help from the Staff, work at their hobbies. Girls from the fourth forms upwards could also indulge in their hobbies rather than take part in compulsory games. Classes included Art, Fretwork, Leatherwork, Music, Needlework, Pottery and Raffia work.

Examinations, Prizes, Successes and Competitions

The courses all focused on the Cambridge School Certificate, taken at around the age of 16, and the Higher School Certificate taken two years later.

> Everyone seems especially sympathetic to the fifth forms before the Cambridge. We were petted and spoiled by Miss Sheldon, our Form Mistresses, and the Staff. While the rest of the School were doing School examinations, we revised for the Cambridge. As revision was done in School time, we were told not to do homework, not to go to cinemas, and to take care of our health. As a special treat, Miss Sheldon allowed us to go swimming every morning, during this time, at 10.30 a.m.

As has already been explained, some Leaving Scholarships for higher education were available. They were necessary because there were no mandatory grants, but only high flyers could apply with any realistic hope of success. Here again, there may well have been girls with considerable ability who did not fulfil their full potential for financial reasons. Educational ideas have a habit of resurfacing and it is interesting to note that, in the 1930s, the County Council were offering loans 'to assist students to undertake courses at an approved Training College, University, or other Institution'. The Bursary system was still in place for pupils who aspired to become teachers. They provided 'free tuition, cost of books and travelling and, where necessary, a maintenance grant'.

Within the School there was a culture of competition and awards. From 1932, categories in the House Competitions, which were judged each June, were combined to include Science, Arts and Crafts, Gardens and Good School Work. The external judges were very pernickety and expected an excellent standard at every stage. Originality and finishing off were particularly scrutinized. All the points gained by competitors at Sports Days were also added to the annual tally.

Houses

School life was still strongly focused on the Houses and their high level of commitment to fund-raising and support for selected charities. There were donations and collections of clothing, books, used stamps, silver paper, old toys, *Daily Mirror* tokens and particular coins such as farthings (960 to the £). New activities included the sale of NSPCC bluebird badges to girls in Fry House and a project by the Darlings to support a Home for little boys in Royston. Mrs Mitchell, the School secretary, was called upon to buy presents for the children at Beech Hill House on behalf of the Nightingales. Miss Sheldon took up the earlier correspondence with Helen Keller and wrote to ask her to visit the School. Miss Keller regretted that she would be unable to do so, but promised to come the next time she was in England. (No record has been found to say that she did so.)

Another major project was the production of House Banners for a deadline in June 1932. Funds were raised and good needlewomen were chosen to do the practical work. Creativity and imagination were paramount.

Boadicea The girls tried to decide the best ways of dealing with obstacles such as horses' legs, Boadicea's flowing garments, scrolls and Old English lettering. But she 'triumphed over all these difficulties' and was there to be seen, riding in her chariot.

Darling Staff and girls decided on 'a gallant ship ploughing her way undaunted through the waves, her sails swelling before a breeze'.

Fry The banner showed a grey anchor on a red background.

Keller's banner was made of dark green fadeless linen 'on which, in pale yellow, was a flaming torch superimposed upon an open book'. These were intended to be symbols of Helen Keller's struggle and success.

House Banners.
(*Photographs by Bob Norman*)

Nightingale displayed a black lamp on an orange background.

As the number on roll grew, new houses were needed and the Curie and Garrett Anderson Houses came into being at the beginning of the Autumn term 1934. The girls soon entered into the spirit of competition and joined in all the traditional activities. There was a combined party to raise funds for banners.

Marie Curie (1867–1934)

Marie Curie was a Polish scientist who, with her husband, studied radioactivity. Together they won the Nobel Prize for Physics in 1903 and, in 1911, Marie was awarded the Nobel Prize for Chemistry.

Colours: Mauve and cream.

Perseverando Vincimus – We overcome by perseverance.

Girls wrote to the Curies' daughter, Madame Curie-Joliot, who sent details of her mother's life. She also suggested planting trees and, as a consequence, 30 poplars were planted on the far side of the hockey field. The chosen charity was the Luton Children's Hospital. By the end of their first term, the girls had sent a donation and, soon afterwards, they equipped a baby's cot.

Banner: Radiating star design in cream on a mauve background

Elizabeth Garrett Anderson (1836–1917)

Elizabeth Garrett Anderson was an English physician who fought for the admission of women to the medical profession.

Colours: Yellow and black

A Cheerful Heart Doeth Good Like Medicine.

The House charity was the Bute Hospital and the girls were soon busy making Christmas gifts, blankets, babies' vests etc. Money was collected as part of the 'Schools' Centenary Purse' to provide buildings at the Garrett Anderson hospital in London. The House Mistress and House Captain attended the opening of the new Nurses' Home there.

Banner: Snake and staff in black on yellow background.

Magazine Articles

As always, the articles in the *Sheaf* add colour to an account of life in the School. They also give a background picture of life in Luton and the rest of the country during the 1930s. In 1938 there was a new format: on the cover was a line drawing of the School by Miss Oldham who also provided a picture of a 'Maiden with her Sheaf' for the first page. Melita Neal and Elizabeth Alcock produced diagrams to go at the end of each section.

There was pressure on every girl to write an article, primarily for the form magazines.

The Magazine article! What shall I write?
It will certainly have to be finished tonight.
Oh! shall it be poetry? Shall it be prose?
I just bite my pen and look hard at my toes.

With my thinking cap on, I feel ready to do
A page full of prose, or a small verse or two,
Of the sun in the day time, or bright moon by night,
Of the flowers in my garden so pretty and bright.

Of the horse in the stable, the sheep on the hill,
Of the bright gurgling stream that runs close by the mill.
But, alas and alack! The clock now has struck nine;
I must put it away and do better next time.

[Mary Bates]

Line drawing by Mrs Smithwhite (Miss Oldham) to represent the
School Motto, used in the *Sheaf* from March 1938.

Life in the 1930s was certainly changing. However, there is an uncanny similarity between some of the pieces written for the magazine and life in the twenty-first century. There is the weather of course, always a good topic of conversation, and another interesting theme is the changing fashion in first names.

So much is happening in our world today; so much of wars, changes, political crises, inventions and football cup ties ...

So much has been heard lately about modern madness and the increasing tendency among young people to make new codes and to violate the manners and customs of the older generation ...

Look at the weather: Where are the winters and summers of the past? ... But not only are the winters milder in these days, but the seasons themselves are so jumbled and indistinct that hardly can we call them Spring, Summer, Autumn and Winter.

[C. Craddock]

Rebecca, Susan, Kate, and Tilly,
Sound out-of-date and rather silly,
Many names we can confuse,
While others we to-day abuse.
Many old folks say all the same,
'We like a good old-fashioned name,
Like Bridget, Julia and Sophia,
Eliza, Charlotte and Maria.'

Sylvia, Marguerite and May
Are modern names we hear today.
Some people say 'Short names are tame.'
And others cry 'What's in a name?'
Many old folks say all the same
'We like a good old-fashioned name,
Like Harriet, Rachael, Jane, and Clara,
Esther, Naomi, and Sarah.'

[Cicely Hull]

Background to Life in the 1930s

With one world war in the recent past and another on the horizon, there was a real hope that another war could be averted. Some of the girls offered their own solutions.

When travelling ... often one sees beautiful and interesting things, of which one reads in history and modern books, and of course there is not a better way to learn another language, than to mix with the people of the land in question ... I think one loses that superior attitude, which is so often adopted when speaking of or dealing with foreigners. [M. Verdcourt]

It seems as if wars can never be eliminated from the earth until nationalism is put in its right place, and stronger bonds are made between the countries ... The best ways to form a union between the countries of the world are to facilitate travelling, and international trade, and to increase education even further. Most people who travel a great deal are broad-minded; and those who travelled would form friendships with other nations, and feel a kinship with them. [E. Kingham]

National Life

In 1931, in the face of national economic gloom, members of staff were obliged to accept a 10% cut in their salaries. Miss Sheldon appreciated the fact that the Governors wrote individual letters to explain this but commented that the staff would have preferred to make voluntary offers of abatement. Everyone, young and old, was expected to economise.

> Each daily paper that I see
> With blackest heading cries –
> The country's going to the dogs –
> We must economise.
>
> Each day the Parliament, I hear,
> With worried frowns and sighs,
> Puzzles o'er our currency –
> We must economise.
>
> The mistresses in schools now say
> Our costs to minimise
> You must not waste your paper, girls –
> We must economise.
>
> For if we wish to rule the waves –
> The pound to stabilise –
> To smooth our Premier's worried brow –
> We must economise.
>
> [Greta J. Simms]

A darker side to life prompted an article which anticipated the coming of the Welfare State. It describes a scene in which a blind ex-service man went singing in the street.

His little daughter was with him and it was her job to collect any money offered.

> Why should a blind man, who had served his country so well (the medals testified to that) have to sing in the streets, in the pouring rain? How grossly unfair life is to some people. He must have become blind as the result of his service. Why could he not be looked after by the State? It is impossible, you say, for the State to look after every blind man who served in the war. Perhaps it is, but if only it were not impossible! We can only hope that the day may come when all ex-service men will be comfortably provided for – and I suppose by that time a great many of them will be dead.
>
> How topsy-turvy things are. Good seems to triumph over evil, and we can only hope that at some future date, there will be no sightless street singers – perhaps even no poverty in the whole world. [M. Barnes]

National events, for example the death of King George V on 20th January 1936, were grieved over or celebrated.

> The School was hushed during the days that followed. Wireless had just been installed in the Hall, on the Saturday before the Funeral. So on the Twenty-eighth we gathered there. We listened in to the Procession through London and, in the intervals, prayed and sang hymns and listened to brief Readings.
>
> In the afternoon the School was closed, but those of the Staff who remained assembled once more in the Hall to listen to and to take part in the Burial Service through which the King 'Our brother' was commended to the Mercy of God.

On a happier note, there was a holiday for the Coronation of George VI. In Luton, the 'main streets were gay with red, white and blue poles on either side of the road and banners hanging from them, flapping in the wind.' There was a procession from Park Street to Wardown Park and, in the afternoon, a swimming Gala at the Open Air Pool. Concerts were held in the Park and there were fireworks on the School Field. Miss Sheldon and one of the Senior Prefects were present at the Town Service on the Football Ground and, later, selected girls represented the School at the Youth Service in Westminster Hall and the Empire Youth Rally in the Albert Hall. The school celebrated by planting trees on the School Field.

Life in Bedfordshire

Bedfordshire, though still to some extent a rural county, has nevertheless changed considerably in the 70 or so years since this was written.

> A field of golden corn and poppy heads,
> A skylark singing in a cloudless sky,

The toiling horses strain each nerve anew;
They give their lives to man, and ask not why.

The polished harness glitters in the sun,
The binder mercilessly fells each ear,
While deep amid the corn a rabbit screams –
Chased by a poaching dog – in deadly fear.

The shadows lengthen, and the golden field
Is slowly turned to rose by setting sun,
The old church clock sounds forth the hour to cease,
Then home, with thankful hearts that work is done.

[Marie H. Gilman]

Life was more peaceful in many respects and, in what was still a mainly Christian era, Sundays had a character of their own. A subject for debate by the Literary Society in 1936 was: *That places of Amusement should remain open on Sundays.* The motion was defeated by 76 to 35.

Sunday is a peaceful day, when even the milkman whistles hymns instead of dance tunes. After a leisurely breakfast, families might take a stroll but this was not altogether a pleasant time for children. 'They may not pick flowers, because they are wearing their best gloves, and the most tempting hedges and banks must be left alone for fear of scratching their Sunday shoes.'

[Muriel Tyson]

The constant war with insects, fungi and blights, ceases for one day, the church bells ring out clearly in the morning air, best clothes, even to uncomfortable stiff collars, are worn, for it is Sunday. Down the quiet road, hymn books under their arms, a crowd of villagers file quietly into the churchyard as did their ancestors in years gone by. From within, the organ peals out its messages of goodwill and peace to all. The tinkling of sheep bells is heard as the shepherd drives his flock down the road.

[Vivienne Poirier]

Background to Luton

The girls were granted a holiday for the opening in 1936 of the new Town Hall by the Duke of Kent.

His Highness stepped from the car. Necks were craned forward, and spectators leaned perilously from windows. An old gentleman behind me informed his neighbours, superfluously and ungrammatically, that 'this was him' and began a rambling anecdote of personal acquaintance to which no one paid the least attention. The troops were inspected, and the cheers doubled and redoubled as the Duke mounted the gaily-decorated platform. Camera-men agitatedly manipulated their machines; and a little boy seized the opportunity to yell vociferously – then silence … The speech was short, and at the final words, 'I declare this Town-Hall open', the clapping broke out again.

[Irene Allen]

Creativity

While many of the articles from the *Sheaf* reflect on different aspects of life at the time, others were examples of the girls' creative and literary talents.

The Jazz Band

Twilight casts a veil of purple peace
   Over the glistening cliffs and tranquil hills,
The brilliance of the sky has paled, and stars increase
   The calm serenity of banks of cloudy rills
All tinged with palest pink. The sea is grey,
   And shining with mysterious gleams that speak
Of things unearthly. A little sobbing edge of spray
   Whimpers o'er the shadowy sands inside the rocky creek,
And sighing gently, like the softest evening breeze,
   With haunting melodies the ripples wash the rocks,
Lapping so gently as if to try to please
   The hard grey, cruel overhanging cliff that mocks
Their child-like kiss and bids them turn again
   To sterner sport … But harshly, suddenly,
With discord wrapt in grating squeaks as if in pain,
   The jazz of a cliff-side band shouts to the murmuring sea,
Of noise and traffic, horns and sudden squalls;
   Where gentle peace and happiness had reigned a while ago.
Din is king, upon these sloping hills, the halls
   That once were filled but with the pleasant men who sow
The seeds of beauty and guard their errant sheep
   Upon the verdant hills, are now a riot –
A struggling, joking mob, who care not, neither weep
   To see the placid, humble hills that once were quiet,
Awaken sufferingly from their sleep; but on
   Goes the band and on the dancing crowd,
Until with midnight's echoing chime, the tunes are gone
   And quietude again returns to heal the proud
     Unprotesting night.

[M. Woods]

Social Life and Social Conscience

Miss Sheldon never wavered from her ideals and high on her list was duty. Duty to the School was mandatory but duty to the outside world was also expected. This became acute as war threatened to engulf the country. Concern for others less fortunate was epitomized by the continued collection of flowers co-ordinated each May by Miss Easton for children in the slums of London. Fathers who ran hat factories provided cardboard boxes which Mr Mandley, the caretaker, filled, tied up, labelled and despatched by rail. Carriage was paid for from a collection made amongst the girls. In 1938, 98 boxes were sent to 45 different London schools. In addition, enough money was collected to send 1,650 handkerchiefs. A letter of thanks from Green Street noted that 'the joy of receiving lovely flowers from a real school in the country never grows less'. In 1936, one family went a step further and took one of the children into their home for a fortnight's holiday and, in 1939, by special request, flowers were sent to 14 Salvation Army hostels, so that older people could also enjoy the sight and smell of the flowers.

Collections were made within Forms and throughout the School. Over £2.10s

Each May, girls brought flowers to send to children living in deprived areas of London. The custom was revived after the Second World War. This photograph was probably taken in the early 1950s. (LN)

[£2.50] was contributed to the Mayor's Appeal for the new hospital and £9 went to the National Trust for the preservation of Sharpenhoe Clappers. The £2.6s [£2.30] raised at a social and a concert was sent to a fund for Chinese refugees. A Fête organized by the Lower School brought in £18 for the Waifs and Strays Society and, when the submarine *Thetis* sank, £2.11s.1d [£2.56] was collected for the widows and orphans.

Apart from these special collections, money was given on a regular basis. 'That halfpenny or penny a week, given by each member of our community, though it may seem very little, is yet capable of doing far more good than is often realised. And let us all remember that in His eyes, even the smallest mite is never despised.'

Talks and Visits

Horizons were widened by visits outside the school and also by speakers from different walks of life who were invited into the School. Many of these specialized activities were organized by the various clubs or societies.

Use was made of the new epidiascope when the Science Club hosted a talk on Photography in 1931. The following year, the Literary Society invited Mrs Tessa Wheeler, the eminent archaeologist, to talk about the history of St Albans. Mrs Wheeler later sent fragments of pottery which she had found in Italy and Greece. Thoughts of the Empire were never far away and, in 1933, Captain Hay of the Navy came to talk to the School about trade routes: 'there are many naval ships all over the Empire, guarding the ships which bring food to us, who live on the small but mother island which cannot grow food for itself'.

In 1934, Miss Cherry Garrard gave practical advice in her lecture on Rock, Ice and Snow Climbing. She told the girls that her preferred dress was 'breeches and a short skirt, a hat with a brim all the way round, and climbing boots which are very large, allowing for several pairs of socks to be worn. She also advised them to take plenty of food, including several lumps of sugar.

Girls from the Science Club attended a lecture in 1932 on the Research ship *Discovery II* which explored the Antarctic during the summer months. In May 1935 they took a trip to Whipsnade Zoo, opened in 1931. Visits were made to Vauxhall Motors to observe the manufacture of cars and Laportes Chemicals. There was a trip in 1934 to see *The Tempest* at the Open-Air Theatre in Regent's Park.

Debates

The first recorded joint activity between the girls from the High School and the boys from the Modern School took place in 1936. This was a debate between the High School Literary Society and Modern School Literary and Scientific Society. The proposition was *That England is on the Downgrade*. Perhaps because of the scintillating subject or, much more likely, because the boys were involved, the event attracted an audience of about 250. On one side, it was pointed out that England had lost a real sense of values and of proportion, that leisure was much misused, and that a true appreciation of good music, painting and literature was fast dying out. Those against the proposition pointed out that tremendous advances in the standard of living and public welfare had been made during the last century and England seemed to compare favourably with other nations. Apparently, England was 'enthusiastically defended'.

The two schools had joint debates in subsequent years. In 1937, the proposition was *That it is Justifiable to keep Animals in Captivity* (carried) and the following year the majority voted against *That Newspapers are a Harmful Influence*. By 1939, the boys had moved into their new School in Bradgers Hill and it was there that a debate *That the Progress of Science is a Menace to Civilisation* was held.

Fêtes

School fêtes and garden parties were impressive occasions with no energy or feat of imagination spared. Everyone seemed to take part with real enthusiasm, but no doubt that was expected or even demanded. The description of the 1935 Fête is typical. There were stalls, sideshows, fishing for bottles, throwing darts, guess the number of peas, exhibitions, letting off balloons, a coconut shy, joy slide and a palmist and her black cat. In the Hall were old-world shops. Miss Flecknoe's class 'had prepared a ballet in which more than a hundred spring flowers danced on the grass' and there was a mass drill. Students from Bedford Physical Training College gave a fine display of swimming. There was a tennis tournament, an auction in the Junior Quadrangle and a Flannel dance in the hall. As always, refreshments were laid out. The total amount of money raised: £250.1s.4d [£250.07].

Plays

Miss Sheldon was always an enthusiastic producer of plays, many of which she wrote herself. She was ably supported by Miss Fuller who supplied the music and Miss Easton who designed and cut out the dresses. The first play to be performed in the new school (1930) was *Hereward the Wake*, which was one of Miss Sheldon's own creations and seems to have represented a battle between good and evil. Joyce Patterson, a pupil who had already won praise for her poetry, wrote the words to a beautiful song: *Dark Shadows of the Future*. Mr Clift, a writer and producer, reviewed the play and depicted such an exciting spectacle that it seems a pity that video cameras had not been invented: 'A great clanging gong-expectant silence, and then from every corner, rushing howling figures, a pushing, jostling multitude, desperate with hunger and with injustice, brave with the recklessness of despair, straight up to the castle wall, into the castle itself'. He described the dialogue as 'sometimes quite Shakespearean'. Proceeds from the play were shared between the Bute Hospital (£40), the School Reference Library (£40), an extension to the stage (£55) and lighting (£22).

In December 1932, *Briar Rose* was performed. This time there were seven writers, including Miss Harris, and 350 in the cast. There were fairies, witches, gypsies, country folk, great folk and the court of the Fairy Queen, all held together by a thread of allegory and wonderful costumes. Mr Clift claimed that 'the whole performance bears the mark of a master producer: Miss Sheldon, Staff and the whole company I congratulate you once again'.

The *Sheaf* does not mention any plays between 1932 and 1934, possibly because everyone's energy was concentrated on the swimming pool fund. But, in 1935, another spectacular show was produced. This was *Cophetua and Arsinoe* by Drinkwater and was based in Egypt, the Irish Court and amongst the Ice Maidens and Fire Maidens. Arsinoe was little, pretty and plaintive but Cophetua was bombastic, arrogant and sneering. When, apparently, they married, Arsinoe had no need to fear because, if Cophetua resorted to evil, the lusty beggars were with her to a man. At Christmas 1936 the School presented *The Tempest* and, the following year, *A Midsummer Night's Dream.* Betty Shaw (Dickinson) remembers that, on 11th December 1936, everyone stood at the end of the play for the National Anthem as usual. But it wasn't played for this was the evening when Edward VIII abdicated.

When I was in the Vth form I was cast as Lysander in the production of *A Midsummer Night's Dream*, a highlight in my time at Luton High School as I was extremely stage-struck. For the whole of that term all spare time was taken up with rehearsals, involving, if not a cast of thousands, at least a large proportion of the school population. The speaking parts were all doubled, and most of the First Year became the fairy court of Oberon and Titania. We rehearsed at lunch times, a difficulty for me as during the whole of my time at school, I went home to Dunstable on the bus for dinner, a practice which probably ruined my digestive system for ever. We were also called in on Saturday mornings.

Helen K. Sheldon could have given tips to Cecil B. DeMille on crowd control. We all sat for long periods on the hard fold-out wooden chairs in the hall and woe-betide any poor fairy who fidgeted and caused the chair to creak. Miss Sheldon had that evolutionary development of teachers – eyes in the back of the head – to a remarkable degree, and would whip round and unerringly fix on the culprit. A look was enough, we all froze to immobility.

Our Greek costumes, all homemade, consisted of ankle-length linen tunics with Greek key patterns in braid around the hem for female characters, and knee-length versions for males. Our footwear was also hand-made, the soles cut from felt hoods donated by a hat-manufacturer father, and attached by ribbons which criss-crossed round the ankle. On my first entry, full of Thespian adrenalin, I emerged from stage-left and as my felt soles met the polished stage floor, I took off at speed across to stage-right where I collapsed ignominiously in a heap, my uppermost thought being 'Now I'm in trouble'.   [Denise Barber]

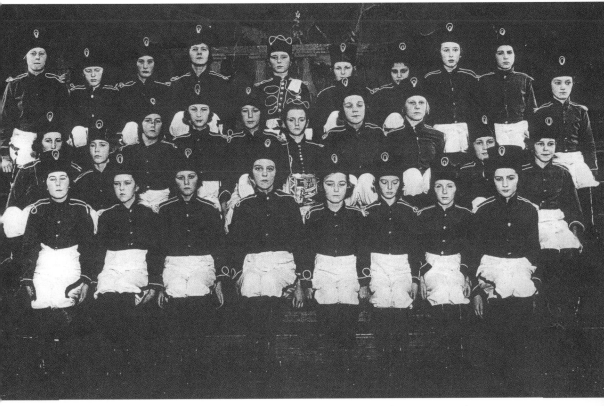

Lower School Play *The Stranger*, December 1938. (*Mrs E. Groom*)

In 1938 there was a Triple Bill: the Lower School presented an operetta *The Stranger* and the Middle School a composite mime *Be warned by me*, based on Hilaire Belloc's *Cautionary Tales* and Lear's *Nonsense Rhymes*. The choice of the Upper School was: *The Prince Who Was a Piper* by Harold Brighouse. In the same year, the boys from the Modern School came with their production of *St Simeon Stylites*. Girls from the High School were impressed by the lighting and other effects and envied a company who could, from their own number, produce such competent electricians.

Old Girls

Thoughts on a career.

A girl is leaving school and is called upon to make a great decision that will affect the rest of her life. She must choose a career. Now there are innumerable careers open to women that before were only taken up by men, and thus she has a large range from which to choose. This seems however, to make the choice more difficult.

The various careers run through her mind. Does she want to take up commercial work, and be regarded as a piece of office furniture by an exacting employer, or does she want to strike out an entirely different career for herself? Is it her wish to help alleviate human suffering by becoming a nurse or a doctor, or to better the present world further by devoting herself to one of the many branches of research? But no! she may desire to teach.

Perhaps, however, she prefers an outdoor life and to the hardy open-air loving girl many careers are open. She can become a dairymaid, or do farm work – a strenuous life which few modern girls seem desirous of taking up. Then horticulture is open to her as a career, or she may be a dog lover and desire to be a kennel maid. If she is very hardy and strong and likes the work, she can become a woman policeman, though this career has few attractions for the modern maiden, unless she is very fond of hard lonely work in all kinds of weather.

Perhaps she wants to travel, to see the enchanting foreign lands one reads so much about. To this end she can become a stewardess on a liner or in an air-liner, although this entails much hard work, and little time for sightseeing. Unfortunately, commercial aviation is not yet open to women, and if it were, she would perhaps prefer this career (I know I should).

Lastly, there is the girl who does not want to go out to work, but who wants to stay at home to lead a dull sheltered existence. Girls of this type are few in these modern enlightened days. Most girls prefer to be independent, to carry out their school tradition in the world, and to fight their way in the world, and to do their bit towards increasing the prosperity of their country. Surely it is better to help to do some active good in one's limited corner of the world, than to lead a sheltered existence under the protection of one's parents.

These are some of the careers a modern girl is faced with on leaving school. Though money plays a large part in her choice, she will surely find a career congenial to her and will be able to fight her way upwards with the knowledge that she likes it, for to-day the world needs the active help of every woman and of every girl. [Margaret M. Madigan 1937]

As this article indicates, girls' horizons were widening. The Inspectors' Report (1935) gives specific figures for the career choices for the years 1931–1934.

University	3%
Training Colleges for Elementary Teaching, Art Schools and Agricultural College	5%
Commercial Posts	
Secretarial	2%
Shorthand Typists	25%
General Office Work	29%
Civil Service and municipal offices	2.5%
Shop assistants	8%

Millinery trade	4.5%
Remained at home	9%
Left the district	8%
Unknown	4%

The Old Girls Society continued to flourish. Members were encouraged to wear the new blazer badge, price 6s.9d [34p] from Alexanders in Wellington Street. There were socials, dances, enthusiastic contributions to the Fêtes and support for particular appeals such as the swimming bath fund. Engagements, marriages, births and, sadly, deaths were reported in the *Sheaf*. The death of Freda Currant, in a climbing accident in Switzerland, caused particular shock and grief. A portrait of her was hung in the School and a round seat was erected under the chestnut tree as a memorial.

The magazine printed letters from former pupils and members of staff who described their homes, their family life and a variety of chosen occupations. Some girls were living or working abroad and enjoying a much wider choice of career but the perception that the world of work was not a place for married women was still strong. For example, in 1937, Keller House said farewell to Miss Thomson who had been a member of the House for years: 'the hearty good wishes of every Keller will go with her both now, when she takes up a new teaching post in Scotland, and later, when she enters upon her new career of matrimony'. Yes, there were still constraints on girls' expectations but there was an independence of spirit which was not to be checked.

"What does she want to be, mother?
What does she want to be?
A teacher, a nurse or a fishmonger's wife,
Lead a useful, a gay, or a prosperous life,
What does she want to be?

"Hasn't she made up her mind, mother?
Hasn't she made up her mind?
   A college, a shop, or a hairdressing store?
   There's no time to waste as I've told you before.
Hasn't she made up her mind?

"Why does she need to wait, mother?
Why does she need to wait?
   A typewriting job, or a dental degree?
   Come! Music or dog-breeding, which shall it be?
Why does she need to wait?

"What is your daughter's taste, mother?
What is your daughter's taste?
 Politics, cookery, art or the soil,
 Med'cine, mathematics or manual toil?
What is your daughter's taste?

"Please, I'll reply for myself, mother.
Please I'll reply for myself.
 Jobs in the world aren't easy to pick
 So I'm staying at School till I've passed my Matric.
And then I'll decide for myself, Auntie,
And *then* I'll decide for myself.

[V.]

Chapter Six

It is to Youth that the Future Belongs 1939–1945

By 1938, Luton High School had a strong, well-established staff, a tradition of 'unselfishness, honesty and hard work' and a reputation as a centre of academic achievement. The Governors certainly appreciated Miss Sheldon's work for 'in view of the conspicuous success which has attended [her] work as Headmistress at Luton for twenty years' they recommended that her salary be raised, as from September 1939, from £750 to £800 per annum. The School had evolved a steady routine and an accepted way of life. However, the equilibrium was about to be shaken for Europe was in turmoil.

The threat of war

On greying winter days when all the heavens cry
Their sad rain-tears down to the earth below;
When gusty little showers run to and fro
For fear, because the winds are shouting through the sky;
When clouds, like restless birds of passage, flying high
Menace the land like messengers of woe;
When Nature wails and winds of weeping blow,
I will remember when the world was all awry.

The days when there awoke throughout the land
The slow yet mighty spirit which is England's core.
The fighting spirit which we understand

> And yet which lay asleep beneath our hand
> Till some poor fool kindled afresh the fire of war
> And lit our Youth into a flaming brand.
>
> [Joy Handby]

The memory of the First World War was still keen and another European war seemed likely to break out. On 29th September 1938, the Munich Agreement was signed. On a national and international level, there was consternation and this affected life in the School. Staff and girls prepared themselves to be of help if troubled times came.

> The anxious days of last September have passed, and although complete calm reigned in School, they left all of us perhaps a little older, sadder and more thoughtful. World affairs rarely trouble youthful schoolgirl brains unduly, but the 'Crisis' became a thing personal to each one of us, a grief and an anxiety brought home with as much force to the youngest in our community as to the eldest.
>
> [Megan Evans and Joy Handby, Editors]

By the summer of 1939, it was no longer a question of 'if' but 'when' war would be declared. Air Raid Precautions were in place and, on 24th August, teachers in areas affected by evacuation were recalled by radio. Luton had been declared a 'reception area', which meant that billets had to be found for the hundreds of London children who were expected to arrive. The High School hall was prepared and tables were piled with food, biscuits, tinned meat, corned beef and chocolate. On 31st August notice was given that evacuation would take place the following day.

The first day in September was also the date marked for the beginning of the blackout. Members of staff and senior girls were given the job of reinforcing and blacking the windows. One former prefect has remarked that she was up a ladder in the School Hall on Sunday 3rd September 1939 when the Prime Minister announced that War had been declared.

> It is no mean feat to balance a beaker of water on a narrow ledge fifteen feet from the ground, and to cut and to stick strips without saturating the willing advisers below … The next thing was to darken the windows. The paint was procured and, swathed in overalls of various sorts and sizes, we mounted – a motley crew – on to the flat roof over the cloisters. We all threw dignity to the winds and tackled our job barefoot … we all, irrespective of age and position, soon closely resembled the finest breed of 'Dalmatian'.
>
> [Winifred Platt and Christine Smith]

Later, windows were covered with muslin, or scrim, which created 'the effect of a permanent mist' outside. This scrim remained throughout the war and it was not until VE Day that the School could return to its 'pristine luminosity'. Windows without blinds were blacked out with dark paper. To counteract the persistent gloom, Mrs Evans collected money and supervised the planting of bulbs to decorate every form room.

Working under Difficult Conditions

School opened on 21st September as planned, although the trenches had not been dug. So girls were told to gather in the safer areas, for example the Hall or the Annexe, whenever there was an alert. As an extra precaution, windows were shut and curtains drawn. Every girl had to carry, at all times, her gas mask, a case for books etc. and a warm coat or blazer. Many girls brought knitting or did homework.

One consequence of the war was the reduction in the size of the *Sheaf* which meant that the opportunity to publish girls' creative work was limited. It also means that this chapter is the poorer for having few contemporary poems to add atmosphere to the text. Fortunately, the editors of the 1939 magazine, Megan Evans and Joy Handby, decided to make it a record of first reactions to war-time conditions and hoped that it would 'stand as an interesting record for future generations'. Subsequent editions described how the war affected, and frequently hindered, day-to-day living.

By the autumn of 1940, trenches had been dug at the far side of the field and the School was experiencing a period of 'sudden wild alarms'. These air raid warnings had the irritating habit of coming 'just in the middle of an interesting lesson, or just after a dull one'. When the sirens sounded, the girls had to crouch under their desks or move downstairs until a hand bell signalled that they should make their way to the trenches. According to Miss Stalker, Miss Sheldon used to marshal girls with a bugle.

Sirens often sounded during the night as well and, when necessary, provision was made for girls to rest for half an hour after Prayers. The School survived unscathed until 6th November 1944 when, according to the book *Luton at War*, a V2 rocket fell 'like a bolt from the blue' in Biscot Road, about half a mile away. There was extensive damage to buildings, 19 people lost their lives and 196 were injured. Many windows, particularly in the Cloisters, were blown out. Fortunately, the girls had been given a day's holiday and so were spared any kind of injury from flying glass.

Clothes rationing caused problems. No doubt much skill and enterprise was employed in overcoming them and the School Prospectus for 1941 noted some concessions. Old gym tunics were acceptable, even if they were not the regulation pattern. Science overalls could, if necessary, be made from any coloured old material to avoid the use of coupons. However, new overalls had to be the regulation ones.

'Aliens' appeared in the form of girls from other schools who were allowed to wear their own uniforms. There were also a number of girls whose families had fled from Europe when their lives were threatened by the Nazi regime.

There were changes in the appearance of the field. Land backing onto Blenheim Crescent was used for the production of vegetables and there were also good yields of salad crops, onions and marrows. Tomatoes grew both out of doors and in the conservatory while the old House gardens were given over to peas, radishes, leeks, celery and turnips. A static water tank, to hold water for fire fighting, appeared near the Argyll Avenue entrance.

Social life was affected. One regulation stipulated that no activity could take place if it involved more people than the trenches could accommodate. This meant, of course, that there were none of the spectacular dramatic productions, so dear to Miss Sheldon's heart. Over-crowding again became a problem because there was no budget for extending buildings. This was not helped by the need to fill the balconies of the Hall and the Gym with beds and bedding for emergency use. Thankfully, the Baptist Church in Blenheim Crescent assisted by opening its doors to various classes.

Significant changes had to be made in family life. Many fathers were away in the armed services and mothers often contributed to the war effort by working outside the home. Consequently, domestic duties frequently fell to the lot of older children. At the Speech Day on 19th March 1945, Miss Sheldon said:

> Another way in which this School … is suffering is from the *home* calls that have to be made upon girls, even upon the youngest here – they used to be absent when they themselves were ill, now they seem to have to be absent almost whenever anyone in the family is ill – for there is no-one to take on the home – and here I might mention another matter that grieves me over and over again – when younger girls are ill and really need a bed and not a couch in our 'sick-room' – they cannot go home, because there will be no-one there till late at night. It is not seldom, too, that girls have to stay at home to carry on the business when father is ill and workpeople away.

The North London Collegiate School

One important effect of the war, as far as Luton High School was concerned, was the arrival of girls who had been evacuated from the North London Collegiate School. This was the celebrated school which had been founded by the pioneer Frances Mary Buss. On 1st September, girls from the 'North London', each with a rucksack, a blanket and a gas mask, walked 'in crocodile' to Kentish Town station and caught a train to Luton. They were taken to Luton High School and given chocolate and biscuits before being escorted through the streets until every girl had been found a safe billet.

The process of evacuation and billeting was difficult for everyone. Hosts and

The North London Collegiate School shared the School accommodation at the beginning of the Second World War. *(NLCS)*

hostesses had to adjust to strangers sharing their homes and evacuees had to overcome homesickness and familiarize themselves with a completely new environment. Miss I.M. Drummond, Headmistress of the North London Collegiate School, wrote in the *Sheaf* that 'it might all have been disastrous had not hundreds of thousands of private individuals set about this particular bit of personal service with such abounding good will and determination. That generous goodwill and that determination to succeed has met us again and again here in Luton.' It is certainly true that lifelong friendships were formed.

The combined number on roll was in the region of 900, 600 from Luton and 300 from London, which was more than the Alexandra Avenue building could accommodate. So, for the first weeks of September, girls from the London school had to gather wherever they could and occupy themselves however they could. They met in Wardown Park, sat in the bandstand, had lessons in the Museum and assembled on the stone steps in the cricket ground. They also learned the 'history of the town and blistered their hands filling sandbags at the Emergency Hospital'.

Fortunately the weather that September was fine and warm and, well before the bitter winter arrived, a scheme had been devised whereby the two schools were able to use the building on a time-share basis. Luton High School girls attended from 8.45 a.m. until 1 p.m. (still having six lessons) and the girls from the North London Collegiate School from 2 p.m. until around 6 p.m. As the evenings were dark, 'the staff took it in turns to escort crocodiles of pupils round Luton in the dark, with torches turned down not to break the blackout, delivering girls to the right billets'.

The High School prefects gave up their room for the staff of the North London and the medical room was made into an office for Miss Drummond. Luton girls could play games in the afternoons and London girls used the sports facilities on Saturdays. There was also some flexibility in the system because the Annexe could be used by the High School in the afternoon for special study or tuition and the Luton School of Art on Park Square and the Baptist Church in Blenheim Crescent were opened to the North London.

The two schools did not share the same ethos for the London school prided itself on not needing rules! One story is told about a group of London girls who, as they left school, were pelted with snowballs. They were called back by Miss Sheldon and were 'stood on the carpet in her study and lectured by her until darkness fell, for playing with boys'.

Meanwhile, a new school was being built for the North London Collegiate School at Canons, Edgware. This was in a 'neutral area' which meant that is was considered safe for the School to reassemble under its own roof. Therefore, soon after Easter 1940, the Luton contingent returned home to join others who had not taken part in the evacuation and Luton High School reclaimed the Alexandra Avenue building as its own.

Organization

Administration

Fees at the school were £12 a year although the 'special place' system was still in place. Bedfordshire Education Committee paid fees and differing annual maintenance grants, based on parents' weekly income and the number of children in the family. For example, if the family income was £4 a week and there were four dependent children, the BEC would pay full fees and allow £5 a year maintenance for a girl under 14, £7.10s (£7.50) for a girl between 14 and 16 and £10 for a girl over 16 years of age, on condition that she had passed her School Certificate.

However, changes were about to be made as a result of one of the most important Education Acts ever introduced. Under the terms of the 1944 Butler Education Act, fees were to be abolished and every child was to receive the type of secondary education suited to his or her age, aptitude and ability. There were to be three kinds of secondary school: grammar, technical and modern. The leaving age was to be raised to 15 and later to 16. This re-organization meant that a High School education would no longer largely depend on a family's financial status but would be replaced by a different form of élitism based on a child's ability to pass the Eleven-plus examination. Also, for the first time, there was to be a Minister for Education at Westminster.

Staff

There was still a considerable turnover of staff as a result of promotions, transfers, marriages and entrance into the armed services. After Miss Macfarlane's retirement in 1939, Miss Easton took over as second mistress but, sadly, she died on 18th December 1945. In 1945, Miss Deas became the first member of staff to join His Majesty's Inspectorate. Between 1939 and 1945, Miss Sheldon received two acknowledgements of her status in the town and as part of the wider world of girls' education. She was made a Justice of the Peace for the Borough of Luton in 1939 and was awarded an OBE in the 1945 New Year Honours List. To mark this award, the Old Girls commissioned a portrait of her from Miss Amy Drucker.

Miss Easton died while still in her post and her death was a great shock to the girls and the staff. On 20th December 1945, the School assembled for a service in her memory. This was a particularly emotional occasion. Readings were from *Samson Agonistes, The Pilgrim's Progress* and Psalm 23. The hymns were *Who would True Valour See* and *Lord of all Hopefulness*. Miss Wesley sang the *Nunc Dimittis*. There were plans to convert the land around the static water tank (beside the path leading to Argyle Avenue) into an Open Air Theatre and Memorial Garden. As far as is known, the theatre never materialized but the garden was built and dedicated in the 1950s. It was a delightful and peaceful retreat with ornamental shrubs, flowers and seating. However, it was destroyed when the School ran short of accommodation (again) and the land was used for building.

Curriculum

The problem of choosing 'options' for examination subjects is still with us in the twenty-first century. In the first half of the twentieth century, specialization took place in the High School at a very early age. Some girls were directed into Domestic Science and others had to choose between arts and sciences. Anyone who was being groomed for an academic career would probably need to take Latin since many universities required it. This option shut the door firmly on some other choices. One girl, who admitted at the age of 11, that she did not know what she wanted to be, was shunted into Latin – no argument.

That turned out to have been a happy decision. Latin may be thought of as 'dead' but it opens up a whole new understanding of English which can never be regretted. Another blessing was Miss Dickson's story-telling. She was a hard taskmaster but, every now and then, she would say, 'Of course, you know about Antigone' or whoever. 'No', we all chanted. Now, she knew that we were lying and we knew that she knew. However, the next hour or so was given over to the telling of wonderful

Mrs Smithwhite (Miss Oldham) in the Art Room c.1940.

Greek or Roman legends, never to be forgotten. Many thanks, Miss Dickson.

Lessons continued more or less normally and academic standards were not allowed to slip. The focus was on external examinations and many girls took up places in universities or training colleges. By 1945, the Sixth Form was growing steadily; there was a course of study for prospective teachers and a pre-nursing programme was set up. In 1945, girls from the Commercial VI form began to attend the Technical College in the morning and returned for non-commercial studies in the afternoon.

The gloom created by the scrimmed windows was lightened by work produced in Mrs Smithwhite's Art classes. The 1943 *Sheaf* noted that 'the upper corridor, with its ever-changing display of designs, figure studies and every kind of experiment in Art, is a joy to those who have eyes to see'. Miss Veitch's work in the Craft department was also commended. In 1945 the magazine reported that 'during the past year music has held a more prominent position in School life. Most girls have had the advantage of two singing lessons a week and, in the Upper forms, this has facilitated a brief study in musical history.' There was a musical appreciation group on Friday morning and Miss Fuller gave piano lessons to a few girls as well as running three choirs and an orchestra.

Miss Sheldon wrote in the *Sheaf* that she had been glad to see how many girls had learnt about First Aid on Wednesday Evenings. 'Indeed, our Wednesday Evenings have been helpful generally to the development of a sense of responsibility, and a feeling of comradeship that should help us all to face with a more even spirit, any troubles and stresses that may befall us'.

Extra-curricular Interests

The 1941 Prospectus set out a scheme for voluntary homework.

> As it is felt that some kind of private and individual study is a necessary and vital part of education ... certain carefully selected tasks are set for out-of-school hours, and the girls are asked to do these tasks, as a voluntary exercise in the training of character, and of independence of thought.

Rule No 5 in the Prospectus states that no girl should be allowed to work for any reason after 9 p.m. but, considering all the academic and philanthropic commitments which also occupied their time, it is probably reasonable to assume that this rule was frequently ignored.

The curriculum was broadened, as always, by visits from outside speakers. There were talks on missionary work in India and the work of *The Resistance* in France. Mrs Churchill sent a speaker to receive money collected for an X-ray unit in a Russian hospital and a group from the Norwegian Secondary School in London paid a visit. There was a talk on *Science and Religion* and another, with slides, about *Pictorial ideas and their Development*. Recitals were given: the Pilgrim Players performed *Tobias and the Angel* and there were presentations of verse speaking, mime, poetry and scenes from plays. On another occasion, there was a concert involving *Old Music with Old Instruments*.

Outside visits still took place: the VI form went to the Royal Academy, to a ballet and also to see *Hamlet*. A weekend reading party took place at the Youth Hostel in Houghton. Although large-scale entertainments were suspended, smaller shows were staged. For example, in March 1942, the lower school form mistresses and girls put on a 'nautical' production for Luton's Navy Week. There were Nativity plays, dramatic competitions and Art Exhibitions.

No doubt everyone who was a child in Luton at the time will remember the massed choirs which gathered on the concrete steps of the Cricket Ground at Wardown. On 21st July 1943 girls from the High School were among the 3,500 performers who took part in the Musical Pageant with massed choirs, orchestras and 'Contingents of Youth Movements with Colours'. Arthur Davies from the Luton Girls Choir conducted and Uncle Mac (Derek McCulloch) of *Children's Hour* fame gave a talk. The Bands of the Air Training Corps and of the Bedfordshire and Hertfordshire Regiment performed.

A 'Selection' was played by the Luton Junior Prize Orchestra together with the combined orchestras of Denbigh Road Senior Boys, the High School for Girls and the Modern School for Boys. The programme of songs celebrated different parts of the British Isles, the Empire and the armed services. This was wartime and how patriotic we felt as we sang songs like this!

Motherland
She stands, a thousand wintered tree,
By countless morns impearled;
Her broad roots coil beneath the sea,
Her branches sweep the world;
Her seed, by heaven's wind conveyed,
Has clothed the distant strand
With forests from her saplings made,
New nations, fostered in her shade,
And linking, linking land with land.

Sports Day 1942. (Margaret Attwell)

Junior School Entertainment *A Patriotic Saga*, 1941. (*Margaret Attwell*)

Games and Gymnastics

The war affected the Physical Training curriculum. One serious problem was the shortage of staff and, for some time, Miss Horn had to carry the burden of responsibility for all gymnastic and games activities with the help of students from the Bedford Physical Training College. Gym lessons were routine although taking showers was stopped for fear of an air raid warning sounding at an inappropriate moment. Athletics practices continued and Sports Days were held. In the summer months, tennis and rounders were played and swimming was soon resumed. Cricket became popular, as it had been in the early days of the School's life. Apparently this was because, in those days of austerity and shortages, it was becoming more and more difficult to obtain tennis balls.

While the school was sharing the facilities with the North London Collegiate School, practices could take place in the afternoons but there was a need to see that girls left school long before dark. The two schools played hockey against each other and there were matches against the Old Girls. House matches continued to be played and netball matches against other Luton schools were arranged. It appears that inter-school games were cancelled in the early days of the war but, later on, visits were made to nearby towns like Bedford, Hitchin and Letchworth although 'there was much cancelling of fixtures, for obvious reasons'. These were probably transport and blackout difficulties as well as dangers from air-raids.

Houses

Annual House Reports show that activities were proceeding normally but the wartime environment meant that, if anything, the emphasis on charitable work was even greater. In 1942, a new house was created.

<u>Jane Austen</u> (1775–1817)

Jane Austen was a famous English novelist.

Motto: The Pen is Mightier than the Sword.

Colours: turquoise and rust.

Banner: Quill pen and an ink-well.

Austen House chose the Luton and Dunstable Maternity Hospital as their charity and lost no time in finding ways to help. They collected money, visited the hospital, knitted vests for babies and sent toys.

An eighth House, Jane Austen, was introduced in 1942.

(*Photograph by Bob Norman*)

Twenty-First Birthday Celebrations

In the Special Anniversary Edition of the *Sheaf* in 1940, Miss Harris wrote about the rather subdued 21st birthday celebrations.

> The twenty-one years of the life of the Luton High School cover a disappointing period of the world's history, with a grim ending. The Peace of Versailles was three months old when the School was opened; the latest 'Great War' had passed its first year when the School attained its majority. Yet its history has been one of steady progress and of broadening ideals – progress and ideals which have so far survived the strain of war conditions. May this prove an omen for our nation's future as well as for our own!

'Grandiose schemes' had been planned but these had to be modified for several reasons. The School would not be allowed to crowd in more than the trenches could accommodate and a service in St Mary's Church had to be abandoned in case of air raids. The celebrations became, therefore, 'on a small scale and purely domestic'. Work by students past and present was exhibited, services were held and short holidays granted. Miss Sheldon was given flowers from each form and also a book containing everybody's signature. It was announced that, in future, a service was to be held annually in the School Hall on the nearest Sunday to 30th September.

In 1939 a Twenty-First Birthday Fund was set up to help girls in financial need. A donation of £5 set the scheme in motion, collecting boxes were placed in each form room and, by 1942, £225 had been raised. £105 of this had been used to help girls pay for school dinners, uniforms, examination fees and the fares of girls doing service in the community during the holidays. In 1943, the fund helped to send older girls to Conferences, for example one on *World Citizenship*. Ingenious plans were devised to boost the fund; staff, parents and Old Girls contributed and girls frequently made donations as a 'parting gift'.

Social conscience

In 1944, Miss Sheldon wrote about 'three happy aspects' of School life: the increased interest of our young people in the world outside the School, in the peoples of other lands and in home and in home-life. The war years made such awareness even more keen and ever more urgent.

Much of this social conscience was linked to the Christian religion. During the Luton *Religion and Life Week* in June 1942, Miss Sheldon wrote that religion is not 'something that belongs to one day out of seven and is left there'. Nor is it something

Speech Day 24th July 1942 – Prizewinners. (*LN*)

that is 'considered earnestly in one special week and is left there'. It is something that 'belongs to all day and every day' and must 'make a difference to our every action to every subject that we study, to every thought that we think'. Parents were invited to attend a regular service which was held every Sunday at 3 p.m. in the school hall.

The ideal of women as homemakers was taken up after a number of prams appeared at the 1943 Sports Day. They reminded everyone that the most important job of all was 'the task of keeping homes together and of bringing up families in circumstances which become more difficult year by year and month by month'. Miss Sheldon had been known to say that her pride in the School rested chiefly on the good wives and mothers it produced.

Obligation to the community took on a different aspect during the war years as a result of government regulations. From April 1942, girls between the ages of 16 and 18 had to register and, under the terms of the National Service Act 1941, unmarried women between 20 and 30 could be conscripted into the armed forces. As Miss Sheldon said: 'we live in troublous days. We are for the first time in the front line of defence of our country.'

> The Land Girl
> Picture if you can a Land Girl,
> In November's icy freeze,
> Making whoopee with the carrots,
> Learning why the chickens sneeze.
> Seven days a week she's working
> Thirty cows to milk each day,
> Muddy clothes and boots too heavy,
> On her back she carries hay.
> She jitterbugs among the brussels,
> Picks potatoes in the rain
> Soaking wet and often hungry
> Lots of laughs and plenty rain.
> The GIs sent us pancake make-up,
> Hair like straw blown in the breeze.
> We are working for our country.
> Now we know why chickens sneeze.
> [Pauline Holmes (Wilkinson),
> who became a Land Girl.]

Retirement was no excuse and Miss Graham wrote to the *Sheaf* telling of her contribution. Before war was declared, she had trained in First Aid and finished a gas course in time to help with fitting the masks. She helped out with clerical work and serving cups of tea at the Child Welfare Clinic and became secretary to the High

Town Ward NSPCC. She was also committed to night duty in a First Aid Post and helping with Flag Days but was able to say that 'life is as full of interest as ever'.

Training for Citizenship and the Company of Service

A large proportion of the wartime *Sheaf* magazines was devoted to citizenship. However, the pressure to work for the community and for the good of the country was greatly increased when a 'Company of Service' was set up. This was a scheme devised by Dr Happold at the Bishop Wordsworth School. Mrs Evans, accompanied by another member of staff, paid a visit, presumably to this School, and came back fired with enthusiasm to set up a dedicated group at the High School. In 1944, Miss Sheldon was able to report that, after a trial period, first with a very small, very carefully picked Company of Service and then with a very much enlarged group, certain clear and valuable ideas had emerged.

> The thing that matters is not spectacular deeds or attainments, not even the attendance at meetings nor the doing of special tasks, but the everyday life of the individual, the quiet striving after an ideal, the desire, with God's help, to use one's talents in the best way for true citizenship, with our fellow men.

The experiment proved successful and, by 1944, girls were eligible for membership when they had been at the School for more than a year. In fact the whole School was 'in training' and some girls had taken the Promises. From these, certain older girls were chosen to form 'The Sixty', the officials of the School. 'The Sixty' held regular council meetings and were, in practice, the élite. Company of Service members had a red on black emblem to sew on their tunics while the 'Sixty' had a yellow badge. It has to be said that the pressure on girls to conform to the service expected of them was considerable and the demands on their time significant, especially when the burden of examinations was taken into account. Life became particularly difficult for girls who also had commitments to other voluntary or religious organizations.

The Federation of the Companies of Service
Luton High School Company

1. I promise to keep myself clean and to observe the rules of health.
2. I promise to try to find out how I may best serve the community of which I am a member and to do thoroughly, methodically, cheerfully, and at the right moment, everything I undertake.
3. I promise to try to find out about the world in which I live in order to fit myself for world citizenship.

Declaration of Intention

> I acknowledge my debt to the community into which I have been born, and which
> demands of me my full and devoted service. So that I may serve that community
> faithfully and effectively, I undertake at school a threefold task, the training of my
> body so that it may be perfectly fit and controlled, the training of my mind so that
> I may understand the world of which I am a part, and into which I shall go and
> particular training according to my particular ability, so that I may play an active
> part in the life of the community.

The Company of Service was divided into groups and the courses undertaken fall roughly into four categories. These were duties in the home, duties to the School, social and civic responsibilities and active commitment to the community. Much of the training took place during 'Friday Four', the last period on a Friday morning. This was the official Citizenship period but there was a considerable overlap between this subject and grooming for membership of the Company of Service.

Learners
One of the first tasks was to learn the meaning of the Promise. Then girls learnt the first rules of health and hygiene, safety first, darning, polishing and first aid. Practical work included digging up dandelions, cleaning the Gym and getting to know Luton, while social life was enriched with school bees, dramatic work, nature activities and ballroom and country dancing. It was also considered essential to teach the importance of giving dinner tickets in on time.

Juniors
Juniors were taught make-do and mend, mothercraft, home nursing and food values. They also learnt how to spell the names of the staff and the meanings of the house mottoes. They polished the silver and undertook to provide flowers for the two main corridors. Interest groups included music and art appreciation, talks on speech therapy, current affairs, central and local government, travel and the lives of great scientists, common sense and map reading. Social graces encouraged were chess, wireless talks, play reading, country dancing, French conversation, swimming and discussions. Some girls were given pen friends in California.

Middle
Among other things, these girls helped in the School kitchens and went out and about collecting wastepaper. They visited the Children's Hospital and the salvage depot and went on a town-planning course. Serious discussions and debates were held and a new responsibility was laid on them, namely, that of preparing themselves to become involved in the leadership of youth movements.

Senior

Senior girls were expected to have a high level of expertise. First Aid included passing examinations and helping out in Red Cross week. They were taught how to manage household budgets and the way to look after rabbits and chickens. Dr Grundy, Medical Officer of Health, gave lectures on pre-natal clinics, maternity hospitals and childcare. Girls learnt about civics and careers, discussed ethics and visited local industries and the police courts. On one occasion ten boys and girls from the Norwegian State School were entertained as part of a joint project with the boys' school. From a practical point of view, girls acted as messengers during a practice invasion, worked in Nursery and Infant Schools, war centres and the new play centres and helped to sell flags for Army and Navy days.

Some girls became members of the Luton Girls' Service Company, later the Girls' Training Corps. This was a Town Company, not a School Company, but was run almost entirely by High School staff; and meetings and parades were held on the School premises. There was also a Junior Service Company which girls leaving Luton Senior Schools were invited to join. Classes were similar to those taken by members of the Company of Service but also included Morse, ARP and Aircraft recognition.

The focus on Youth Clubs is worth noting. The school leaving age during the War was 14 and there was a four-year gap before boys and girls were eligible for conscription, so schemes were organized and young people were not so much directed as recommended to join groups which suited their interests. Some of these, for example the Air Training Corps, served as apprenticeships for the armed forces but others were set up at High Town, Beech Hill, Chapel Street and Stopsley under the aegis of the County Education Authority. They became very popular and, naturally, expertise was required to run them.

Six girls represented Luton High School on the Luton Youth Council. They also helped out in the canteen at the headquarters in Guildford Street. March 1944 was Youth Month which aimed to make the public aware of Youth activities and the *Sheaf* reported that a High School team won the netball tournament and then went on to defeat a team representing Watford Youth. Miss Sheldon had reservations about the Youth Movement; at the 1945 Speech day, she said: 'I could wish personally that there were a winter curfew of 8 for all girls under 15 (unless with parents). Once a week is enough to my mind, and *one* movement – none at all for delicate girls. We must not exploit our young people.'

Demands on Girls' Time

Everyone was busy in a variety of altruistic activities some of which involved helping in Miss Sheldon's home and garden! Girls knitted 'comforts for the troops' and squares for blankets. There was limited heating in hospitals so girls knitted white stockings for patients undergoing operations. Samples of 'how to darn' and 'how not to darn' were prepared and, on one occasion, a huge number of woollen union suits (vests and knickers combined) were sent from America 'to cheer our darkest hour'. Fay Weighall (Fryer) recalls how Miss Wolverson supervised their transformation: from each suit the girls managed to produce one man's vest, one pair of men's undershorts, one baby's vest (from the sleeves) and one child's vest (from the legs). 'They then disappeared – I believe to blitz victims. We could herring-bone [embroider] for Britain by then – on the beaches, in the fields etc etc.' Not all the activities were so arduous, however.

> Writing cards reminds me of the flurry at the High School in wartime. We used to take used cards in to school and remove the base, double paper lining from the posher ones, and write a suitable greeting on the card. Those of the lesser sort would be treated with typing error fluid (no Biros then) and similarly re-cycled. They were then sold on (to each other, teachers etc.) for 1d or 2d in aid of the Red Cross Ambulance appeal. I don't remember how we went on about envelopes – re-cycled with labels I expect. Each form had a cardboard Post Box. <u>No</u> presents to staff or girls allowed … Christmas at the High School … really <u>was</u> lovely. Very simple, inexpensive but lovely. The carol services were such wonderful oases in wartime.
>
> [Fay Weighall]

Fire watching was a popular, once a week, occupation amongst the 17 plus age group. Firewatchers, who patrolled on top of the School, needed to have a First Aid Certificate, did not have to be involved with exams and earned themselves 5s (25p) a night. Supper and breakfast were taken in the domestic science room and 'a good time was had by all'.

Sometimes girls were called upon to keep form rooms clean and much of the responsibility for growing and harvesting the crops on the school grounds fell on girls' shoulders. The homegrown vegetables were used in the School canteen. There were also land parties for girls over 13 and good workers could boast a green armband displaying 'Dig for Victory'.

> During the Summer Term organised parties of girls from the Lower Vths and IVths have been helping on farms at Toddington and Woburn. At 9.30 a.m. a van draws up outside the School, and twenty to forty-five girls, dressed in dungarees, trousers, shorts or other suitable clothing, climb into it and are taken to the farm. On arrival, we are met by the foreman, who either divides the party or attaches us to another squad of workers composed of land girls and farm workers.
>
> The chief work that has been done is potato picking …
>
> A whistle is blown at one o'clock and we are given half and hour for eating our sandwiches and for resting, although some prefer to explore around the farm. We work again at the same jobs until four o'clock, when the lorry fetches us, and we

return to School very dirty and with our hands stained with potato. We are glad to report that the farmer says we have done 'a grand job'.

[E. Evans, N.C. Sillar M.L. Tanner]

Another very popular source of income was the Christmas post round which remained a seasonal joy for years to come, long after the war was over. It was a sad day when, in December 1965, Luton's Director of Education announced that he saw no good reason why VI Form pupils should be allowed to cut their autumn term short to help out with the Christmas rush.

Each day was more or less a repetition of the previous one – get yourself signed on; collect the paper slips for the registered letters and parcels; join a queue in order to obtain these … wait until your letters were sorted, and then begin the delivery. When this was done you were free to go home (unless someone caught you, and asked you to deliver some on your way home!). There was, however, one noticeable difference – as the days went on, the bag became decidedly heavier.

[Eileen Ellis]

Philanthropy

Besides the House charities and the Twenty-First Birthday Fund, there were frequent demands on the pockets of girls and their families, as this list of appeals (1945) demonstrates:

The usual weekly charity collections from September 1944 to June 1945, apart from 'Special Efforts', amounted to £204.5s.9d

In addition to our usual donations of £15.15s to the Luton and Dunstable Hospital, and the £10.10s to the Children's Hospital, we have been able to send: £5 to the Rehabilitation Clinic; £11.11s to Great Ormond Street Hospital; £15.12s.6d to the Tuberculosis Campaign; £4 to the Princess Louise Hospital; £3 to the Fund for Helping the Dutch; £5.5s to the Queen Elizabeth Hospital for Children; £5.5s to the Yugoslav Relief Fund; £11 to the Overseas Tobacco Fund; £10.10s to the Cancer Campaign.

In the Christmas holidays we made a collection of £345 for the Kalinin Hospital in Russia.

We are at present busily engaged in collecting clothes, toilet requisites and sewing materials ready to send to the Channel Islands – and our appeal, as always, has met with a wonderful response from parents and girls.

Other appeals were for the: Red Cross, aid to China Fund, Nursing Association, Blind, Governesses' Benevolent Institution, NSPCA, Waifs and Strays, National Association for the Prevention of Tuberculosis, Salvation Army and Public Assistance

Miss M.E. Redman, Matron of the Luton and Dunstable Hospital, at the Harvest Festival, 1942.
(Mrs I. Wagstaff)

Institution. Vegetables, fruit and other provisions were sent to the Luton and Dunstable Hospital, probably as Harvest Festival offerings. A variety of articles from sweaters to razor blades, was made up into 26 parcels for Russian soldiers. Sacks of books were collected for merchant seamen. Soft toys were made for nurseries and the WVS and, in 1941, an ambulance was donated to the Red Cross.

National Savings stamps and certificates were sold on Thursdays. £179.9s.6d was collected during a special 'School Saving Week' in 1941. Nearly £3,000 was saved for 'Warship Week', £3,365 for 'Wings for Victory' and £2,346.4s for 'Salute the Soldier'. In June 1945, a grand total of £28,038.19s.9d was reported.

Into the Wider World

Girls who left school during the war, went out into a totally different world. Employment was controlled through the Labour Exchanges and conscription was introduced. Some girls worked in reserved occupations and those who had successfully applied to colleges or universities could continue with their education. Everyone worked unless they had dependent children. Luton's factories were very much involved with the war effort and it is reasonable to suppose that Old Girls from the High School played their part. The 1944 *Sheaf* lists the walks of life which had attracted girls from the School: university, training college, secretarial life, civil service, music, art, social welfare, mathematical computing, laboratory research, war nursery and the armed services.

Thoughts on leaving school
(with apologies to Rupert Brooke)

These I have loved:
The sudden jarring of the frequent bell
That marks out lessons, tells us hours of play;
The cheers, the clapping and the long array
Of prizes, shields and cups and honours won –
The majesty of Speech Days and the fun
And sweet anticipation Sports Day brings;
The joy of watching those who shine at things
That I can never do; the honest pride
In praise received when one has really tried;
The solid satisfaction that is gained
From sheer hard work; the matches lost and won –
The feel of stick and ball – the breathless run
To tackle, hit and save the side; the glow
That warms numbed fingers in the wintry blow;
Long summer days, and lessons out of doors;
The burning tennis courts; and blessed cool
That comes from dipping in the swimming-pool;
The adventure of exams, the endless weeks
Before Results. (Poor mistress who still seeks
The work one should have done long days ago!)
The empty School on Saturday; the crowd
Which teems anew each Monday morn; the loud
Insistent clang of hand-bell, heard again
Now Peace has come to Britain's shores; and then
The sunlit silence of the Hall at prayer;
Then the light touch of sadness always there
In Lord dismiss us …"; All the joys and fears
That make up days, and terms, and all one's years
At School;
    All these have been my loves.
[Daphne F. Dennis]

Hilary Reed (VI A)

Brush and line drawing to celebrate the Coronation of Queen Elizabeth II. (*Sally Gurney*)

Chapter Seven

Homely Changelessness
and Valuable Change 1945–1953

Some of you say, 'School seems just the same'. It is, in so many ways; there is the same orderly sequence of hours and days; there are the same games, the same meetings after School, and there is the same noise as well as the same quiet. Some of you, who perhaps have been away longer, say, 'How people have changed! … So School goes on: it is a mixture of old and new, of homely changelessness and valuable change, to which all of us, from the youngest of the First Years to those who left many years ago, contribute.

[E. Evans]

An atmosphere of 're-awakening' characterized the immediate post war years internationally, nationally and in the narrower sphere of school life. There was the immediate joy of victory and, soon afterwards, an unexpected change of government. Two years later, on 20th November 1947, came the wedding of Princess Elizabeth, which epitomised the country's emergence from the gloom of rationing and austerity. The country celebrated once again in the summer of 1951 with the Festival of Britain. On a sadder note, there was the death of King George VI on 6th February 1952, but the accession of the new Queen Elizabeth II heralded the arrival of a new Elizabethan age.

Hopes for the future were also stirred by the setting up of the United Nations Organization in 1945. Travel became easier and girls from the school holidayed abroad or emigrated. Visitors from other shores came here to talk about their lives and pen friendship schemes were set up. The world had become alive and accessible once again.

Valuable Change

It is probably more useful if the changes which came about in the post-war years are considered first.

The Retirement of Miss H.K. Sheldon

The retirement of Miss Sheldon in 1947 could not exactly be described as 'valuable change' but the departure of such a dominant figure obviously had a great effect on the School. Miss Sheldon had worked hard to fulfil her promise to give Luton a good school and she certainly deserved a happy retirement. Mrs Evans said of her that she has 'guided us through the early years and given to the task all the wisdom and courage and unwavering vigilance which she possesses – qualities of no mean order in anyone, but which in her were heightened to an unusual degree'. Councillor H.C. Lawrence, Chairman of the Board of Governors, believed that she had 'left a record in Luton which will never die'. Tributes and presents were given by governors, staff and parents, among them cheques, book tokens and photographs. The girls presented a handmade bedspread and chair backs, a scroll from the Houses and an illustrated and lettered book, signed by every girl. On June 14th parents and friends were invited to an 'At Home' and, on 20th July, a Thanksgiving Service attended by governors, representatives of the civic life of Luton, Old Girls, parents and members of the School was held at the Parish Church.

OPPOSITE Miss Sheldon says 'Goodbye', July 1947. (LN) ABOVE Presentation to Miss Sheldon by the Old Girls' Association, June 1947. Miss Sheldon had the interior of her house decorated with the money given to her. (LN)

Today August 31st 1947, I lay down my work as your Head Mistress, and so it seems to me the right moment to send you a Farewell message.

These last twenty-eight years have been happy ones for me, and I thank you all for helping to make them so: they have been important and interesting ones too, in that they have contained the first quarter of a century of our history.

We have, since the first term, endeavoured to follow a high standard and to pursue ideals. I now hand on to you the care of the tradition thus formed, and I ask each one of you in the years to come to improve upon our early efforts.

I am, as you know, content and happy to leave the School I love to such a guide as Mrs Evans, but she will need all the help and loyalty and understanding that you can give her, and I beg you to give them to her even more unstintingly than you have given them to me.

If you will always remember that only the Best will do, and that little things matter desperately, then no Head Mistress that you may ever have will need to fear the Future.

I look forward to many happy visits to the School, and to welcoming many of you to my new home: those, who have already seen me in it, will give you news of me.

Good-bye – and God bless you all,

I am,

Your affectionate friend

Helen K. Sheldon   [Written from Ashtead, Surrey]

Miss Harris had retired to Ashtead the previous year, although she did return to teach advanced classes on a voluntary basis during a serious staff shortage.

> I have by now found quite a number of interests here, and am so kept busy and happy. The Afternoon Townswomen's Guild, to which one of my sisters, Miss Harris and I belong, meets monthly, and I am now on the Committee.
>
> It is lovely to be living so near to my sisters, as hardly a day passes that we do not see something of one another, while Miss Harris spends every Wednesday with me.
> [H.K. Sheldon]

Eileen Evans

Eileen Evans (Threlkeld, b.1901) attended the prestigious Manchester High School for Girls. Between 1898 and 1924, the Headmistress of this school was Miss Sara Burstall, whose name is celebrated in the history of girls' education. In 1907, Miss Burstall wrote *English High Schools for Girls: their aims, organization and management* which described almost exactly the system which was followed by Luton High School for Girls, especially in its early days. Mrs Evans went on to study at Manchester University, graduating with a first class B.Sc. Hons. in Zoology. She returned to teach for a while (1922–24) at her former school while another of her teaching appointments was as Biology mistress at Penistone (co-educational) Grammar School. There is no doubting the fact that Mrs Evans was an extremely talented class teacher. Her discipline was firm but gentler than Miss Sheldon's had been and her 'pep talks' were legendary. Miss Ling recalled that she would always be remembered for 'her enthusiasm, her energy and her infectious laugh.'

She was appointed to Luton High School in 1938 as Biology teacher, VI Form Mistress and Careers Mistress and, in 1945, succeeded Miss D. Easton as Deputy Head. When she was appointed Headmistress, she told the *Telegraph* that, although there were bound to be developmental changes, she was 'looking forward with enormous interest to seeing the new Education Act implemented so that every child is given an equal chance in life'. She declared that one of her keenest aims was 'to maintain the ideals and traditions built up in the School over the past years'. Apparently, she also bore in mind the advice given to her by the Revd. Carlisle, Vicar of Christchurch, 'Now remember, Mrs Evans, a school is like a fish: it goes bad from the head downwards.' An Inspectors' Report in June 1949 stated that 'the Governors are to be congratulated on choosing a natural leader of staff and girls who, while preserving warm human sympathies, unostentatiously inspires in others her own high standards of character and scholarship'.

Mrs Evans became a JP in 1955 and was a Governor of the Dame Alice Harpur School in Bedford between 1968 and 1978. A former member of that staff recalled Mrs Evans 'coming to the Staff Room to talk with staff and listen to any comments and was well liked as a Governor'.

Staff

Between the two World Wars, there had been a 'marriage bar'; this meant that Education Authorities were extremely reluctant to employ married women teachers. However, this was relaxed during the Second World War and officially removed under the terms of the 1944 Education Act. Miss Oldham, a talented Art teacher, returned as Mrs Smithwhite and then left again at Christmas 1945 to await the arrival of her baby son. For the next two terms, her husband took over her post. He seems to have been the first male member of staff – amongst about nine hundred females.

Other members of staff became involved with official exchanges. Miss M.R. Mallett switched posts with Miss S. Woliver from Cincinnati, Ohio. Two of her letters were published in the *Sheaf*; one described the differences between English and American schools and the other a ten thousand mile, coast-to-coast, journey which she made in the summer before her return.

High School Staff c.1947. *Left to right:*
Back row: Miss Liddle, Miss Horn, Miss Stalker, Miss Stableford, Miss Stephenson, Miss Sturgis, Miss Hudson, —, —, —, —, Miss Edge, Miss Dickson, —. *Middle row:* Miss Smith, Audrey Sare-Soar (secretary), Beryl Taylor (secretary), —, —, Miss Potts, Miss Woods, Miss Rose, —, —, Miss Burton, Miss Reed, Miss Middlehurst, Miss Chamberlin, —. *Front row:* Miss Wolverson, Dr Frankenstein, Miss Flaherty, Miss Sillar, Miss Harris, Mrs Evans, Miss Sheldon, Miss Smewing, Miss Macnab, Miss Dowdall, Miss Wesley, Miss Ling, Miss Fuller.

No school uniform is worn here, and most of the girls are wearing make-up. Few of the boys wear ties, and their most common garments appear to be a pair of navy blue jeans and a brightly coloured shirt. Two bells ring and it is time to take register, but first I make sure that all chewing gum has been deposited in the waste-paper basket. Gum chewing is universal here.

Miss Barbara Middlehurst taught Mathematics between 1942–3 and 1950. When she left, she worked in astronomy and Sir Patrick Moore has confirmed that they worked together on 'transient phenomena on the moon.' They contributed to a Report on the subject which was published by NASA: *NASA Technical Report TR R-277 (NASA, July 1968). A catalog of 579 Transient Lunar Phenomena.* Sir Patrick Moore said that she was 'a delightful person'.

The 1944 Education Act

The 1944 Butler Education Act brought important changes to schools throughout the country. Luton High School, together with the Grammar School and the Technical School, had been under the control of Bedfordshire County Council, while the other schools in the town were managed by the Luton Education Committee. When the 1944 Act came into force, all schools became the responsibility of the Bedfordshire Education Committee and the High School became part of the northern group of county secondary schools in Luton. However, while the Bedfordshire Local Authority allocated places, the general control of the School passed, in 1947, to the Luton Scheme of Divisional Administration. One of the most welcome changes introduced by the Act was the abolition of fees in April 1945.

> In less than a fortnight's time all State education for children over 11 will set out on the path upon which our type of girls' school set out … years ago – the path of what is now termed 'Secondary Education for Girls', and just as there must have been difficulties in those days, so there will naturally be in these – but just as a miracle has in these not-so-many years been effected for some of our sex, so we trust and hope that a miracle may in due course be brought to pass for all those others who now join us. And if there is anything at all to help towards this 'miracle' that we in this School can do, then I for one should wish to try to do it. But it is important, if we are not all to be disappointed, that we should face up to the fact that miracles in Education are not sudden ones brought about by an Act of Parliament or by a stroke of the pen, but the outcome of years of thought and endeavour. [H.K. Sheldon Speech Day 19th March 1945]

The Eleven-plus System

At the time, it was generally believed that a child's intelligence and future capability could be correctly measured at the age of 11. Theoretically, an 'average' child would have an IQ (intelligence quotient) of 100, while grammar school children would have a higher score. Depending on the number of grammar school places available in any given area, a cut-off line was drawn; those above were allocated grammar school places while those below would attend secondary modern schools. Children who showed promise in technology could be offered a place at a technical school. Later research established that testing at 11 was by no means an exact science and it was particularly difficult to be fair to borderline children who just failed the examination for whatever reason. The eleven-plus examination came to dominate the lives of children, especially in their last year at primary school. The day when the pass list was published was extremely traumatic for parents and children since so much depended on it. Opportunities were provided for children to transfer to the Grammar Schools at 13 or 16 but only a few were able to take advantage of this. The following account will help to demonstrate the problems associated with deciding children's future at the age of 11.

Personal Observations on Entering the School at 13

One day when I was in the second year at Denbigh Road Senior Girls School, Miss Parish the headmistress came into my class which was the top stream and asked if anyone who had not taken the 11+ wanted to apply to take the 13+ examination. At the end of the afternoon my Form teacher asked me to stay behind. She gave me a note to take home to my parents suggesting that they should apply to the Examination Authority for me to be allowed to take the 13+ examination.

The 13+ examination was held at Luton Technical College and my mother and I had to attend an interview at the High School with Miss Sheldon. For some reason the results did not come through in time for us to start at the High School at the beginning of the school year. By the time I heard I had passed I was already in the Third Year at Denbigh and had just been made a prefect and House and Form Captain …

The High School was quite a culture shock. Twelve girls had been accepted and we were called 3rd Year X. Our Form Teacher was Miss Williams but we did not have a Form room of our own but were put in with 3rd Year W, Miss Wesley's Form in the Geography Room a the top of the stairs. We felt very inferior to the 3rd Year W girls who were very self assured and so much cleverer than us. I think they were the top stream. In the 4th year the 12 of us were still a separate class but our form room was now the Bridge and we were no longer X, the unknown quantity or quality, but were 4S, our form teacher being Miss Stephenson.

The first few weeks were very bewildering, the school seemed vast … We were not used to changing classrooms for every lesson or having to carry satchels loaded with books … The work was very different and we had three years' work to catch up. Some subjects were completely new to us i.e. French, Algebra, Geometry (we had only studied basic Arithmetic), Biology and Physics. Even subjects we thought were familiar like History and Geography were studied in so much greater depth they seemed almost like new subjects. Of course we had to try to learn the High School style of Handwriting.

There was a big change in our status; we had been the top pupils in our old school, prefects etc, the big girls who would have been leaving school in a year's time. Now however, we were the lowest of the low, even the youngest girls in the first year had been there longer than us and knew their way around the buildings. We were always getting into trouble for breaking rules that we were not aware of. However, by the end of the first term, we were quite at home. We had been accepted by our old friends and started to make new ones. We were beginning to master the new subjects and getting used to different ways of working, enjoying the challenge and we wore our uniform with pride. 3rd Year X won the Voice Speaking Competition for the Classes own choice section with our recitation of an excerpt from *The Rime of the Ancient Mariner*. (I can still recite it.)

Careers advice for VI Formers left a lot to be desired. The only careers the staff seemed to be aware of were: teaching (academic VIth), nursing (pre-nursing VIth), or secretarial (VI commercial). When I said that I wanted to be a hospital almoner, it stumped them. They decided that an almoner sat in an office and put me in VI Commercial! The School obviously did not think I was university material and worthy of going into the academic VIth to study for Higher School Certificate. I was hopeless at Shorthand and Typing and hated it and left school after about six months to take a clerical job in the Almoner's Office at Luton and Dunstable Hospital where I would have a lot of contact with people. When I was 18, I passed the entrance examination for the London School of Economics where I graduated in Social Science and Social Administration (so I was university material after all!). I had a career in Community Development work.

Having had the unusual experience of being a pupil at both and elementary senior school and a grammar school, I am a firm advocate of the comprehensive system … I think all of us at Denbigh Road felt we were failures and inferior to our former friends who now went to the grammar schools. I know that, as the system was then, if I had not taken the 13+, I would never have got to university and had the successful and fulfilling career. [Margaret Rowley (Marsom)]

Examinations

The value of examinations as opposed to regular assessment by the staff of schools was a topic of considerable debate. At the 1945 Speech Day, Miss Sheldon made her feelings on the subject clear.

As I really do believe that this kind of outside testing [School and Higher Certificates], which today really does give a good chance to even the poorer candidates, is enjoyable and a spur to effort to our young people – *I am in favour of it*, provided that due allowance is also given to School Records. We in this School have always kept these most exactly. I cannot think that an outside testing can do any harm to anyone, because we can always leave out the rare girl who gets overdone or over-excited, and in her case rely on record alone. I find parents, staff and girls keen and I have a strong idea that no-one would really like as much the School Record system only. Standards in different schools vary so greatly.

[H.K. Sheldon 1945]

The School Certificate, taken at around the age of 16 and the Higher School Certificate, taken two years later, were grouped awards. Candidates had to pass in a number of different subjects according to set rules. However, a system was under consideration whereby candidates would take separate examinations and receive a certificate for each subject. This became a reality in 1951 when the General Certificate of Education was introduced. Ordinary level examinations were taken at the age of 16 and Advanced level examinations at 18. There was also a higher Scholarship level (S-level). It was possible to avoid the O-level examination altogether and concentrate on getting good results at the higher levels.

Not surprisingly, there were teething problems. In the early days, there were only two grades: pass or fail. Also no one could take the examination under the age of 16, thus making it almost impossible for children in the secondary modern schools who, from Easter 1947, left school at 15, to follow the necessary curricula. Even in the High School there was confusion for some girls who were too young to take the O-level examinations. As still happens in educational circles, amendments had to be made and it became popular for students to take seven, eight or even ten subjects at O-level, while A-levels became the instrument of selection for university entrance. The new system, therefore, soon began to resemble the old.

Parent Teacher Association

In the autumn of 1948 Mrs Evans and the school staff decided to form a Parent Teacher Association. The inaugural meeting was well supported and a keen and conscientious committee appointed. Mr E. Greaves, the first honorary secretary, was succeeded in 1952 by Mr A.C. Terry. It was decided that two meetings would be held each term, one would be a general meeting to be addressed by a prominent speaker and, at the other, topics of interest would be discussed. Social evenings were held in the spring and garden parties in June. At the second AGM in October 1950, it was reported that 'upwards of £130 had been donated to various school funds'. There were social activities such as whist drives and brains trusts and well-known speakers included Mr L. Plewes from the Luton and Dunstable Hospital and Mr Freddie Grisewood whose subject was 'Behind the scenes at the BBC.'

In 1952, the PTA welcomed Freddie Grisewood, a well-known broadcaster, who spoke on *Behind the Scenes at the BBC*. (*LN*)

It is good, too, to have news in this magazine of our Parent-Teacher Association. Its activities have already greatly enriched our School life. And it makes it even easier to understand and to rely on the constant liveliness and generosity and co-operation of you girls in school as we realise in what full measure you inherit it from your fathers and mothers.   [E. Evans 1950]

Homely Changelessness

Mrs Evans' use of the words 'homely changelessness' indicates that there was a structure to the way of life in the School which would have been recognizable to generations of girls.

One of my most vivid memories is of the first day of each School year – the whole School gathered in the Junior quadrangle; Miss Sheldon surrounded by prospective form-mistresses; the breathless hush of anticipation as the lists are being read; the scramble for a favourite desk in the form-room; a new timetable and finding out which mistress is to teach us …the smell of Dettol in the Sick

Room; the reading of the Charity List on Thursday mornings … the strange smell emanating from the Chemistry Lab; the minutes at House-Meetings … the Staff lockers filled with books in the corridors … that unforgettable place – School.

[Gwendoline Fowler]

A sense of continuity was encouraged by the presence of a group of long-serving members of staff, not only teaching staff but also Mr Mandley, the caretaker and Mrs Richardson, the cook.

Is it worth it?

When I first unlock the door,
Survey the empty corridor,
And think what I have come here for,
I wonder, is it worth it?

Bric-a-brac lies all about
Waiting to be carried out!
Makes me want to turn about –
I wonder, is it worth it?

From Kitchen comes the cry of old
That the water's nearly cold.
I make rejoinder, feeling bold,
And wonder, is it worth it?

Seeing to the milk and straws
Looking to the sticky doors,
Doing this and that I pause,
And wonder, is it worth it?

At eve to Staff Rooms I must roam.
There I stop and give a groan,
Haven't people any home?
I wonder, is it worth it?

When my toil is done at last,
As I leave the building vast
I think about the day that's past
And wonder, is it worth it?

I think of all the children's faces
Filing each into their places.
To beat the bell some poor child races.
I wonder, is it worth it?

As I see them at their work,
Maths and Art and Needlework.
And in the Library they lurk.
I wonder, is it worth it?

Then I see the Honours Board,
How pupils past gained High Award
For working hard – a just Reward.
I nearly think it's worth it.

You know what work in school is done
By Head and Staff and everyone ..
Light hearts in work, light hearts in fun.
I'm sure it's really worth it!

We all come in this great big scheme
Where learning is the Vital Theme,
And work in Harmony, one big Team.
OF COURSE, it's really worth it!
                              [The Caretakers]

          Mrs Richardson

This Figure, that thou here seest put,
For Mrs Richardson was cut;
In her Domain with loving Care
Our daily Meals she doth prepare.
O, that our Artist here could place
Her Character, drawn in her Face;
And shew the kind Heart's golden Core
Beneath her snowy Pinafore.
But, since she cannot, Friend, be looking,
Not on her Picture, but her Cooking.
                    [Norma Meacock
             (with apologies to Ben Jonson)]

Organization

Staff meetings were usually held before School on Tuesdays. These extracts from the minute books, 1951 to 1953, reveal the code of behaviour expected and will probably sound familiar to hundreds of girls.

18th September 1951

Points which need noticing and enforcing:

a) Non-use of crush hall except for essential purposes.

b) Single lines in corridors, on the right. Silence in lines waiting outside form rooms.

c) Silence in the cloakrooms during lesson periods.

25th September

All children who are not in the form room when the register bell rings must be marked late. Nothing absolves them from this.

23rd October

Detention – children should make out their own slips with the full reason for the detention.

20th November

Children must not go into the cleaner's cupboard.

Staff were asked to be very careful in the giving out of stationery which was becoming increasingly difficult to obtain.

10th January 1952

No talking in corridors rule would be relaxed during the dinner hour but … remained in force daily until the 4 o'clock bell.

Children must use the special No. 7 buses and not the service bus.

Girls on the Eastern National Dunstable bus were not behaving sensibly and must be spoken to.

15th January

It was agreed that a scheme should be devised whereby the prefects would have more responsibility on break, dinner and cloakroom duties, with members of staff available and on duty in case of necessity.

Wet days. It was agreed that there should be two rooms available for those wishing to do homework and two rooms for the talkers and knitters.

Games could be organized by the prefects in the gym.

Routine matters to be dealt with

a) General notebooks.

b) Lingering in cloakrooms.

c) Hair too long.

d) Coloured coats and mackintoshes.

22nd January

A regular inspection of tunics by form mistresses was urged, as many were very dirty.

The suspension of the silence rule at dinnertime did not mean that the corridor could be used as a promenade.

7th May

Empire Day fell on a Saturday, so it was suggested that flowers should be sent to reach the London schools on the following Tuesday.

11th June

Mrs Evans asked for the support of staff at prayers. It was set down statutorily that prayers must be held for the girls and Mrs Evans felt that she needed the co-operation of members of staff who should not absent themselves for finishing marking etc.

9th October

Detention. This was for work not done or badly done. Where large numbers were involved the subject mistress herself should take charge. For work not given in, detention should not be automatic. Members of staff should use their own methods.

12th February 1953

Girls late three times should be sent into detention to make up lost time. Coronation souvenirs. Girls could choose from the following: spoon, glass beaker, each suitably inscribed.

12th March

Members of staff were asked to be more careful and helpful about cups and trolleys as the girls found it difficult to get the washing up done. There had been complaints from the girls.

April 23rd

No short-sleeved cardigans were to be worn.

Sandals could be worn both to and in school in the summer term.

Hats. Girls were very bad at wearing these and staff should be on the look out for lapses.

There were shortages of staff and of accommodation. The Inspectors' Report noted that Science classes were to be found in form rooms, the Junior Library, the dining room, company room, sick room, the Bridge and the senior cloakroom. The Inspectors were particularly appalled because there were no music rooms: 'the present arrangements for the subject would be makeshift in a small modern school; in a school of this size and character with girls of this age range, they are deplorable'. Music classes were taken either in the Hall or at the Chapel in Blenheim Crescent. There were 20 beginners who were being taught to play the violin by Miss Flint in the hope that they would help to build up the orchestra. Their lessons were held in the store room of the Junior Library.

Curriculum

The standard of work and achievement had not been allowed to lapse during wartime and girls were, as ever, expected to study hard. The Inspectors called the High School a 'Grammar School of sparkle and polish of which the town may rightly be proud' and expected that it would 'continue to grow in the best tradition of the girls' schools of England'.

Each academic year was divided into five mixed ability forms which, in the early years, followed a similar curriculum. Later, some subjects were taught in sets. In the second and third years, girls opted for Latin, German, Chemistry or Cookery. During this era, a six-day week was introduced. This did not mean Saturday classes but the timetable began on a different day each week: day one would be on Monday one week, Tuesday the next week and so on. This was to allow time for a greater range of subjects, for the younger girls to do homework and for the V and VI Formers to undertake independent study.

The VI Form became larger and its curriculum wider. The academic VI Form prepared girls for the Higher School Certificate or General Certificate of Education while the General VI Form followed a broader curriculum 'designed to be useful for girls who will go on to nursery or infant teaching, horticulture, agriculture, physiotherapy, radiography, nursing, physical education and other careers'. Girls from the VI Commercial group went to the Bedfordshire College of Further Education in the morning and returned to the High School in the afternoon for 'cultural and academic subjects'. For their benefit, the 'Friday-Four' citizenship period was moved to 'Thursday-Seven'.

The importance, which was attributed to different aspects of school life, is reflected in the particular prizes which were handed out on Speech Days.

> James Cup for Handwriting
> Appleby Prize for Oral German
> Best articles or poems submitted for publication in the *Sheaf*.
> Lord Luke's Prize for Knowledge of the Commonwealth
> Seaward Cup for Music
> Drama Cup
> Helen K. Sheldon cup for Spoken English
> John H. Staddon cup for Good Citizenship
> Headmistress's Prize
> Major Games awards:
>> Royal Life Saving Society; School Full Colours in swimming, netball, hockey
> Major House awards:
>> Netball; Jack Cup for Hockey; Payne Shield for Swimming; Barnes Cup for Tennis; Bateson Cup for Athletics

Games took on a new lease of life once the war was over but the standard of play in hockey and netball was thought to be lower. Travelling to schools further afield became easier and practices could be held more frequently since there was no need for girls to hurry home to avoid the blackout. Whereas the High School had preferred to play against similar teams from more distant schools, now the netball teams also competed against local secondary modern schools and girls took part in the Luton Town Schools' Sports Day.

There were House tennis tournaments and rounders became popular. The 'Rapley bat' was awarded annually to the girl showing the most promise in cricket. Swimming was as popular as ever, and a considerable amount of time went into preparation for Royal Life Saving Examinations. In the annual Sports, girls competed for individual medals and also helped to accumulate points for the House championships. There were inter-form gymnastics competitions and experimental ballroom dancing classes (with the Grammar School boys) were held for the VI Forms in the Autumn of 1950. Hockey enthusiasts travelled to the Oval to watch international matches.

RIGHT Prefects' Hockey Match, High v. Grammar, 1951. *Left to right: Back row:* Muriel Gunn, L.J. Harlatt, R.D. Clark, Jean Osborn, B.R. Baker, Shirley Benson, Les Young, Sheila Crossman, D.T. Thompson, Jocelyn Randall, Ruth Garrett, Geoff. Stott, Jacky Hargreaves, A.M. Grayston, G. Wray. *Front row:* Janice Swallow, J.M. Bates, Janet Mariner, T.B. Vaughan, Shirley Simpson, R.E. Martin, Peggy Collier, D.F. Webb.

OPPOSITE ABOVE c.1949. (*LN*)   ABOVE Sports Day, arranged for 24th May 1949, had to be postponed because of rain. On 13th June most events were run, but hurdles and circular relays had to be left until the following day, again because of rain. (*LN*)

ABOVE Swimming Sports 1949 (*LN*) BELOW Probably Sports Day 1952. Some events were altered that year in order to conform to SAA regulations. A Slow Bicycle Race was included instead of the House Team Races. (*LN*)

Extra-curricular Activities

Mrs Evans wrote in the 1953 *Sheaf*:

> The steady core of learning must be our foundation, and to success our results testify in some measure. That work honestly done is the first need in the building up of personality. These pages will show that to that core you have added many, many other qualities and activities – qualities like generosity, community feeling, willing service, and activities reflected in all the clubs and societies in which you are wise to play so enthusiastic a part. These are the building units of a whole personality and in so far as you use them you will be the more valuable women – better wives and mothers, better in any sphere of activity where your future lies.

After the war ended, the 'societies' sprang to life again. At the Literary Society meetings, there were talks, readings and quizzes. One game devised by the staff 'discovered a decided talent for impromptu comic verse.' Miss Hudson, an enthusiastic new member of staff, was influential in the establishment of a lively and very committed Dramatic Society which put on a variety of plays.

> During the twenty-seven years of its existence the High School has produced many plays and pageants of many kinds, but nearly all of them had certain features in

Quality Street April 1945 (Margaret Attwell)

common; they made use of large, often very large, numbers of girls – they were usually efforts of the School as a whole – members of the Staff acted with the girls; the dresses were designed and cut out in the School; and crowd scenes were an important feature of the action. *Quality Street* did not, of course, lend itself to such treatment; it was the work of the Dramatic Club only; costumes had, for obvious reasons, to be hired.

[D.M. Harris]

Quality Street set the pattern for the dramatic productions of the next few years. Grammar School boys were enlisted to help with the staging but, by 1949, Miss Hudson and Mr Williams from the Grammar School were producing joint performances of well-known plays such as *Pygmalion* and *St Joan*. Much more has been written about the joint activities in the companion book on Luton Grammar School.

ABOVE *The Ivory Door* performed by the Dramatic Society Spring 1948. Brand: June Gladman; Captain of the Guard: Cynthia Oakes; Chancellor: Joyce Chapman; Perivale: Sheila Dean (*LN*)
RIGHT *Snow White* Lower School operetta July 1948. Produced by Miss Hudson, music by Miss Fuller. Snow White: Marion Jones; Wicked Queen: Pamela Smith (*LN*)

I would like to add a word of thanks and commendation to the Stage Managers. The boys' School produces quite masterly stage hands. They are efficient, capable and unfailingly good-humoured.

If we have taught our players nothing else, we have taught them that 'there is quite a lot in this drama business' as one of them remarked last term, and that when you really get down to acting it has an interest and a fascination of its own.

[K. Hudson]

In 1953 there was a Staff Review entitled *Staff and Nonsense*:

Who will readily forget the sensational entry of Mrs Evans as the sinister but incongruously-attired villainess, Evelyn Tent, or Miss Stalker as Fairy Rosencrantz, the Guardian of Lost Property or the Toulouse-Lautrecesque ladies who danced the can-can or the American co-ed class under its English Exchange teacher or Miss Hardy as that Late Victorian beau, Handsome Hector, or Miss Kidd as High School Ophelia or Miss Scott's Grandma Buggins or Miss Sherwood's Cora or the unavailing efforts of the Singing Cowboy to mount Old Faithful or the spruce dowdiness of Miss Wesley's Vicar's Wife?

The School took part in the 1947 Bedfordshire Dramatic Festival which was part of the annual British Drama League Community Theatre Festival. Amateur groups

throughout the country prepared short plays to be submitted to expert criticism. Miss Hudson and the LHS Dramatic Club presented *Red Queen, White Queen* by T.B. Morris. The programme notes that 'owing to the Fuel and Lighting restrictions the Saturday performance has been cancelled'. However, Doreen Gray (Hill) recalls that the group was invited to the BBC to do a recording afterwards.

Only those who have acted in plays know the joys, hopes and fears of the girl privileged to be in a school play.

The work of learning parts, studying characters and rehearsing, scene by scene, brings its own reward of happiness and satisfaction. As the cast slowly begins to memorise its parts and the action and trend of the plot emerge, so the acting becomes more vigorous and spontaneous …

On the arrival of the costume-hamper (if indeed it arrives at all!) excitement grows. Squeals of laughter and stifled giggles can be heard as costumes are fitted. Pins and tape measures are now to the fore and alterations begin apace! When all the alterations are complete and every costume has had its pressing they are carefully stored until the great day.

On the opening night, everyone is tense. Sudden spasms of loss of memory shake the bravest heart, but hurriedly examined scripts soon dispel these and restore confidence.

Making up has a thrill of its own! Blue grease-paint on eyelids, lamp black on eyebrows, rouge on cheeks, a liberal sprinking or powder – and recognition is impossible.

All is now ready; a final push from fellow-actors and you find yourself in the glare of the footlight and the play is under way!   [Janice Swallow]

Concerts

The beautiful School Hall was the focus of much of School life. Miss Fuller and Miss Flint were responsible for choral and instrumental concerts which also included vocal and instrumental solos.

An enjoyable annual ceremony was the Harvest Festival when the platform was adorned with the gifts of fruit and vegetables and the smell of apples filled the air. It also became a tradition for the third year forms to present an annual Festival of Nine Lessons and Carols.

LEFT Staff play 1952, chosen by Miss Brown *The Importance of Being Earnest.*
Lady Bracknell: Miss Reed; Canon Chasuble: Miss Dorling; Cecily: Miss Emery;
Ernest: Miss Wood; Algy Moncrieff: Miss Mallett; Miss Prism: Miss Brown (LN)
ABOVE *A Hundred Years Old* December 1952. Antonin: Rex Boston;
Doña Filomena: Janet Richfield; Papa Juan: David Sturman; Young lovers: David Oldroyd and
Christine Livesey. (LN)

The Choir singing in Wardown Park 1949. (*LN*)

The grave pilgrimage of the three kings through the centre aisle of the Hall, and the solemn chant of the chorus, telling once again of the fulfilment of the prophecy … 'God who at sundry times and in divers manners spoke in times past unto the fathers by the prophets, hath in these days spoken unto us by his Son' … are memories which will return whenever Christmas with her fir trees and beaming holly berries lightens the monotonous gloom of winter.   [Janet E. Cook]

Clubs and Societies

Also revived was Le Cercle Français which became very active indeed with competitions, play-readings, French conversation and visits to France. In the summer of 1948, many girls went on exchanges as a result of a linking of the School with the Société Nationale des Chemins de Fer Français (French railways). One girl remarked that, when she left, the whole village turned out and kissed her on both cheeks. Another later attended her French pen friend's wedding and, inappropriately, gave a rendition of a speech from Henry V (compulsory learning at LHS) between two of the many courses of the meal. Fortunately, there did not seem to be any English speakers present! At least one of the pen friendships started under this scheme is still alive and well in 2004. Spanish was introduced and an associated society, La Sociedad Española, was set up.

In the Summer term 1951, a Music Society was formed to hear recitals and talks on composers. One of the visiting speakers, Mr Ludovic Stewart, came to 'make an opera' with the group and it was reported that 'nothing daunted by being asked to sing at sight in two, three or four parts, everyone rose to the occasion with an enthusiasm which quite made up for any lack of professional artistry'.

There was also a Chess Club which met regularly each week to learn and to play, with a cup being given to the winner of the Club's competition. For some time, bridge became popular with the VI Form and considerable amounts of time were spent before, during and after school hours, on what was considered to be a social skill. Things came to a head when a member of staff noticed a pile of money beside a group of players and, mistakenly, thought that they had progressed to gambling.

In 1947, a party of staff and four girls went to Westminster Hall for the 25th anniversary of the Bible Reading Fellowship. Then, in 1951, a Student Christian Movement was formed. Membership was open to girls from the IV, V, and VI forms and meetings were on alternate Wednesdays. A film *Dust or Destiny* was shown and debates included *What difference does it make if you are a Christian? Is suicide a crime?* and *Should duty to one's country be put before one's religious beliefs?* That same year two members went to a Summer Camp at Würtemburg, Germany. The purpose of the Camp was to help girls, through the varied activities of a holiday, 'to understand the Christian faith and to enter into the fellowship and service of the Christian Community'. During 1952–53, Miss Osborn gave a talk entitled *Evolution and the Bible* which 'aroused many discussions in the form-rooms afterwards'.

Visits and Visitors

We have to imagine ourselves in another world, more adventurous than the one that existed before the Second World War but still very different from life as we know it in the twenty-first century. The accounts written in the *Sheaf* magazine are fascinating sources for a study of the social history of the day.

The VI Form went out for visits and, with the war over, trips abroad were again feasible. An article in the magazine described a trip to France (1950) when a group of girls spent a month with hosts in Lyon.

> As we drew in we had on our right our first glimpse of a Parisian landmark – the wonderful Oriental basilica of gleaming white stone standing high up on the hill of Montmartre – the cathedral of Sacré-Coeur. At last the train halted, we clambered down the high steps of the railway carriage on to the platform, entrusted our cases to a French porter whose number we carefully noted and walked out of the station to find two taxis to take us to our hotel … this was the real France at last.
>
> [C.M.Scott]

The Meteorological Office was based in Dunstable. A group of girls went there to observe and wrote a Report which would probably be unrecognizable by the forecasters of today.

> We viewed with particular interest the weather maps of Great Britain for that day, for a new one is drawn up every hour. We also saw the map which had already been plotted, forecasting the weather for early the following morning. Weather reports from the Dunstable Meteorological Office are sent during the day by dispatch riders to Broadcasting House, to be read in the news bulletins.

The following account of a visit to Luton Airport describes a much smaller centre of activity than the International Airport we know today.

> The first port of call was an enormous hangar, and with one accord all eyes turned to a striking scarlet plane – an Airspeed 'Envoy' – ever ready to take moneyed holiday-makers to any of the Butlin Holiday Camps ... Two engineers then came to explain everything and showed us the smooth-lined Proctors, the compact little Auster, its flashy American rival, and re-converted warplanes being serviced to continue in their peacetime role ... Of the wireless room few impressions remain but a mass of confused wires and switches and the unsuccessful attempt to establish contact with a training-plane.

The London Docks were still the focus of trade and commerce with routes across the world.

> In the grey fog of the morning the river came to life once more, as every day. The mournful sirens of the large cargo-boats could be heard. Small barges began to chug along among the drift-wood which floated on the water. Men, who were still yawning, came tramping along the dockside to begin yet another day's work. As the fog lifted, the gigantic cranes hauled loads of timber, tea and sugar from the gloomy holds of the boats on to the concrete dock-side. The river police came speeding along in their motor-launches tooting 'Good morning' to the larger boats. A rowing boat appeared, taking the dockers to one of the floating docks anchored to a buoy. A dredger came to clear the river-bed. The huge arm was lowered into the water, and a few moments later came to the surface with a squelchy noise, bringing a load of wet rubbish, including paper bags, lemonade bottles, and ice-cream cartons that people on the pleasure-steamers had thrown overboard the previous day. The rubbish was transferred to the deck of the dredger, which then moved slowly on.
>
> Tower Bridge lifted up its arms to allow a steamer to come up to its landing-stage, where, later on, people could board it and go down the river. Everything on

the vessel was shiny, and all the sticky fingerprints had been wiped off the wheel and rails.

Further down the river huge pylons passed electricity from one bank to the other. Passenger-ships leaving London looked huge and regal as they went down to the sea. Yes, the river was really alive now! [Marjorie Heathfield]

In 1948, a group of girls spent a week in Stratford. Visits were made to places of historical interest in and around the town, but the highlight of each day was a play at the Shakespeare Memorial Theatre. These included *A Winter's Tale*, *Hamlet*, *Othello* and *The Merchant of Venice*.

One of the most popular out-of-school activities was the annual trip made by members of the VI Form to study the flora and fauna around the Youth Hostel at Houghton Mill, near Huntingdon. Other field trips were made to a Harvest Camp at Halstead, Kent, in August 1948. Here the girls were kept busy picking peas, hoeing cabbages and stooking corn.

On our arrival we were greeted by our Headmistress, attired in a white overall, preparing our evening meal. This was delicious, as were all our meals throughout the week, and I feel sure that if ever Mrs Evans wished to leave the teaching profession, she would get forty heartfelt testimonials which would enable her to obtain any post requiring culinary skill. [Pamela Grieve]

Among the guests invited to talk to the School were Miss Margaret Tempest, an author and illustrator of children's books, Mr Gibson-Martin, whose subject was Plastics, Mademoiselle Marquis and Monsieur Rex, who spoke about Jean de la Fontaine, and Mr Jackson, a missionary, who talked about life in Ceylon (Sri Lanka). Mrs Burston performed extracts from plays, recited poems and

HOUGHTON MILL.

Houghton Mill. (1953 Sheaf)

demonstrated mime and Mr Robert Speaight, an actor, talked about Shakespeare and the Elizabethan theatre. Rosemary Rappaport (violin) and Else Cross (piano) performed pieces by Mozart and Brahms.

Notable visitors were invited to Speech Days. In March 1946, the honoured guest

The Visitors' Book for 22nd March 1946. Note the signature of R.A. Butler, famous for introducing the 1944 Education Act. (DH)

was the Rt. Hon. R.A. Butler MP whose name is linked to the 1944 Education Act and who was thought by many to be a future Prime Minister. Miss Sheldon wrote that this was a red-letter day.

Miss Vera Brittain, best known for her book *Testament of Youth*, which describes the experience of her generation during the First World War, spoke at the December 1951 Speech Day. Her advice was to keep an independent mind, to 'learn to question everything and work out for yourself each problem you encounter'. She also spoke of the importance of breadth of mind and recommended everyone to 'cultivate a wide perspective' and not to 'judge things from your own circle and background, but widen your outlook by travel and reading'. Mr Vezey Fitzgerald, BBC naturalist, came in July 1951 and advised everyone to keep a pet.

Magazine

This book owes a great debt to the various editors who produced the School magazine. Its pages have plotted the life of the School and given insights into the ideas and attitudes of staff and pupils. Creative writing in the form of poems and articles has opened up the atmosphere of the times for posterity. The *Sheaf* was also appreciated by a wider audience. *The Times Educational Supplement* included some material in one of its issues (1951), an Army cadet training college asked for a copy and another was included in an exhibition of school magazines in Germany. The wartime editions had been limited in size and the 1947 magazine was a special record of past years but, in 1949, the editorial committee decided to return to the style of pre-war years. Mrs Evans explained that it was intended 'to give an honest and lively picture of what we think and do, not only for ourselves but for former members and all our friends in whom it will kindle the warm glow of remembrance'.

Mist

[This poem was awarded first prize in the 1951 Sheaf competition]

A rolling damp blanket of pearly grey
Descends on the brown dripping trees;
It is silent and cold like forgotten ghosts
As it floats on the cold autumn breeze.

Over fields and houses and lanes and streets
It floats like a great white shroud,
And all around me a whirling grey wall
Shuts me away from the crowd.

Cars and buses loom out of the grey
Like fiery dragons of old

And their soft gleaming lights as they pass in the gloom
Turn the watery mist to gold.

People drift near, then they disappear,
Away, past that damp drifting wall
And it seems I'm alone in the soft silent world
And there's nobody else at all.

[Pamela Cowtan]

After the First World War, the School had taken an interest in the League of Nations Union and, in another post-war world, hopes for a peaceful future were focused on The United Nations Organization which was celebrated each year on 24th October. The *Sheaf* reflected Vera Brittain's advice to travel and read, as it published personal stories from girls who made journeys to other lands.

Ceylon (Sri Lanka)
The last stop before we came to Australia was Colombo in Ceylon. It is quite a large town and there are many things to see. The temple especially is very beautiful. If you wish to enter it you must first remove your shoes, as the ground on which you walk is holy … [Maureen and Margaret Sheehan]

Australia
Australia … is a country that offers wonderful opportunities to people who are willing to work hard and put up with things until they can get established. No one should come to us with the idea that it is just a glorious carefree land with huge pay-cheques and not much work to do.

[E.M. Jones, a visitor from Queensland]

Canada
The next day we went to Niagara Falls. Never shall I forget my first glimpse of them – the most wonderful sight of my life …
On our homeward journey, on the Empress of France, the sea was very rough. We passed one large iceberg which glistened in the sun. During the night we saw the northern lights. [Janice Higgs]

Denmark
If you want to speak to the master or mistress (it was a mixed school) you called him or her, and if there was no answer you walked round and tapped the teacher on the shoulder until you had the information you wanted …
I am all in favour of the Danish system of ending at two o'clock. It leaves plenty of time for homework in the afternoon and leaves the evenings free.

[Elizabeth Morris]

France
Pendant mon séjour à Biarritz, j'ai visité Lourdes, lieu de pèlerinage, surtout pour

les malades. Biarritz est à voir. Si vous avez de l'argent, allez-y cette année!

[Margaret Morrad]

Germany

The kindness and friendliness of the German people to English visitors is a wonderful experience which I hope many more girls will have the opportunity of sharing.   [Gillian Odam]

Japan

In July 1947, we left England and sailed to Japan. My mother, my sister and myself were going out there to join my father, who was serving with the troops in Iwakuni, which is on the south-west coast of Japan.   [Hilary Taylor]

Nigeria

On the walls of the house there are always one or two lizards, basking in the sun. We share our dining-room with a pair of tiny fire-finches, busily building a new nest in the thatched roof, and the other morning, while driving through the bush we saw an aribi (a type of antelope) and a whole family of baboons, who loped effortlessly across the road.   [Margaret Crosskey]

The Thirteenth World Conference of the Guide Movement in Oxford

There were six of us in my dormitory from America, Holland, Wales, New Zealand, Scotland and myself, England. It was very nice to be able to get to know girls from other countries so easily …

Over ten thousand Guides from miles away had come for this wonderful and never-to-be-forgotten Camp Fire …   [Moyra Seaward]

Social Life and Social Responsibility

Although the war years had heightened philanthropic awareness, social life had been somewhat subdued. After 1945, the mood changed and the School could be used for Fêtes and other activities once again. On 4th June 1946, children from Denbigh Road Junior School came to share a Victory Celebration. This seems to have been carefully prepared with the younger children in mind since the school was divided into 12 lairs, or home bases, with animal names. Almost everybody was in fancy dress. There was a Punch and Judy Show, presented by two members of staff, and also demonstrations, singing, dancing and, in spite of rationing difficulties, food.

A month later, the first Fête for many years took place. All kinds of stalls were set up and raffles were organized. One form undertook to do jobs such as cleaning shoes, silver, bicycles and cars for the staff (cars – a sign of changing times). There were exhibitions, choirs, massed drill and, of course, refreshments. At the end of the day, £359 had been made. Christmas parties for the Lower School were re-introduced and, from 1947, the VI Form entertained the Grammar School VI Form for social get-togethers.

Part of the ethos of the High School was to look at the wider world and, whenever possible, to assist the unfortunate members of society. The 1949 Inspectors' Report noted that there was 'an unusually strong training in social graces and service to others'. The custom of sending flowers to schools in London was revived and a new undertaking was the 'adoption' of a little Indian boy, Rupchand Boragi. His sad story was told by Nesta Soddy (Burditt), an Old Girl of the School, who had married a missionary and who was herself a teacher. She 'saw many pitiful sights in the course of her and her husband's work, but none that touched her heart so much as the young child who had some musical talent, but was blind'. He was doomed to a life of begging, unless money could be found to send him to the School for the Blind in Calcutta.

On a visit home, Nesta Soddy spoke to the girls of the High School who agreed to pay his school fees of £10 a term for four years. At the end of this period, Mrs Evans said 'we cannot abandon him now. We shall continue to support him until the end of his school life.' And so, money-raising events continued to be held for his support. In July 1956, the *Luton News* reported:

> For eight years, LHS girls have been supporting a blind Indian boy at the Blind School at Calcutta. Now he is 15 years old, and is growing deft in basket work and weaving.
>
> He is also gifted musically, and is being encouraged in this direction.
>
> Recently, the High School had a first-hand account of the boy's progress from an old girl, Mrs Nesta Soddy, who works in Pakistan with her husband, who is home on leave … she brought photographs of him for the girls to see.
>
> The girls are very conscientious in their efforts to raise money for him, and hope to go on helping him until he is really independent.
>
> Their aim is that, unlike many blind persons in India, he will not be driven to begging when he returns to his own native village.

Widening Horizons

As befitted the freedom of the post-war era, Old Girls from the High School were stretching their wings. Some left School to study at Universities, Teacher Training Colleges of different kinds and the prestigious Music Colleges and, as usual, there were girls who chose to train as nurses. However, other careers in the medical world were represented, for example medicine, radiography and veterinary medicine.

Between 1935 and 1946–49, the proportion of leavers who took up secretarial or clerical jobs fell from 58% to 38%. During the years 1946–49, only 1% took up millinery and 2% became shop assistants. 8% entered the nursing and allied professions while 4% became laboratory assistants. Of the 13% who went on to further education, 6% (28 girls) went to Teacher Training Colleges and 3% (14 girls) to universities.

Although the war was over, some girls were happy to join the women's sections of the armed services and civil aviation attracted a few. Others opted to work in the more traditional branches of Commerce or the Civil Service, but there were more unusual choices such as working with Esperanto and even motor rallying.

The Old Girls continued to meet regularly for social gatherings and the *Sheaf* published up-date lists of engagements, marriages, births and deaths. However, more and more former pupils were leaving these shores for a life overseas. This was often to marry or to accompany husbands to employment abroad but some girls, notably teachers and nurses, were taking up work overseas on their own account. By 1953, there were former High School girls living in Africa, America, Australia, Canada, France, India, Kenya, Malaya, Mexico, Nigeria and Sweden.

As Mrs Evans observed, there was a changelessness about life in the school but nothing is set in stone. The middle years of the twentieth century marked a time of transition and anticipation. The School had many good reasons for looking to the future with confidence and assurance.

Geographical Society

Widening Horizons. (1954 *Sheaf*)

In May 1957, Sir John Burgoyne (left) unveiled a memorial bookcase in Miss Sheldon's memory. It contained her OBE. Also pictured are Mrs Eileen Evans (centre), Mr R.J. Hill, Vice Chairman of the PTA, and Miss Amie Farr, President of the OGA (right). (*LN*)

Chapter Eight

A Happy and Rewarding Place
1953–1965

By 1953, Luton High School was one of the largest, if not the largest, Grammar School for girls in the country and Mrs Evans' description of 'a happy and rewarding place' is echoed in the observations of other members of staff. In 1957, a group of Her Majesty's Inspectors of Schools published an 'outstanding and complimentary report' and Mrs Evans was thanked by the governors for 'her splendid leadership of the staff and pupils'. This high standard was achieved in spite of a shortage of staff, cramped conditions and the very large numbers of girls attending. The School was well thought of in the wider field of education and several senior members of staff were promoted to the headships of other, similar, girls' schools.

Staff

Miss Sheldon died in 1955 and, in May 1958, a memorial to her was unveiled. This consisted of a specially designed bookcase and reading desk. Her OBE insignia was given to the school 'for safe keeping in the school archives'. Where is it now?

> The beginning of the Spring Term has been overshadowed by the sad news of the grave illness [and death] of our revered Founder Headmistress … It is the earthly end of a vital and compelling personality who gave herself completely to the devoted service of our School, and who built it on so true and strong a foundation that we who follow have cause for abiding gratitude and profound respect. As her successor and loving friend I would wish to salute the rich memory of one to whom I owe a great debt.
>
> [E. Evans]

Farewell to Miss Macnab. (*LN*)

Some older members of staff, who had contributed to the stable background and strong tradition which the school enjoyed, retired during this period. They were Miss C. Dowdall (1926–59), Miss L. Fuller (1926–63), Miss M. Macnab (1920–53), Miss C. Stableford (1930–62), Miss K. Stephenson (1928–55) and Miss A. Wesley (1929–56). Miss Ling became Deputy Headmistress in 1956 and, in 1952, a significant new member of staff, Miss M. Irvine was appointed. She supervised the department of Modern Languages before leaving, in 1961, to become Head of Great Yarmouth High School and eventually returning to Luton High School as its third Headmistress.

It is interesting to note that most senior posts were filled 'in-house'. Miss J. Macfarlane, the first senior mistress, came from the mixed school in Park Square. Miss D. Easton, who succeeded her, was a serving member of staff, as was Mrs E. Evans, who took on Miss Easton's responsibilities when she died. Mrs Evans then became Headmistress. Both Miss Wesley and Miss Ling were already on the staff when they were promoted to Deputy Head while Miss Irvine was also a former member of staff.

The 1957 *Report* of Her Majesty's Inspectors commented that 'almost without exception the members of the assistant staff are extremely sound teachers, with enlightened interest in their pupils' development'. They were, however, working under very great difficulties. The Inspectors commended them for the way they coped. 'That the school continues to make sound progress in such adverse conditions is a measure of the stature of the Head Mistress and her staff'. There was particular praise for Mrs Evans. The Governors had been congratulated in the previous report (1949) for their excellent choice of Mrs Evans as a successor to Miss Sheldon. The 1957 *Report* remarked that to 'her distinguished scholarship and inspiring personal qualities' could now be linked 'great energy, independence of mind and breadth of vision'. The last few years had enabled her 'to acquire a deep understanding of her pupils and of the means by which they may best serve their generation. Cheerfully accepting material conditions which lesser head mistresses might find overwhelmingly discouraging, she carried her staff forward in stimulating education developments.'

The problem was, to some extent, a shortage of staff. The proportion of full-time staff to pupils was only 1 to 24 which was lower than nine out of ten of the country's grammar schools. There was no specialist Physics teacher and the School was seriously understaffed in Science and Mathematics.

At this time of staff shortages, it became necessary to take on male members of staff to make up the numbers. The first of these was Mr A.J. Frost who came in 1958 to teach Russian. The following year Mr J. Dukes became head of Mathematics.

Non-teaching members of staff showed great loyalty. There was, of course, Mr W. Mandley, the second school caretaker, who stayed until 1950, having obtained permission to stay on past the normal retirement age.

> He never refused a request for help ... When it came to fixing things up for the school plays Mr Mandley was indefatigable and his resourcefulness limitless. When all was finished and ready he stood sentinel at the door in black jacket and tie collecting the tickets, and by his look warning all that no nonsense would be tolerated within.
> [F.J. Stalker]

But the longest-serving of all was Mrs Richardson, the school cook, who was appointed in 1919 and stayed until 1960. Her successor as canteen supervisor was a former pupil, Edith Burgess, née Densham.

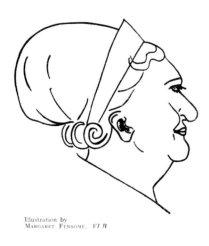

Illustration by
MARGARET FENSOME. VI B

Mrs Richardson, School Cook.
(1951 *Sheaf*)

Such cheerful and single-minded service as Mrs Richardson has given to School generations for the past forty-one years cannot be measured in words ... Her task has never been an easy one. She has had to grapple with problems of number, space and time that have grown ever more and more exacting. But from the beginning she identified herself so closely with the school and its needs that, as it has grown, so have her grasp and her cheerful courage grown to meet the challenge – and she has never been too beset to take on readily those many extra voluntary jobs that have done so much to make our living pleasant and gracious, for in a school, no less than in a home, it is of inestimable value if warmth and graciousness can flow from the kitchen.

THE MARCH OF TIME
E. PLUMMER, V A II.

The School's fortieth anniversary was celebrated in 1959. On 2nd October, a Service of Thanksgiving was held at the Parish Church and, on 21st November, a special lunch was laid on at the School. Those attending included Dr J.C. Corbett, the Borough Education Officer, Alderman Mrs F.M. Brash, the Chairman of the Governors and Alderman Mrs R.O. Andrews, the Mayor of Luton. To celebrate the occasion, the staff gave a clock for the crush hall and the girls had a collection to buy a ceremonial chair for the platform. The Parent Teacher Association presented a table and a second, matching, chair.

Celebrating the Fortieth Anniversary of the School. BELOW Gifts to the School. Assembly 2nd October 1959. (LN) OPPOSITE ABOVE The girls attended a Thanksgiving Service at the Parish Church on 2nd November 1959. The First Year girls had a service at St Andrew's Church. (LN) OPPOSITE BELOW Celebration Lunch, Saturday. 21st November 1959. (LN) ABOVE 'The March of Time' (1960 Sheaf)

Organization

The 1957 *Report* of the School Inspectors noted that 'happily for the interests' of the girls, the Governing body included seven women amongst its numbers. However, they were all heavily committed to serving in other Luton schools as well, so the time they could spend on the welfare of the Girls' High School was limited.

The *Report* was particularly critical about the building and the shortage of equipment although they conceded that 'the trim state of the premises, the compact nature of the buildings, and the easy orderliness with which the pupils move within them leave a first impression of a large school most admirably housed'. In fact, playing fields, buildings and services were 'quite inadequate to the present number of pupils'. There was a catalogue of deficiencies.

There was not even one laboratory which reached the minimum standard required. There were no rooms 'which would accommodate a whole form as well as the apparatus and equipment needed for sound modern teaching in Geography or Mathematics, and Music lessons were still confined to a corner of the Hall or the Junior Library. Similarly, Art, Craft and Cookery were 'handicapped by deficiency of subject rooms'. Toilet facilities were inadequate, the electricity system was in danger of overloading and the central heating needed up-grading.

The problem was aggravated by the rising numbers admitted. In 1955, the School opened its doors to six first year forms while only a few girls left from the higher forms. The number on roll on 31st August 1957 was 1,050. Attempts had been made to create more space: the Upper School took over the Annexe and the two cloakrooms in the main corridor were converted into four form rooms.

In February 1956, the new dining hall, a 'fifteen-year-old dream', was formally opened. The Inspectors remarked that 'with the provision of the new canteen the school dinnertime has become a pleasantly gracious occasion. Originally the canteen was extremely poor acoustically, but now that the girls, by voluntary effort, have provided it with curtains, they can chat without the noise level becoming too exhausting for the 200 or more girls who take the meal at each of the three sittings'.

Then, in 1960, work began on a new Science block which was completed at the end of the following year. The vacated laboratories were converted into even more, badly needed, form rooms.

> It began, so to speak, with a fanfare of pneumatic drills. All day and every day they
> screeched incessantly, giving girls and staff alike headaches and bad tempers, and
> driving the poor 'A' level candidates to distraction. Huge lorries churned up our
> grounds and dumped tons of soil in our static water tank [frightening away the
> ducks]. Men, whistling, smoking, drinking tea, shattered the cloistered aura of
> academic serenity which had previously surrounded us. [Z.X. & Q.Y.]

More about those ducks!

> It was a discontented, unhappy little drake that brooded upon his misfortunes one winter's day. If ducks were able to sigh, then he would have sighed, as he thought nostalgically about his beloved static water tank, of which he and his wife had been the sole occupants. Some ducks might not think much of it, but to them it had been home. Now he would never see it again … The River Lea might suit some ducks, but it wasn't the same as a pond of your own.   [Cherry Ewington]

Work on the Science block was completed at the end of 1961 and some girls volunteered to give up a day of their Christmas holidays to help move all the apparatus from the old rooms to the new where, as yet, no 'Dave, Pete or Elvis' had been carved into the shining new bench tops.

> How does one carry a skeleton? However hard one tries to carry it in one's arms, there always seem to be extremities dangling in an undignified manner. Our solution to this problem was to have four bearers – one supporting the head, a second holding an arm, a third grasping the rib-cage and the other arm, and a fourth holding the knees to stop them knocking together. Thus, in a fairly reverent procession, the skeleton was transported from old haunts to new.
>
> [Angela Revell]

Yet more building work was undertaken (1960–61) when it was decided to cover and heat the swimming pool. During that time, the girls practised at the pool in Bath Road and, when the work was completed, girls (not boys) from other schools in the town were allowed to use the High School facilities. The arrival of the heated pool was a life-changing event.

> My enduring experience is of one occasion when I was so cold that it took me longer than usual to dress. This was a worry because the next lesson was French and we were in awe of the teacher who was very strict about punctuality.
>
> I was not the only one late as my classmate was even further behind. She was shaking so much that she could not dry herself, added to which she had lost all her colour and her lips were blue. The PE teacher asked me to wait for her and escort her to French which meant that we would be even later and in even deeper trouble. Horror of horrors, it might even mean a detention! However, we eventually arrived at French and we felt that the end of the world had come. The teacher took one look at my friend and 'hit the roof'. In the tirade that followed we gathered that she totally disapproved of girls having to swim in such conditions. Someone lent her a blazer and she still had to do the French dictation despite the fact that she could not write legibly.   [Frances Smith (Gardner)]

Mrs Evans always responded to changes in society and, in 1959, decided that girls in the VI Form should no longer be compelled to wear school uniform. This decision caused enormous interest locally and nationally and, very soon, the national and local press arrived asking for statements and pictures. Mrs Evans agreed to appear on the BBC TV programme *Town and Around* to answer questions about her unusual decision. No doubt the freedom was appreciated but some girls seem to have preferred to stay with the uniform, one reason being that games and similar awards could be attached to uniforms. About the same time, a differently shaped hat, more in the boater style, was introduced. Deportment ties replaced deportment girdles.

> Last April, Mrs Eileen Evans, headmistress of Luton High School, interested newspapers as well as her ninety sixth-formers when she told the latter that she would no longer insist on their wearing the school uniform of gym-slips, white socks and elastic strapped hats because of the expense of their maintaining a double wardrobe. Before long, visitors found it difficult to distinguish between pupils and teachers. But the sixth-formers have had enough of it. They have found themselves unable to keep up-to-date with the fashions worn by girls at work, who have more money to spend on clothes, and are going back into uniform.
>
> [Charles Freeman in the *Bedfordshire Magazine* Winter 1959]

Another short-lived idea which involved girls in the VI Form was the decision to do away with sub-prefects and allow every girl with VI Form status to do their jobs. After a while, the prefects asked for the old scheme to be re-instated. All prefects were allowed to leave lessons promptly in order to fulfil their duties provided that they 'excused themselves gracefully'.

Curriculum

Enjoy every minute of the seed-time, for the harvest will surely come.

The School offered a wide curriculum which prepared girls for an ever-increasing choice of careers. During her talk at the 1954 Speech Day, Mrs Evans emphasised the importance of a sound education. She believed that 'shorthand and typing exercise a fatal fascination on the female young' but that 'firms are better pleased with a girl of good general education and no proficiency in commercial skills than a girl who has neglected her general school work to acquire a smattering of typewriting and shorthand'. She also thought that matrons of hospitals held a similar attitude. The emphasis in the School was, not surprisingly, on the academic subjects demanded by the examination boards. 'A milestone was passed' when, in 1960, six girls passed 'O' level Russian. Opportunities were always taken for girls to educate themselves in other directions. A visiting student from Switzerland explained how

LUTON HIGH SCHOOL
SUMMER DRESSES

The new school dress, first introduced in 1953, is in "Evernew" gingham, a high quality cotton fabric specially shrunk and dyed for school wear.

The special check design is retained, by the manufactures, for the exclusive use of the High School in Luton and district, and there is a choice of three colours :—Blue, Pink or Gold.

We are pleased to announce this material has now been reduced in price to

4/6d. per yard

The prices of the ready made d[...] reduced to :—

30"	32"	34"
27/6	28 11	30 6

38"	40"	42"
33 6	34 11	36 6

For those wishing to make their own ga[...] hand-cut paper patterns have been re-d[...] are available at 2 - each.

ALEXANDERS (LUTON[...]
31/33 Wellington Stree[...]

Advertisements for School Uniform from the 1954 and 1958 School magazines

ALEXANDER'S *for*

DISTINCTIVE CHILDREN'S WEAR by :
PETER PAN
MARCHETTE
BAIRNS WEAR
CHILPRUFE
JUDY
Etc.

COMPLETE
SCHOOL OUTFITS
Colours & Badges

Ubi Semen Ibi Messis

WE accept it as an honour and a responsibility that our name should be linked with that of the Luton High School in the supplying of its " uniform " and " colours ".

The School is jealous of its reputation: so, too, are we: we believe that the school motto " UBI SEMEN IBI MESSIS " can be our guide and we aim to give a standard of service and reliability that will reap the reward of continued confidence and support.

Uniforms and the "Old School Tie" are Symbols of Unity and " Esprit de Corps ", but the austerity of their limitations serve only to enhance the joy of relaxation and we cater, with equal diligence, for the holiday and the " every-day " occasion when it is good to feel well dressed.

Youth reaches its maturity: the school-girl is, in turn, the "Old Girl", but still we offer our Service in the realm of Fashion.

We trust our reputation will survive the years and, on the foundations of the past we build our hopes for the future—that we may be of service

EXCLUSIVE LADIES' WEAR by :
BERKERTEX
HORROCKSES
STEFNEY
LEDUX
MARTINEX
WOLSEY

LADIES' & CHILDREN'S
FASHION WEAR
*

ALEXANDERS (LUTON) LTD., 31/33 WELLINGTON ST., LUTON

much she appreciated the general lessons 'where all sorts of problems were discussed freely. Especially for me they were very advantageous, as I got involved in fervent discussions, and came to talk, and talk without noticing it.'

An unusual and very successful feature of the curriculum was the division of the whole VI Form, irrespective of year or course, into small groups which studied for two periods a week, under different members of staff, a subject of the teacher's own choice. The groups were changed twice a term so that during two years in the VI Form a girl had the benefit of sharing the enthusiasm and interests of twelve different mistresses. These courses included Music, Art, Italian, Modern Dance, Science, Needlecraft and Current Affairs.

Girls in the lower forms had, as always, to make choices about the subjects they wished to follow. Some of the brighter girls in the 'Transitus' forms were able to fast-track through the Middle school and complete their examination syllabus in four years instead of five.

There were two flourishing libraries, now supervised by teachers whose formal responsibilities included the post of Librarian. There were more than 2,000 books in the Junior Library and 4,000 in the Senior Library. Unfortunately for the younger girls, the Senior Library was reserved for the VI Form's private study during the day, which limited access for the rest of the School.

Once again the awards which were given out on Speech Day give an excellent indication about the values placed upon the different aspects of the curriculum and school life in general.

These were the awards for 1954–1955:
> James cup for handwriting
> Appleby cup for oral German
> Prefects' cup for dramatic work
> Seaward cup for music
> Helen K. Sheldon prize for spoken English
> John H. Staddon prizes for good citizenship
> Lord Luke prizes for knowledge of the Commonwealth
> *Sheaf* prizes
> Needlework prize in Middle School
> Lines prizes for English
> Form prizes
> School games colours
> House awards
> Form prizes
> Headmistress's prize for leaving head prefect

By 1961–62, other awards had been added:
> Spicer plaque for chemistry in fourth years

Rogers prize for mathematics
Prizes for special progress in mathematics and science
Connolly prize for science
Stableford prize for religious knowledge
PTA awards to senior prefects

The House Shield was the ultimate award. Fry House holds the record for having won it the highest number of times.

Founded	Name	Winners of the House Shield 1919–1968	
1943	Jane Austen	1946,47,48	3
1919	Boadicea	1921,24,28,30,31,53,64,66,67	9
1934	Marie Curie	1945,54,64	3
1919	Grace Darling	1923,26,35,36,37,38*,39,40,41,44	10
1919	Elizabeth Fry	1925,32,34,43,55,56,57,58,	
		60,61,62,63,65,68*	14
1934	Elizabeth Garrett Anderson	1949,50,51,52,59,68*	6
1919	Helen Keller	1933,38*,42	3
1919	Florence Nightingale	1920,22,27,29	4
		*Ties	

Sports

The Inspectors complained about the limited amount of playing space, especially since new building projects had encroached on the land available. By 1957, there was only one hockey pitch, a small practice area and six tennis courts which were badly in need of re-surfacing. The area around the School was now built up and there was no realistic prospect of acquiring any more open land which would be practical in terms of distance and travelling time.

Sports were, as always, an important part of school life. Teams and individuals took part in inter-school, county and national events. Girls took examinations for the Royal Life Saving Society and some became qualified netball umpires.

Ninety girls visited Wembley for the annual Hockey International; forty girls enjoyed an afternoon at Wembley watching fierce play of county and international netball teams; a small group were inspired by a visit to Wimbledon to see both the annual tournament and the Wightman Cup ... the prefects this year have organized badminton ... many girls are interested to follow other forms of sport, and some may go on courses, run by the Central Council of Physical Recreation, in canoeing, hill-walking, and sailing ... Mrs Robinson is taking six VI form girls to learn to ski in Austria. (1961)

1959-60 Under-15 Hockey XI. Left to right: Back: Leslie Aldridge, Rita Deverick, Pauline Moore, J. Faiers, J. Bowler; *Left:* Christine Gurney; *Seated:* Doreen Fletcher, Anne Mills, Barbara Trustam, Lynn Sturgess, Dorothy Moulding *(Pauline Moore)*

Eighty-two girls visited Wembley to see the exciting match between England and the United States of America ... Three girls have enjoyed Lawn Tennis Courses at Lilleshall [Shropshire], and four gained experience at a hockey coaching course for teachers. A VI form group went to the International Dance Festival. (1963)

Modern educational dance made an appearance and, in April 1960, a demonstration was put on for parents and staff. Miss S. Coates explained that this form of dance was 'expressive movement without rigid steps and gestures which could be performed to piano-music, recorded music, percussive sound, the spoken word or without any accompaniment at all'.

There was a break with tradition in 1961 when it was decided that no girl could be in the first hockey XI as well as the first netball VII. The girls solved that problem for themselves by organizing their own team under the name of 'the hocknettes'. Another significant change was the introduction of new netball rules which meant that greater stamina was needed 'in order to maintain a high standard of play throughout an entire match'. In 1961, there were badminton courses for the VI

Junior Tennis VI, probably 1960. *Left to right: Back:* Rita Deverick, Doreen Fletcher, Maureen Eldon? Front: Christine Whalley, Pauline Moore, Barbara Trustam, Mary Cook
(Pauline Moore)

Form, run by the Central Council of Physical Recreation. There was also talk of arranging fencing, judo and golf.

However, the most radical break with tradition was probably the abandonment, in 1964, of athletics in favour of swimming and tennis. A survey was held to see what the girls thought about the idea and most of the 504 answers received indicated approval. One comment was that 'anyone can run and all you need it for is catching buses' but there was also regret about the passing of Sports Day because it was a chance to spend an afternoon without lessons.

In May 1964 and with the co-operation of the Central Council for Physical Education, golf appeared on the curriculum. Mrs Evans said that 'Games, like badminton, tennis and golf are much more socially advantageous to girls than athletics'. To begin with, a group of 24 VI Formers spent regular PE sessions at the Dunstable Downs Golf Club where the lessons were offered for a special low fee.

We should like to thank Mr Glennister, who continues to coach VI Form girls on Friday evenings in badminton; Mr Field, who gave 24 VI Form girls some enjoyable lessons in golf during the Summer Term 1964; and Mrs Parsons who has just begun to give fencing lessons to VI form girls. Some Senior girls once again enjoyed a day at Bisham Abbey last May. We should also like to convey our thanks to Mrs Scanes for our fixture lists, to Mr Duncan who tests our hockey umpires, to Mrs Richardson who helps with after-school swimming, to the School and House games and swimming captains, to our games secretaries, to girls in the VI and IV Years who help with match refreshments, to girls in Upper IV who help with games equipment, to umpires, linesmen, ballboys, and timekeepers. Lastly our very grateful thanks for all the help given to us in their various capacities by Mrs Burgess, Mr Titchmarch, and Mr McCarthy.

[M.G. Coleman, E.R. Boskett, B. Twitchen (1965)]

Extra-curricular Activities

The formal curriculum was supplemented by an increasing number of extra-curricular activities. These varied from year to year; new ones were founded and others appeared to fold, but there was surely no girl who was at a loss to know what to do with her time! Life in the school buzzed. However, these activities were not for interest alone, for it was accepted that membership of school societies was necessary for a satisfactory leaving testimonial.

Readings, talks, debates, mock trials and scientific films could all be enjoyed in the Literary, Scientific and Debating Societies. VI Form debates ranged from the 'light-hearted to the serious' and were often held in conjunction with the boys' school. Some of the more interesting subjects were *That Britain should join the Common Market*, *Sex equality is impossible* and *That Britain should ban the bomb*. Four members of staff debated the motion that *It would be good to be young again*.

In 1960 the newly-formed Scientific Film Society began fortnightly shows of films about Chemistry, Physics and Biology. Chess enthusiasts started a club which then became a part of Luton Chess Club. They were invited to play in the Bedfordshire Junior championship and entered the *Sunday Times* National School tournament.

Interest in Drama was high. Parties of girls went on trips to see first class shows, for example in London and Stratford-on-Avon. Then, of course, there were the plays which were produced by the Dramatic Society, now supervised by Miss Brown. Some of those put on during this period were: *Alice in Wonderland and Alice through the Looking Glass, She Stoops to Conquer, Time and the Conways, Tovarich, Quality Street, The Admirable Crichton, Androcles and the Lion, Toad of Toad Hall* and *Pilgrim's Progress*. The boys from the Grammar School often took part and these plays are described in much more detail in the companion volume on the boys' school.

RIGHT Staff Revue: *Evans Above* 1958.

"EVANS ABOVE" Staff Revue 1958

Opening Chorus

1 Mrs. Thomas	9 Miss Vaughan	17 Miss Whinnett	25 Miss Ling
2 Miss Kidd	10 Miss Dorling	18 Miss Flaherty	26
3 Miss Stalker	11 Mrs. Yossava	19 Miss Carpenter	27 Miss Griffin
4 Miss Sherwood	12 Mrs. Boskett	20 Miss Brown	28 Mrs. Marshall
5 Miss Bunnage	13 Miss Coleman	21 Miss Broomer	29 Miss Parry
6 Miss Lloyd	14 Mrs Richaud	22 Miss Colmer	30 Miss Whiteley
7 Miss Gribble	15 Miss Fuller	23 Mrs. Wharton	31 Miss Mulholland
8 Miss Peacock	16 Miss Flint	24 Miss Stableford	32 Miss Badcock

As ever, visitors came to the School; the Inspectors were shocked to hear that, when they did so, Mrs Evans was obliged to entertain them 'out of her own pocket'. One visitor was Miss Lyn Oxenford from the 'British Drama League' who gave a lecture and demonstration on period movement. Verse Speaking and Spoken English competitions continued to be held. The staff were not excused; this happy and enthusiastic group of ladies willingly gave their time, not only to the different societies but also helped to entertain the school with staff reviews containing selections of songs and sketches. One of the liveliest of these was given the title *Evans Above*.

The prefects of 1961 also produced a Revue. Within a fortnight of finishing their A levels, they had whipped up 'a delightful concoction for (we hope) their own refreshment, certainly for the delectation of the rest of us, and principally to help wipe out the deficit on the *Sheaf*, whose sales cannot, in these days, fully cover the cost of production'. One of the photographs in the magazine shows a 'terrifyingly accurate staff room' with the caption: 'O would some power the giftie gie us, to see ourselves as others see us!'

In 1963, the 'Lower Sixth Belles' presented a *Review* with items such as: *Consumer's Report*, *The Bisto Kids*, *Alley Cats* and *That was the Year to Come*.

The Geographical Society hosted speakers who described countries they had visited, showed films and arranged quizzes. The Historical Society 'for which there has long been a need' began in 1962. One of their activities was listening to a series of records entitled *The Sounds of Time* 'which presented some of the important events and voices of the years 1939–47'. However, one of the most enthusiastic and well-supported groups was the Student Christian Movement which also held joint activities with the Grammar School. In 1964 a group went, with Miss Ling, Miss Dorling and Miss Hibbett, on a visit to Israel. According to the *Luton News*, the party left on 16th December and travelled to Venice where they boarded the *Dunera*. They docked at Haifa in time to reach Jerusalem for Christmas Eve. Christmas dinner was to be 'sandwiches eaten on a trip on the Sea of Galilee'. The girls took with them knitted baby clothes which were forwarded to the Edinburgh Missionary Hospital in Nazareth.

To what extent has the *Dunera* been an educational window on the world? For me, the classic beauty of the Acropolis, the thought-provoking scenes in Israel, and the romance of Pompeii have been the realisation of something hitherto only read about and imagined. I loved most of these places, and had mixed feelings about others, such as Jerusalem with its vicious and tragic division. But over and above the physical, it was the people in these places that interested me most, and I feel most strongly that my education has been broadened and enriched for the fleeting but invaluable contact with them.

[Judith Darby]

The Nativity Play for 1953 was the *Coventry Mystery Play of the Shearmans and Taylors.* (LN)

Christmas Eve, 1964
Come and adore Him,
The Prince of Peace
Born in a land now torn,
Split by the wire and gun,
Split by the new and old,
Split between Jew and Arab,
Kiosk jostling shrine,
Greed jostling reverence.
Come and adore Him,
Christ, the Lord!

[Jo Atwell (extract)]

SCM debates included: *The responsible society, Is heaven a myth and hell a joke? Is suicide a crime?* and *Should one's conscience come before one's loyalty to one's country?* Films from the *Fact and Faith* series were shown and Miss Osborn gave seven talks on *What do Christians believe?* Christian music and Christian art were appreciated and an annual passion service was held. The 1957 *Sheaf* described how the group organized a collection of clothes for Hungarian refugees. In 1961, an *Any Questions* meeting was held when subjects debated included: *Ban the Bomb, Mercy killing,*

Mrs Evans and Miss Osborn at the Parents' Fête in June 1956. *(LN)*

Bingo, *Church unity* and *Hire-purchase*. This was so successful that an *Any Answers* follow-up was held.

The Music Society enjoyed all kinds of music: classical, jazz and traditional. There were recitals at the school and, since the wonderful orchestral concerts which used to be held in Luton had been stopped, girls took trips to concerts in London. A Madrigal Group and a Lower School Music Society were initiated in 1964 and 'exotic instruments such as bongos, maracas, and a glockenspiel' were used in the performance of a work by Malcolm Arnold. Fathers, uncles, brothers and boy friends provided the tenors and basses for a presentation of the *Song of Simeon*.

Annual concerts were held. At the performance on 3rd June 1954, the orchestra, which was conducted by Miss Flint and accompanied by Jean Godfrey, played *Marche Militaire*, *Christmas Pastorale*, pieces by Lulli and Haydn and old English dance tunes. The choirs, trained by Miss Fuller, sang a variety of songs such as *Orpheus with his Lute*, *Blow the Wind Southerly* and *The Keel Row*. There were vocal solos and duets, cello solos and piano solos.

Languages were always an important part of life in the school and the French

Club thrived. Aspects of French culture were experienced in a variety of ways: films about France, musical evenings, play and poetry readings and French competitions. During 1954, the Third Year girls dressed dolls in national French costumes and the Fourth Years made up crosswords. Exchange visits continued to be made through the 'Amitié Internationale des Jeunes'.

German was a new venture and, again, the focus was on the culture of the country. Spanish students had their own club; they took trips to London to watch Spanish dancing and some girls went on a holiday course held by the Hispanic Council. Speakers came to talk about, among other subjects, bull-fighting. The 1964 *Sheaf* gives a Russian Circle in its list of school societies.

The Classical group was not a formally constituted society. However, girls entered for the Schools' Greek and Latin Reading contest at University College, London.

> 'Vetus es, pater Marce,' iuvenis inquit.
> 'Canities candidissima est;
> continua tamen in capite stas,
> putasne decere senem?
> 'Juvenis,' pater Marcus filio dixit,
> 'timui ne cerebrum laedat.
> Deinde decrevi nullum habere,
> ac saepissime ita accidit.'
> ['You are old, Father William', with apologies to Lewis Carroll
> Carole Henderson and Erica Beswick]

The trip on the *Dunera* was not the only cruise undertaken. In 1962, 35 girls together with Miss Dorling and Miss Ling, went on the *Devonia*, a floating boarding school. The weather was not always kind and Miss Ling wrote that 'it was strange to feel the blackboard receding and then advancing once more'. There were lessons, deck games, swimming and interest groups. The group visited Vigo 'with its palm trees and interesting shops' and the 'wide green parks and wonderful scenery' of Lisbon and made a tour of Carunna.

Bodies as well as minds were catered for. In 1956, a Gymnastics Club was formed which aimed to help girls to increase their understanding of movement and to improve their standard of performance.

> The mover learns to control her body weight, to move with varying shapes, speeds, and strengths, and to direct her strength in varying directions. Having mastered some of these techniques, she can, through guidance and through experimentation, build up a vocabulary of movements ... she is not, as in pre-war days, made to move in exactly the same way as all the other members in the class.
> [M.G. Coleman]

In February 1961, a demonstration was held which was enlivened by a challenge from the Club President's brother who had declared that girls would not be able to complete a movement nicknamed 'Touchdown'. This involved 'a double vault over horse and box at two different levels at one feel swoop'. There were classes in ballroom dancing and folk-dancing. A Riding Club was begun. Perhaps sun-bathing cannot exactly be counted as a profitable activity but some girls from the Upper School, having found out how to get onto the roof, made their way there on sunny days. Just enjoying life can be thoroughly recommended.

> During dry lunchtimes we ranged around the sports field and the many exciting and, of course, forbidden spaces to explore. In those days a large square water cistern filled space beyond the back entrance lane (from Biscot Road) partly hiding the remains of a rose garden. At the opposite end of the school, the tennis courts were our boundary although we loved The Rough, a scrubby area beyond, which also housed the biology pond. Across the sports field … lay the Bumps [site of wartime trenches], a wonderful territory inhabited by the daring and those who fancied trying out smoking – instant detention for anyone caught, on either count.
>
> [Jeannette Ayton (Likier)]

ARGYLL AVENUE FROM THE PLAYING-FIELD   MARGARET KINSEY (I S.)

The 'Bumps' were the mounds left at the site of the old air raid shelters. (1957 *Sheaf*)

Luton and the Wider World

Articles in the *Sheaf* continue to give us glimpses into Luton life. One poem conjures up a picture of the corner shop, soon to be replaced by the supermarket. On the other hand, the country was about to enter the motorway age.

> The General Stores
> The shop on the corner is painted in blue,
> The mat spells a welcome for me and for you.
> The shelves are chock-full with all manner of things,
> From ladies' silk stockings to gold curtain-rings.
> Washing detergents line all of one wall,
> 'Surf', 'Tide', 'Omo', this shop sells them all.
>
> [Extract from a poem by Ruth Hall]

M1

I never saw countryside change so quickly. Before the men came the hills were green and beautiful. Then they came with the yellow machines called 'Cats' … they dug and loosened all the chalk, and many lorries came and carted it away. By the end of the first week we saw little but chalk when we looked from our window … The roadway was ready now except for the finishing touches. Tarmac was put down … and the steep sides were flattened with earth and grass-seeds … And so, one Monday – I was on my half-term holiday – I went up the Bradley Road bridge to see the first traffic come along since the motorway was officially open. Cars came only rarely at first. Now they come and go all the time.   [Mary Nash]

The High School had become very much a part of the wider world. Former students had moved far away and Mrs Evans regularly received letters describing careers and telling of family news. As Miss Stalker remarked, 'Our seed has been well and truly sown.' These two contributions to the *Sheaf* mark historic milestones: Ugandan independence and the infamous Berlin wall.

Letter from Uganda
We have just celebrated 'Uhuru' or Independence; it was very exciting! … The Uhuru celebrations began on Monday evening (8th October 1962) with a Tattoo held at a huge stadium on a hill outside Kampala … At 12 midnight the Union Jack was lowered to the playing of the National Anthem and the Ugandan flag was raised in its place – amidst much cheering! A wonderful firework display then followed which set the whole sky ablaze with a succession of brilliant colours.

[Margaret Bradley]

The Berlin Wall
I stand here gazing,
The wall, topped with barbed wire
Splits my view to only a few yards.
As my eyes are drawn towards the gap,
I see cheerful smiles on the people's faces.
But how long will this last?
'Open for the Christmas period'.
These excited people laden with gifts and food
Bustle their way through the gap
With carols ringing, bringing Christmas cheer to all,
The choir sing to keep spirits high.

[Kathleen Punter (extract)]

Several members of staff from the High School went on exchange trips to schools in other parts of the world and all seem to have taken advantage of the opportunity to see as much of their host countries as possible. The importance attached to these links is reflected in the choice of Mr H.F. Collins as guest speaker for the 1959 School Speech Day. He was the Chairman and Director of the British Committee for the Interchange of Teachers between the United Kingdom and the United States of America. This description of Luton in 1957 was written by Miss Jean Birt, an exchange teacher from Australia.

I even enjoyed going to school at sunrise, seeing the water tower silhouetted against pink clouds and, returning at sunset, looking down on Luton lights shining through a mauve mist. The fact that grey smoke helped to make the picture did not spoil it for me.

I have half-a-dozen still transparencies of the swans on Farley Pond, all of them lovely, others of white farm cottages with steeply pitched shingled or thatched roofs ... I like the tinkling tunes of ice-cream vans, the good-nature of bus conductors, the sensible way pedestrians treat traffic-lights, the jokes about the weather, the meticulous regard for half-pennies and fractions of an ounce ...

I love the way you English live and let live – accept all comers and quietly let them absorb your ways, or, if not, go their own. Where is that aloof, taciturn Englishman with his 'sang-froid habitual?' I have never met people more soft-hearted, or received a warmer welcome anywhere.

Miss A.E. Greasley left for Newfoundland in 1952. She made some good friends during her stay in St John's but did not enjoy the long, hard winter. Miss C.M. Scott spent a year teaching at Port Credit High School in Canada (1955), while her counterpart, Miss E.V. Toth, taught at Luton High School. In 1962, Mr L. Rising, a French teacher from California, changed posts with Miss C. Broomer. Miss M. Whiteley went to Australia (1961) in the place of Mr P. Palmer.

> I came to Luton on a Fulbright plan exchange. Fulbright was a US Senator who, after World War II, devised a plan to bring the US and Europe a bit closer together through teacher exchanges. As an exchange, I was paid by my regular US employer, plus travel expenses paid by US funds.
>
> I must confess that I was ill prepared for a year at a girls' high school, with much younger students, and a different system of schools. At my college then, we taught students mostly 18 years plus, as well as some adults returning to school in their middle ages to begin new careers …
>
> I remember enrolling our son, Alan, in Luton Grammar School. The headmaster asked what subjects he had had. He had not had Algebra, Geometry, Foreign Language, Chemistry or Physics which were taught only in Senior High School in the USA. But he loved England and did very well in sports, rugby and athletics. Some of his records in Athletics were put up on the wall at Luton Grammar School. Are they still there?   [Leonard Rising 25th August 2002]

> Naturally, despite their strong common bonds, England and Australia are two very different countries; their peoples and their ways of life are also different … but … when you remove the superficial trappings of accent, custom, habits of thought, and other characteristics developed mainly as a result of background and upbringing, all people seem to be much the same underneath.   [P. Palmer]

> Towards the end of my stay I crossed the continent, having lunch in Sydney, tea in Melbourne and supper in Perth. The total flying time was less than seven hours. Outstanding among my travels was undoubtedly the trip to the Centre, our winter holiday. During the day we enjoyed temperatures of 80° F, but the cool evenings of 60° F were much appreciated. The fortnight was, of course, rain-free … Air transport has helped too, and to fly the three hundred miles to Ayers Rock before breakfast, in the front seat of a Beachcraft 'plane, was indeed a highlight of my year.   [M.E. Whiteley]

Mr A.J. Frost described his 1960 trip to the Soviet Union with 24 other teachers of Russian. They spent about five weeks there, while a similar number of Russian teachers of English came over here. In Russia, women played a very prominent role and the officials who met the English group in Moscow were surprised to find that there were only two women in their party.

The *Sheaf* describes many of the visits paid to the school. For example, in February 1960, Miss Ruth Pulford came to talk about her work with refugees. She explained the 'political causes driving vast sections of communities to become

refugees, and touched upon the dire plight of those in Korea, Hong Kong and Jordan, as well as those nearer home in Western Europe'. Groups of girls frequently made trips into the wider world; these visits fell into four main categories: work-related, field trips, cultural and overseas.

In 1954, a group went to the Vauxhall Rehabilitation Centre where men who had been injured or were ill, were able to do useful work by using specially adapted machines. They went on to observe patients in the physiotherapy department. In the

Easter in Paris 1959. (*Pauline Moore*)

same term several would-be Infant teachers went to Leagrave Infant School to observe and, in 1956, a small group went to the official opening of the Ludun workshop where disabled workers were able to find employment.

Flatford Mill, in the heart of Constable country, became a popular centre for field trips when girls fished for pond specimens and studied the plant and woodland ecology. In 1957, it was the base for a group which went to sketch and paint. An organized trip to Rye in 1960 was also for budding artists. There the River Rother 'provided ideal conditions … to study the problems of light refraction'. Another field centre visited was Preston Montford in Shropshire. Then there was Slapton in South Devon where girls could study in a fresh-water lake, in mountain streams and woods, on the seashore and amongst the rocky outcrops and bogs of Dartmoor. In 1957, a group went on a geographical trip to Ambleside, in the Lake District, where most of the time seems to have been spent climbing in the Fells. Another geographical expedition was made to explore Snowdonia in 1961 and, by 1964, Outward Bound courses were being organized.

Apart from the regular 'exchanges', there were group parties to different parts of Europe. A trip to Champery in July 1959 made history as the group was the first to use air travel for part of the journey. A holiday to Austria and Switzerland during Whitsun 1960 also marked a milestone because it was the first joint party to be organized by the High School and the Grammar School and the first from either school to fly to and from the continent. Then, in May 1962, a 'pioneer' party of thirty-five girls and two members of staff set off from Tilbury on the *Devonia* for a cruise to Spain and Portugal.

As ever, there were frequent trips to France. One of these is particularly remembered for a mini-disaster. One of the coach parties missed the boat train from Victoria Station by five minutes so the coach driver offered to take the girls to Newhaven instead. Alas, they also missed the ferry and had to wait for the night crossing. They eventually arrived at their hotel in Paris at an unearthly hour to shatter the sleep of the girls who had arrived, according to schedule, the night before.

Germany had been added to the list of regular places to visit and the first skiing party left for Austria at Easter 1961. In 1959, three members of staff accompanied a group visiting pen-friends in Denmark and Sweden. Another group spent Easter 1958 in Amsterdam. Miss Stableford took a party to Oberammergau in 1960 and wrote about it for the *Sheaf*. She ended with the prayer of St Ignatius Loyola which is familiar to generations of High School girls:

> Teach us, good Lord, to serve Thee as Thou deservest; to give and not to count the cost; to fight and not to heed the wounds; to toil and not to seek for rest; to labour and not to ask for any reward save the joy of knowing that we do Thy will.

A party went to Montreux in 1961. Trips out included: Geneva where the girls visited the Palais des Nations, a Prix Unique Store, the St Bernard Pass and the Rochers de Naye. They also visited St Gingolphe which was a centre of the French Resistance during the war.

The 1959 edition of the *Sheaf* describes visits to London. The Art Department went by coach to the National Gallery and then the Natural History Museum. The History and Geography students went, this time by train, to the Imperial Institute and the British Museum and a very large group travelled to the Planetarium. Some girls with 'small Latin and less Greek' paid a visit to Bradfield College to enjoy a production of *Agamemnon* in Greek and there were regular trips to London to see plays.

Widening Horizons

The financial attractions of local employment had not decreased but the efforts of the staff and of the Youth Employment Service had almost eradicated the problem which had been experienced throughout the life of the School, namely the irritation caused by girls who did not complete the recognized grammar school course and who, thereby, deprived other girls who might have benefited by the opportunity. The Inspectors gave these figures (1957) concerning the activities of girls who left the School. About 38% proceeded to full-time further education, 7% to university, 11% to Teacher Training Colleges and 10% to nursing and other professions related to medicine. However, the contribution which the School made to society was not limited to this tangible outcome, for the ethos of the School was one which aimed to reap the hoped-for 'harvest of good citizens'. The 1957 Inspectors' *Report* acknowledged this.

> Very careful consideration has been given by the school to its objectives and policy. It hopes to send out girls who have a scale of values based on Christian principles; who will develop into women who can think for themselves and have poise and balance; who have learnt something of how to organise themselves and take responsibility; who will continue to want to learn; who have worked hard to develop their own gifts and are prepared to use them in service for others; who have knowledge of and feeling for the best in literature, music and art; and who will have some understanding of the world of today and be prepared to take their place in it as helpful citizens. The general activities have been planned so as to supplement the formal classroom teaching in attaining these objectives, but naturally vary a little from year to year according to personal tastes and enthusiasms.

Luton High School had a splendid building, a strong tradition, national recognition, excellent leadership and an enthusiastic and happy staff. The girls had wide interests and high academic expectations. At this stage in its life, the School was on the crest of a wave but political forces were at work which meant that the wave was about to crash onto the shores of an unknown land.

Mrs Evans' Retiremen. Signatures of Staff at the Presentation Dinner, 27th March 1965.

Chapter Nine

Co-existence and Demise
1965–1970

Mrs Evans' Retirement

In her last Speech Day address in 1965, Mrs Evans described how life had changed during the previous twenty years.

> Twice as many girls took O Levels as then took School Certificate examinations.
>
> Four times as many took A Levels as took Higher School Certificate examinations.
>
> More and more doors had been opened to girls, 'though some of them can still only be said to be ajar'. For example, it was at least three times harder for a girl to get a place in a medical school than it was for a boy.
>
> There were interesting new factors in the lives of girls: the particular in place of the general boy friend, part-time work in the evenings, weekends and holidays and travel abroad.

Mrs Evans was concerned about the danger time, at the end of the second year, when a 'disturbing minority' of 12–13-year-old girls became obsessed with outside interests, late nights, unwise companionships and worthless pursuits, and squandered their opportunities of realising their best gifts until it was too late.

At Easter 1965 Mrs Evans retired but still lived nearby in Barton and continued to take an interest in the life of the School and the town. She had presided over some of the happiest days the School had ever known and was respected by governors, parents, pupils and staff. Miss Irvine, her successor, said that 'she gave to all of us, both girls and staff, encouragement, gaiety and a high ideal of service which we tried sincerely to achieve'. At her last Speech Day, Mrs Evans spoke endearingly about the girls 'who are the school'.

Mrs Evans. (*Parkwood Studios*)

With all their faults – with all my faults – I have loved them and trusted them. Indeed it has sometimes been their more engaging faults which have been so lovable. Their good efforts and good will, their liveliness, their reasonableness, their innate kindness, their ingenuities and dodges, their serious thoughtfulness have altogether made up a rich and unforgettable pattern of days. But more than that I have respected them – for their gifts and abilities, for their powers of organisation of themselves and of affairs, for their capacity to persevere in the face of discouragement, and for their gallantry in the midst of real trouble.

Mrs Evans' Retirement
OPPOSITE ABOVE Mrs Evans' dog was called 'Corrie'.
OPPOSITE BELOW Celebration meal with Miss Dowdall, Miss Ling, Mrs Evans, Miss Wesley and Miss Stephenson.

Marguerita Eileen Irvine

Miss Marguerita Irvine (b.1917) was educated at Portsmouth Southern Secondary School for Girls and King's College, London, (1935–38) where she obtained a BA degree in Latin, French and History. She taught in Lancashire and Epsom before coming to Luton High School in 1952 to replace Miss S. Smith as head of Modern Languages. In 1961 she took over the headship of Yarmouth High School. Then, in 1965, she was selected from a short list of five to be the third Headmistress of Luton High School for Girls. She held this post until the summer of 1967 when she transferred to the Sixth Form College as Vice-Principal. It was later revealed that this post had been promised to her at her interview in 1965. Miss Irvine is remembered as being an exceedingly strict disciplinarian.

Miss M.E. Irvine c. 1976.
(Mr R.D. Whalley)

Life in the School

The examination

Tick-tock; tick-tock:

In never-ending monotony

The clock in the room ticks

And tocks away the minutes.

Pens are filled, papers named and numbered,

And pencils are sharpened to church-spire points.

All wait and sigh or pray for inspired thoughts.

Still the timepiece mechanically marks the passing seconds, annoying
everyone.

Suspense and anxiety diffuse through the room,

And silence reigns unbroken but for breaths and creaking chairs.

'You may begin!'

A stern voice breaks the silence.

Papers rustle as question sheets emerge from snowy coverlets of foolscap,

And with faces paper-white and trembling hands,

Pens are poised for action.

Thoughts at first muddled and indistinguishable

Arrange themselves in ordered sentences.

Heads are scratched, nails bitten, and brains racked.

For those few words the inspired Miss X
Delivered to your class while you were dreaming,
And which here would be so apt.
Spellings of divers words are scrawled on blotters,
And who before this day finds twenty ways
To spell that word so common yet irreplaceable?
Tick-tock; tick-tock:
The clock ticks away the precious answering-time,
The invigilator sighs, stretches out her legs.
The well-revised scrawl away at fifteen sheets an hour,
And the not-so-well-revised regard them thoughtfully,
Wondering if what they write is worth the effort.
'You have half-an-hour left.'
Only thirty minutes more!
It is not enough to write
Your pounding thoughts on the paper,
With flying nib
Inking its way through reams of glaring white,
You finish,
A line is ruled, the questions numbered,
Papers tied.
'Stop writing!' Just in time!
Everyone sits back with sweet relief.
The ticking clock is now ignored,
Or cursed for having kept the time too strictly.
Once from the room, the candidates chatter,
Laugh and shudder as text-books reveal the truth,
And return home, thankful it is past,
To wait for the result.

[Marilyn Jones]

Under Miss Irvine's headship, the curriculum, lifestyle and extra-curricular activities flourished much as they done while Mrs Evans was head. She only had seven terms in which to make her mark but her attitude to thorough learning is indicated in her Speech Day talk, 1965. She also commented on the wide number of general activities in the school.

It is always disappointing to see some girls at too early an age allowing themselves to become absorbed by other distractions which are of fleeting value, so that they do not have time to enter wholeheartedly into their school life.

This sharing in all that the school has to offer cannot be too strongly stressed, because much will ultimately be gained from it by the girls themselves. I would ask them to remember this because I am convinced that it is most essential for their future lives … the achievements of a large number of girls have been of a high and satisfactory order and we congratulate them.

For those who had done less well than they had expected, she emphasised the need to give more care to the solid learning that none of us can escape.

She spoke of the need for steady, thorough learning of facts, so that it was possible to lay a firm foundation on which to build our own ideas later. 'This firm foundation is essential', she said 'and there is no easy way for any of us of doing this humdrum learning, and I would ask the girls to remember this'.

[*Luton News* 22nd July 1965]

The 1966 edition of the *Sheaf* is the only one to give a picture the School during the short time that Miss Irvine was in charge. There is no mention of any innovations but this was not, of course, the time to be making radical changes.

Drama

The *Trojan Women* was presented.

The production of the Greek tragedy, with its concentration on human emotions and situations and its almost complete lack of action and movement, is an ambitious venture on any stage. That it should have been so successful on this occasion is a great tribute to those concerned, and not least to the producer.

The set, lighting, costumes and grouping are of the utmost importance when the movement is limited and the chorus is an integral part of the play, and all these were extremely effective on what is a difficult stage. The music, too, added to the atmosphere.   [J.W. Sherwood]

Art

In the summer of 1965, there was an exhibition of very unusual and interesting paintings and drawings in the main corridor. They had come from Japan in exchange for the work of about fifty girls from the High School which had been sent to Tokyo.

This correspondence began several months ago when the school was asked by a member of staff of Halyard School, who has friends in Tokyo, if we would be willing to arrange an exchange of work.

Consent was given, and a letter was duly received from Mr Yokoi, the Librarian at Aichi Syukutoku Gakuen, acknowledging the arrangement …

This exhibition gives us an excellent opportunity to notice the differences and similarities between the English and Japanese approach to art in schools.

[Elizabeth Marriott]

Societies, Clubs and Extra-curricular Activities

Various items elsewhere in the magazine will testify to the activities of the Music Society, the Camera Club, and the Dramatic Society. Besides visiting the Dead Sea Scrolls Exhibition, members of the Student Christian Movement have had various interesting speakers, including the Bishop of Bedford, and a number of girls regularly visit elderly house-bound folk to do shopping and give companionship. The Chess Club continues to flourish under the eye of Miss Aspinall, and the French Circle has had a variety of interests, including a visit to see *On ne Badine pas avec l'Amour* and a party where the speaking of French was 'de rigeur'. The Debating Society has had a stimulating time in encounters involving able opponents from both Grammar and Technical Schools.

Visits

The visit to the Dead Sea Scrolls Exhibition

We arrived at the British Museum, exhausted but hopeful, only to see crowds of other people, also exhausted but hopeful. Undaunted, we persevered elbowing our way through a dense jungle of humanity, and eventually emerging to be given an informative lecture on the subject of the Dead Sea Scrolls … The lecturer gave us an idea of the background and importance of the Scrolls, and also some insight into the their origin. The lecture having finished, we joined a seemingly never-ending queue in order to see the Exhibition, passing on the way the Codex Sinaiticus.

[Vivienne Ward and Irene Paton]

Music

Among the activities of the Music Society were a programme of light classical music and a talent competition for Juniors. Mr Michael Marsh-Edwards came to give a talk on percussion, illustrating it with recordings and unusual instruments which were passed round for all to see. One party from the Society went with the German Circle to hear the Vienna Boys' Choir at King's College, Cambridge and another joined the French Circle at a Recital of French Songs by Monsieur Jan Rosol. A Madrigal Group was formed in 1963–64; their most ambitious venture was their entry in the Bedford Music Festival in March 1966. They managed to take fourth place even though most of the competing groups were much more experienced.

The Society held a Music Festival in September 1965 which was, apparently, a great success.

After the initial announcement, the whole School seemed to be buzzing with musical activity. For weeks there was not a piano unused in any break or dinner-hour. Even if you came to School at 8 a.m. in order to practise, you were not alone, for even at this early hour the corridors echoed with the sounds of trumpets, clarinets, strings, pianos and voices … girls whom you did not associate with 'Music in School' produced recorders from the depths of their lockers, and one Upper Sixth Folk Group diligently gargled in the dinner-hour.

[Marilyn Jones, President]

Girls from the High School also teamed up with boys from the Grammar School to form an orchestra, later opening the membership to children from other schools in the town. They worked hard to become a harmonious group and, in 1965, felt able to enter the St Albans Music Festival with Chabrier's *Joyeuse Marche*. All felt that they had acquitted themselves well and were disappointed to learn that they had only gained second place (out of two), falling behind by just two marks.

The Choir was under the supervision of Miss Lewis. They sang at Mrs Evans' Leaving Service at the Parish Church and joined with the Luton Choral Society to sing *The Dream of Gerontius*. In 1966, they sang some of Brahms' *Liebeslieder* at the School Concert, being joined once again by fathers and friends who sang the tenor and bass parts. The most important event of their year was the performance of Schutz's oratorio *The Christmas Story*.

The orchestra was decreasing in numbers owing to the smaller intake of members of the lower end of the School. On the other hand, the expertise was growing; 'whereas two years ago the orchestra consisted solely of violins and three clarinets, to this have now been added a viola, two cellos, a double-bass, two trumpets and a flute'. Collections were made at their concerts so that even more instruments could be bought. They were fortunate in having the use of a harpsichord which had been lent by Bedford School. On another level, home-made instruments were produced: an egg-slicer harp, comb and paper, a box covered with rubber bands, a cake-tin drum and a maraca made from a tin and some rice.

The Interviews

The atmosphere in the waiting room is tense. There are vague murmurings about 'O' Level results, and stifled whispers about the situation in Rhodesia. Victims depart, sped upon their way with cries of 'Good luck', and one wonders if they will emerge hereafter. Suddenly a familiar name resounds through the stifling air. Glazed-eyed, you stagger to your feet, vague murmurs follow you, and you arrive at the formidable door. You receive an image of musty books encircling the spacious room in whose midst sits an ogre with horn-rimmed spectacles and a few grey tufts of hair. He critically peruses your application form, and you almost hear him groan with the tedium of interviewing candidates, who to his sprightly intellect can but appear morons.

The moisture drains from your mouth as he bluntly demands to know your reasons for invading his domain …

[Mary Northwood (extract)]

Games

The Games teachers wrote that

> table tennis has been added to the VI Form choice of physical recreation, and it is
> hoped to begin some form of tuition in canoeing at some later date. The Central
> Council of Physical Recreation provide many exciting courses and holidays, and
> we hope that girls will make the effort to keep up some form of physical recreation
> when they leave school and maybe help to build up a club in the district in which
> they live. [M.G.C. E.R.B. B.T.]

In 1966, a group of girls went to spend Christmas skiing in the Swiss Alps.

> To those of us who spent Christmas in the Swiss Alps the word 'snow' conjures up
> a magical scene: sparkling white crystals, dry, powdery and XuVy, clinging to every
> object, capping roof-tops, and transforming hotel and cow-barn alike into palaces
> garlanded with glistening icicles. This was real snow, feet deep, into which one
> could jump and dive, roll and swim, yet emerge dry and glowing with warmth! …
>
> It is surprising how, in just seven days, those seemingly ungainly six-foot
> planks of wood, with complicated 'safety release-bindings' attachments, suddenly
> become a desirable appendage to the body!

There are other interesting articles in the *Sheaf* written by girls who went on
individual visits, not organized by the School. They make fascinating reading.

> A visit to Russia by coach
> We had a modest blue-and-white 1952 coach with a reconditioned engine,
> various-sized tents, and our rations for the weeks ahead – bulk supplies of
> powdered milk, coffee, sugar, jam, margarine, dehydrated potatoes, dried peas, tins
> of corned beef, spam, tomatoes, rice pudding, plums and rhubarb, and packets of
> cornflakes and porridge – all packed in the boot with the spare cans of diesel oil.
> [Barbara Twitchen]

Then there was the Comex expedition to India, again by coach, for a Youth Festival
which, in the event, did not take place because of hostilities.

> Well, we got to India at last, travelling through Pakistan, gazing at the beauty of
> the Khyber Pass, by-passing a cholera epidemic in Irak [sic], enduring the wet-heat
> of Bagdad [sic], only to find ourselves plunged into the middle of a war. The
> British Press, it seems, was pro-Pakistan, so the Indians were feeling anything but
> friendly towards their erstwhile rulers. They treated us nevertheless with all the
> courtesy and hospitality for which the East is famous …

Perhaps we did not do much to restore the Commonwealth. But we saw how the East lives. We learned to appreciate a little its point of view, and the journey was not wasted in spite of our weariness and the hardships we went through – travelling for a month in a coach that is not air-conditioned is sometimes very like hell – because we have come to see with our own eyes that the world is more than just England, more than just Europe, more than just our Western civilization, a fact that we all acknowledge in theory but often find very difficult to believe.

[Carole Henderson]

Pauline Juffs wrote a piece for the *Sheaf* describing her summer holiday work on a kibbutz in Israel. In these communities, 'everything is done for all the inhabitants by all the inhabitants, and as a community they share the profits of the industrial and agricultural industries equally'. Work for the students involved clearing stones and rocks, planting grass, picking fruit and ironing shirts.

Politics and the Comprehensive System

Throughout its relatively short history, Luton High School had been influenced by major changes in educational ideas. The 1902 Balfour Act laid the plans for its foundation, the Butler Act of 1944 opened wide the doors but, in the mid 1960s, political moves combined to bring about the School's demise. On 1st April 1964, Luton achieved County Borough status which meant that it assumed control over all the schools in the town. As a result, Bedfordshire County Council ceased to have any input into the running of the High School, Grammar School and Technical School.

In February 1964, the Town Council adopted a new 'Education Charter' devised by Dr J.A. Corbett, the town's Education Officer. This stated that, from September 1964, only 15 per cent instead of 20 per cent of the town's 11-year olds (about 90 children) would be admitted to each of the grammar schools. The others would attend a new type of secondary school where they would be able to take O level examinations and, if successful, transfer to a VI Form in one of the selective schools. A representative of staffs at the grammar schools wrote to the *Luton News* in early 1965 to say that the scheme was 'widely praised outside Luton for being realistic, fair and sound'. In November 1964, Mrs Evans also observed that

of all the many plans afoot in the educational field this seems to me to show the greatest wisdom – certainly for Luton. Paradoxically perhaps, it appears to come nearest to a real implementation of the Education Act which set out as a goal 'equal opportunities for every child according to age, aptitude and ability'. I feel that our authority has shown both courage and insight in its plan which does provide such opportunities for all, even for the child of greater ability, and which avoids the necessity of over-large schools, where there is, I believe, a real danger of loss of personal care for, and knowledge of, the individual child.

Academically bright children benefited because it was possible for them to fast track through the system and even take O level examinations a year early, while children at the top of the non-selective schools gained confidence as leaders among their peer groups. It has been observed that children who transferred to grammar schools at the age of 16 were often more mature than their counterparts who transferred at the age of 11.

However, the 'Corbett plan' had had no time to prove itself when, in January 1965, the Luton Education Committee let it be known that an alternative, fully-comprehensive, plan was being presented to the Ministry of Education. This plan was set against a background of educational ideas proposed by the new Labour government at Westminster. The Eleven-plus system was, in fact, very much a political hot potato.

On 12 July 1965 Mr Antony Crosland, Secretary of State for Education and Science, issued *Circular 10/65* which stated that

> it is the Government's declared objective to end selection at eleven plus and to eliminate separatism in secondary education ... the Secretary of State accordingly requests local education authorities, if they have not already done so, to prepare and submit to him plans for reorganizing secondary education in their areas on comprehensive lines.

This is not the place to attempt to justify either the advantages or disadvantages of grammar schools versus comprehensive schools. Indeed, no consensus of opinion regarding the ideal secondary school has yet been reached and we are now in the twenty-first century. However, the Luton Education Committee had decided in favour of the comprehensive system and set out plans to

- put an immediate stop to 11+ examinations. This included the second part of the examinations for entry to the grammar schools in September 1965.
- set up a number of secondary schools (High Schools) of about equal size. These would offer O level and GCE examinations.
- provide A level courses at two Sixth Form Colleges. This would be a pioneer scheme because Sixth Form Colleges were an entirely new concept. [In the final arrangement, there was only one such College, the one at Bradgers Hill which was the first or one of the first of its kind in the country.]

A political storm greeted Luton's plan for comprehensive education; a major concern was the undue haste with which it had been introduced. Crowds filled the gallery for a meeting of the Town Council and an action group was formed. Shocked parents convened discussion groups in all parts of the town. The *Luton News* was full of letters, most of which criticized the scheme for one reason or another and one spoke of 'Machiavellian methods'. Grammar School staff warned of the loss of experienced staff from Luton. Councillor Mrs K.M. Milner (Conservative) was concerned that 'when you have once destroyed a thing, it is extremely difficult to build it up again' but Alderman Hedley Lawrence (Labour) talked of 'a great and exciting time'.

The new plan had to be put to the Secretary of State. He welcomed it but advised the Town Council to wait before introducing it. However, it was to be implemented 'as soon as it is practicable and possible'. Meanwhile, the Education Officer was told to go ahead with the second part of the Eleven-plus examination and, for one more year, the Corbett plan was followed. It was also resolved that the necessary legal procedures for the closure of Luton High School for Girls were to be set in place. Reorganization came into effect in September 1966 and, by July 1970, the transition from selective to comprehensive schooling was complete.

In practical terms this meant that pupils who, in September 1966, were halfway through an A level course were left in their schools to complete it. After that, all A level work took place at the Sixth Form College in Bradgers Hill (formerly the boys' Grammar School). The High School was allowed to continue for one more year so that girls could complete their A levels but, in September 1967, Denbigh High School took over their fine building in Alexandra Avenue. Mr E. Whitaker became Headmaster and the School worked from two sites, Alexandra Avenue and Denbigh Road. This School incorporated children from Denbigh Road Secondary Modern School as well as the remnant of Luton High School for Girls. Every July one year group of former High School girls left or transferred to the Sixth Form College, the last leaving in July 1970.

Mr Eric Whitaker

Mr Whitaker was born in 1919 and educated at Todmorden Grammar School (1930–1938) and Goldsmiths' Training College (1938–1940). He served in the Army, becoming a sergeant REME (England and Western Europe) between 1940 and 1945. In 1951 he obtained a BA degree in History at London University. During his career he taught at:

Townsfield Secondary School, Hayes, 1945–1947
Beech Hill Secondary School, Luton 1947–1948
Stopsley Secondary School, Luton 1948–1954
Denbigh Road Secondary Boys' School, Luton

LEFT Mr E. Whitaker 1956. (C.W. Parrott)

1954–1955 (Headmaster)

Denbigh Road Secondary Mixed School, Luton 1955–1967 (Headmaster)

Denbigh High School, Luton (Headmaster)

His interests included:

Membership of the NUT

Teacher Representative on Joint Consultative Committee 1955

Member of Luton Juvenile Employment Committee 1954

He married Margaret Mander, b.1915, who was a former Head Girl at Luton High School for Girls and who also became a Headteacher in Luton.

Numbers on roll at each school in January 1964–68

	1964	1965	1966	1967	1968
Selective Schools					
Luton Grammar	854	825	746		
Luton High	937	905	815		
Barnfield Secondary Technical	623	590	587		
Sixth Form College (mixed)					
a) VI Form elements				181	204
b) Grammar School element				400	388
Barnfield High (mixed)				594	441
Denbigh SM (mixed)	628	637	664		
Denbigh High (mixed)					
a) Luton High School element				558	317
b) Main School element				726	820

From July 1967, the girls from the Luton High School for Girls were officially members of the new Denbigh High School but they remained a distinct group and had their own Senior Mistress because it was essential that there should be someone on the staff who was responsible for the organization of their external examinations. They also kept their own Houses, Speech Days and games teams but, as time went by, the schools became more integrated.

The first of the Senior Mistresses was Miss Flaherty who had been at the School since 1943/44. She is remembered by generations of girls for her distinctive hairstyle and for her History lessons. Apparently she could be distracted from her planned lesson by being asked 'What was it like during the War'? She would take up the challenge and 'Lo and behold, forty minutes had passed and not one word on the Treaty of Utrecht or the Bill of Rights'. Mrs Burness was in charge of the girls after Miss Flaherty retired in July 1968 and, the following year, Mrs Thomson (Griggs) became Senior Mistress.

A very real problem was the merging of the two cultures. The High School girls were part of a very precise tradition which had been carefully nurtured since 1919 and they saw the School as their own. Then the boys and girls from the Denbigh Road School, with a different kind of history, came along to claim it as theirs. Differences of opinion naturally occurred and some found the transition exceedingly trying. Others, however, were happy and saw the changeover as 'seamless' and exciting.

This was a particularly difficult time for members of staff and some problems occurred when lines of communication broke down. Each School had a time-honoured routine and, with the best will in the world, confusion can easily arise in this kind of situation. Time and energy also had to be spent travelling between the three sites: Denbigh Road, Alexandra Avenue and Bradgers Hill. However, as time went on, the two schools began to gel.

> For many of us [staff] it was a difficult choice. A fair percentage of the High School staff had never taught mixed ability classes, and the prospect of mixed ability classes and boys was, for some, quite daunting. Others of us did not want to have to choose between losing senior pupils or juniors, but being peripatetic and belonging in neither establishment did not appeal ... At that stage my concern was that there should be as much continuity as possible for the remaining pupils as far as their education was concerned ...
>
> And then it was D-Day, Denbigh Day, in other words! In September 1967 the doors of the old High School opened to Forms 3, 4 and 5 of the High School girls and Forms 1 and 2 of Denbigh High School and, try as I may, I cannot adequately find words to express the turmoil of emotions we all felt that day ... For some of the more senior teachers, the changes must have been quite distressing. For the rest of us, there was a determination not to let the side down, so to speak, and we did our utmost to carry out our duties as best we could in the manner to which we were accustomed, and our girls were urged to do the same ... As the year progressed and tensions eased, many friendships were forged and a certain community spirit flickered into life ...
>
> September 1968, and a new school year began. For the High School it was its penultimate year, with only Fourth and Fifth forms, but it was to be an easier session with good relations throughout both schools. We had reached a stage where most staff taught both Denbigh and High School pupils and there was a young and enthusiastic group of teachers to complement more senior and established staff. For my part I was ably supported by some of the kindest, friendliest, most hard working people with whom I have ever had the good fortune to work. We enjoyed our time in school, and I would like to think that the High School pupils did, too. We could not manufacture a whole school of High School pupils, but we tried to continue, as far as possible, the traditions that generations of pupils had handed on and on Prize-giving day at the end of the year, the award

winners lined up and moved forward with the same military precision that, for years, had been a feature of the ceremony. As for the singing of the school song and hymns, *I Vow to Thee, My Country* and *Jerusalem*, though they were sung lustily, I swear there were few dry eyes in the hall. To the girls of the school who that year, worked so hard and made our jobs so rewarding I offer my heartfelt thanks. I hope we did not let you down.

Many years have passed but I still recall with great affection the staff and pupils of the High School, a number of whom became lifelong friends and, although the manner in which comprehensive education was implemented in Luton gave cause for concern, I have to be glad that I was given the opportunity to teach in Denbigh. There, too, were friends to be made and to this day it is a source of happy memories.

[Moyra Preece (Burness)]

In June 1968, a combined *Sheaf-Blue Jacket* school magazine was produced. Mr Whitaker took the opportunity to express his feelings about the co-existence of the former High School girls and the children from Denbigh Road:

Change there has been in many spheres not least in education. Here, the change has been fundamental, providing new challenges and a sense of fresh adventure. We are now firmly set along this road creating a new exciting school which has much greater opportunities than its predecessor. Our progress benefits tremendously from the traditions of the past and, in our case, this is two-fold. On the one hand, we have the sound foundation of Denbigh and on the other, the equally respected history of the Luton High School. Each has gained from the other and it is fitting that this magazine should be a joint effort. I feel it right to place on record my most grateful thanks to everyone for the assistance so freely given during the past twelve months.

Change, then, there has been and this is inevitable, as without change there would be no progress. It has been a peaceful change, a natural change, a change that has been accepted. I feel that our ability to absorb these innovations springs from our solid traditions of school and of country. In this age when violence erupts so easily, often without sufficient cause and certainly without ultimate advantage, it is good to know that we can work together peaceably creating our own personal traditions to add to those of the past.

Here then is our joint effort – the story of two schools merged together. We have one aim – the best opportunity for all and everyone's best effort overall.

The High School had collected a wealth of memorabilia. In May 1967, Miss Irvine sent letters to people who had donated cups and trophies to ask whether they should stay at the Denbigh High School, be transferred to the Sixth Form College or remain the property of the most recent winner. The replies varied and the collection was dispersed. However, a few of the sports cups have recently been found and added to a small collection of High School memorabilia. Some of the house banners are also being cared for; they are not only important because of their relevance to school life but are also valued pieces of excellent needlework. Documents will be accepted at the Bedfordshire and Luton Record and Archive Service or Luton Museum and Art Gallery but these are not appropriate homes for the other artefacts. It is of concern to everyone who has worked towards the production of this book and the centenary celebrations that what still exists to remind us of the vibrant life of the School should find a suitable home.

The Sixth Form College

What of the girls who transferred to the Sixth Form College? The fact that Miss Irvine also went to the College brought some continuity but there were many practical problems for girls who moved into a purpose-built all-boys establishment with no facilities for girls. In the opinion of some, the move would have gone more smoothly if Barnfield School had been chosen as the Sixth Form College instead, because it was already co-educational.

In the 'olden days' at the Alexandra Avenue School, the arrival of a group of boys on the scene would have set the jungle telegraph buzzing, but now the girls had to get used to sharing their school lives with them on a daily basis. This, not unexpectedly, proved to be somewhat of a distraction. However, it appears that the girls enjoyed their new freedom and saw the move as an exciting challenge. They felt honoured to be the pioneers of this experiment in education which was new, not only to Luton but also to the country as a whole.

Farewell

On 23rd July 1970 the *Luton News* published a farewell to the Luton High School for Girls.

> Luton High School for Girls is no more. It ended its life at 4.0 p.m. on Friday (17th July) when the doors closed behind the last of its pupils to complete the grammar school course after selection at 11.
>
> There were, it is true, rather premature last rites when three years ago it merged with Denbigh High School, the new comprehensive which took over the buildings of the old Luton High School. The two groups, under the same headmaster Mr Eric Whitaker, then began a three-year period of co-existence.
>
> As he made clear at the last prize giving of the High School on Wednesday evening, there was no question of the High School losing its identity in the much bigger Denbigh School.

'These girls had a character of their own,' he said. 'Once we began to know each other there was an increasing demand on all sides for a great deal of unification.

'I am sure that the outcome in terms of work and enjoyment of school life has been one of rich dividends'.

The school hall was packed with present school-leavers, old girls, parents of the present generation of school-leavers, and past and present members of staff.

Mrs Eileen Evans, who in 1947 succeeded the founder headmistress Miss Sheldon, was present, together with her successor, Miss M.E. Irvine …

The Head Prefect, Ruth Hall, made her report on the school's activities and presented to Denbigh a gift from the High School leavers – eight banners for each of the eight houses. They had been designed and worked by the High School girls in the two and a half weeks since the O level examination …

The evening ended with a comedy melodrama *Temptation Sordid or Virtue Rewarded* by Winifred Phelps and performed by girls of the Luton High School.

And so, the life of the Luton High School for Girls came to an end. The euphoric joy of the first pupils, the determination of Miss Sheldon, the infectious laughter of Mrs Evans, the dedication of the staff and the successes of many hundreds of girls were just memories. It has been a pleasure to enter into the life of the School once again.

Five Years Hence
(*After Ozymandias of Egypt, by P.B. Shelley*)

I met a scholar from that happy band,
Who said, 'I've passed the eleven-plus and shown
I'm worthy of it, ready to put my hand
And brain to nobler studies yet. And grown
In years and knowledge, still I onward wend
To University. I thought it good
That 'twas for me the High School to attend,
And take upon me all for which it stood.
Alas, nought of that system now remains.
'Ubi Semen, Ibi Messis', only brings
A sob of grief, a cry of deep despair.
Nothing beside remains. Round the decay
Of that most noble High, revered and fair,
The Comprehensive system now holds sway.

[Patricia Hawkins]

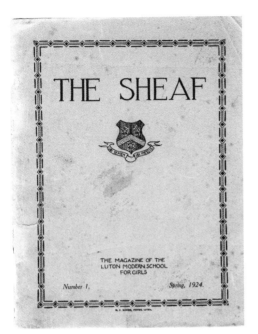

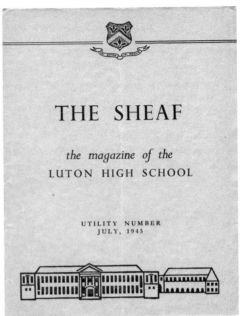

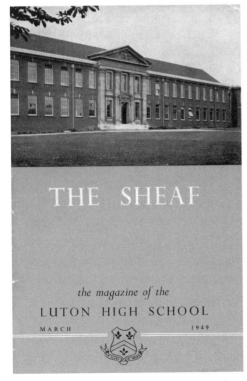

The changing face of *The Sheaf* magazine. (*Pat Gillespie*)

Chapter Ten

Ibi Messis

Old High School Girls
(With really profuse apologies to the late Mr Rudyard Kipling.)

'Oh where are you going to, all you old High School girls,
     Very grown-up since we saw you last term?'
'We are going to sew, or to teach, or to typewrite,
     To take down dictation, or pin up a perm.'

'And where will you do all this, all you old High School girls
     And where shall we find you now you are away?'
We're swallowed by hospital, office or schoolroom,
     Address us … well! 'Anywhere. Thick-of-the-fray.'

'But if anything happened to all you old High School girls,
     And suppose you had nothing to face but the dole?'
'Why you'd have no first-class young women in Luton,
     And wouldn't big business just be in a hole?'

'Then we'll pray for an opening for all you old High School girls,
     Plenty of jobs and some easy exams.'
Oh want of a job doesn't worry old 'High Schools'
     And anything's simple when once you're through Cambs.'

'Then what can we do for you, all you old High School girls,
     Oh, what can we do for your comfort and aid?'

'Just plead with your fathers – so oft our employers –
  To give us a chance just to show how we're made.'

'For the notes we transcribe and the jobs we are doing,
  Are often enough to exhaust or perplex
An Einstein, a Socrates, Pankhurst or Plato
  And YET we are called the Sub-dominant sex.'

[V (1936)]

Although the day-to-day life of the School ended in 1970, the whole story has yet to be told. This is a difficult proposition, for thousands of girls have passed through its doors but we do not know where they are or what they have done. The harvest is not yet not fully gathered and there are still former pupils 'out there' living and working and having an effect on life. Many have made their homes in other parts of this country and others in lands across the globe. How many families have we raised? How many of us have worked or are working in occupations undreamed of by the girls who went to the school in Park Square? What influence have we had on the world? Were we a 'harvest of good citizens' as was fondly hoped?

The *Sheaf* magazines regularly printed information about careers and much input has come from former students who have willingly shared their wealth of observation and experience. Thanks are due to all these people, whether they recorded their accounts in the distant past or whether they have helped directly with the production of this book, but it cannot be emphasized strongly enough that this is not intended to be a celebration of the few, for the life of every girl who ever attended the school is of value. Each, in her own way, has reaped her individual harvest.

At first it was intended to match the careers of boys from the Grammar School to those of girls from the High School but it very soon became apparent that this would not be the best way to approach the subject. One hundred years ago, when the School in Park Square was first opened, 'sexual equality' had hardly been dreamed of and girls were seen in a completely different light from boys. Boys were expected to have good careers; girls, meanwhile, were destined for a domestic role and their employment was usually seen in terms of 'a good job' instead of a fulfilling career. In 1930, Alderman H.O. Williams reminded the girls that they should not only learn the law of the study and the science of the laboratory, but also the art of home-making. Girls who did want a career, for example in teaching, had to make a painful choice. By the 1960s, doors were opening but, as Mrs Evans said in her last Speech Day, some were still 'only ajar'.

By the end of the twentieth century, the doors had been opened wide and it has been said that girls today have their own set of difficulties because they are faced with too many choices. One feature which is significant is that many Old Girls have exercised their new freedoms by changing the direction of their lives, particularly after they have raised a family. This chapter will therefore concentrate on the evolution of girls' and women's expectations; it could stand alone as a social history of women's lives in the twentieth century.

Over the years, different year and friendship groups have kept in touch and others have been rekindled by energetic organizers. It is now possible to find names of some former pupils on the Internet and there is plenty of information on the *Friends Reunited* website. However, most of the reunions described in this book have survived without the help of modern technology. Considerable excitement has been engendered by the planned celebrations to mark the centenary in September 2004. One former pupil heard about the occasion and went out the next day to book flights home. That says it all!

Employment and Careers

Apologies are offered for any dates that are not quite accurate. Articles from the *Sheaf* often do not carry a particular date and those given here are usually the date of publication rather than a specific date. Any revised information received will be kept and noted. Apologies are also offered to former pupils whose names are not included in this chapter. It would have been impossible to include everyone and it has to be emphasized that the accounts listed below are intended to be examples. As has already been observed, it would be wrong to regard the life of one person more highly than that of another, for everyone has something to offer to life.

It is fair to say that some occupations were considered highly acceptable. First and foremost was probably teaching, closely followed by nursing, banking, the civil service, librarianship and office work. From the perspective of girls in other schools in the town, it no doubt appeared that a kind of class distinction was in operation for some of these occupations were closed to them for many years. One of the marketable qualifications of High School girls was, so it is said, the legendary neatness of their handwriting.

University

The ultimate prize was a university education but, in the early days of the School's life, this privilege was only accorded to a small minority and the 'Congratulations' section of the *Sheaf* magazine took care to list the names of girls who were successful. In October 1923 it was reported that Vera Stanton, the first head girl, had gained a BA degree making her the first from the girls' school to graduate. Ten years later the *Sheaf* noted that she was now Gräfin [Countess] von Schweinitz and had a three-year-old daughter, Sylvia, who was able to speak both English and German.

The so-called 'redbrick' universities were favoured for the obvious reason that Oxford and Cambridge Universities did not exactly welcome women with open arms. Women could sit for Oxbridge examinations but, even if they out-performed the men, could not earn a degree. It was 1920 before Oxford gave degrees to women and 1948 before Cambridge followed suit. Miss Sheldon studied at the Royal Holloway College in London where girls were offered the chance to sit for a London degree or the Oxford Final Honours. She chose the Oxford qualification.

Many of the girls who took university degrees undertook a further year's study to gain a teaching certificate. Others took a combined four-year course which qualified them both in their chosen subject and in teaching. The first to be named in the 'Congratulations' column for taking the longer course was Elma May who studied at London University.

Over the years, girls studied a range of subjects: English, German, French, History, Sociology, Botany, Chemistry, Zoology and Geography and, in 1933, five girls were given university places: Phyllis Carpenter and Lilian Odell at London University; Joan Stalker at Liverpool, Kathleen Brooker at Birmingham and Joyce Patterson at Leeds. These graduates often took up teaching posts in other parts of the country or in countries overseas. Letters to the *Sheaf* indicate how university life changed over the years.

1924

We are expected to continue working till 10 o'clock, and then to have our milk and go to bed. At 10.25 p.m. a bell is rung, and lights go out in all public rooms at 10.30 p.m. After this, there must be no noise anywhere, and with all the corridor lights as low as possible, people look more like ghosts than anything, as they glide stealthily, silently along.   [Ellen L.M. Hills Royal Holloway College]

1954

The seventy or so different clubs and societies cater for a very wide range of tastes and interests. In these societies we find ample opportunity for discussion – which occupies so much of our time – and it is this discussion which, in my opinion provides the 'broadening' influence which is so integral a part of University education. It may cover any one of a vast range of topics, from the frivolous to the most fundamental problems of life, thrashed out usually over a cup of coffee ... At college we meet people of such opposing ways of thought that, to avoid being hopelessly muddled, we have to think things out for ourselves and form our own opinions. It is here that the background of fact acquired at school falls into perspective as a basis for these opinions. [Anne Richards King's College London]

1954

Much has been written about Oxford, for there are almost as many views on it as there are people interested in this, the oldest of our Universities. To a bewildered 'fresher' the first indication of the variety of interests catered for is the circulars which arrive on the very first day from many of the University societies extolling the advantages of being anything from a bellringer to a heretic.

[Kathleen Potter St Hilda's College, Oxford]

In the course of time, former High School girls started to work for higher degrees. Mary Hamilton Hart planned to study for a Ph.D. in 1954 and the *Sheaf* notes (1959) that, after Moira Shaw had gained a BA in English from London University, she was awarded a Fulbright Scholarship by the United States Educational Commission. She took up a post as teaching assistant at Minnesota University where she expected to stay for three or four years and also planned to obtain the higher degree of Doctor of Philosophy.

Teaching

There was, historically, a cultural divide between teachers in secondary schools and those in elementary schools. In 1904, when the mixed school was opened on Park Square, elementary school teachers learnt their skills under the Pupil Teacher system. This was much criticized because teachers were seen to spend all their lives within elementary schools and one of the reasons for opening schools like the Luton Modern School was to educate potential teachers to a higher standard. In 1908, the Student Teacher scheme was introduced in Luton; children from the Modern School were given bursaries to stay at school for an extra year and they could then learn teaching skills at the chalk face and at classes run by the County Council. When pupil and student teachers had completed their initial instruction, they became uncertificated teachers but in-service tuition and correspondence courses gave them the opportunity to study for a teaching certificate. Edith Webb was a 'bursar' from the Girls' Modern School and began work as an uncertificated teacher at Surrey Street Girls' School in September 1924. Many years later, she became Headmistress there.

> Soon after starting there it was announced that the external examination for full qualification would be held for one extra year only. So began a correspondence course over the next two years. This meant study and school work every evening and Saturday mornings, leaving Saturday afternoon and Sunday free. The examination, which lasted a week, was taken at Watford and covered twelve subjects. Fortunately I passed with a distinction in History. So I became what one person described as 'Certified' and my salary leapt up 50% from £8 to £12 a month.

There were also Teacher Training Colleges and the *Sheaf* regularly reported the names of girls who were accepted by them in order to become trained as well as certificated. For example, in 1933, 'Congratuations' were extended to Ethel Worth and Flora Humm who were going to Hockerill College in Bishop's Stortford, Phyllis Darnley who was accepted by Furzedown, Norah Worthington and Muriel York who chose Stockwell and Joan Throssell and Joan Machin who had places at St Katharine's. A significant number of High School girls who went to Training Colleges became head teachers.

> 1924
>
> The first bell rings at 6.45 a.m. ... at 7.45 we have breakfast ... Chapel is at 8.30 in our very own chapel ... Then lectures start at 9 and go on till 1 o'clock with a break of fifteen minutes at 10.30 ... We are all expected to go out somewhere every day even if it is only to walk round the grounds. Tea is at 4 o'clock and then lectures again from 4.30 to 7.30. After supper which is at 8, time is taken for various societies – Dramatic, Literary and Debating and so on. In the winter months we have inter-dormitory socials in the day-room and usually once a week somebody from outside comes to give us a lantern lecture.
>
> [Ella King, St Katharine's College]

In 1951, Ella took up a lecturer's post at a Teacher Training College in Sierra Leone and held a high position in the country's education service.

Between the two world wars a 'marriage bar' was in operation. This made it almost impossible for a girl to choose to marry and, at the same time, remain in the teaching profession. However, the demand for teachers during the Second World War meant that the 'marriage bar' was ignored and, in 1945, it was abolished. After the war, when the leaving age was raised and the numbers of children of school age increased, 'married women returners' were encouraged to up-date their skills and return to the classroom. Since then there has been no problem for married women who wished to stay in the profession. Another scheme to alleviate the shortage of teachers after the War was the one-year Emergency Training scheme.

There was progress in 1953, when the principle of equal pay for women teachers was accepted, although it took several years to be fully implemented. Then, in 1960, the standard course was increased from two to three years. Three years later the names of these institutions were changed to Colleges of Education and aspiring teachers eventually followed degree courses.

The Luton Education Committee was acutely aware of the shortage of teachers and decided to open Putteridge Bury College of Education (1966). Many former students of the High School decided to change direction and become teachers. The College took students from Luton, Bedfordshire and Hertfordshire. Mr G.W. Humphries DFC B.Sc., formerly Principal of a Teacher Training College in Nigeria, was appointed Principal and Mr R.A. Swallow, headmaster of Maidenhall School, was one of the first members of staff. The Report of the Luton Education Committee

(1963–1968) stated that 'the main purpose of the College was to provide non-residential training for mature students who wish eventually to teach in primary schools'. These were allowed to take a shortened two year course. Post-Graduate Certificates of Education were also offered.

> I never regretted it for one minute even though we were the first intake and literally went in with the builders working all around us … I did Science but the following term I switched to Biology and thoroughly enjoyed it … The students there with younger children reckoned that they were better off than we were as they got their little ones to bed early and had the rest of the evening for their studies. But I must say that both my children were marvellous to me, humping great books from the library … My most vivid memory from Putteridge was walking into a lecture hall and seeing the blackboard covered with white chalk saying 'goodness knows what' and the senior English lecturer told us that it was Greek and that we must never forget that a page of print looks exactly the same to any five-year old – and I never have.
>
> [Jean Munn (Lawrence)]

Girls from the High School also specialized in different areas of teaching such as Physical Training, Art, Domestic Science and the teaching of the deaf. From its early days, Luton High School had strong links with Margaret Stansfeld, the first Principal of Bedford Physical Training College, and several former students of the School trained there. In 1954 three girls went, one, Janet Mariner, following in the footsteps of her sister, Evelyn.

Physical Training

> Owing to limited space I am unable to tell you of all that occurs during a three years' course at a Physical Training College, so I will try and summarise the few important points that occur chiefly in our first year.
>
> On the theoretical side of 'things' we devote most of our time to physiology, hygiene, physics and mechanics, and anatomy. Later on, in the second and third years, School of Remedial Exercise and pathology are added to the above list.
>
> Dancing also plays a large part in the College curriculum, incorporating Greek, National and Country dancing..
>
> Now I come to the part of the syllabus which to most people is so closely connected with P.T. – namely games. Throughout the winter, hockey, lacrosse and netball are the principal games played … During the summer months, tennis, cricket, swimming and rounders fill in the spaces left by the winter games in the timetable, and a very good combination they make.
>
> [Patricia Fussell Queen Alexandra Training College 1938]

The theory of movement forms an important part of the course and Biology, Anatomy, Physiology and Health Education are all closely linked into the chain of Physical Education subjects. Perhaps the most important of all is the practice of teaching which goes on throughout the three years in college.

[Shirley Benson wrote from Bedford for the *Sheaf* in 1955]

Domestic Science

During our first year we do one chief subject each term, such as Housewifery or Cookery with about half a dozen other subjects of less importance. Last term we did Housewifery and had quite an exciting time learning various housecrafts from the upholstering of furniture to the cleaning of pots and pans, not to mention wrangling with 'accounts'.

This term we are endeavouring to become (expert?) laundresses ... I thought 'ironing looks quite simple' when I watched it being performed in a demonstration class. But woe betide me when I began, for I burned my fingers, scorched my clothes and altogether made a good mess of things.

[Irene Webb Battersea Domestic Science Training College 1930]

Private Schooling

Private schools attracted girls from the High School. In 1928 the *Sheaf* noted that Myrtle Jenkins was joint Principal of Cleveland House, Dorothy Gent was Principal of York House School, Barbara Aylott was teaching at the Convent School and Doris Clarke had a school for children under seven. Doris Fountain was teaching at a private school in Tintagel. Josephine Juett was more adventurous and went to be a children's governess in a wealthy home near Hollywood. She described the charms of California for the *Sheaf* (1933).

I have heard San Francisco termed 'The Bagdad [sic] of the West', and for myself California holds the charm of a beloved fairy story. It might well be painted in gold upon the maps; this land steeped in sunshine; sunburnt faces against glowing hills; ancient hills golden with poppies (in Springtime); golden in the sunset light, or the mists, which rolling in from the Pacific at evening are so transfused with light that to walk in them produces in me an ecstasy akin to bathing in a rainbow.

The eucalyptus trees, like giant silver birches, rise straight and tall above the gardens. Their discarded bark dangles in strips around their trunks, ready to come clattering down upon our housetops in the next gale.

It is Spring and the air is heavy with the scent of peach blossoms and mimosa. What a joy it is to lie beneath a tree and gaze up through masses of softest yellow into the infinite blue. A humming bird pauses trembling on a flower nearby – a flicker and it is gone.

The monotonous rasping of grasshoppers, punctuated by the hoarse screams of the Blue Jays, are nature's only sounds by day. Later the robins will begin to sing.

Missionary and Church Work

Girls who intended to become missionaries often gained teaching certificates before they left this country. Nesta Soddy (Burditt) took a degree in French at Birmingham and then went (1933), with her husband, to India to work for many years for the Baptist Missionary Society. She maintained links with the High School and, in particular, organized the School's support of a blind Indian boy. Annie Baldock, who had been teaching in an elementary school in Birmingham, began training to be a missionary in 1933.

After the Second World War travel became easier. By 1950, Penelope Carlisle was in East Africa and, in 1964, she had left her school in Kampala, Uganda, to do relief missionary work among refugees further in the interior. She was working in 'the most primitive conditions'. 1960 found Joan Stephens (Harlow), a former Head Girl, living in West Bengal where her husband was a missionary. Three years later the *Sheaf* reported that they were working in Durgapur, the 'Steel City' of Western Bengal. Miss Hardy, a former member of staff, left the school in 1945 to train as a missionary and went to work in China.

There were opportunities for church work in this country as well. In 1937, Dorothy Gent gave up her school, York House, to devote herself to lay work in a poor parish in London and, in 1961, Phyllis Brock was reported to be a Methodist Deaconess near Leamington Spa with about a dozen churches in her area. The last years of the twentieth century saw enormous changes in the roles of women within the Church.

Where the seed, there the harvest. When I first went to the High School, I thought that was a pretty good motto for a school; with the sheaves of corn on the badge and school magazine, the *Sheaf*, it made a good 'package'. One of the amazing features of seeds, I was to discover later, is that they are full of potential. Within that grain of wheat, or peanut, or corn, or dust-like speck, there is that which, given the right conditions, can grow and change to become a mature plant which might well itself bear seeds. I hope the motto was chosen in the first place in recognition of all the potential that was there in us young people.

It was through the teaching of Biological Sciences in the Sixth Form at Luton High School that 'seeds' were sown in me which led to my fascination with the created world. A Biology degree and a postgraduate teaching certificate later, I began communicating that fascination as a Science teacher. I had always wanted to teach and I enjoyed teaching. After marriage and the birth of two children I returned to teaching and expected to continue as a teacher until retirement.

But, over the years, something new was growing in me – the conviction that I should no longer be a school teacher. A complete change in direction led me to join a team establishing a Children's Hospice at Milton, Cambridge, and, over a few years, to see that hospice opened and functioning. How I was challenged over that time! Challenged by the need to raise £1 million each year to run the hospice; challenged by the sick children the hospice helped and their devoted parents; challenged by the very suffering the hospice was there to relieve – physical, mental and spiritual. My Christian faith, too, was challenged; for the first time I really asked many deep questions, and found much hope and comfort in knowing that Jesus, the Son of God, has shared our human suffering and death and has overcome them.

Those deep hospice experiences changed me to the extent that, when we moved away from Milton, I felt that I was being called to ordained Christian ministry in the Church of England. Others agreed with my feeling and now, ten years on, I am a 'vicar'.

Seeds grow to maturity. It is so easy in our lives to try to predict what that maturity will be. I am grateful to those who saw potential in me all those years ago at Luton High School and, later, I am grateful to God for the potential he saw and still sees in me – for all he has given me and continues to give me.

[Valerie Kilner (Evans) 1953–1960]

Medicine

The first reference in the *Sheaf* to a former pupil who qualified as a doctor was in 1959 when it was reported that Cynthia Heymeson 'recently qualified as a doctor, obtained her M.B., B.S. at London Hospital. She is now House Surgeon at East Ham Memorial Hospital'. Janice Rimbault (Swallow), having studied at St Bartholomew's (Bart's) in London, qualified at about the same time. In 1959 she was awarded the prize for the outstanding student of the year, which had never been awarded to a woman before. Jane Clark also studied at Bart's and qualified in 1964.

I eventually went back to work at Bart's for some time before I became a Ship's surgeon for British India Steam Navigation Co on the educational schoolships, *Devonia*, *Nevasa* and *Uganda*. I had the interesting task of fitting out the medical department on both *Nevasa* and *Uganda* when they were first commissioned as schoolships, the former in Falmouth and the latter in Hamburg …

It was when we came to Lymington that I started working in Palliative Care at the Macmillan Unit at Christchurch and I have been committed to this field of medicine ever since.

The most wonderful happening for me, was the request from a local philanthropic lady that if she financed the venture I would start a Hospice in

Lymington. She gave her croquet lawn for a site and the wherewithal to build and equip it. I was responsible for the layout, furnishing, staffing and ultimately being its Medical Director for the first six years …

Soon after retirement I went to teach palliative care for a short time at the first Moscow Hospice. This was an eye-opener and a never-to-be-forgotten experience.

I gained so much more than an academic education from the High and I know it shaped much of what I have done since. Equally important was influence of home where my schoolmaster father sowed seeds of enquiry and respect for plain hard work which spurred me on not to be beaten in my determination to study medicine.

[Janice Rimbault (Swallow)]

Professor Dame Lesley Southgate (Carter) has had a distinguished career in medicine and was made a Dame Commander of the British Empire in the 1999 Queen's Birthday Honours for services to primary care and standards in medicine. She trained at Liverpool University Medical School and spent 33 years in general practice. She has also been a member of an impressive number of committees and working parties and has run courses for receptionists, pharmacists and nurse professionals. As well as being a prolific writer, she has been a consultant, lecturer and professor and has received many honours from universities in this country and abroad.

I was the first person in my family ever to go to University and still refer to myself as 'a nice girl from Luton made good'. I now realise what a good education I had but it was also combined with a very normal and free teenage life as a working class girl in the town.

[Lesley Southgate (Carter)]

Anne Oates (Riegelhaupt) trained as a doctor and became a Member of the Royal College of Physicians, Member of the Royal College of General Practice and Diplomate of the Royal College of Obstetricians and Gynaecologists.

Veterinary Medicine

Molly Hyett (Fardell) ran a well-known veterinary surgery in Luton.

I went to the Luton High School in 1943. Miss Sheldon ruled the day. I left Luton when I was 13 to go to Burnham on Sea, attending Bridgwater Grammar School. From there I obtained my veterinary degree at Bristol University in 1957. I returned to Luton in 1960 …

One day Miss Ling brought her animal to see me. She always terrified me as a child, maths never being my strong point. I attended her dog and added up the account incorrectly. She gave me a much remembered look and said 'you never could add up correctly!'

Our Brook Street practice was very much a family practice, many staff staying with me for many years. With the help of the *Luton News,* we never put a fit animal to sleep – many an owner came out of the surgery with more animals than they came in with …

It was a different age … I think we ran the practice by common sense and a love of animals as well as our veterinary skills and we were always available to our clients.

Nursing

Dr Margaret Currie (Lodge) (1948–54) has written about the changing face of nursing in the twentieth century. She spent most of her career in clinical practice and nurse education and is now a senior research fellow (hon.) at the University of Luton and Health Care Historian at Luton and Dunstable Hospital.

The year 1919 was not only a memorable one for the girls of Luton High School (LHS) but also for the nursing profession which finally achieved state recognition under the Nurses Registration (England and Wales) Act, 1919. Under this Act, a General Nursing Council (GNC) was set up which, among other functions, was required to standardise schemes of training in all major hospitals and asylums which had gained the necessary GNC approval. Small local institutions were, therefore, unable to offer recognised courses. The GNC was also required to keep a Register of qualified nurses, training for which was of three years' duration for the prestigious general part and the Supplementary Registers: for male nurses; the nursing of sick children; the mentally ill and mentally defective. Fever nursing was a two year course.

Even before the school moved to Alexandra Avenue, the Modern School had donated a cot to the Bute Hospital (1882–1939) in Luton c.1908. This was one of the first tangible links between the school and a local hospital, probably established as Miss Evelyn St S. Poulton was a mistress at the school and her sister, Miss Fanny Harcourt Poulton was Matron at the Bute (1904–25). Each House at LHS adopted a particular charity relevant to their patroness; for example, Curie raised funds for cancer charities. Nightingale focused initially on Luton Children's Sick and Convalescent Home (Luton Children's Hospital in 1931) and the deprived children and orphans at the Beech Hill Homes and, after 1933, the Winsdon Girls' Home.

Relatively few LHS girls took up medicine; more entered training for the professions allied to medicine, such as physiotherapy, radiography, speech or occupational therapy, chiropody and pharmacy. For many years only small grants were available for these, but in nurse training, a small salary was paid and board and lodging was provided. Girls from all social classes became nurses, but it was a more feasible option for the less financially secure. Although some old girls occasionally gave information about their new careers, there was little formal advice about which of the caring professions to join or where to train. As the Bute was not a nurse training school, most girls opted for one of the large teaching hospitals in London or the provinces. When they began training they moved from one female dominated society to another. Until the permissive society, nurses were required to live in nurses' homes and, if they got pregnant or married in training, were usually required to resign.

The *Sheaf* gives a glimpse of some nursing careers in the period 1919–66, but there are, unfortunately, no exact quantitative data regarding numbers, places where they trained or their subsequent careers. What is known is that earlier links between LHS and local hospitals, fostered by the friendship between Miss Sheldon and Miss Redman, Matron of the Bute (1928–39) and the Luton and Dunstable Hospital (L&D) (1939–49), benefited LHS girls as a new opportunity for training locally began in 1939. On 14th February, Miss Sheldon was proud to be the only LHS representative in Ward 1 at the L&D where the official opening ceremony of the new hospital by Queen Mary took place although about 400 LHS girls helped to line the royal route.

In September 1939, the same month war was declared, the L&D became an approved training school for female nurses. That year, Miss Sheldon wrote a farewell to girls leaving in the *Sheaf* and mentioned Joyce Gingell, a Harpenden girl, who was 'so gentle and friendly'. Following general nurse training at the L&D (1940–43), she went to Oxford to take an orthopaedic nursing course. Miss Redman who, like Miss Sheldon, took a kindly interest in many girls, wrote to Joyce there in 1944 'I could not be more satisfied had you been my daughter'.

During the Second World War, LHS teachers and pupils took first aid courses and it appears that more girls than usual entered nursing in 1941 and 1942, perhaps, because 140 local people had been injured and 59 people killed when the worst air raid on the town took place on 30th August 1940. First-aiders were in demand for the wounded, although the seriously injured were conveyed to the L&D, which was almost overwhelmed. Towards the end of the war there seems to have been a VI Nursing class as the prize was won by B. Hine in 1946. She was also awarded School Honours.

In September 1953, LHS began a new scheme for six girls, selected from local secondary modern schools, to take up nursing. They entered the fifth form aged 15 years and in the three years at school took O-levels and Human Biology A/O level, which exempted them from the GNC State Preliminary Examination, Part I. These girls, in particular, are known to have flourished educationally and psychologically due to the tremendous support available to them. Although one girl was unable to become a nurse because of illness, the other five made the most of this wonderful opportunity.

It appears that most girls who took up nursing or midwifery enjoyed a worthwhile career. One who did very well was Shirley Jones (Phillips) who left at the end of the fifth form in 1966 to undertake cadet nursing at the L&D. This included compulsory day release to Luton College of Further Education. Following nurse training, marriage, midwifery training and a move to the Midlands, she continued her career.

> To cut a long story short, I went back to work as a Midwifery Sister on day duty for 2 years while I gained more O levels and was accepted onto the Advanced Diploma in Midwifery. I passed and then undertook a full time year of a joint course – the Cert Ed (FE) with the professional body teaching qualification in midwifery.
>
> Soon after that I joined the Birmingham and Solihull College of Midwifery as a tutor ... along the way I published a book *Ethics in Midwifery* in 1994, the first of its kind in midwifery ... In October 2001, I became Head of the School of Women's Health Studies in the University of Central England, then in February 2001, I had my professorship conferred upon me.

Professor Shirley Jones had a difficult start at the High School on account of illness. However, that did not prevent her from making a success of her life and she has this advice:

> young people should not be written off if, for some reason, they do not perform as well as originally expected. All I needed was to be in an area where I felt I belonged ... which then developed my self-esteem and confidence, and I have not looked back ... I also acknowledge that I was lucky to have been in the right place at the right time, with someone who listened to what I had said and helped me follow my leanings.

By the end of the twentieth century, nursing and midwifery students had moved into higher education; they were no longer 'pairs of hands', but predominantly students. With a greater knowledge base, they were capable of new and challenging rôles.

Health Services

Radiographers
The first radiographer to be noted in the *Sheaf* (1950) was Margaret Holland (Green) and in 1963 three former students qualified at the Luton and Dunstable Hospital. They were Jill Symonds, Susan Willett and Mary Copperwheat (Pearce). In 1956 Wendy Tomlin wrote about her experiences.

The theoretical work entails a detailed knowledge of anatomy and physiology, some physics, and a working knowledge of the apparatus being used … Radiography is essentially a practical subject whose requirements, besides scientific School Certificate, are tact, sympathy, gentleness, a tape measure, a plumb-bob, a marked pair of scissors and last, but not least, a sense of humour; anyone with all these qualities, plus strength, a straight eye and conversational ability with difficult private patients will be welcome anywhere – especially in radiography.

Almoner

Jean Farmborough (Osborn) described the work of an almoner (1956).

Before actually commencing work in a hospital one must obtain a social science diploma at one of the universities. This course takes two years, and consists of practical work as well as theoretical.

Whilst I was a student at the London School of Economics and Political Science I spent one month in a residential children's home looking after small boys, another month in the almoner's department at the Luton and Dunstable Hospital and finally two months working with a family welfare agency in London …

An almoner's work is really concerned with the personal problems connected with illness that trouble the individual patient and may hamper his recovery. Her function first and foremost is to help in the treatment of the patient, and to do this she must work as a member of a team and co-operate effectively with doctors and other members of the medical staff.

The work is definitely varied – interviews are carried out in the Out-Patients Clinics, on the wards and sometimes in the patient's own home. As a result of one interview it may be necessary to buy a dressing gown for a patient who cannot afford to do so, as he has four young children at home to look after. After another interview, perhaps, there will be arrangements to make for young baby to be temporarily looked after whilst his mother comes into hospital.

Apart from variety in the work, an almoner also has the opportunity of meeting people from all walks of life, and finding out about their different modes of living.

Pharmacist

During the early years of the twentieth century, training in pharmacy could take place in a chemist's shop. Ida Mason, who started at the School in Park Square in 1905, left to become a chemist's apprentice and two dispensers are noted in the 1933 Sheaf. Paddy Barber studied under the Boots scheme in the 1930s but left during the war to join the armed services.

Caring Occupations

In 1924, M. Benney was training to be a Norland children's nurse, a very highly respected occupation. By 1950, the care of children was becoming more complex. The *Sheaf* noted that Phyllis Ride was, 'after leaving Girton, taking a course at the London School of Economics with a view to becoming a Children's Officer'.

In 1968, Rosamond Hayward (Lane), together with her husband Reginald, started the Dunstable and District Handicapped Persons Typing Club in Dunstable. This is believed to be the only group of its kind in the country and has been successful in giving handicapped people confidence and typing skills for the last thirty-six years. Since 1973, they have organized accommodation, transport and carers for an annual holiday. There are regular outings, for example to garden centres, and a church service is held each year. In 2000, Rosamond and Reginald Hayward were each awarded the MBE for their services to the community.

In 1970, Betty McKean (Hickman) joined the committee of Luton Churches Housing Ltd. – a housing association formed in the sixties because of a widespread concern over lack of housing in Luton and the growing feeling that churches should be involved in social problems. From a small beginning with less than 20 units, the association now has over 400 units and is instrumental in helping many people in housing need – families, single homeless people, unmarried mothers and senior citizens needing sheltered accommodation. In 2002 the association changed its name to Luton Community Housing Ltd to reflect its wider, community aims and its determination to remain an independent locally based housing association meeting local needs. Since 2000, Betty has been Chairman of the Board and, in 2003, was honoured by an invitation to a Buckingham Palace Garden Party in recognition of her work for the association.

Margaret Rowley (Marsom) also pursued a career in the caring services. In the early 1950s, she graduated from the London School of Economics with a degree in Social Science and Social Administration and spent her working life in Community Development. She was, for a time, Executive Officer of Luton Council for Voluntary Service.

Judi Rowe (1966–69) recently wrote a letter to the *Luton News*, with the aim of making contact with girls who had been at the High School and Sixth Form College with her (1969–70). She is now working in a home for abandoned children in Nairobi, Kenya.

Josephine Wrighton (Figgins) has contributed a great deal of time and energy to the community. She is a Trustee at the Pasque Hospice, a non-executive member of Luton Primary Care Trust and a founder member (1989) of Luton Hospice at Home and, for 14 years, she has been Magistrate in the town.

Jennifer Moody (Southgate) attended the School between 1944 and 1950. She hoped to become a nurse but, after raising a family, took up social work. She opened a refuge for abused women in Luton which was visited by HRH Princess Diana. Later, she was invited to take lunch at Luton University with HM The Queen and HRH Prince Philip. After 'a tussle with her conscience' she accepted the award of MBE which she received from the Prince of Wales.

So, there I was, accepted into the hallowed halls of Luton High School for Girls … It did not take long before I blotted my copy book. VJ Day came; a big celebration was arranged for us all to go in fancy dress. Having just been told about the bomb being dropped on Hiroshima and then on Nagasaki, I really did not see what cause there was for celebration and said so. I would not go to the ball. My parents were called up in front of the formidable Miss Sheldon. How dare they allow their daughter actually to have thoughts of her own? She was considering expulsion. Somehow an agreement was reached and I was talked into going, as a pretty little butterfly. That episode, I feel in lots of ways, set the scene for my life, clearing for me what is truly meant by compassion, equality and standing by one's own morals …

A direction that seemed to cover all my needs and my abilities became apparent. The need for abused women to have a voice and be treated more as equals, particularly when they were constantly being put down physically and mentally. So, against everyone saying it was too large a task and I would never be able to do it, I opened up the first refuge for abused women and their children in 1973. The main philosophy was to help women learn to value themselves, to take control of their lives and to become what they want to be. Sadly, I have learnt that you cannot help everyone but at least I could tell many stories where women have changed from being victims to survivors.

Through the 30 years, the organisation grew from one tiny refuge to five much larger ones catering for all ages, classes, colours and creeds, all being treated equally … Apart from the many 'gifts' that I have received, those of women saying we had turned their lives around, that they felt so much better about themselves and they now felt pride in their achievements, were other unexpected pleasures, meeting people I would never have dreamed of meeting, such as our President, Dame Cleo Laine …

The good bit about accepting public recognition was the wonderful letters and phone calls that I received; they were my true accolade … I think that I would like my epitaph to be just 'The woman who refused to take 'no' for an answer'.

Commerce, Civil and Diplomatic Services

Secretarial Skills

Office work was once the prerogative of boys but gradually girls moved into the business world, usually paying to learn their skills at private establishments such as

PLASTICS DIVISION

YOUR FUTURE NEEDS THOUGHT

So why not think about the Plastics Division of I.C.I. for stimulating and interesting jobs with excellent prospects to offer.

Opportunities exist in the laboratories of Welwyn Garden City for Laboratory Assistants, and there are openings for Shorthand Typists, Clerks and other Office Staff.

A 37½-hour five-day week, pension fund, profit-sharing scheme, and excellent restaurant facilities are coupled with opportunities to pursue a wide range of recreational activities.

For information about current vacancies write to:

The Personnel Manager,
IMPERIAL CHEMICAL INDUSTRIES LIMITED,
Plastics Division,
Bessemer Road,
Welwyn Garden City, Herts.

An advertisement for a Laboratory Assistant.

(1966 *Sheaf*)

Berridge's and House and Williams. A Commercial department was set up at the High School in 1930 although there is evidence to suggest that there were classes before that. Mary Owen (Rollings) still has the RSA bookkeeping certificate she was awarded in 1938 as 'a candidate of the Luton High School'.

In 1951 Audrey Hathaway was awarded an Institute prize by the Chartered Institute of Secretaries for the high standard of her work and Rowena Harris, having obtained a degree in French and undertaken secretarial training, went back to work in the office of her College, Bedford College in London.

In 1954, Patricia Morgan shared first place in the whole country in an RSA examination in shorthand with 120 w.p.m. She was awarded a silver medal. By 1958, she had increased her speed to 150 w.p.m. Brenda Cumberland also gained a silver medal for coming second in the country in an advanced typing examination. Margaret Macpherson was awarded the Luton and District Chamber of Commerce Prize (1958) for being the best student in office arts.

Thelma Salmon was employed (1957) at Salisbury, Central Africa, as Secretary to the Public Relations Adviser of the Rhodesian Selection Trust Group Copper Company and Joan Young (Siriett) wrote from Suva in Fiji (1959) to say that she was teaching commercial subjects at the girls' Grammar School to a class made up of Indians, Fijians, and 'part-Europeans'. She said that she obtained 'more work and results out of them than I ever got from an equivalent class at home, and it is a pleasure and a satisfying experience to teach them because they want to learn'.

Local Industry

In 1933, twenty-five former pupils were working at Electrolux Ltd, although the *Sheaf* did not state in what capacity. There were particular incentives for working there:

> Congratulations to Electrolux Ltd. for having their playing fields improved with a view to making hockey and netball pitches for their employees. Practices for both games are being held weekly, and we hear that our old girls are well to the fore. Twenty-five hold positions on the firm, so the High School is well represented!

By 1933 nine old girls were working at the General Post Office and others, Marjorie Thorn, Enid Lambert, Lorna Gladwin and Marjorie Warren, travelled to London to work. In fact, there were eventually so many girls commuting to London that the train they travelled on was dubbed the 'High School Express'. Others used the line to get to St Albans (1937) where Jessie Warren worked in a bank and Marjorie Pinney in Customs and Excise. By 1953, girls stretched their wings even further; Marjorie Sinfield, who was formerly working in Barclay's Bank, Luton, went out to a similar post in Melbourne.

In 1931, the Home department of the Civil Service was opened to women and the diplomatic service from 1946, although they still had to leave on marriage. In 1955, equal pay was accepted in principle.

The *Luton News* (27th June 1936) mentioned 'an unusual and outstanding achievement': three pupils of the High School gained the first three places in the district in the recent Civil Service examinations.

> The total marks gained by Dorothy Edwards was the second highest in all the provinces out of 581 candidates, while Dorothy was also placed second of all candidates in handwriting with 86 per cent marks; her fellow scholars, Margaret [Giddins] and Joyce [Round] gained 75 per cent and 79 per cent respectively.

Libraries

Helen Gething (Slater) who attended the High School between 1937 and 1945, was a librarian and explains here how changes have taken place over the years.

> Pre-war there were two ways to become a Librarian. One way was to go to work in a Library and do the exams by Correspondence, taking many years. The alternative was to go to London University for a two-three year course in Librarianship. Either of these then qualified one to apply to become an Associate of the Library Association and put ALA after one's name.
>
> I got a Saturday job at Leagrave Branch library and Miss Sheldon told the

Luton Librarian, Frank Gardner, of my ambition. He asked to see my Father and me and explained that because we were near the end of the war, a new system had been set up to train ex-service people as quickly as possible.

First of all, a preliminary exam had to be taken, after a period actually working in a Library. This was to give practical experience. Then there were about six courses in Librarianship at a number of Technical Colleges round the country, taking one year to achieve Associate of the Library Association (ALA) and a second year to become a Fellow (FLA).

I chose to go to Manchester College of Technology. In a way we were guinea pigs as this was only the second year of the Courses. There were six exams to be taken at the end of the year. This was really tough as they were over a mere three days which gave no time for revision in between. In the past, people had taken them one at a time, year by year, so this did not matter. Later, they spaced the exams over several days.

I passed three exams and failed three, but because of the way they were linked together, I had to resit five. I left after the first year and went back to Luton Library. Eventually I passed all the exams and then had to wait until I was 23 years old before they would give me the ALA. This made me a 'Chartered Librarian'. There was no obligation to go on to FLA.

I decided to specialise in Reference Library work and, when my parents moved to London, I got a post as Reference Library Assistant at Hampstead Library. Any further promotions depended on applying for vacancies. I left in 1952 to get married.

As long as I maintained my membership of the Library Association, I could continue to call myself a Chartered Librarian and could apply for a job in any library.

In the late 1960s, I wanted to help a friend to classify some books and files. I went to the local Library to get out some books on Cataloguing and Classification. The books I had originally studied were now referred to as 'classical'. The subject had become 'Information Retrieval'.

I realised that my knowledge was so out-of-date that no one would want to employ me. Life in the libraries had moved on beyond recognition with punched cards, then computers and information retrieval. So I let my membership to the LA drop.

In 1954, Mary Hamilton Hart gained a First Class degree in Latin with subsidiary Greek at London University. She then began a post-graduate course with a view to taking up University Librarianship. In 1959, it was noted that Grace Long (Cameron) became assistant county librarian in Leicester and, in the early 1960s, Margaret Holdstock was children's librarian at Luton Public Library after which she became Regional children's librarian for Buckinghamshire.

Trade, Light Industry and Retail

Luton was the centre of the hat trade, which, during the early days of the School's life, engendered much of the wealth of the town. A large proportion of girls who went to elementary schools spent their working lives in the industry and the early records indicate that some girls from the High School did the same. Many of the parents of girls who went to the Modern School in those early days were owners or managers of hat factories and it was not uncommon for daughters to join the family business. The School records show that other girls also entered the millinery trade.

Although this does not have a particular bearing on girls' employment, it is interesting to note that there were strong links between the High School and the Swedish firm of Skefko since several girls whose fathers came

Pretty heads *can* have reasoning brains!!
(1961 *Sheaf*)

to Luton as managers became pupils at the School. In 1950, one girl applied for a temporary post and was asked why High School girls did not usually look for work there. On reflection, the answer probably was that, at that time, such jobs were not on the unwritten, but nonetheless real, list of 'acceptable' occupations.

Shops were frequently family concerns and girls often left to help. Some of the first school records note that girls were working for costumiers, chemists, drapers and hairdressers, all no doubt considered to be 'respectable' occupations. Later lists add bakeries and confectioners. A former pupil recalled that T.A.E. Sanderson's daughters kept a teashop on Park Square and, in 1933, Mildred Stevens ran an attractive little tea-shop 'Whipsiderry', almost opposite Dunstable Town Hall. The cakes were reputed to be excellent and the *Sheaf* asked 'Why not drop in and taste? '

Jean Howatt (Preece) was a former pupil who set up in business herself. In 1953, she won first prize in the Professional Florists' Class for a bouquet of flowers at the

Evening News Flower Show at Olympia. Ten years later she obtained a Diploma of the Society of Florists, the highest award for her craft. She gave a talk on her work at an Old Girls' meeting in October 1962.

Armed Forces

A CAREER IN THE W.R.A.C.
CAPTAIN JULIE MELVILLE, W.R.A.C.

A Career in the W.R.A.C. (1964 *Sheaf*)

A large number of boys from the Modern and Grammar Schools were conscripted into the armed services and, sadly, far too many of them lost their lives. The Girls' School has no boards in the corridors listing the names of the fallen but the call to support the war effort was still there. During the First World War girls in Luton worked in munitions factories and Pamela Stafford, who was admitted to the Modern School in 1905, worked in a Munitions Office. By 1939, attitudes had changed and girls were required to 'register' for work of national importance. Those without family commitments were called up for active service.

However, the armed forces attracted girls from the school long after hostilities had ceased. All three of the main women's services were represented and members served at home and abroad. The 1963 *Sheaf* noted two Old Girls who had joined the WRAF: Betty Moulton, a corporal, was enjoying life in Hong Kong where, besides having holidays for English festivals, they celebrated the Chinese, Muslim and Hindu festivals. Helen Lewis, who had taken a mathematics degree at London University, was a Flying Officer working in the educational side of the service.

Rita Lewis's career changed direction several times and, after teaching, she had the distinction of working for all three services.

> There was a job at a local RAF camp Swinderby so I applied to work for the Civil Service … Contractorisation by the government ended my time at Swinderby but I was recommend by the Commanding Officer for a job at Main Building of the Ministry of Defence in Whitehall … This meant dealing with extremely sensitive

government documents classified from confidential to Top Secret. I was security cleared, enabling me to deal with this material which had to be recorded and accounted for from the time it arrived on my desk until it was filed or destroyed … After the most exciting job of my life I was offered a transfer across the road to the Admiralty working in Naval Promotions … The Promotion Board sat in the Admiralty Boardroom with its beautiful carving and large compass on the wall … The Admiralty was a listed building and much of it was just as it had been in Nelson's day … One morning I was walking along Whitehall on my way to work when I heard this deafening bang. It seemed to come from across the road and as I looked two sausage shaped objects exploded out of the top of a white van parked on the corner in front of the main MOD building. They went over my head and then exploded – as I was later to learn in the garden of 10 Downing Street … All good things come to an end and when the Promotions department was transferred to Portsmouth I retired … I took a trip to Hong Kong and China and when I came home my retirement ended and new career began in the Crown Court. One bonus was that I was invited to cocktail parties on board naval ships on the Thames.

The Creative Arts

Here are just a few names but there must surely be many more former pupils who were successful in the field of the Arts.

Art

The *Sheaf* notes several successes: in 1955, Dorothy Walker had a painting hung in the Royal Academy and, two years later, Brenda Clark had two pictures hung in the 'Young contemporaries' Exhibition at the RBA Galleries, London. Over 40 pictures were sent in from her Art College, but only four were accepted, two of them hers.

The 1963 Luton Art Exhibition in Wardown featured oil paintings by Sylvia Mousley and Freda Mantz. Pauline Clarke, who was only 19 at the time, had a wood-engraving in the Royal Academy Exhibition in London in May 1964. The engraving, which was sold almost immediately, was of three dolls from the ballet *Petroushka*. Pauline and Freda also had some pictures in the Wardown Art Exhibition of 1964.

Writing

A career in journalism was possible from an early date. In 1928, Winifred Ball obtained a diploma in the subject from the London School of Economics. In 1936, Vera Day (Sharman), who had been a reporter for the *Luton News*, was congratulated on having stories broadcast under her pseudonym of Shamus O'Day. By 1952 Mary Paul (Bone) has replaced 'Krov' (Margaret Brown) as music critic at the *Luton News*.

The previous year she had won the British Amateur Mandolin Championship and, in 1958, gave a short talk on the BBC's *Woman's Hour*. Later, Margaret Brown took over the column again after Mary Paul moved to Liverpool where she wrote weekly humorous columns for the *Liverpool Daily Post* which she illustrated herself.

The 1955 *Sheaf* noted that June Gladman had had various pony stories accepted by a national children's newspaper, and had been asked to write a series. Eileen Hobbs took up a secretarial post in Northern Rhodesia and hoped to make a career in free-lance journalism. By 1962, Jane MacLatchy was working as a journalist in Perth, West Australia.

Music

Several Old Girls, as well as Mary Bone, made their name in the field of music. Mary Bass was a talented soprano who won prizes at many competitions and festivals. In 1955, she went to study at the Guildhall School of Music where she gained the Lord Mayor's Prize and also the Sydney De Vries Memorial Prize. In 1963, she became a member of the staff. Joyce Gillam also attended the Guildhall School of Music where she studied the violin.

Eileen Gaskin, a gifted pianist, studied at the Royal Academy of Music where she won the chief piano prize for her year. In 1955, she was made a Sub-Professor. She returned to the High School to give several recitals. Judith Henry studied violin at the Royal College of Music. Rosemary Ganderton and Wendy Router (Harrison) both won national awards for their mandolin playing.

The *Sheaf* (1964) noted that Beverly Smith has taught on several music courses (recorders) in England and France with the Dolmetsch family. She was awarded a Netherlands Government Scholarship and went to Amsterdam where she studied the recorder and the viola da gamba.

Marion Jones was a member of the Luton Girls' Choir for many years and, in the 1950s, was chosen by Sandy MacPherson to sing children's hymns on the regular Sunday morning radio programme *Chapel in the Valley*.

Theatre and The Media

By 1937 Thelma Payne and Lorna Gladwin were working at the BBC. In 1961 Patricia Pedder was in charge of one of the Photographic Libraries there. Acting also appealed. In 1955, Avril Roberts (Goring) was reported to have become the first woman producer of Luton's Community Theatre Movement. The 1957 *Sheaf* reported that Helen Wynter had gained a London University Diploma in Dramatic Art, the Central School of Speech and Drama's Teaching Diploma and the Sylvia Strutt Memorial Prize for Poetry Speaking. Valerie Bland worked with the Perth Repertory Company and the Bristol Old Vic. In 1963, she appeared in the ITV programme *Emergency Ward 10*.

Photography

Marjorie Thorn wrote to the *Sheaf* in February 1928.

> I believe I am the first Old Girl who has taken up photography, and so I hardly know how to begin to describe our work at the Regent Street Polytechnic. After the LMS the Photography School seems quite small, for there are only about forty students, in our class there are eleven girls and a solitary boy, the youngest of us all.
>
> Two periods a week we spend in the Studio, taking photographs of each other … Quite a long time is spent in practical work, making negatives, printing, enlarging and so on … Quite different from this is the 'finishing'. This includes 'retouching' negatives, to remove freckles, straighten noses, make the expression more pleasing, and generally to beautify the sitter's appearance. When the print is made there are often white spots or scratches upon it; these all have to be filled in with paint so that they are quite invisible, and it is not nearly as easy as it sounds!

In 1963, the *Sheaf* noted that Anne Simkins (Kathleen Thursby) had become an expert amateur photographer. 'Altogether, forty-seven trade-processed transparencies chosen from all over England, Scotland and Wales were shown at this Exhibition and Anne's success in having three entries included is a most remarkable achievement'.

Anne Simkins' prizewinning photograph, 1962 'Winter's Mantle'. (*Anne Simkins*)

(Anne's names may sound confusing but they remind us that the School had some kind of ruling, for a while at least, that girls should be known by their first Christian name. Anne was one of these.)

> Despite my protests of not being worthy of any space in this book, I had to give in to persuasion! Academically, I consider myself to be a failure when, during my year of dairy farming, prior to a course at an agricultural college, I became engaged to an arable farmer, cancelled college and began a hobby with cameras instead of a career with cows!
>
> Being a founder member of *The Shillington and District Camera Club* in 1960, photography became a more serious hobby with area and national competitions becoming the target for club members. Over a period of three years during the early 1960s, five of my colour transparencies were amongst 27 entries from all the East Anglian clubs to progress onto *The Photographic Alliance of Great Britain* exhibitions that were staged in nineteen cities.
>
> The photograph entitled *Winter's Mantle* was, as a colour slide, one of my three successful 1962 exhibits and, in 1964, it also won a competition organized by *University Cameras* in Luton, making it my own personal favourite then and still, to this day.
>
> On reflection, a career in photography would have suited me well though I cannot regret my 48 years of farming life.

Gardening

Danae Johnston (Wright) has used her creative skills to make a very beautiful garden which has won considerable acclaim. Every year in June, Old Girls from the High School gather for an evening in her garden and all of them can vouch for the fact that Danae's is indeed a very splendid garden. In 1999, she won the *Gardener of the Year* for the East and South of England in a competition organized by the BBC.

Sport

Here again, it is not possible to do justice to all the girls who have excelled in one kind of sport or another. Some went on to play in local teams, college teams and even county and national teams. The *Sheaf* noted some successes but there must have been more.

Margaret Smith was elected Captain of the Netball Team at Bedford College, University of London (1935).
Muriel Smith 'continues to add to her victories on the running track'.
Patricia Fussell obtained her hockey colours and a place in all the games teams at the Queen Alexandra Training College (1938).

Doris Scammell was Captain of Women's Hockey at Manchester University (1952).

While Deborah Kheifetz was at University College Hospital, she took up athletics and represented Middlesex in 'throwing the javelin'. Later, she became a Lieutenant in Queen Alexandra's Royal Army Nursing Corps (c.1955) and was Victrix Ludorum at one of their Annual Sports Days, being first in the 100 yards, discus, and javelin and third in the long jump.

Janice Swallow studied at Bart's Hospital in the 1950s. She represented the hospital and university at hockey while she was there and once played for an England side in Holland. She also played tennis for the hospital team.

Brenda Dodgson, in her final year at Bristol University, was Captain of the Women's Rowing Club and saw her team win the Weybridge Challenge Cup and obtain full rowing colours – the first time Bristol University has achieved this (1961).

Beryl Harrison, who left the High School in 1946, played County hockey for 18 years and captained Bedfordshire for many seasons. She became a County Selector in the early 1960s and later a Selector for the Midlands Counties Women's Hockey Association and match secretary from 1973 until 1978.

Susan Morgan studied mathematics at St Hilda's College Oxford, and won a University Hockey Blue (1963).

Jane Clark, who studied at Bart's, was captain of the women's team in tennis and lacrosse (1964).

Domestic Science

Zena Skinner, who spent some of her school life at the High School, has carved out a career for herself as a cookery expert. In 1958, she became an overseas cookery demonstrator for the General Electric Company and completed extensive tours in Africa and in the West Indies. At the time, she specialised in demonstrating electric cookers and other appliances to native women. Between 1959 and 1989 she was a well-known contributor on television cookery shows, such as *Looking at Cooking*, *Know Your Onions* and *Ask Zena Skinner*. She also talked to Her Majesty the Queen at Sandringham. Zena took part in radio programmes, for example, *Start the Week with Richard Baker* and was interviewed on *Desert Island Discs*. Her articles have appeared in the *Radio Times*, *The Listener*, in other magazines and in local papers and she has 13 cookery books to her name.

Jean Gillis studied Domestic Science at the National Training College and became (1950) the Assistant Cookery Demonstrator and Home Service Adviser with the Gas Company in Luton.

Melita Neal was head of the Domestic Science Department at Dunstable College of Further Education and published textbooks on cookery and needlework (1962).

Law

It seems that Constance Mott (Craddock), one-time secretary of the Old Girls Association, was the first former pupil to study law.

> Since her marriage, Constance Mott has lived in Kenya, where her husband is a farmer … She has built up a flourishing practice as a barrister, specialising in property cases and International Law: this is a much-needed line in Kenya, where there are people of many nationalities, who often own property in the original countries as well as in their new country. (1956)

In 1961, the *Sheaf* noted that 'as far as we know, Maureen MacGlashan is only the second Old Girl to obtain a degree in Law' and reported that she was one of only two successful women, out of five thousand candidates, who took the relevant examination for entry into the diplomatic service. She received the honour of Companion of the Most Distinguished Order of St Michael and St George which is awarded for services to British interests abroad, particularly in the Diplomatic Service.

> In my day (1949–56) the employment of choice for women was still perceived to be marriage.
>
> After leaving LHS at Christmas 1956, I spent a couple of terms teaching before going to Girton College Cambridge to study law (BA 1960) and international law (LLM 1961). I then entered the Foreign Office. My posts included Tel Aviv (6-day war), East Berlin (setting up the new embassy), Brussels (UK Presidency of the EEC), Belfast (hunger strikes), Bucharest (Ceausescu), Belgrade (Milosevic) and finally (as British Ambassador) the Holy See. Along the way, I also worked in the Cabinet Office Think Tank (on such things as regional policy, vandalism, planning policy) and spent two years pre-retirement, four post-retirement selecting candidates for entry to the senior branch of the Civil Service. I also spent four years in the 1980s setting up the Research Centre for International Law in Cambridge. Since retirement in 1998, in addition to selection work for the Civil Service and now also for the Anglican Church, I have been more or less a full time indexer, specializing in law books. I am currently President of the Society of Indexers.

Sciences

Teaching and research

Girls who studied for science degrees often went on to become teachers. Jean Godfrey, a former head prefect at the High School and the daughter of second master at the Grammar School, studied science at Cambridge. Her sister, Mrs R.W.

Crosskey, taught science at the High School before joining her husband, an entomologist, in Nigeria. Other graduates went on to do scientific research. Doreen Boston passed the final examination in Bacteriology of the Institute of Medical Laboratory Technology and worked (1959) in the public health department of the Luton and Dunstable Hospital (1959), Rosemary Fiddick gained a B.Sc. in Biochemistry at Sheffield University and then did post-graduate work on the blindness which can develop in diabetics (1964) while Ann Terry, former Keller House Captain, did veterinary work (1965) at Sandwich in Kent for Pfizers. Paula Allsopp (Groom) now works at Onderstepoort Research Institute in South Africa.

> The school was unashamedly élitist, but aimed at bringing out the best qualities in everyone, no matter what their abilities. Science studies were particularly emphasised, perhaps because Eileen Evans was a scientist herself, but as I had been interested in things scientific from an early age, this just served to push me to find out more and ended with my studying chemistry – a far cry from what I am now doing, which is identifying intracellular pathogens of ruminants in a veterinary research establishment. My particular field and one which fascinates me and at which I am recognised as an expert, at least in the USA, is detection and molecular characterisation of some of the many as yet unknown tick-borne organisms affecting both domestic animals and wildlife, some of which cause disease and may even, under exceptional circumstances, be pathogenic to humans. These things occur in Europe too, so watch it if you go walking in the forests of Spain or other wild places where there are ticks.
>
> [Paula Allsopp (Groom)]

Technicians

There were others who chose to follow a scientific curriculum in the VI Form and then found employment as laboratory technicians. For example, Eve Middleton-Jones passed examinations to become a Laboratory Technician and (1954) 'hoped to work in the International Health Organisation at Geneva'. Gwendoline Lintern was a medical laboratory technician at Paddington General Hospital for three years and then emigrated to Canada to take up a similar post at Vancouver General Hospital (1955). It appears that local firms, such as Electrolux, would contact High School staff who then matched jobs to girls. Rothamstead Research Establishment in Harpenden also looked for girls with a scientific background. Elizabeth Carlisle worked there (c.1950) and seems to have become a specialist in the study of bees.

Verna Steward explained that the Careers Officer at the High School recommended her to apply to the Services Electronics Research Laboratory, a Naval Scientific Research Establishment. She went on day release to study Physics. 'My job (1953) then was concerning new semi conductor materials, some of which were at that time being invented, and my career was mainly crystal growth, and assessment of materials'.

Agriculture and Horticulture

Girls sometimes chose to study at these colleges before or after working on the land. Frances Hills went (c.1936) to Swanley Horticultural College. Jocelyn Randall did a year's practical work on a farm at Markyate, before going to Studley Agricultural College (1954). The 1957 *Sheaf* noted that she had gained a Diploma in Dairying and became 'assistant herdswoman to a championship herd of Guernsey cows'. Josephine Burton received the same Diploma from the same College and then worked for United Dairies as a bacteriologist. In 1957, Elizabeth Toyer gained her National Certificate in Agriculture and was awarded Landsman's Prize for first place. She specialized in cattle work.

Engineering

Over the years, opportunities began to widen. Wendy Phillips gained her Ordinary National Certificate in Mechanical Engineering (1957) with a distinction in mathematics. Judith Rogers obtained a Diploma in Technology in Applied Physics, at the Northampton College of Advanced Technology in London. She was one of the first Old Girls to obtain graduate status (1963) by means of a 'sandwich course' working some of the time in industry and some of the time in college. As part of her degree course, she had to build a computer.

Penelope Dudley and Beryl Hulley were the first girls to become apprentices (1959) in the engineering section of Hunting Aircraft. Penelope became the first girl to win a prize, the Lawes Rabjohns Prize, for technical drawing. By 1961, Beryl Hulley, having worked her way through the test laboratory and drawing office, was in the aerodynamics section. Penelope Dudley was awarded a silver medal under the portal scheme, one of the

---

THE ENGLISH ELECTRIC AVIATION LTD.

(*A Member Company of the British Aircraft Corporation*)

THE AIRPORT, LUTON

*can offer varied and interesting careers
to girls leaving school this Summer.*

The positions available include:-

Laboratory Technicians - for which an 'A' level in Mathematics and Physics is required. Opportunities for promotion to engineer status are available to girls who obtain a Higher National Certificate in either Electrical/Electronic or Mechanical Engineering.

Mathematical Assistants - An 'A' level in Mathematics at least is required for entry into this grade and there are splendid opportunities for girls with real ability to progress to a Senior post in this grade.

Computers - these positions require an 'O' level in Mathematics, Physics, English and preferably two other subjects. Opportunities are available for promotion to the Mathematical Assistant grade.

Engineering Apprenticeship - girls with 'A' level passes in Mathematics and Physics will be considered for a student apprenticeship and those with 'O' level in Mathematics, Physics and English with two additional subjects for entry as Technician Apprentices.

If you wish to discuss the possibilities of a career with this Company, please write for an appointment for interview to the Senior Personnel Officer at the above address.

Careers in Industry. (1961 *Sheaf*)

highest awards given to employees of firms within the British Aircraft Association.

Janice Hawkins, after taking a degree in mathematics, studied aeronautics at Southampton University – the only girl in the class (1964).

Sandra Ringrow (Kennedy) was employed in one of the major international automotive design agencies and, later, Jaguar Cars.

Meteorology

Aileen Martin (née Mann) … worked (1964) in the Meteorological Department of Northern Rhodesia as an Aviation Forecaster at Livingstone Airport, the only woman of that rank.

Politics

By the 1950s the *Sheaf* was reporting the activities of former pupils who were working for the different political parties. Rhona Turnbull (Backshall) was appointed a Justice of the Peace in South Shields and others were involved in local politics. Constance Dunham (Young) became a governor of the School (1962).

Most notable was Barbara Andrews (Aylott) who, in 1959, was the first Old Girl to become Mayor of Luton. The *Sheaf* reported that 'in this high office, Mrs Andrews has been conspicuously successful, and has shown both dignity and charm'. At the School's fortieth anniversary service in the Parish Church in October 1959, Mrs Andrews read the lesson. She was also the guest of honour at the Anniversary Luncheon in November and her 'lively speech must have brought back many memories to all who were in The Huts'. In 1962, she was awarded an OBE in the New Year's Honours List and was thought to be the first Old Girl to receive the honour. The editors of the *Sheaf* congratulated her heartily on the award 'which she so richly deserves because of her many public services'.

Travel and Tourism

In the 1950s, travel became easier and many girls took up careers as Air Hostesses. Others trained to work in hotels. Dawn Moore was given a £100 grant for foreign travel as student of the year at Westminster Technical College (1962). She was the top girl in the Hotel School, and was working as a receptionist at Ariel Hotel, London Airport. In 1963 she went to study at the University of Tours and planned to go on to the Bordeaux vineyards to learn about wine.

Jeannette Games (1964), after studying at the Westminster Hotel School, worked in hotels in London, Copenhagen and Paris. She was able to speak some French, German, Danish and Italian, and her ambition was to manage an hotel. Jean Merry worked as part of the editorial staff of the firm which produced 'the ABC of Airway Travel' (1955).

Various

The 1933 *Sheaf* included congratulations to Alweena Hafner who set up a practice in Luton for massage, Swedish remedial exercises, medical electricity, light and electro-therapy. She had become 'bio-physical assistant to the Chartered Society of Massage and Medical Gymnastics'. Freda Currant had intended to follow in her footsteps but unfortunately died at a young age.

Gill Sentinella (Horley) studied to work with silver at Sheffield. (late 1960s)

Olive Gouldthorpe became president of the Luton Esperanto Society (1951).

Hazel Dunham was winning prizes in International Motor Races, including one in the Monte Carlo Rally (1953).

Patricia Hully had a varied career: within a period of five or six years, she had been a police woman, a BOAC air hostess, and a secretary in Geneva with the finance department of the WHO (1963).

Dianne Parker (Ogglesby) began her working life interpreting and translating in Spanish and French but has, for many years, been a professional driving instructor in the driving school which she runs with her husband.

Opportunities for Changing Direction

For a reunion in 1996, girls who attended the High School between 1961 and 1966 completed Curricula Vitae forms. These figures, gathered from the forms, are not mathematically precise but they do give a reasonable impression of the career choices former pupils in this year group have made.

Girls who worked in education topped the list (21) and were followed by those in financial establishments (14). Next came those working as secretaries (13), in nursing (9) and the Civil Service (5). There was considerable representation from former pupils working in modern careers like management (4), the media (3) and IT (2). Then there was an accountant (1), a driving instructor (1), an air traffic controller (1), workers in aviation (2) and charity workers (1). Laboratory work, local government, pharmacy, engineering, languages, travel and agriculture and gardening were represented. Significantly, 25 girls had had varied careers and 15 had gone on to further study.

Emigration

The *Sheaf* magazine has pages of announcements from abroad and letters from former pupils who had made their homes across the seas. There were some who seemed to suffer from wanderlust, even in the days before a 'gap year' became an accepted way of life. In the early days, it was frequently noted that it was the husband of a former pupil who had emigrated but soon girls were making their own decisions.

Missionary work or voluntary service was often the motivation but jobs in teaching, nursing or commerce seem to have been easy to find. No doubt a 'good education' such as the High School gave, helped many a girl to find employment.

In the dying days of the Empire, people from the 'mother country' were welcome in countries which still owed allegiance to the Crown. America was also popular and mention was made of girls living in Europe and South America. The list of countries compiled from the 1996 CVs is similar but there are significant differences. With the setting up of the European Union, countries in that group seem to appeal. So do the Gulf States.

In 1962, Hilary Hawkins (Thompsett) and her husband were responsible for all the teaching of Science at a school in Ghana. The labs were wonderful but the equipment consisted only of one Bunsen burner and a flask or two. They found that the Ghanaian language had no equivalent for scientific words. They also mentioned that all the water for the school and for their bungalow had to be brought in by lorry twice a week, 'so the weekly bath is an event'.

In the same year Jean Faikesch (March), who was married to an Austrian, wrote to describe her life in Vienna, especially the problems she encountered when shopping before she became proficient in German.

Margaret Bradley returned home in 1964, having spent a year in Uganda, working with Voluntary Overseas Association, at a place on the shores of Lake Victoria. She had been running clubs, teaching English, and generally making herself useful to the native population.

Margaret Lincoln (Scuse) wrote to describe her career which, she notes, turned out to be more interesting than the one she had first envisaged. Her account is interesting because it demonstrates that, although women have been glad to shake off the label of domesticity, the responsibilities of family life do not have to be burdensome but can be a joy.

> I left the Luton Sixth Form College with excellent A levels and got a place to study at the then swinging new University of Sussex. At the age of 22, I was given a BA First in German Studies and set up with a three year grant to write a Ph.D in the field of Comparative Literary Studies, my visions fixed on one day attaining academic fame or at least some comfortable chair as professor in some not too remote university. The fact that I married a fellow student, who had similar ambitions to mine, and that we had in the course of our studies managed to produce two daughters did not at first deter me from my course. In fact, quite the contrary. We were both young, living at a time when, at least in the student world, women and men were equal, and on the basis of this sense of equality we decided to share the rearing of our children, dividing our time between library and home, each of us acquiring an allotted amount of time to pursue work on our separate Ph.Ds. However, what I had not envisaged was the pull of the maternal instinct in

me. Almost imperceptibly the time allotted for my study got less as I began to see my priority to be more and more with my children rather than with my studies, these living creatures with their immediate needs rather than with the minds and writings of poets long since dead. There were also two quite pragmatic reasons for the shift. Firstly, on the basis of the shared arrangement, neither I nor my husband were actually progressing very far with our research. Secondly, it was the 'reign' of Margaret Thatcher, who doggedly pursued a policy of reducing, even eliminating, unprofitmaking university departments. I could see my dreams of a quiet professorship slowly but surely diminish. My grant was coming to an end. One of us would need to earn some money. I decided to do a postgraduate course in teaching. If the worst came to the worst I could teach German to secondary school kids.

In 1977, though, we followed an invitation to Germany to teach English at the University of Münster. The idea was to stay for just two years and then return to England. These two years have become 26 years. In these years I have been teaching free-lance mainly at adult educational centres and at universities, I have given birth to two more daughters, written a book on German poetry and helped my husband as a voluntary worker to set up an advice centre, which is also a school and a café to help the integration of foreigners coming to Hamburg. I now have a permanent post in an adult education centre in Hannover, teaching a variety of courses which I have developed myself.

Thinking about it, I have had a really interesting career, as mother, as wife, as free-lance writer, teacher and social worker and I must say I don't regret a minute of it.

So many Old Girls have contributed towards the production of this book and sincere thanks are due to them all. There are articles and poems from the *Sheaf* which were written while the School was alive and flourishing. Then there are the many reminiscences which were specially written. However, Sally Siddons (Overhill), who was at the School between September 1957 and July 1962, has had a special part to play, for it has been her responsibility to turn all the initial text into a published book. It seems highly appropriate that this should have fallen to the lot of another High School girl.

After achieving O levels, I took up a career in banking, which lasted 12 years. I retired from the bank to bring up my family of three sons and, several years later, the opportunity came to work at *The Book Castle*. At this time *The Book Castle* had just ventured into the world of publishing, specialising in local interest titles. In the early days my tasks were numerous, from serving in the shop to being a sales rep. out on the road. My boss, Paul Bowes, then invited me to be more involved in the publishing of the books rather than the selling. This meant understanding

IT to the extent of dealing with graphic designers, print companies, and mainly the authors who vary from young football fans to octogenarians who have written their life story in long hand. Definitely, for me, one of the most enjoyable parts of the job is making new friends of all the authors and contacts I meet in the course of a day's work. Hence my life has come full circle; I have contributed to this book and am also responsible for the production of it. In conclusion I have to say that any publishing errors are possibly my fault, so please excuse!

RIGHT A career in Banking.
(1966 *Sheaf*)

Old Girls

A Report in the *Sheaf* (1947) described the life of the Old Girls Association which was inaugurated at a meeting held on 1st June 1921. 'It was decided to hold one meeting in each term of the school year, and this procedure has been continued to the present day'.

The activities of the Association included functions for charitable purposes and social welfare in the town. One of the most successful annual events was the Dance, the first of which was held in 1928. Dances continued without a break except for the war years. Since the early days, many former pupils have worked hard, as presidents, secretaries or treasurers, to ensure that the Association continued to flourish, but particular mention must be made of Janette Scanes. Anne Simkins has written an appreciation of her work which, incidentally, also included typing up lists of games fixtures over the years.

To think of the Luton High School *Old Girls' Association* without Janette Scanes seems impossible for those of us who have continued their support of the

Old Girls' Social Evening 1953. Miss Macnab was presented with a cheque and life membership of the Old Girls' Association. (*LN*)

Association but sadly she died, aged 86, in April 2003.

Janette left the High School in 1935 having been a prefect and school captain of netball and tennis. She was an Honorary Treasurer of the Old Girls from 1949 until 1968, when she was elected on to the first committee of the newly formed *Old Lutonians Club* of which she became President for the 1971–1972 year, yet still keeping together the *Old Girls' Association*.

Thanks to Janette's efforts as our unofficial secretary and treasurer, there has been an annual June 'get-together' since 1967.

Following her death, a letter was sent to all those who had supported the meeting over the past four years, inviting them to the 2003 'get-together' as a special tribute to Janette. A wonderful summer evening was enjoyed by 42 'Old Girls' who met up with friends whilst taking in the delights of Danae's garden. Without Janette's dedication over the years, this annual reunion would, I am sure, not have taken place. We will always remember her friendly and happy presence at our meetings and hope that, in her memory, they may long continue.

Maureen Hawkes wrote a piece for the *Sheaf* in 1962 in which she explained that the Old Girls' Association was not just a crowd of old dears reminiscing about the 'good old School in our day, and criticizing the modern generation'.

How often have I heard this remark? It was with no great enthusiasm that I went along to my first meeting of the Association, and maybe it was only the thought of a free swim that finally persuaded me! I soon realised how wrong I was. They are certainly not old dears (at least the majority are not!). They are extremely active in organising the Association's meetings and outings etc. …

At my first meeting a speaker from the BBC gave us a very entertaining informal talk about his job and the inevitable incidents occurring in sound radio and television. We were then escorted by Mrs Evans round the new Science Block and covered Swimming Pool. There were certainly no cries of 'the good old days' then, only of envy! The Pool looked wonderfully inviting, and everyone was very pleased to hear that members of the Association would be able to use the Pool every Wednesday evening throughout the year. I should think that in itself is more than sufficient incentive to join the Association. Also the Tennis Courts can be used on certain evenings during the season, and there is Badminton in the Gymnasium during the winter …

For the really 'sports-minded' there are the annual Hockey, Netball and Tennis matches against the School, which always produce great rivalry, but are nevertheless very much enjoyed.

Then for everyone, particularly the less energetic, there are the theatre visits and outings organised by the Committee.

Photograph of Janette Scanes (left) and Beryl Harrison (right), June 1993. (*Anne Simkins*)

Reunions

Recently several reunions have been organized. This one, which took place in November 1989, was organized by Pauline Keen (Moore).

> Everyone seemed to recognise someone they knew and it went from there … Background music was eventually turned off after being drowned by the 66 former students catching up on the last thirty years … One former pupil came from the British West Indies to catch up on who's done what. Other guests came from Cornwall and Scotland … Friendships were rekindled and addresses were swopped in the school hall – now known as Denbigh High School … You could almost feel the satchel on your shoulders.   [*The Citizen* Nov 9th 1989]

Patricia Gillespie (Evans) has described a gathering of the Class of 1947.

> September 1997 was approaching! Would it really be fifty years ago that I, with my peers aged eleven, embarked upon 'the ways of learning' at the Luton High School for Girls? Why not celebrate with a reunion – at Alexandra Avenue? In hopeful anticipation the School Hall was booked.
>
> Then began the search! Almost miraculously, by advertisement, by word of mouth, through the small groups of friends that had stayed in touch over the years, through chance encounters (selling flags for charity outside Sainsbury's!) the message spread and about one hundred contemporaries were traced – many still living locally, others in all corners of the United Kingdom and some as far afield as Australia, New Zealand, Germany, Canada and Spain.
>
> At 2.00 p.m. on Saturday 5th 1997 some fifty friends began to gather. There was an air of excitement and, understandably, a little apprehension. Would we recognise each other? What would we find to talk about? Would the old school building have changed out of recognition? In the event, the years rolled away and the ice melted as Yours Truly, dressed in her school uniform, greeted the guests, stimulating the laughter and happiness that became the hallmarks of the afternoon as we retraced the 'roads we trod together' and discovered 'where the ways of learning' had taken us.
>
> Firstly a 'do you remember this?' session chatting over memorabilia – reports, tradition cards, the long photos, sports achievements, even the House shield – indeed 'the records as we wrote them'! Then a tour of the buildings, guided so sympathetically by a member of the Denbigh High School Staff. We were amazed, and somewhat comforted, by how little had changed in the 'E'-shaped block and wondered enviously at the covered swimming pool (it was freezing in our day!) as well as the new science facilities. Next, out through the main doors for a souvenir photo on the front steps.

Reunion in October 1989 of girls who started at the High School in Sept 1956. *(Pauline Moore)*

The strains of Trumpet Voluntary welcomed us back into the Hall for afternoon tea, the highlight of which was a celebration cake, decorated with the School badge, kindly donated by the late Miss Laurie Fuller and cut on the day by the late Miss Betty Read, who was form-mistress to some of us in 1R. We were pleased that Miss Christina Scott was also able to share the occasion with us.

Finally we assembled at the foot of the stage to sing the School Song. Despite many a tear in the eye and a catch in the voice, the rendering was lusty as we felt that we too had 'come rejoicing with our sheaves'.

All too quickly our celebration was over but its memories live on in photos and the video made and subsequently sold in aid of the Children's Hospice here in Luton. Its memories live on too in the friendships it rekindled and in the annual informal get-together that has taken place ever since at the beginning of October. Out there, somewhere, are others of our year group we would love to trace. Do get in touch via the Publishers of this book.

Reunion of the Class of 61–66, October 1996. (*Patricia Gillespie*)

Girls who joined the High School in 1951 were invited to a Reunion Lunch at Putteridge Bury on 8th September 2001. In the same year Shirley Hobbs discovered a photo of her class of 1949 and sent it to the *Luton News*, asking fellow pupils to get in touch. They decided to call themselves the 49ers and arranged a party with a birthday cake and even an arrangement of flowers in the school colours of maroon and gold. Between them, they have discovered what happened to 90 out of the 150 former pupils. 74 are on the mailing list for their newsletter. Most live in other parts of England but some are in America and Australia. They are keen to meet up again and find any schoolmates still not in touch.

Danae Johnston (Wright) continues to host the annual meetings which began with the Old Girls' Association.

'Old Girls' Today

As the LHS ceased to exist in 1967, many of us are now <u>really</u> old girls – but never say die! We continue to hold an annual social evening. This pleasant affair was started by Mrs Evans; she invited us to her charming period cottage in Barton in June each year for an evening of reminiscences and getting up-to-date with the lives of friends we rarely saw otherwise. Her garden was as attractive as her house – a real cottage garden and my rose-tinted memory does not recall any gatherings spoilt by rain. I do remember a pink tamarisk that was always in full bloom; waving its arms across the drive to welcome us. It was a bit like 'Brigadoon'; it did not exist for us apart from that magic June night.

When Mrs Evans' health began to fail, I volunteered my garden as the venue for our get together to ensure that we all stayed in contact with each other.

While the school was still the LHS an energetic nucleus of us were not satisfied with meeting once a year, we met every Wednesday up at school, in the summer. We swam and played tennis. In the dark months we borrowed the gym and played badminton. About a couple of dozen regularly supported these activities and great fun it was, although not many of us were hardy enough to use the pool before it was given walls and a roof!

It was all very casual – no rules – no lifeguards – just the caretaker rattling his keys to hurry us away at the end of the evening. Sadly, once the School became Denbigh High School, we were chucked out. For a while, Pauline Davis, who taught at the 'new' school, invited us to swim as her guests, but it rankled that we, who had helped to raise money to have the pool enclosed, were now officially excluded!

We were reluctant to give up our Wednesday night out and began to go to one or another's homes for coffee, biscuits and a gossip. As the years passed most of us were married and glad to leave the domestic scene for a while. We changed from talking about films and boy friends to good recipes and nappy rash. I recall one of our number wanting advice from the other mums about her baby son who woke her every night. She confided in us that she tried to settle him with a milky drink, a biscuit and a cuddle!! I can still hear the howl of laughter that greeted this disclosure. 'You give him milk and biscuits – no wonder he wakes up!'

Happy days. Now the topics are likely to be our ageing parents, or our own aches and pains. The twenty-four has dwindled to half a dozen regulars and two or three who come occasionally. We still meet on a Wednesday evening and our husbands who are convinced that they are the main subjects of our conversation (how wrong they are) call us the 'Mafia', a title we rather enjoy!

The June meetings attract around forty Old Girls who enjoy my garden if the weather co-operates. I do not seem to have Mrs Evans' luck, but the coffee and biscuits are consumed indoors, if need be, to the deafening noise of female voices, all talking at once. Although I have provided the place, Janette Scanes has been the driving force of these gatherings, rounding every one up and finding any more stray OGs to join in.

Brenda Tiley, Glynis Miles and Linda Litchfield have managed to contact most of the 'class of '66' as well as some former members of staff. This group has had several reunions.

It would seem from the letters we have received that you enjoyed the Reunion on 20th October (1996) and felt that the journeys you made, some of which were very long, were worthwhile. This gives us a lot of pleasure and makes all the organising worthwhile. We also understand that many of you have renewed friendships which had faded away, as these things often do through the ups and downs of life. We hope you will continue to keep in touch with each other, and with us … Wasn't it amazing that once we all started to sing, the words [of the school song] just came back.

The biggest reunion was probably the one which was held on 4th November 2000. It was organized by Mrs Kathy Green, Treasurer of the Denbigh Association, with the permission of the present Head teacher of Denbigh High School, Mrs Yasmin Bevan. This was to celebrate the 70th anniversary of the school building and was open to former pupils of both the Girls' High School and Denbigh High School. It was very well attended; in fact it was oversubscribed. The celebration took place in the School Hall. There were 'speeches, guided tours, a chance to look at a display of memorabilia, some entertainment, refreshments and a light buffet and, to round off, a grand firework display'. Kathy Green wrote afterwards that they sold over 400 tickets to ex-pupils and staff, who all seemed to be having a great time. Over 350 cups of tea and coffee were consumed and £282 was spent at the bar. There was immense interest in the display of photographs and much reminiscing about the past. A central feature of the day was the cutting of a birthday cake by Miss Mary Woods, a former pupil, head Girl and member of Staff at the Girls' School and Emily Pemberton, Head Girl of Denbigh High School in 2000.

The School may be no more but hundreds of us are very much alive and well.

An Assessment

So, was the High School a good school? The answer to that question is not straightforward because we can only judge a school in its historical context. By the standards of the early twentieth century, it was a pioneering school and, throughout its life, was well thought of in the educational world. Schools similar to Luton High School still exist in the private and grammar school systems and the prototype of girls' High Schools, the North London Collegiate School, is still hugely successful. However, much more is expected from schools in the twenty-first century and it is not at all useful to try to make comparisons.

The School was élitist on two counts. In its early life, it catered for the daughters of people in Luton who could afford to pay the fees and so a barrier was put up between them and most of the other girls in the town. A divide there most certainly was and High School girls were often viewed by other Luton schoolgirls in an unfavourable light. The other divide was based on academic ability and, later, intelligence testing but, when Luton adopted a comprehensive system of education, many were grieved for the demise of the town's 'centres of excellence'. However, others rejoiced and welcomed what they saw as a fairer way of life.

Whether or not it was a good school also depends on personal opinion. Some girls have said that they 'loved every minute'. Others were thoroughly unhappy.

Sometimes this was because of the exacting curriculum but many a girl with an individualistic streak rebelled against the strict regime and the conformity that was demanded. What would now be called 'life-skills' did not feature widely on the timetable but, to be fair, it is probably true to say that the School hoped to bring out the best in everyone.

One generally accepted observation is that there was very little constructive career advice and girls had to rely on their own initiative. It does seem strange that, considering the size of the School, it has been difficult to locate proportionately long lists of girls who reached the heights in their chosen careers. This raises 'many questions about expectations and roles and the difficulty of applying changing perceptions across the decades'.

It would not be fair, however, to be negative. There were many dedicated staff, led by strong head teachers, who worked hard over the years to give to generations of girls a sound and thorough education which has stood them (and, without doubt, still stands them) in good stead. Girls could also enjoy excellent facilities for sport and extra-curricular activities. It is probably true to say that most girls look back on their time at the High School with a measure of appreciation. Some personal observations are appropriate here and the last word will be given to Mr E. Whitaker who was at the helm as the School disappeared for ever from Luton life.

> The reading has brought back many memories of my time at the High School, and makes me realise what an important and lasting effect the gaining of a scholarship was in my life.
>
> [Denise Barber]

> I have to say that it provided an excellent education.
>
> [Brenda Tiley]

> If I have a criticism of Luton High School it was that … it did not actively broaden your expectations of what might be possible, or challenge you to greater ambitions. What it did give you … was a lot of independence and a realization that if you wanted to achieve anything, you could, but that you would need to make all the running yourself.
>
> [Maureen MacGlashan]

> I gained so much more than an academic education from the High and I know it shaped much of what I have done since.
>
> [Janice Swallow]

On the last day of the last month of the School's life Mr Whitaker acknowledged the distinctive spirit and vitality of the High School when he said that those 'girls had a character of their own'. It is probably true to say that we still have.

Appendix I
Head Girls

(Known as Senior Prefects in the early years)

1919	Vera Stanton	1944	Jeanne Clark
1920	Ella King	1945	Sheila Evans
1921	Ella King	1946	Gwendoline Fowler
1922	Marjorie Oddie and Edith Smith	1947	Gwendoline Fowler
1923	Edith Smith	1948	Gwendoline Fowler
1924	Gertrude Mitchell	1949	Joan Harlow
1925	Gertrude Mitchell	1950	Joan Harlow
1926	Rhoda Scott	1951	Eileen Gaskin
1927	Louie Griffiths	1952	Jean Osborn
1928	Joan Stalker	1953	Janice Swallow
1929	Freda Currant	1954	Marjorie Horley
1930	Phyllis Carpenter and Mary Woods	1955	Jean Godfrey
1931	Mary Woods and Thelma Payne	1956	Maureen McGlashen
1932	Mary Woods and Greta Richardson	1957	Angela Connolly
1933	Bonita Payne and Olive Janes	1958	Annette Gazeley
1934	Olive Janes and Margaret Mander	1959	Judith Rogers
1935	Margaret Mander to December, Margaret Knight from January, Margaret Impey from September	1960	Susan Morgan
		1961	Penelope White
		1962	Carole Wilson
1936	Joan Payne and Norah Watts	1963	Lucy Alcock
1937	Joan Payne and Norah Watts	1964	Margaret Smith
1938	Penelope Carlisle and Gillian Harris	1965	
1939	Gillian Harris and Megan Evans	1966	
1940	Megan Evans and Judith Carlisle	1967	
1941	Barbara Brown and Joan Watkins	1968	Beryl Whittaker
1942	Joan Watkins	1969	Ruth Hall
1943	Betty Clutten		

Appendix II
Games Honours

Many girls gained enormous pleasure from just from playing Games and others were proud to break records or to represent the School. Certainly, Games and Athletics played a very important part in the life of the School. It has not been possible to print a complete list of every achievement but some successes can be acknowledged. The wartime magazines, in particular, gave scant information.

In addition to these awards, many girls won Life Saving Certificates and netball and hockey umpiring certificates. There were also cups and House points awarded on Sports Days.

House Games Colours were awarded. More prestigious were the School Games Colours (C): a.– athletics; g.– gymnastics; h.– hockey; n.– netball; sw.– swimming; t.– tennis.

These lists have been compiled (with one or two slight discrepancies) from the *Sheaf* magazines and also from a board which is still (2004) on the wall in the School Crush Hall. The board was placed there in 1936 by members of the Old Girls' Association in memory of Freda Currant. No records have been found for the years after 1965.

School Games Honours

1921	Junior Sports Cup	Marion Costin
1922	Junior Sports Cup	Hilda Stewart
1923	Senior Sports Cup	Barbara Aylott
	C.	Marjorie Simmonds – n.
		Marion Costin – n.
1923–25	C.	Agnes Jack – n.
		Thelma Smith – n.
		Maggie Rudd – n.
1924	Senior Sports Cup	Hilda Palmer
1924–25	C.	Agnes Jack – n.
		Maggie Rudd – n.
		Thelma Smith – n.
		Marion Heady – n.
1925	Sen. Championship – Sports	Freda Barber, Marion Westmacott
	C.	Marion Headey
1926	Sen. Championship – Sports	Nora Benns, Hilda Stewart
	C.	Mary Sanderson – n.
		Hilda Stewart – n.
		Aline and Edna Rhaidr-Jones – n.
		Gertrude Mitchell – h.
		Florence Griffiths – h.
		Sylvia Robinson – h.
1927	C.	Aline and Edna Rhaidr-Jones – n.
		Hilda Stewart – n.
		Florence Griffiths – h.
		Evelyn Dixon – h.
1928	Senior Sports Cup	Alweena . Hafner
	C.	Evelyn Dixon – h,
		Edna Rhaidr-Jones – n. t.
		Vera Sharman – n.
		Joan Arnold – t.
		Constance Cherry – t.
		Agnes Turner – t.
		Thelma Payne – s.

1928–29	School Hockey Captain	Freda Currant
	School Netball Captain	Freda Currant
	School Swimming Captain	Thelma Payne
	School Tennis Captain	Agnes Turner
1929	Senior Sports Cup	Alweena Hafner
	C.	Thelma Payne – s.
		Freda Currant – n.
		Greta Richardson – n.
1930	Senior Sports Cup	Ida Gray
	C.	Mary Norwood – n.
		Kathleen Hucklesby – n.
		Phyllis Darnley – n.
		Eileen Cole – n.
		Thelma Payne – s.
1931	School Netball Captain	Greta Richardson
	School Swimming Captain	Thelma Payne
	School Tennis Captain	Phyllis Darnley
	Senior Sports Cup	Mary Norwood
1931–32	School Netball Captain	Greta Richardson
	School Swimming Captain	Thelma Payne
	School Tennis Captain	E. Herbert-Burns
1932	Senior Sports Cup	Marjorie Pike
1932–33	School Hockey Captain	Greta Richardson
	School Netball Captain	Greta Richardson
	School Tennis Captain	Lisbet Inglis
	C.	Eileen Cole – n.
		Greta Richardson – n.
		Joan Machin – n.
		Lisbet Inglis – t.
		Thelma Payne – s.
		Bonita Payne – s.
1933	Senior Sports Cup	Marjorie Pike
1933–34	School Hockey Captain	Margaret Mander
	School Netball Captain	Lisbet Inglis
	School Swimming Captain	Bonita Payne
	School Tennis Captain	Lisbet Inglis
	C.	Greta Richardson – h.n.
		Lisbet Inglis – h.n.t.
		K. Evans – n.
		Janet Letham – n.
		Patricia Fussell – h.
		Joan Oakley – n.
		Bonita Payne – s.

		Georgina Lane – s.
		Bonita Payne – s.
		Georgina Lane – s.
		Sheila Lacey – s
		Margaret Mander – n.s.
1934	Senior Sports Cup	Dorothy Brown, Grace Gibbs
1934–35	Athletics Champion	Grace Gibbs
	Junior	Florence Chalkley
		Audrey Holden
	Prize: Excellence in Games	Margaret Mander – h.n.s.
	C.	Janet Letham – n.
		Margaret Mander – h.n.s.
		Dora Hill – n.
		Eileen Jordan – h.
		Winifred Merrett – h.
		Sheila Lacey – s.
		Eileen Smith – s.
1935	Athletics Champion	Grace Gibbs
1936	Prize: Excellence in Games	Patricia Fussell
	Athletics Championship	Patricia Fussell, Eileen Atzema, Audrey Holden
	C.	Eileen Jordan – h.
		Patricia Fussell – h.n.
		Gwendoline Tripp – h.t.
		Dora Hill – n.
		Elizabeth Dickson – n.
		Nancy Jupe – n.
		Eileen Smith – s.
		Margaret Impey – s.
		Mary Hunter – s.
1936–37	School Hockey Captain	Patricia Fussell
	School Netball Captain	Nancy Jupe
	School Tennis Captain	Patricia Fussell
	C.	Patricia Fussell – h.n..
		Nancy Jupe – n.
1937	Athletics Champion	Eileen Atzema
1937–38	School Hockey Captain	Edith Densham
	School Netball Captain	Patricia Tompkins, Eileen Atzema
	School Swimming Captain	Mary Hunter
	School Tennis Captain	Patricia Tompkins
	C.	Mary Hunter – s.
		L. Atzema – n.
		Edith Densham – h.n.

		Patricia Tompkins – n.
1938	Athletics Champion	Jean Butcher, Joyce Gingell
1938–39	School Hockey Captain	Pamela Park
	School Netball Captain	Patricia Tompkins
	School Swimming Captain	Pamela Park
	School Tennis Captain	Patricia Tompkins
	C.	J. Gingell – n.
		Pamela Park – h.n.s.t.
		Patricia Tompkins – n.
1939	Athletics Championship	Joyce Gingell
1939–40	C.	Pamela Park – h.n.s.t.
		P. Hazel – h.s.
		H. Higginbotham – h.
		H. Hunter – s.
		J. Shaw – n.
		Patricia Tompkins – h.n.
		C. Smith – t.
1940–41	C.	J. Alexander – s.
		J. Carlisle – h.
		Kathleen Dawe – h.n.
		Evelyn Mariner – h.s.
		J. Shaw – n.
		C. Smith – n.t.
		M. Thripp – s.
1941–42	School Athletics Captain	Evelyn Mariner
	Deputy	Kathleen Dawe
		Evelyn Mariner – h.n.s.
		Kathleen Dawe – h.n.
		J. Shaw – n.h.
		J. Wood – h.
		Claudia Davies – n.
		C. Smith – t.
		P. Burley – s
1942–43	School Athletics Captain	Kathleen Dawe
	C.	Claudia Davies – h.n.
		K. Dawe – h.n.
		M. Ball – s.
		C. Darnell – s.
1943–44	C.	Eve Middleton-Jones – s
		Diana Williams – n.
		M. Green – s.
		J. Clark – s.
1944–45	School Athletics Captain	Diana Margaret Williams

1945–46	School Athletics Captain	Gwendoline Fowler
1946	Athletics Champion	H. Gardner
1947	Athletics Champion	Deborah Kheifetz
1947–48	C.	Mary Lintern – h.n.
1948	Athletics Champion	Eunice Beaumont
1948–49	C.	Jean Stokes – h.
		Joan Kerry – h.
1949	Athletics Champion	Jean Osborn
1949–50	C.	Patricia Heap – g.
		Monica Summerson – g.
		Avril Harding – g.
		Annette Bragg – t.
		Jean Stokes – t.
		Anne Cruttenden – s.
1950	Athletics Champion	Jean Osborn
1950–51	C.	Joy Bass – a.
		Avril Harding – s.
		Patricia Heap – t. (singles)
		Janice Swallow }– t. (doubles)
		Patricia Heap }– t. (doubles)
1951	Athletics Champion	Joy Bass
1951–52	C.	Norah Martin – s.
		Margaret Brunning – n.
		Jean Osborn – h.
		Shirley Simpson – h.
		Dorothy Head – n.
		Margaret Ibbett – n.
		Shirley Benson – h.
		Sheila Crossman – h.
1952	Athletics Champion	Jean Osborn
1952–53	C.	Jocelyn Randall – s.
		Peggy Collier – g.h.n.
		Sheila Crossman – g.
		Janet Mariner – g.
		Muriel Gunn – h.
		Janice Swallow – h.t.
1953	Athletics Champion	Sheila Peters
1953–54	C.	Patsy Willett – s?
		Norah Martin – s?
		Eleanor Gee – n.
		Hilary Reed – h.n.t.
		Ruth Garrett – h.
		Kathleen Thursby – t.

1954	Athletics Champion	Hilary Reed
1954–55	C.	Joan Middleton – h.
		Gillian Raines – h.
		Hilary Tompsett – h.
1955	Athletics Champion	Brenda Conley, Gillian Latch
1955–56	C.	Jane Murray – s.
		Joan Middleton – h.n.t.
		Patricia Pinchon – h.n.
		Hilary Tompsett – h.
		Beryl Coe – h.
		Ann Shortland – n.
1956	Athletics Champion	Brenda Conley
1956–57	C.	Moya Miller – s.
		Janet Hunt – t.
		Jean Stable – h.
1957	Athletics Champion	Janice Bonner
1957–58	C.	Jennifer Lawrence – h.
		Jennifer McArthur – h.n.
		Anne Payne – a.
		Susan Morgan – a.
1958	Athletics Champion	Anne Payne
1958–59	C.	Florence McLaughlin – h.
		Mary Kightley – h.
		Susan McKenzie – h.
		Margaret Burns – h.
		Carol Henry – s.
		Jane Gilbert – a.
	National Standard in Athletics	Susan Morgan
1959–60	C.	Aileen Cross – h.
		Silvia Glen – h.s.
		Susan Morgan – h.n.
		Ann Boston – n.
		Christine Rutter – n.
		Pamela Clark – s.
1959	Athletics Champion	Anne Morgan
1960–61	C.	Maureen Hawkes – h.
		Shirley Nicholl – h.
		Janet Parsons – h.
		Lillian Rickett –h.
		Brenda McArthur – n.
		Helen Murray – n.t.
		Jennifer Waller – t.
1960	Athletics Champion	Susan Morgan

1961–62	C.	Margaret Bradley – h.
		Marjorie Harrison – h.
		Suzanne Blackbourn – n.
		Rita Deverick – n.
		Mary Eastland – n.
		Shirley Nichol – t.
		Gillian Carney – s.
		Carolyn Thomas – a.
1961	Athletics Champion	Susan Morgan
1962–63	C.	Doreen Fletcher – h.t.
		Christine Robson – h.
		Ann Burgess – n.
		Margaret Davies – n.
		Mary Evans – n.
		Tandy Davies – a.
		Wendy Dickinson – s.
		Suzanne Blackbourn – g.
1962	Athletics Champion	Carolyn Thomas
1963	Athletics Champion	Carolyn Thomas
1963–64	C.	Glenys Crowther – h.
		Helen Medlock – h.t.
		Jane Morgan – a.g.h.
		Barbara Robinson – h.
		Caroline Thomas – h.
		Cynthia Ashworth – n.
		Helen Muller – t.
		Christine Robson – t.
		Elaine David – s.
		Mary Goodman – g.
1964	Athletics Champion	Carolyn Thomas
1964–65	C.	Vivienne Banks – h.
		Helen Muller – h.
		Valerie Rudd – h.
		Gaynor Waller – h.
		Mary Lavelle – n.
		Barbara Robinson – n.
		Penelope Brittain – s.
		Mary Goodman – g

Appendix III
Staff

Relevant members of staff from the time of the Mixed School.

(Many thanks to Mr John Gillespie who compiled the list for the Mixed School.)

Thomas A.E.Sanderson	Headmaster	1904–33
Frederick F. May	Art	1904–36
William Otter	Woodwork	1904–33
John B. Hoblyn	Chemistry	1904–15
Became chief chemist for Vauxhall Motors.		
Edward W. Edmunds	Science/English/Maths	1904–16
Second Master		
Miss C.S. Gardner	English/Languages	1904–16
J. Bygott	Eng/Maths/Geography	1904–08
Miss Rose Moylan	Languages/English	1904–06
Miss Jane Macfarlane	French and German	1907–
Transferred to Girls' School.		
Miss E. Webb	English/Languages	1907–11
G.J. Denbigh	Science/Maths	1908–17
Miss E. St S. Poulton	English/Senior Mistress	1908–18
Miss B. Daysh	Cookery/Needlework	1908–12
A. Jordan	Science/Maths/Geography	1908–16
A. Kirsch	Languages	1906–08
J.M. Forbes	Mathematics	1909–39
J. Plummer	Drill	1910–14
E.I. Barrow	Mathematics/Science	1911–14
Miss Daisy Rose	Games/Drill	1912–
Transferred to Girls' School		
Miss H.G. Forsaith	Needlework/Cookery	1913–19
A.P. Frost	Mathematics/English	1913–42
T. Huffington	Eng/History/Languages	1913–14
Miss C.K. Thomas	Eng/History/Languages	1914–
Transferred to Girls' School		
Miss Lucy Stafford	Mathematics, Latin	1916–18
Former pupil		
H.W. Gilbert	Science	1914–20
Miss E.T. Lewin	Science	1914–19
Miss C. Bell	Mathematics/English	1915–19
J.W. Findlater	English/History	1916–50
Miss E.M. Boby	Languages	1917–18
Miss M.M. Netherwood	Latin/Maths/Eng/Geography	1917–
Transferred to Girls' School		
Miss V.M. Barnes	English/Maths/Languages	1917–
Transferred to Girls' School		

Miss F.M. Jackson	Mathematics/History	1918–20

Senior Mistress, remained at Boys' School
Became Senior Mistress at Redlands School, Bristol

Miss A.L. Price	English/History/French	1918–

Transferred to Girls' School

Staff at the Girls' School

This list, which is incomplete, has been compiled from a register held at BLARS, copies of *The Sheaf* and Bedfordshire Education Committee Minutes. This has been a particularly difficult undertaking. Former members of staff have very kindly given it their attention and have succeeded in filling in some of the gaps. Dates may not be accurate as they often refer to an academic year and not a precise date.

Other inaccuracies may occur because

there were two members of staff with the same surname,

a member of staff may be included under her maiden and married name,

human error,

some members of staff left and later rejoined.

Apologies are given to members of staff whose names have been omitted.

Members of staff who are known to have married but whose names are uncertain are marked with an asterisk.

Part time and occasional teachers are recorded in smaller type. Some of these returned more than once.

Miss H.K. Sheldon	English	1919–47

Headmistress

Miss B.L. Bracey	Geography/History	1919–21

Miss Bracey, one of the original members of staff, worked on behalf of the Religious Society of Friends for the welfare of refugees and was awarded the OBE in 1942.

Miss H.G. Budge	Art	1919–20
Miss A. Cooper	Maths/Latin	1919–26
Miss M.A. Newton	Science	1919–21
Miss P. Peacey	Domestic Science	1919–24
Mrs P.L. Polishuk (Rickards)	French/History	1919–20
Miss V.M. Barnes		1919–24
Miss J. Macfarlane	German	1919–39

Miss Macfarlane became Senior Mistress.

Miss M.M. Netherwood		1919–20
Miss A.L. Price		1919–21
Miss C.K. Thomas		1919–20
Miss D.C. Rose	Drill/PE/Games/Needlework	1919–39
Miss D.M. Easton	General/English/Drama	1920–45

Miss Easton became Deputy Head; died 1945

Miss A.M. Littler		1920–24

Miss E. Macdonald	PT	1920
Miss G.M. Trump		
Miss I. Wilson 1920		
Miss M. Bickerdike	Maths	1920–26
Miss M. Davies		1920–21
Miss H. Graham	French	1920–37
Miss M. Macnab	English	1920–53

Inspired and inspiring English teacher.
She and Miss Wesley collected information about Old Girls for the Sheaf.

Miss G. Russell		1920–22
Miss P. Sailman		1921–22
Miss D.G. Cope 1921/22		
Miss E. Finch	Junior Science	1921–26
Miss G. Titmuss		1921–24
Miss M. Barrowman	Geography	1921–26
Miss D.B. Petrie		
Miss K. Murphy		
Miss E.R. Breakell	History	1922–28

Sister of M. Breakell

Miss E.B. Kingston	Art	1922–29
Miss A.M. Raisin	Senior Science	1922–28
Miss I. Wills	Junior French	1923–25
Miss M. Whelan	Singing/Junior Maths	1924–26/27
Miss M.I. Tubby		1924/25–26/27
Miss Pettit		1925/26–26
Miss M L Breakell		1925–29

Sister of E. Breakell.

Miss C.A. Dowdall	Maths	1926–59
Miss D.E. Hazell		1926–27
Miss L.M. Sharp		1926/27–27/28
Miss W. Cray		1926–27
Miss N. Watson		1926–28
Miss L.G.C. Fuller	Music/Choir	1926–63
Miss K. Blakeman		1926–27
Miss M.J. Radford		1926–28
Miss A. Rees		1927–28
Miss D. Gregg	Science/Biology	1927–37

Became Lady Tunbridge.

Miss J.D. Hunt		1927–30
Miss E.M. Smewing	Chemistry/Physics	1927–46
Miss M.M.J. Stott		1928
Miss F. Hines		1928–29
Miss E.M. Smith	French	1928–34

Miss K.S. Stephenson	Maths	1928–55
Miss M.H. Waller		1928–29
Miss M.E. Wolverson	Needlework/Domestic Science	1928–47
Miss W.A. Caldin		1929
Miss D.M. Harris	History	1929–46
Miss E. Hollis		1929–30
Miss A.W. Wesley	Geography/RE	1929–56
Became Deputy Head in 1947.		
Miss D.H. Cooper	Art	1929–41
Became a nun.		
Miss C. Stableford	French/RE	1930–58
Responsible for Christmas and Easter services.		
Miss N.D. Horton		1930–32/33
Miss M. Smalley		1930–31/32
Miss H.W. Cooper	Commercial	1930–35
Miss M. Kerry		1931–32/33
Miss E. Hare	Maths	1931–39
Miss K.F. Puttock		
Miss A.E. Hubbard		1932–33
Miss V.C. Ling	Maths	1932–
Became Lower School Head then Deputy Head in 1957.		
Miss D.M. Skerry		1932–34
Miss M.de la Mare	PE/Games	1932–36
Miss M. Watson		1932–33
Miss M.G. Davison		1933–35
Mrs C. Fisher		
Miss M. Bartram	Domestic Subjects	1934–37
Mrs H.M. Pike*		–1958
Miss A. Groves		1934–36
Miss M. Yardley*	Latin or History	1934–41
Miss J.R. Hills	French	1934–36
Miss G. Parker-Gray		1935–38
died 1938		
Miss M. MacLean		1935–38
Miss H.A. Thomson	Science	1935–37
Miss E.W. Parker		1935–36
Miss E.G. Aust		
Miss E Burton		1936–38
Miss I. Oldham	Art	1936–45
(Mrs Smithwhite)		
Miss J.M. Skittery	PE	1936–41
Joined WRNS		
Miss J.A. Evans	French	1936–42
Became a headmistress in Keighley.		

Miss M. Glanville-Greysmith		1937–40
Miss E.M. Pattenden	Science	1937–39
Miss N.B. Sillar	Domestic Science	1938–46

Became an organizer for Bedfordshire County Council.

Miss V. Mason		1938
Mrs E. Evans	Biology	1938–65

Became Deputy Head and then Head.

Miss M. Woods	English	1938–47

Former head girl. Became a Head teacher in Shaftesbury.

Miss M.T. Flatman		1938–39
Miss J. Macdonald	PE	1939–42

Became a private physiotherapist.

Miss A.W. Hawksley	German/French	1939–41
Miss S.E. Broadberry		1939–42
Miss M. Bishop		1939–41
Miss G. Milner	Commercial	1939–43
Miss E.L. Vernon		1939–39/40
Miss M.J. Stanley	Science	1939–41
Miss P. Brass		
Miss Dyson		
Miss Shaw		1940–42
Miss D.S. Watt		1941–42
Miss H. Thomas	Latin	1941–44
Miss D.V. Scott	French or English	1941–44
Miss A.M. Chorley		1941–42
Miss J.M. Trewhella		1941–43
Miss M.J. Quarterman	French	1941–44
Miss S.M. Cobern		1941–42
Miss K.E.M. Palser		1941–42
Miss W.E. Hardy		1941–45

Became a missionary in China.

Miss C.K.H. Dunsby		1941–43
Miss M.E. Horn	PE	1941–47
Miss Eaton		1942–45
Miss B.M. Middlehurst	Maths	1942/43–50

Miss Middlehurst was a mathematician. She studied astronomy and worked with Sir Patrick Moore on transient phenomena on the moon.

Miss M. Williamson*		1942–
Miss M. Pim		1942–43
Miss D.J.R. Heard	French?	1942–43
Miss R.W. Rabey		1942–43/44
Miss J.H. Deas		1942–45

Became a School Inspector

Miss P. Veitch	Craft	1942–45
Miss M.L. Tanner	Maths	1942–
Mrs J.M. Butler		
Miss N.C.A. Flaherty	History	1943/44–68

Became Senior Assistant in the Lower School 1952.
Head of LHS girls 1967–68.

Miss A. Prout		1943–
Miss M.B. Asher		1943–
Miss M. Haworth	English	1943–
Miss E.M. Hiscock	French	1943–45
Miss N.G. McKenna		1943–47
Miss M.H. Wilson		1943–
Miss W.M. Edge	Latin	1943–46
Miss I.K. Atkins		
Miss Fleming		1943–
Mrs Beckley*		1944–

an 'old friend back'

Miss M. Dickson	Senior Classics	1945–55

Became a Headmistress on the Isle of Man.

Miss I.F. Allen	Craft	1945–49
Miss M. Burton	German/French/Latin/Library	1945–59

died 1959

Miss Burton left her own library and royalties on German books she had written to the School.

Miss D.F. Chamberlin	English	1945–50
Miss I.W. Hall		1945–48
Miss Liddle	PE	1945–46

Went to Kenya

Mrs Padden		1945–
Miss Pearson	Biology	1945–46
Miss Spencer		1945–46

Returned to studies

Miss Sturgis	English	1945–46
Miss Tingle		1945–47
Miss Roberts		–1946
Miss B.J. Williams	Geography	1946–50

(Mrs Seale)

Miss K. Hudson	Drama	1946–50
Dr L. Frankenstein	German	1946–48
Miss O. Rose	Biology	1946–49
Miss Evans		1946–

(Mrs Fry)

Miss J. Stalker	History	1946–66

Former head girl, active in Old Girls' Association
Family firm: Briggs and Stalker's bookshop
Speech Day Prizes selected there

Miss B.I. Reed	Needlework/Science/English	1946–56
Miss A. Potts		1946–47
Mr Smithwhite	Art	
Miss Davies	History	1947–48
(Mrs Brindley)		
Miss C.O. Gooderson	French	1947–48
Miss M.R. Osborne	Science	1947–53

Became a head teacher in Stevenage.

Mrs I.M.M. Saunders		1947–48
Miss M.E.Y. Barrow	Gymnastics	1947–49
Miss Bromwich		1947–49
Miss J.B. Briggs		1947–48
Miss K.M. Goodwin	Science/Nature Study	1947–48
Miss E.V. Lake	Physics/Maths	1947–61
Miss T. Thomas		1947–48
Miss M.W. Thompson		1947–48
Miss Gabb		–1947
Miss K.M. Bellew	English	1947–49
Miss D.M. Flint	Music, Orchestra	1947–
Miss E.R.C. Astbury	French	1947–50
Miss P. Carlisle	Geography	1947–48
Miss M.E.C. Hazell	English	1947–49
(Mrs Barter)		
Mrs R.D. Graham	PE?	1947–48
Miss M.H. Brown		
Miss M. Barton or Benton		
Miss S. Smith	French	1947–51

Became a head teacher at Newcastle-under-Lyme and wrote a French course.

Miss V. Ashwell	Biology/Science	1948–49

Became a head teacher in Manchester.

Miss P.E.K. Fletcher	Needlework	–1950
Mrs A. Harper		
Mrs L.H. Munby		
Miss N.J. Chedzoy	Science/Biology	1948–50
Miss D.M. Garbutt	Geography	1948–51
Miss M.R. Mallett	Geography	1948–54
(Mrs Brewer)		

Went on an exchange to Cincinnati 1950.

Miss M. Marchant	History	1948

Miss E. Mariner (Mrs Oakley)	PE	1948–50
Miss E.E. Weston	Biology	1948–50
Miss H. Fried	French	1948–49
Miss J.W. Sherwood	English	1948–66
Went to College of Further Education, Park Square.		
Mrs E.S. Stainton	English	1948–49
Miss Baker	English	
Mrs Street	Art	
Miss M.E.C Baxter		
Miss G.L. Bowditch	French	1949–50
Miss R.D. Joseph		1949
Mrs F.M. Attree		
Miss P. Western	English	1949–66
Helped to edit the *Sheaf*		
Miss J.M. Wood	PE	1949–53
Miss N.J. Nutman		
Miss Deadman		
Miss D.F. Dennis		1949–51
Mrs N. Gallimore	German	1949–56
Miss L. Green	English	1949–52
Miss J.M. Hindle	Art	1949–
Miss N.A. Marten	History	1949–51
Mrs L.P. Cole		
Miss Bromwich		
Miss J. Miller	History?	1949–52
Mrs O.M. Perryman	Science	1949–50
Miss C.M. Scott	French	1949–56
Went on an exchange to Canada.		
League of the Commonwealth Interchange of Teachers Scheme.		
Became a head teacher in Dunstable.		
Miss J.I. Beeby	Spanish	1950–54
Miss A.C. Coles	English/Latin	1950–
Miss D.F.N. Dorling	RK	1950–
Went to the VI Form College		
Miss A.E. Greasley	PE	1950–52
Miss J.M. Kidd (Mrs Smith)	Biology/Botany/Zoology/Physics	1950–58/9
Miss M.T. Read	Craft/Art	1950–61
Miss P.M. Tanner	Maths	1950–54
Miss G.E. Brown	Voice Production/Drama	1950–
Went to Australia in 1955.		
Went to the VI Form College.		

Miss G.R. Davis	French	1950–53
Miss M.E. Godfrey	Science/Biology	1950–52
Miss A. Sharpe	French	1950–51
Miss M.G. Butler	Domestic Science/Needlework	1951–
Miss P. Ellam	Science	1951–55
(Mrs Gott?)		
Miss C.M. Ough	Chemistry	1951–55
Miss F. Newton		
Miss A.M. Howell	Home Economics	1951–53
(Mrs Thomas)		
Miss E. Shilton		1951–
Miss K. Underdown	Junior Library/English	1951–55
Miss R L. Emery	Geography	1951–
Miss M.J. Chandler	Chemistry/Physics	1951–60/4
(Mrs Candler?)		
Miss W.E. Hardy		1952
Miss M.E. Irvine	Modern Languages	1952–61
Became a head teacher at Yarmouth.		
Returned to LHS as head teacher.		
Miss D.M. Bland	Geography	1952–
Went to the VI Form College		
Miss E. Everley*		–1952
Miss M. Jones		1952
Miss M. Brough	Classics	1952–55
Miss E.L. Colston		1952–53
(Mrs Walker?)		
Miss J. Durham	French	1952–57
Mrs S.E. Futrell		1952–53
Miss C.I. Meacham		1952–
Miss D.A. Wippell	Games PE	1952–
Miss R.A. Russell	English	1953–55
Miss M.M. McCarthy	Science	1953–55
Mrs R. Palmer*		–1952
Miss C.E. Broomer	French	1953–
Went to USA 1961–62.		
Miss E. Griffin	Cookery/housecraft	1953–59
(Mrs Pearson?)		
Miss J.A. Sanders	PT	1953–56
(Mrs Keen)		
Miss E.B. Godwin	English	1954–63
Became a head teacher in Walsall.		
Miss M. Gwynn		1954
Miss S.A. Benson		

Miss J.M.E. Reaburn		
Miss A.F. Bond		1954–
(Mrs Hughes?)		
Miss A. Carpenter	History	1954–60
Miss M. Hooper		1954–55
Miss M.E. Peacock	Maths/Physics	1954–
Went to the VI Form College.		
Miss J. Brierley	Biology/Botany/Zoology	1955–57
(Mrs Shipway?)		
Miss M. Lawman		1955–
Miss M.E. Robins	Physics/Biology/Hygiene	1955–66
Miss J.P. Badcock	English	1955–58
Miss J.M. Smith		1955–58
Miss J.V. Earwaker	Spanish/R.I./French	1955–62
(Mrs Thomas)		
Miss C. Colmer	PE	1955–58
(Mrs Morris)		
Miss A. Searle	Maths	1955–58
Mrs J.M. Butler		
Miss M. Lawman		
Mrs R. Morris	Classics	1955–57
Miss M.E. Whiteley	Geography/Maths	1955–62
Went on an exchange to Australia and New Zealand.		
Miss C.M. Whinnett	English/Hygiene/Needlework	1955–64
(Mrs Theodorson)		
Miss J. Lloyd	French/Italian/English/Latin	1955–62
(Mrs Payne)		
Miss B. Golding	Botany/Zoology/Biology	1955–58
(Mrs Marshall)		
Miss E.V. Toth		1955
Exchange Teacher from Canada		
Mrs M. Stebbing	Housecraft/Needlework	1956–66
Mrs M.D. Eborall		
Mrs J.M. Hill*		–1956
Miss M.H. Webb		1956
Miss M.G. Coleman*	PE	1956–
Went to the VI Form College.		
Miss B.I.Reed		1956–
Mrs E. Boskett	PE	1956/57–
(Miss Hone?)		
Mrs E. Whitaker		
Mrs J.M. Dell*	Art	–1956
Mrs Bawdon*	Botany	

Mrs Butler*	Chemistry	
Miss V. Graber	German?	1956–57
Miss J.M. Molland	R.I./English	1956–58
(Mrs Coombes)		
Miss J.O.P. Vaughan	Geography/Cricket	1956–66
Believed to have played netball for England.		
Miss M.J. Galbraith	Art/Craft/Housecraft	1956–59
Mrs S. Williams		1956–57
Miss H.H. Hampson	Latin/Greek	1956–
Mrs M.R.O. Ellis		
Mrs M.M. Humphries		
Miss J. Birt	English, History	
Exchange Teacher from Australia		
Mrs M.R. Corby	English/French	
Mrs E. Henderson		1957
Mrs Hughes*		–1957
(Miss Bond?)		
Miss H.E.M. Parry	French	1957–62
Miss G. Gribble	Maths/Physics/Human Biology	1957–71
Mrs E.K. Richaud	Spanish/French	1957–66
Miss M.E. Bunnage	Needlework	1957–60
Mrs A.W. Pedder		
Miss D.H. Eddon		
Mrs R. Corby	French	1957–58?
(Miss Crewe)		
Mrs M.E. Jones		
Mrs M.C. Whitfield		
Mrs N. Gallimore		
Mrs D.E. Yossava	Chemistry	1957–59
(Miss King)		
Went to VI Form College		
Mrs B.A. Wharton	German	1957–60
Mr R.C. Edwards		
Miss T. Schlingensief		1958
Miss C.L. Walsh		1958–61
(Mrs Stewart?)		
Miss L.A. Salisbury	Classics	1958–61
Miss E. Preston		1958–59
Miss J. Coates	PE	1958–61
Miss H.M. Jones	Library/English	1958–66
Miss R. Garrett	French	1958–
(Mrs Hester?)		
Mrs M.F. Browne		1958–60

Miss P. Stewart		1958–
Miss B.K. Macdonald	English	1958–62
Mr A.J. Frost	Russian/Maths	1958–
Went to the VI Form College.		
Miss M.L. Boatwright	Classics	1958–59
Mrs P.A. Gibbs	Botany/Zoology	1958–59
Miss J.H. Quinn		1958–
Mrs J.M. Smith (Miss Kidd)		
Mrs V.A. Redmill		
Mrs E.M. Lovelock		
Mrs E. Holmes		
Miss P.A. Dean	Modern Languages	1959–60
Mrs M. Dukes	Mathematics	1959–
Went to the VI Form College.		
Mr J. Dukes	Mathematics	1959–
Went to the VI Form College.		
Miss A.R. Woods	PE?	1959–61
Miss J.C. Osland		1959–
Mrs P. Gott*		–1959
Miss G. Johnson		1959–61
Miss S.R. Cowley	German	1959–65
Miss R.R. Harris	Classics	1959–
Went to the VI Form College.		
Mrs T.G.K. Gilbert	Chemistry	1959–64
Mrs M.P. Regan		
Miss F. Green	Cookery/Housecraft	1960–
Went to the VI Form College.		
Miss S.V. Booth	Art/Craft	1960–63
Miss M.A. Burns		
Miss P.R. Edmonds		
Mrs D.F. Stevenson		
Miss B.E. Clarke	German	1960–65
(Mrs Banbury?)		
Miss P.D. Evans	Modern Languages	1960–64
(Mrs Gillespie)		
Miss J.M. Bingham	Maths	1960–64
Went to India.		
Miss E.B. Copp	History	1960–65
(Mrs Wayman)		
Mrs A.M. Chotkiewicz	Biology	1960–62
Miss A. Gazeley		
Mrs T.M. Morgans	Biology	–1962
Miss S.J. Aspinall	French	1960–66
(Mrs Bray)		

Mr L. Rising		1961
Exchange Teacher from USA		
Mr P. Palmer		1961
Exchange Teacher from Australia		
Mrs W.K. Young	Needlework	1961–
Miss M. Del Rosa		
Miss F.P. Stanham	PE	1961–64
Miss E. Hibbett	RE	1961–65
(Mrs Webb)		
Miss J.R. Balshaw		1961–
Miss J.R. Hitchen	Maths	1961–
(or Mitchen?)		
Miss S.E. Miles	Maths	1961–63
Miss A.G. Barnes		1961–62
Miss B. Rollason	Modern Languages	1961–
(Mrs Williams)		
Went to VI Form College.		
Miss D.M. Spratley	Art/Craft	1961–
Miss H. Caplan		1961–62
Mrs J.R. Whitaker*		–1961
Mrs G. Turner	Maths	1962–
Miss M.M. Christie		1962–
Mrs J.E. Robinson	PE	1962–63
Mrs J.R. Cockburn*		–1962
Mrs I.G. Swanwick	Biology	1962
Miss A.J. Rowntree		1962–
Miss R.A. Symonds		1962–63
Miss H.P. Beaumont	Domestic Science	1962–65
Miss F.R. Crabtree		1962–63
Miss C.M. Brindley	Physics	1962–64
Mrs S. Devereau		1962–
Miss A. Foster	French	1962–
Miss E.A/A.E. Marshall	Science?	1962–65
Miss M.M. Kilty	Spanish	1962–
Mrs S. Devereau		
Mr J.B. Henderson		
Miss C.A. Dannock		1962–
Mr E.A. Quinn		
Miss F. Hollitt	RK	1963–66
Mrs M. Burness	Classics	1962–69
(Mrs Preece)		
Miss M.C. Spencer		1963–
Miss G.F.A. Lewis	Music/Needlework	1963–
(Mrs Stebbing)		

There is a gap in the Education Minutes here.

Mrs C.A. Sallows*	Physics	–1964
Miss D. Pritchard		1964–66
Miss B. Twitchen	PE?	1964–
Miss L.M. Evans		1964–
Miss S.L. Dickens	French	1964–
Mrs A.R. Buisson		
Miss L.E. Dunn		
Mrs B. Sharman		
Mrs E.I. Hall	Maths	1965–
Miss E. Watkins	Spanish	1965
Mrs J. Eastwell		
Mrs M. Parsons		
Mrs J. Lucas*		–1965
Mrs A.F. Garner*	Biology/Science	–1965
Mrs A.M. Richardson*		–1965
Mrs J. Tong*		–1965
Miss B.O. Thorne		1965–
Miss J.A. Shreeve		1965–
Miss J. Childerhouse		1965– 66
Mrs K.P. Frost	Botany	1965–66
Mr R.M. Greenhalgh	Art	–1966
Mrs L.M. Flitton*		–1966
Miss M.K. Harrison	Zoology/Biology	1966–
Miss A.I. Piper		1966–
Mrs V. A. Forshaw		
Mrs M.P. Jackson		
Miss A.M. Warren	Music	
Mr I.A. Jones	History	
to VI Form College.		
Mrs Thomson (Griggs)		–1970

Other names – no dates

Miss Caplin	English
Mrs Pauline Dent	Biology
Miss B. Harrison	English
Miss M. Miller	French
Miss Morland	English
Mrs Peddar	Biology
Miss Robbins	Science

Non-teaching staff

This list is far from complete.

Canteen supervisors

    Mrs Richardson 1919–60

    Mrs Burgess (née Edith Densham)

Secretarial

    Mrs C. Mitchell, first secretary, 1919–1931

    Mary Groom OG who left to join WRNS 1941

    Audrey Sare-Soar

    Mrs Bond

Caretakers and groundsmen

    Mr D. Clark

    Mr W. Mandley, caretaker retired 1950

    Mr G. Martin, groundsman

    Mr McCarthy

    Mr S. Sapwell

    Mr A.G. Graffham

    Mr W. Gale

    Mr Titchmarsh

Appendix IV
Numbers on Roll

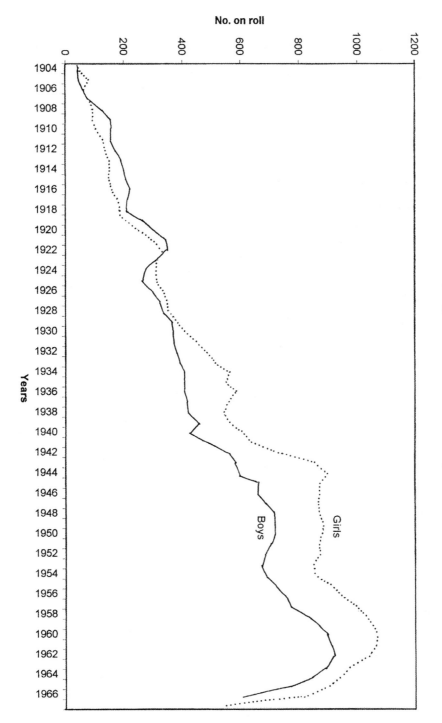

Graph based on figures researched by the late Mrs I. Bond, former secretary at Luton High School.

An aerial view of the school at Barnfield

Luton
Technical
School

1937–1967

Background to Technical Education

Practical and scientific skills used to be passed on in apprenticeship schemes which had their roots in the medieval guilds but, with the coming of the Industrial Revolution and factory production, these traditions began to founder. There was, however, an acknowledged need for artisans to be instructed in the scientific principles of manufacturing.

In 1799, George Birkbeck gave a course of evening classes in science and mathematics in Glasgow, a project which resulted, in 1823, in the formation of the Glasgow Mechanics' Institute. In the same year he opened a Mechanics' Institute in London and many more were set up in other parts of the country. By 1850, there were 600 Institutes with half a million members, mainly in London, Lancashire and the West Riding but, unfortunately, they did not attract the labouring classes in large numbers. A Mechanics' Institute, with a library and reading room, existed in Luton between 1845 and c.1882. The charge for full membership was 2s 6d (12½p) while women paid 1s (5p). Over the years, Mechanics' Institutes began to lose their specialized mechanical bias in favour of wider courses of study. They did, however, prepare the way for the technical institutions and trade schools of the future.

This country had become complacent about its manufacturing superiority but, by 1851, at the time of the Great Exhibition, it was obvious that competition from overseas markets had to be taken seriously. It was recognized that, in order to maintain our industrial might, the subject of technical education had to be addressed. Two years later the Science and Art Department was set up in South Kensington 'as the central agency for the encouragement of technical and commercial education'. In 1856 the Department was transferred from the Board of Trade to the Education Department. This was a significant step in the history of technical education but, unfortunately, the instruction given favoured theory over practice. Schools Boards (set up from 1870) also received support from the Science and Art Department to run evening classes in scientific subjects.

Another significant step in the development of technical education came in 1880 when the City and Guilds of London Institute for the Advancement of Technical Education introduced a system of evening classes with set syllabuses leading to City and Guilds examinations. By the end of the nineteenth century, over 60 subjects were offered.

The Technical Instruction Act 1889 and the Balfour Act 1902

In response to the fear that England was falling behind some European countries in technical subjects, the Samuelson Commission (1882–4) was set up to consider the situation. As a result, the Technical Instruction Act was passed in 1889. This gave County Councils power to establish Technical Instruction Committees and raise a penny rate to pay for technical and manual instruction. The following year the Local Taxation (Customs and Excise) Act allowed money from the increased duty on beer and spirits to be spent by these Committees. This was famously known as 'whisky money'. Under the terms of this Act, teaching a trade was not allowed but teaching 'the principles of a trade' was permitted. Grant money was to be administered by the Science and Art Department.

Bedfordshire County Council was required to oversee and fund technical instruction in Luton; this involved the setting up of the Luton Technical Instruction Committee. Much of the 'whisky money' allocated to Luton was used for subjects with a direct connection with the straw hat industry, such as chemistry and applied mechanics and the principles of advanced straw plaiting. Cookery, laundry work, needlework and basic health care were also offered. Classes were advertised in post offices and other public places and it was pointed out that the best time to hold the classes was during the slack (hat industry) season.

There was another, short-lived, scheme in Luton in the middle of the 1890s which was initiated by F.W. Beck, a local solicitor, with the support of the Luton Chamber of Commerce. It was to be 'based on the system of education, instituted in 1890 by the London Chamber of Commerce, for securing a sound commercial training … and holding examinations in connection with the examination of the London Chamber'. This scheme would have involved local schools, particularly the Higher Grade School in Waller Street, with the responsibility to prepare students for the examination. However, the idea met with little success and was discontinued in 1896.

In 1901, there were plans to build a school for the study of technical subjects in Luton and the Council was prepared to provide a site if the County Council would pay for the 'erection of a Secondary Science and Commercial School in this Town'. The Luton Chamber of Commerce promised their 'hearty support'. However, the Board of Education had plans of its own for secondary education and these made it inadvisable to proceed with any local schemes. As a consequence of the 1902 Education Act, the Luton Technical Education Committee ceased to exist and, in 1904, a Technical Institution was set up in conjunction with the new Secondary School in Park Square with T.A.E. Sanderson as head of both departments. Members of his staff taught in both day and evening classes.

Department of science:
chemistry, physics	Mr Edmunds and Mr Hoblyn
mathematics	Mt Hutchinson
botany	Mr Edmunds and Miss Moylan
human physiology	Mr Edmunds
hygiene, physiography	Mr Hoblyn

Department of engineering
    machine construction and drawing,
    steam, applied mechanics,
    practical geometry   Mr Hutchinson
Department of the building trades:
    building construction, builders' quantities
    carpentry and joinery
    manual training (woodwork)   Mr Otter
    structure and working of trade
    sewing machines   Miss Bone
Department of commerce:
    book-keeping, shorthand
    geography   Mr Bygott
Department of language and literature:
    French, German   Mr Llewellyn
    English   Miss Gardner
    advanced literature   Mr Edmunds
    English history   Miss Gardner
Department of domestic knowledge:
    dressmaking, needlework,   Miss Finlinson
    millinery   Miss Moylan
Department of art:
    light and shade and design,
    freehand, model, blackboard drawing,
    geometrical drawing, perspective   Mr F. May

The subjects on offer did not vary much over the next few years; this accords with the view that the period between 1900 and 1945 was not a time of progress in the field of technical education. Indeed, in 1934, the Bedfordshire County Council Higher Education Sub-Committee noted that the only change had been

> a natural growth in numbers from 482 class entries in 1902–3 to 872 class entries in 1933–34, though this increase is scarcely proportionate to the growth in population … In other words, the facilities for Technical Instruction in Luton, adequate though they may have been thirty years ago, have for some time fallen short of recognised standards and local requirements and no longer meet the needs of modern times.

Another innovation worth noting was the introduction in 1921 of National Certificate courses and examinations by the Board of Education and the Institute of Mechanical Engineers.

Junior Technical Schools

In 1913, the Board of Education recognized the setting up of Junior Technical Schools which could provide full-time day classes for post-elementary 13–16-year olds who were awaiting skilled apprenticeships in engineering and other such industries. These schools gave a general education but their main aim was the 'training [of] skilled employees for the needs of local industry'. They were not to be seen as competing with the grammar schools but were a part of the secondary school system and admission depended on passing an examination.

The *Hadow Report* (1926) recognized the contribution which Junior Technical Schools had made to post-primary education. Then, in 1928, the *Report on Education and Industry* praised the schools, noting that they had received the approval of employers and educationists alike. Three years later, a *Report on Education for the Engineering Industry* paid tribute to the system claiming that children who had been to the schools were 'normally some of the most promising recruits to the engineering industry'. Pupils had a strong sense of responsibility and took a 'pride in good craftsmanship'.

Junior Technical Schools were highly successful in finding employment for their pupils and they, in turn, showed a level of commitment by continuing with their education at part-time day or evening classes. However, by 1937, there were only 220 of these schools in the country.

Luton was a town with strong links to industry and the idea of setting up a Junior Technical School had considerable appeal. As far back as November 1918, the Governors of the Technical Institution met with local representatives from the engineering, dyeing, bleaching and chemical and hat industries to discuss the desirability of setting up such a school. As a result, they

> resolved unanimously that in their opinion the establishment of a Junior Technical School in Luton was eminently desirable and they recommended the Bedfordshire Education Committee to make provision for such a school ... though it was realised that there would be difficulty, if the school were established, in persuading parents to allow their boys to attend when they might be earning good wages.

Unfortunately, the Education Committee responded by saying that financial constraints made them unable to take any immediate action. In November 1920, a similar suggestion was made but, again, the financial situation deterred the local authority. It was also said that employers preferred scholars who had received a secondary education. The Governors of the Technical Institution did not let the matter rest and complained again, in 1932, that there were not sufficient facilities for training engineering apprentices and other young people connected with industries in the town.

In June 1933 the Education Committee, Luton Chamber of Commerce, Institution of Production Engineers, and the Engineering and Allied Employers (Bedfordshire) Association contacted the Education Committee to point out the lack of accommodation at the Technical Institution which had to share a building with the 407 scholars at the Modern School. There were

- no facilities for practical work in the Engineering, Building and Allied Trades Courses of instruction. Without these facilities the Courses of instruction in Mechanical Engineering cannot be jointly approved by the Board of Education and by the Institute of Mechanical Engineers for the award of Grouped Course Certificates in Engineering, certificates which have a professional and national as well as a local value, being highly prized and much sought after.
- no courses of instruction associated with the hat industry. The need for such classes offering instruction in Millinery etc. is a much felt one.
- no provision for Day Classes for those leaving the Elementary Schools and desiring technical training prior to apprenticeship.

In November 1934, the Bedfordshire County Council Higher Education Sub-Committee produced a Report on *Technical Education in Luton*. They resolved that, subject to the approval of the Board of Education, the following provision should be made:

- a new Secondary School for Boys on the Dunstable Road site.*
- additional land for the playing field on the Dunstable Road site.
- the buildings in Park Square, Luton, now used as a Secondary School for Boys, be converted for use as a Technical School providing:
  a) a Junior Technical School
  b) a Senior Technical Institute
- land as a playing field for a Junior Technical School
- a Junior Technical School should have adequate accommodation and suitable equipment.
- evening classes should be made available in Millinery, Engineering, Building and Allied Trades.

[*The Boys' School eventually moved to Bradgers Hill, not Dunstable Road.]

The appeal was supported by details of visits made to existing Junior Technical Schools. They noted that these schools were small because they were specialized and because numbers were expected to bear some relation to the amount of jobs available in local industries. Staff at Junior Technical Schools had usually had experience in industry and links between industry and the schools were strong. The visits indicated that pupils approached their work with 'seriousness and satisfaction' because there was 'no difficulty in realising the direct bearing of their work on their future lives'.

The Sub-Committee explained that the curriculum in a typical school for boys included most of the following: practical mathematics (including arithmetic, mensuration, algebra and trigonometry), drawing (including constructive and solid geometry as well as hand-sketching), engineering and building details, workshop practice in wood and metal, elementary science (including practical work in physics, mechanics and chemistry) English (including reading, composition, geography and history) and physical training.

The School of Arts and Crafts

It is not in the remit of this book to write about the School of Arts and Crafts but a brief reference to it should be made because it eventually shared the same building as the Junior Technical School. The School of Arts and Crafts was opened by Bedfordshire County Council in 1934, on the 3rd and 4th floors of Arthur Day's premises at Connaught House, Upper George St. The buildings were hired for an initial period of three years but, after that time, the School took over rooms on the top floor of the building in Park Square. In July 1936, it was recognized by the Board of Education.

Miss R. Willis	Full-time principal
Mr C. L. Skinner	Full-time assistant art master
Miss J. I. Stephenson	Full-time teacher of millinery
Miss I. Carter	Full-time assistant teacher of millinery

Alderman John Burgoyne

Alderman Burgoyne is regarded as the man who did most to help the furtherance of technical education in Luton. He was born in 1875 at Tipple Hill, Aley Green, near Caddington. His father, Thomas, was a bleacher and dyer who turned to the plait trade and John later became head of the firm. He became a Methodist Sunday School teacher and continued to have a lifelong interest in education. In 1902, aged 27, he married Florence Farrow and they had one son, Jack.

In 1931, John Burgoyne was elected to the Town Council, becoming mayor in 1938. He remained in that post throughout the period of the Second World War and was made a freeman of the town in 1945. He was Chairman of the Luton Education Committee for thirteen years and, from 1934 to 1944, a member of the Bedfordshire Education Committee. In 1946, he was awarded an OBE.

Alderman Burgoyne was a Governor of Luton High School, Luton Grammar School and Dunstable Grammar School. He was also Chairman of the Governors of Luton College of Technology and, to emphasize his interest in technical education, enrolled in a variety of classes. He was influential in the establishment of the Luton Junior Technical School. He was knighted in 1956 and became a Justice of the Peace.

The Setting Up of the Junior Technical School

In September 1937, Bedfordshire County Council set up a Junior Technical School in Luton. The story of the School is a happy and successful one; it is a tale of achievement in the face of many difficulties. In 1937, its 'parent', the Technical Institute, changed its name to Luton Technical College and Mr W.E. Park B.Sc. was appointed head in May of that year. He was in overall charge of Technical Education but the new School was to be the responsibility of Dr Sidney Charlesworth who was appointed to the headship in June. This has led to some confusion about the name of the Technical School. It was often known in the town as the 'Tech' or the 'Technical College'. Officially it was the Technical School but, at the same time, a part of the College so, in a sense, all these names are justified.

Sidney Charlesworth, Dip. Ed., MA, Ph.D., attended the Central School, Sheffield, between 1918 and 1924 and Sheffield University from 1924 to 1930 where, from 1928 to 1930, he was a Frederick Clifford Research Scholar. In both school and university he took a keen interest in sport. Between 1930 and 1937 he

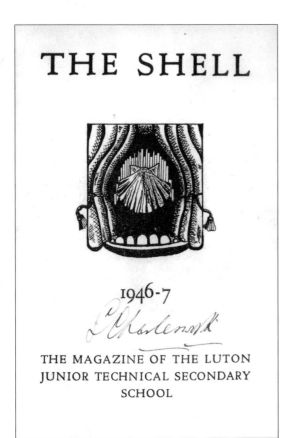

Signatures of staff. The title page confirms that the School was known as the
Junior Technical Secondary School. (1946–47 Shell)

Dr Charlesworth c.1940. (*Patricia Morgan*)

held teaching posts in Sheffield and Doncaster. He married Phyllis Barr and they had two daughters. When they moved to Luton, they lived at 'Westering' 292, Old Bedford Road.

Dr Charlesworth was an active member of several professional associations including the National Union of Teachers and was treasurer of the Luton Head Teachers' Association. He took a lively interest in local activities: he was on the local executive committee of the NSPCC, vice-president of the Luton Rugby Club, a member of the Schoolmasters' Cricket Club, the September Players and the Luton Choral Society. He was a Church Warden at Luton Parish Church (St Mary's) and belonged to the Luton Society of Men of the Trees. As recreation, he listed athletics, gardening and car maintenance.

Dr Charlesworth was held in high regard by all those with whom he came into contact. T.H. Hewitt noted (1950) that, during the war years, the staff found Dr Charlesworth to be a sound administrator. 'I am sure that the students of those days who now look back to that period and are capable to assess the position will agree that our Headmaster was also a wise leader and counsellor'.

> Although he is such a busy man, he is always ready to listen kindly and patiently to any youngster who comes to talk to him; he is always ready to give sound advice; he delights in meeting his former pupils, who call in to see him from time to time for a chat or for help.
>
> [Audrey Whalley (Cole), secretary of the Old Students' Association 1950]

Dr Charlesworth was all that a Headmaster should be. I had the privilege of serving under him for sixteen years and I honestly believe that if a role model for a perfect Headmaster were to be sought he would be included in the top three.

[R.D. Whalley (Staff 1961–66)]

He was always very affable and sociable, even avuncular. I never saw him lose his temper with anyone. It is often said that such a friendly approach is not desirable in someone set in charge who may subsequently need to apply some discipline. The feelings that he inspired in me however were such that I felt that I couldn't possibly let him down. There was no need for discipline; he just had my complete loyalty.

[I. Jones (Staff)]

He was one of nature's gentlemen.

[R. Blacker (Staff)]

Dr Charlesworth wrote (1950) that 'the aim always was, and still is, to establish a good school – not just a Technical School – but a School in its widest sense; and in this community to develop an interest in learning both for leisure and vocational needs – backed by advising the facilities for Further Education'. The happy atmosphere in the School was also due to the fact that Dr Charlesworth took the greatest care to appoint staff who would work well together and who would further his ideals.

On 3rd June 1937, the *Luton News* reported the setting up of the Junior Technical School.

This School is to be opened in September and viewing the modern equipment and the general facilities available for advancement of technical education, I realised that it will provide opportunities for training in industry that Luton previously has never been able to offer.

It is anticipated that most of the pupils will be drawn from the senior elementary schools of Luton, Dunstable, and South Bedfordshire with some transfers from local Secondary Schools.

They will be selected on the results of an entrance examination [in English, Mathematics and Freehand Drawing and an interview] – this is to be held on June 18th – and when they have completed the two-year course they should have a sound general education of Secondary School standard, including mathematics, English, history, geography, science, physical training and drawing.

They will also have received instruction in the principles and practice of engineering and allied industries, and will be in an advantageous position to enter upon the senior part-time courses with a view to qualifying for national certificates.

Changes in the methods of engineering production and in the building industry have stressed the need for a large supply of staff workers possessing a sound technical education with good practical experience. Many firms are finding difficulty in securing suitable candidates for promotion to the drawing office, testing departments and as foremen of production departments.

The School will also provide an excellent foundation training for boys who desire to enter the engineering departments of the Post Office, the Royal Navy or RAF.

The equipment is nearly complete. The building erected in the playground of the Boys' Modern School at Park Square is light and airy and admirably adapted for its purpose. On the ground floor there is a large workshop, equipped on modern lines with lathes, grinding, milling and shaping machines, electrical and oxyacetylene welding plants, and requisite tools. An adjoining laboratory is fitted with a steam engine plant for test work.

The fees for the Junior Technical School are £1.12s.6d (£1.62½) per term, but all boys entering the School are eligible for Special Place admission, with remission of fees as circumstances justify.

Some parents saw the Junior Technical School as more acceptable than the High School or the Modern School, the advantages being that the course was shorter and the curriculum focused on employment. It was not uncommon for children to be refused parental permission to take the scholarship examination but to receive their blessing, two years later, when they had the opportunity to move to the Technical School. In fact it appears that the School was always over subscribed.

Naturally most of the children who went to the Technical School were from the senior elementary schools but the few who wished to transfer from the secondary schools concerned the head teachers, Miss H. K. Sheldon and Mr F. E. Gauntlett, who always had a problem with pupils who failed to complete their agreed five year course. They wrote to the secondary school governors about their apprehension and suggested that

> all applications from parents should be made to us, and should then be considered in the first place unofficially by ourselves with Mr Park;
>
> that, if mutually agreed, the matter should then be referred to our Breach of rules Committee, and considered officially by them in conjunction with the three of us, before being reported to the Governors. In such a way, the interests of all sides would be duly considered; Mr Park should get really suitable pupils: and we on our part should run no risks of having the influence of Secondary Education in general, and of ourselves in particular, jeopardised.

In April 1938 the Education Committee agreed that all applications from pupils at the secondary schools to sit for the admission examination should be brought to the knowledge of the head teachers and that there should be full consultation between them and Dr Charlesworth. Transfers from the secondary schools should only take place in September of each year. However, children from the senior elementary schools were able to transfer at the beginning of any term. This meant that life in the school was very fragmented.

The School was, and remained, extremely popular with families in Luton and the rest of the county. About 70% of the admissions during the first ten years came from Luton and the surrounding areas of Dunstable and Barton, while the rest came from Leighton Buzzard, Stotfold, Bedford and Shefford. Some pupils travelled considerable distances and yet were willing to make extra journeys to take part in out-of-school activities.

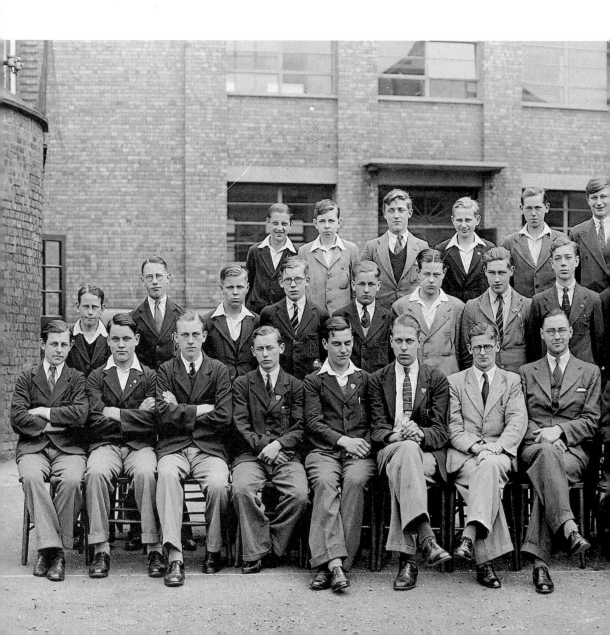

The First Pupils

Seven of our boys were successful at the [Technical School] entrance examination. To the successful seven – D. Draper, D. Payne, D. Farr, T. Clark, R. Butterfield, D. Rolls and W. Wenman – our advice is – make the most of your opportunities and try to create a good impression in your new sphere. Remember Surrey St is watching you.   [The first magazine of Surrey Street School in Luton (1937)]

Probably the first intake of boys (1937) when they had completed their two-year course in 1939. *Background: Extreme left:* The Ark, *Centre:* Jury block, *Right:* downstairs was the woodwork shop, upstairs the French room and paint shop. *Middle row:* 2nd from left, Tom Clarke, 5th from left, John Agar, *Front row :*far left, Geoff Brandham, centre, Dr S. Charlesworth, Ald. J. Burgoyne and Mr Park, 6th from right, Tom Hewitt.

The first student, in alphabetical order, was Vernon Agar. He attended the School between 1937 and 1939 and then became a part-time student at the Technical College from 1939 to 1950. He obtained his Higher National Certificate and then a degree, worked at Vauxhall Motors Ltd and then took up teaching posts, the first of these being at the Technical College (1951–1954). He moved on to other colleges in London and Singapore and finally became Principal of Elizabeth College in South Australia from where he retired in 1988.

I have many memories of the 'Tech' and recall our first morning in September 1937 when 32 nervous boys assembled in the 'ARK' to be introduced to Dr Charlesworth, W. E. Park, Mr Banner, Mr Crofton and others. I recall that the Registrar was Mr Jeffs and the secretary was Lesley Jackson.

A year later we were joined by two groups of girls in Commercial Studies and further groups of boys taking Technical Studies. The teaching staff increased and to quote my favourite 'Tech' lecturer J. E. Cule ' we rejoiced in the presence of' Frank Talbot (Mr Piano), Alf Bourlet, D. A. R. Clark (a real disciplinarian), Miss Hartley and Mrs Talbot.

Among the students in 1937, I recall Geoff Brandon, Eric Crew, Denis Murden, Ivan Talbot, Ron Dear, Derek Draper, Tom Clark, Peter Herrick, Gordon

OPPOSITE & ABOVE Technical School Football Team, probably the first (1938), on the Gas Works Ground. The School beat the Masters. School team, l-r: *Back:* G. Conisbee, H. Fletcher, D. Draper, E. Pennington, D. Culling, D. Murden, *Front:* E. Crewe, T. Clarke, R. Dear, J. Howells, P. Herrick. Masters' team: *Back:* (C. Griggs) N. Goodwin, S. Charlesworth, F. Talbot, W. Price, W.E. Parks, J.H. Jeffs, *Front:* J. Cule, C.W. Baggley, W.E. Barnett, B.J. Banner, C.W. Tinkins
(Thelma Gregory)

Conisbee, Derek Culling and others whose names escape me after 60 years.

Later I recall such characters as Vicky Belcher, Ron Paradise, Syd Jackson, Bob Green, Jim Vass, Bill Gillespie, Revd Dewi Lintern and Jim Whalley (whose father R. T. Whalley was such a fine headmaster at Stopsley Elementary School).

[Eric Millen was also a member of this group of boys.]

Oscar Ballard, from Denbigh Road School, was pupil number five. He contributed a chapter to *A Hatful of Talent*, a book published in 1994 to celebrate the founding of the University of Luton. He recalled being told 'that we would be destined, upon leaving, to be part of a group which had been conditioned in the ways of engineering, and thus would be suitable to take up apprenticeships at local firms'. During the second year they were 'joined by the Commercial School, consisting largely of girls. Our social life improved but our work probably suffered'.

Mr Ballard pointed out, as other students have done, that there were no externally recognized examinations in the Junior Technical School and, at least in the early days, 'the option to proceed to a university degree was therefore all but closed. The alternative was to build up sufficient additional qualifications to enable application for Chartered Engineer status to be obtained.'

Geoff Brandon was the first pupil to register and he became the first head boy. He recalled that

> the School consisted of only the two-storey engineering block at the bottom of the 'Yard' and the classroom above the woodwork shop. The rest of the buildings were fully occupied by the Luton Modern School, as it was then called; while a dye works stood where the basement is now situated.
>
> The Staff was large in proportion to the number of students. It consisted of Mr Park, who taught drawing; Dr Charlesworth, who combined English with History and Geography; Mr Tonkin, who took us for Mechanics and Geometry; Mr Barmer, who looked after our Mathematics, and Mr Crofter, who was our Practical Instructor.
>
> It was a good time to be in the School; all the equipment was new, and if any special jobs were required to be done, we did them as there was nobody senior to us to have the pick of them.

Admissions, Uniform etc

I suppose the first lesson I learned before I actually started at the school was to lie! It was at the oral interview; I'd passed the written exam. I sat feeling terrified and very lonely in front of a panel behind a formidable table. Dr Charlesworth was in the centre. Some simple practical tests and then the dreaded questions – so far so good until I was asked "What do you consider to be your weakest and least favourite subject?" I answered honestly "Maths", which prompted Mr Dawe (I learned his name later) to leap to his feet and immediately, if this wasn't shock enough, to snap out a question as he sucked at his knuckle. "What is a half plus a third?" I was a speechless jelly, frightened out of my wits and shy ... I failed!

Fortunately I was young enough to get another try. The next time I once again sailed through the written exam, and when the time came for the oral I was ready for it. The questions, would you believe, were exactly the same, but this time my least favourite subject was history, and I knew all the answers, but even so I pondered a bit before answering and acted hesitantly ... and passed! What it meant of course was that from being the youngest boy in the class I was up with the eldest boys: perhaps that was not such a bad thing. I will always know without any calculation that a half plus a third is five-sixths!

[W. Rainbow 1947–49]

To be fair, Walter Rainbow went on to contribute willingly to the life of the School. Dr Charlesworth wrote on his leaving report 'whenever there have been tasks for him to do, he has shown a good sense of appreciation, responsibility and efficiency. By his manner and bearing, his interests and application, he has been a very real influence to good in the Form and School'.

The uniform consisted of a maroon blazer and cap, grey pullover and maroon and silver tie. Girls wore a navy gymslip with plain bodice, scooped neck and a double pleat at the back and front. They also wore the maroon blazers and the silver and maroon ties. They had navy hats with maroon band and badge and navy gaberdine raincoats.

The first School Badge, later adopted by the Old Students' Association, was 'derived from the old Bedfordshire insignia of the days before 1951 when the county possessed no coat of arms, and showed the strong association which existed between our school and the county in the days before the 1944 Act'. The shells or silver scallops are derived from the coat of arms of the Russells, Earls and Dukes of Bedford.

The later badge was 'representative of our present links with the Borough of Luton and with the County of Bedford and of our Departments of Commerce, Building and Engineering, together with the School Motto, in Latin, which translated means, *With mind and hands*. The School was divided into four teams: blue, green, red and yellow. The words of the first School Song were written by W. Edward Bowen and the music composed by Kenneth D. Abbott, both members of the staff.

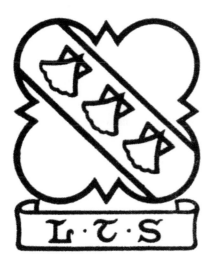

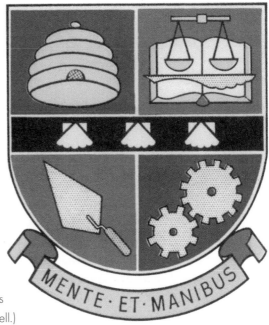

ABOVE The original School Badge. RIGHT The new badge was probably introduced soon after 1948. (Photographs suggest that there was another badge as well.)

Forward! Upward!

Here we challenge now the future –
Trowel, compasses and pen,
Plan the house, design the motor,
Change the merchandise of men.
We will build your stately dwelling
On foundations sure and strong,
Upright, solid, all excelling,
Fashioned to endure long.

We will make you goods exceeding
Past attempts and present means,
Give you power to travel, speeding
By the might of our machines.
We'll record your honest dealings,
Trade to trade as man to man
In a world at peace, revealing
Faith in the eternal plan.

Forward, upward to the future,
Trowel, compasses and pen
Harnessing the gifts of nature,
To the work of God and men.
Forward, Upward, all uniting
Over land and sea and sky,
With a vision pure delighting
In the skills of hand and eye.

Mr Whalley recalls that, when he joined the staff of the School in September 1950, he was faced with a completely new experience, having been previously involved with Grammar and Secondary Modern Schools which taught boys from 11 years of age to possibly 18. The 'Tech', on the other hand, had a 13- to 15-year-old age range and a new intake and exodus each term.

The intake each term consisted of two classes of pupils with an engineering bias, two with a building bias and two with a commercial bias. They would be called E1A and E1B, B1A and B1B and C1A and C1B. In the second term they would become E2A and E2B and so on until they reached the sixth term as E6A etc when they left school. Later, I believe in 1951, engineering and building were merged to be called technical but, looking at a later timetable of mine, I see that although

Mr Whalley and the Engineering Class, April 1950 – April 1952.
Left to right: Back: Michael Thompson, Brian Clark, John Harris, Garry Cook, Rowland Winser, John Keeling, Roger Wood, Arthur Stonebridge,
Middle: Robert Walters, Peter Mardle, Gerald Milton, Alan Peach, Raymond Pickett, Richard Gibson, John Beswick, Leo (Tony) Williams,
Front: Derek Jones, David Doust, Terry Dear, Anthony Loveday, Mr R.D. Whalley, John Gray, Alan Pritchard, Brian Lawrence, Haydn Watkins,
Missing: Geoffrey Beech, Roy Hall, Ramon Mortimer (R.D. Whalley)

most of the forms are T forms, there still remains one E5B and an E6A so it would appear that the original E and B selections ran out over the two years. This system necessitated much extra administration and leaving reports by staff each term.

Another aspect new to me was the size of the classes we had in the large workshops we shared with the College. These required two members of staff in the one workshop. I thought this might be a recipe for conflict between staff but a system of one member taking the lead with one class whilst the other member assisted and the roles reversed for the next group worked very well and was an early runner for team teaching that became a new fashion in the 1970–80s.

Accommodation

Technical schools were always the Cinderellas when it came to accommodation and were usually left with any available empty and unsuitable spaces. The Luton Junior Technical School was no exception. At first the School occupied part of the building which was about to be vacated by the Luton Modern School. They had the use of a room in the Woodwork Block and a new Engineering Block containing a large Metalwork room on the Ground Floor and three classrooms on the First Floor. When the Modern School moved out in January 1938, the Technical School took over the building although, of course, the Technical College used the same premises. The lack of accommodation was an ever-present nightmare. Once Dr Charlesworth is said to have timetabled eight classes for one room with none for another. Changing rooms was chaotic and 'only succeeded with the goodwill of pupils who saw it as some kind of adventure'.

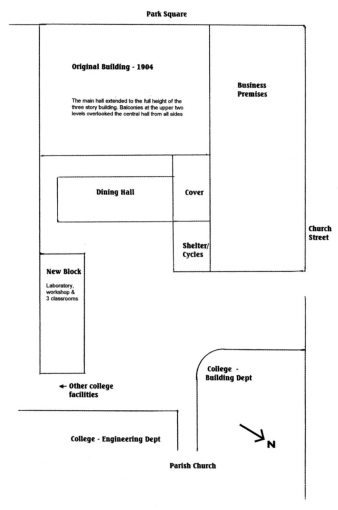

Technical School Layout

Park Square

Original Building - 1904

The main hall extended to the full height of the three story building. Balconies at the upper two levels overlooked the central hall from all sides

Business Premises

Dining Hall

Cover

Church Street

Shelter/ Cycles

New Block

Laboratory, workshop & 3 classrooms

← Other college facilities

College - Building Dept

College - Engineering Dept

N

Parish Church

Plan of the Park Square School. (Peter Goodwin)

However, to give a complete picture, I must go back to April 1938 when the School assembled in Room 103, with the veterans of Forms A and B seated to the left and right of the room, and the new boys from Form C standing in the centre. I well remember the procedure – Mr Tonkin read the lesson, Dr Charlesworth led prayers, while Mr Banner and I stood by. One great feature of those days, which was soon to be lost never to return, was that we had just enough classroom accommodation – Rooms 103, 18 and the woodwork shop. The Staff room was also quite spacious when one considers the number of occupants. It was a strip four feet wide at the end of Room 18; it even had a gas cooker and fireplace! The playground, which also served as playing field, was a strip twenty-five feet wide between the woodwork block and the Dye works – what times we had!

September 1938, saw the entry on the scene of the Commercial School. Before long, the boys were asking for their course to be extended to three years, and so the T3 Form came into being. It is still intended for those who can best benefit by it. At the same time, there was a considerable increase in the number of Staff. The original few welcomed Messrs, Barnett, Talbot, Cule, and Birch and Misses Harley and Cahill.   [T. H. Hewitt 1950 (Staff)]

In 1936, work on a new building was begun. This was known as the Jury block after the County Architect. For obvious reasons, work stopped during the Second World War but was resumed afterwards. Building was again halted in 1948 and the block was eventually demolished in 1959 on the instructions of the Ministry of Education which claimed that it was neither adequate nor appropriate. The site was then cleared to make way for the College of Further Education and eventually Luton University. All that ever existed of the proposed Jury building was an imposing entrance leading down concrete steps to the basement which was used for classrooms and also as a place of safety during air raids. In 1949, plans to build two new Technical Schools, one for 300 boys and another for 300 girls, were approved but were put on hold and never materialized.

The comings and goings of groups of children were seen to be amusing by some people but were not appreciated by members of staff who found them very wearisome. For example, Mr Whalley remembers that, in the late 50s, the technical workshops were 'off site and the responsibility of trudging through snow, sleet, fog and rain and oft-times having to wait on street corners for the arrival of the late class that had travelled some distance to be exchanged for your class … put very great pressure on the staff'.

One venue was the balcony of the Chapel in Chapel Street where different groups occupied the alcoves. The children are said to have listened to the most interesting of the four lessons being conducted. Sometimes groups had to go looking for a 'home' and it was not uncommon for 'changeovers' to be made in the middle of Waller Street. On other occasions, members of staff would stop to pass the time

Staff of the College and the School in front of the Jury building, n.d. but before 1950.
(*Patricia Morgan*)

of day with acquaintances, for example a former pupil on police duty. During his teacher training, Mr R.D. Whalley had been given instructions on how to take children out of school and he tried faithfully to put them into practice.

> Two responsible pupils would be chosen, one to lead and one to be at the rear of the 'crocodile' while walking on the pavements. I was to control this 'crocodile' from the other side of the street by signalling to these two pupils. The lead pupil was to stop at every junction automatically until receiving the signal to proceed, and the rear pupil was to make sure that no-one got behind him.

It was quite a stretch to the games field and we had to pass the Grand Theatre where some 'girlie' shows were presented. The posters displayed outside caused the 'crocodile' to slow down almost to a stop while these were studied with great interest by the pupils. It became quite a feat to overcome this obstacle without too much loss of time and I felt a satisfaction at succeeding very well.

Further along the road we passed the Education Offices. I continued to use the method of control I had been shown at Training College, and the 'crocodile' walked on the pavement visible from the Education Office windows and I walked on the opposite pavement not visible to the inmates of the hallowed building. The inevitable happened! The Headmaster got a rocket for sending classes to the games field unescorted and I was called to explain the situation.

Mr Whalley also took classes for PE at Youth Headquarters. There was 'an adjacent corridor with pegs on the wall and this was used as a cloakroom. I had thirty minutes to transport the class from the playground [at Park Square] to this corridor, get them changed, teach the lesson, get them changed again and transport them back to the main building.' In winter, games were taken on Pope's Meadow. That meant twenty minutes to get there and twenty minutes to get back with very little time for play. No washing or showering facilities were available. Another problem was that the field sloped towards the road and balls were sometimes run over by buses.

Other locations used for classes over the years were: the Fire Station, Waller Street Chapel, Surrey Street School, the Youth Headquarters in Chapel Street and a disused hat factory in Guildford St. This hat factory was hot in summer and cold in winter.

> [It] had consisted of four floors and a basement. Apart from the ground floor where the display showroom and the store room were situated, the other floors had just one large room. These had to be partitioned into workable spaces and the apprentices attending the College classes quickly did the job. [They had to remove the partitions temporarily for City and Guilds examinations.] The Painting and Decorating room was on the second floor and the French room on the fourth floor.
>
> … The Chemistry laboratory … was to be in the display showroom at the front of the building. It had a shop front size glass window that went the full width of the room and from about three feet from the floor to the ceiling. The bottom half of this window was painted. Glass is quite a good conductor of heat so the room was very cold in winter and well into the nineties on a hot summer day. Glass also transmits sound waves well and as this window fronted a busy main street the room was continuously noisy. There were no opening windows but there was an antique extractor fan in the top right hand of the window … any acrid or obnoxious gases that were produced during demonstrations were drawn by the fan across the pupils in the class … I must report though that this room had two great advantages over the old lab for it had a sink and gas taps.   [R. Whalley]

The problem of space became even more critical as building for the new College of Technology took up more and more of the playground area. (During the 1950s, the Technical College became Luton and South Bedfordshire College of Further Education and then the Luton College of Technology.) *The Shell* (1954–55) commented that 'from day to day, Park Square remains the centre of our far-flung battlefields'. Queues form regularly for Chapel Street, Waller Street, Guildford Street, Pope's Meadow, Bell's Close and, once, a humorist was heard to cry 'Line up here for Sandy, St Neots, and the North!'. It was also generally hoped that man would never land on the moon because it was feared that outposts would be set up there.

It's a long lane !!!!

However, Dr Charlesworth looked beyond the problem saying that 'present pupils will ever be remembered for their excellent co-operation in these difficulties'. The promised new building, for the exclusive use of the School, had seemed to be an unobtainable dream but, on 7th November 1955, the footings were dug on a site in New Bedford Road.

LEFT
'It's a long lane!!!'
by T. Dennis
(1956-7 Shell)

Curriculum

Have you ever thought of what might happen if the teachers were suddenly inspired by some power from above, to be kind to pupils? How would it be possible to keep the teachers under control if they once got a chance to launch out on a kindness campaign? Would it not be terrible if, when gently chided with a broken chair or a heavenly body from above, the only result was a broad and sickly smile instead of a shout of rage and the shuddering of the earth as the teacher in question charged madly around the classroom looking for the innocent-looking offender!

No, I don't think it would be at all nice to be given a smile which is nothing short of devastating and worse than any amount of detentions which, although intended for a punishment, are very often quiet half-hours where the bulk of one's homework can be done or for the lazy people a quiet and refreshing game of 'Noughts and Crosses' may be enjoyed. So be warned, fellow criminals, you never know!

Now, if I don't get three detentions for writing this article, then I will eat three copies of the School Song. [R. G. Devonshire]

In the early days of the school the roles of girls and boys were fairly clearly defined: boys followed the technical course and girls the commercial, although a few boys did choose to follow the commercial route. Technical Schools were, ideologically, autonomous, with staff being able to decide the courses which were appropriate for the area. This was not intended to mean that they were able to 'escape from definite and exacting tests of their efficiency'. The lack of any recognized external examinations did, however, narrow the choice for future employment. Girls in the Commercial classes studied for the examinations of the Royal Society of Arts.

In Luton, links between the School and local industry remained strong, with firms helping the School and, later, receiving trained ex-pupils as apprentices or employees. The School also depended on the amount of material available for any particular course and members of staff, for example Norman Garside, head of the technical side, was known to visit local firms to scrounge materials such as angle iron, sand and cement.

Boys' Curriculum
    English
    Geography
    History
    Mathematics (Arithmetic, Algebra, Geometry, Trigonometry)
    Geometrical and Engineering Drawing
    Science (Chemistry, Physics, Mechanics)
    Workshop (Metalwork, Woodwork, Electrical Work, Processing)
    PT

Girls' Curriculum
    Book-keeping
    Commerce
    Shorthand
    Typewriting
    Cookery
    Speech Training
    French and optional German
    Arithmetic with a commercial bias if required

Technical Class 1944–46, Easter 1946. *Left to right: Top:* Roger McLaren, Olive Walker, Margaret Warden, Betty Cole, M. Howard, Thelma Murden, Molly Marsom, Clifford Howe. *Middle:* Mavis Clarke, Molly Faulkner, Thelma Simpkins, Josie Cook, Mavis Litchfield, Pauline Kenny, Freda Robertson, Adine Elliott. *Front:* Betty Blood, Iris Coles, Beryl Taylor, Dr Charlesworth, Miss Ainsworth, Mr Parks, Mary Wildman, Pamela Sharp (*Thelma Gregory*)

Personal Reminiscence

On the 9th of April, 1945 I began my two year commercial course at Luton Technical College. My education to this point had been at Burr Street Junior School and Britain Street Senior School in Dunstable in classes of fifty pupils or more.

At the College I found myself in a class of 25, two boys and twenty-three girls, drawn from quite a large area of Bedfordshire and bussed into school daily. After a couple of terms the number in class dropped to 23. Our form teacher was Miss Z. Lyus, a young woman with whom we could identify, very able and a good teacher.

We were taught English, Geography, History, French, Arithmetic, Bookkeeping, Commerce, Shorthand, Typewriting, Cookery, Speech training, PT and Games. I notice from my report book that, in the second year, we also had classes in Religious Instruction and Music, plus a period allocated to Social Activities: my choice being drama. We put on a performance of an excerpt from *Pride and Prejudice* by Jane Austen; I played Mr Collins! Later in life I was to play the parts of Jane and also Elizabeth, so I know Pride and Prejudice pretty well!

So began the most intensive and rewarding period of my formal education. It was infinitely better being taught in a class of 25 pupils who wanted to learn and by proficient teachers who demanded, and had, our attention. I seem to remember that each class period was 45 minutes, although some subjects were given twice that time. For instance, Games: the College in Park Square didn't have any playing fields so, once a week, we tramped through the town to Pope's Meadow, 20 minutes walk away, for 45 minutes of play, then tramped back again to Park Square. However, PT, for which we took off our gymslips and tucked our white blouses into our navy knickers, took place in the main hall, sometimes with onlookers from the balconies above.

The College building seemed quite old; the main hall comprised a ground floor and two upper floors with balconies overlooking the ground floor. The classrooms were situated around the ground floor and the balconies. Students were allocated lockers. Mine was on the top floor. Those were sought after because they were larger but, of course, necessitated a lot more running up and down stairs. Part of the top floor, and separate from the rest of us, was occupied by the Art School.

The uniform for girls was: navy gymslip, white blouse, school tie, maroon blazer, navy hat with maroon hatband (which I still have) and navy gabardine raincoat.

The lunch hour was staggered. Some of us had only three quarters of an hour, others one and a half hours, but we who had the shorter time, left school earlier in the afternoon, which was nice because we had quite a lot of homework.

I was very proud not to have been absent during my two years at the College and a school friend and I, in the winter of 1947, when heavy snowfall stopped buses from running, walked from Dunstable to Luton so as not to break our record.

My two years at Luton Technical College drew to a close on 28th March 1947. In my last term I had been elected Head Girl by my fellow prefects, and so ended a very happy and rewarding period of my life.

On the third day after leaving, I started work in the office of a newly formed manufacturing company in Dunstable and, for several years, continued to attend the College on a day-release basis. The company prospered, eventually becoming a Public Company quoted on the London Stock Exchange and, in time, I became Secretary/PA to the Chairman and Managing Director.

It was a tribute to the standard of training and commercial education that the College offered that many employers who took on former pupils would look first to the College for new recruits when the need arose. [Lois Counter]

Pupils taking part in a bricklaying class at the back of the School, supervised by
Mr George Tolley. (*LN*)

Building Department

There were political overtones behind the opening, in 1942, of the Junior Building
School, as the government foresaw the need for a large post-war building
programme. The intake was similar to that of the Technical and Commercial forms
although the proportion of country boys was higher.

Workshop practice
      Brickwork
      Plastering
      Painting
      Plumbing
      Concreting
      Carpentry
      Joinery
Electrical Installation
Appropriate Technology

As to general lines of organisation of such a school, [Mr W.E. Park] suggested it should be closely linked with the existing technical schools under the same headmaster, with the same age entry, 100 per cent special places, the same scale of fee remission and special place award and the same type of entrance selection examination.

The course should normally be two years, with an optional third year for more definite training in some related craft, or for selected pupils, to work leading to profession training.

It was suggested that the initial cost for equipment would be small and the annual cost per pupil comparable with that of the existing schools.

The governors adopted the scheme in principle for submission to a special branch of the Board of Education as a basis for consideration.

[*Luton News* March 1942]

At first the Building School was very successful; by 1947, there were over 300 students in the department and several enthusiastic pupils made names for themselves in post-war building. However, about a quarter of the students who joined in the early days did not enter the building trade. By 1948, 60% entered the engineering industry, including about 15% to Vauxhall Motors. These students went into engineering without having studied the correct type of mathematics. So, in 1951, a decision was taken to wind down the Building School and, by 1953, it had completely closed. Potential builders were absorbed into the technical classes, although still specialising in practical subjects.

Significant Landmarks 1938–1958

The Second World War

The first group of pupils had just come to the end of their two year course when the country was hit by the outbreak of the Second World War. A third year of study (T3) was offered to boys who had not been successful in finding employment. Pressure on accommodation also increased when other courses were set up in the College. One of these was for women being trained in munitions work and others were for soldiers on welding courses and army officer cadet courses. Room also had to be found for evacuees from the North Western Polytechnic Boys' School. 'Country children' were given a 'town retreat' in the home of a town child where they could go if there were problems with transport. These homes were also used in the period of evening external examinations.

In common with other schools in the town, children in the Technical School had to practise air raid drill. A plan for basement classrooms which could be used as air raid shelters was submitted. This was approved and financed by the Ministry of Defence. 'War work' was undertaken. For example, about 40 pupils attended a farm camp at Colworth during the summer holiday 1944, something like 3,000 hours being worked in all. In the early part of the autumn term some 50 boys were released on odd days for potato picking.

1944 Education Act

Government Reports, notably the *Hadow Report* (1926), had advocated secondary education for every child. The *Spens Report* (1938) proposed that Junior Technical Schools should become Technical High Schools and enjoy parity with Grammar Schools. The *Norwood Report* (1943) accepted that there were different types of children, academic, technical and practical, and that these different groups should attend schools which matched their ability. All these Reports culminated in the important 1944 Education Act which stipulated that every child should receive the secondary education to which he was suited by age, aptitude and ability. The leaving age was raised to 15 from April 1945 but the age of entry to the Technical School remained at 13.

1948 – The School Becomes Independent

Technical High Schools (with different names but all intended to cater for children

Mr Harrison and Class c.1946.

whose future was expected to be in industry or commerce) began to appear soon after the war but they experienced the same old problems of unsuitable buildings. In 1948, Luton Junior Technical Secondary School separated from the College and became autonomous with its own staff of 29. It became known as the Luton County Secondary Technical School. Although there was still a vocational bias, more time was given to general subjects such as Music and Religious Instruction. Electrical work and processing disappeared. As ever, crocodiles of children were to be seen commuting to and from Chapel Street Methodist Hall, Waller Street Methodist Chapel and Central Youth Headquarters. In 1948, W. E. Park took a post as head of Vauxhall Motors Apprentice School, the school that had been started with the first boys from the Junior Technical School.

1949 – Increasing Numbers

In 1949 came the suggested plans for two new technical schools, schools which never materialized. (The County Development Plan suggested three.) The *Luton News* reported the views of Councillor Hedley Lawrence who deplored the fact that these schools were not to be co-educational. He was critical of the syllabus of the existing School and spoke of 'this pandering to such firms as Vauxhall Motors'.

> The child is spending too much time on the lathe learning to turn out parts for Vauxhall Motors, when more of that time should be spent on education. He can learn more about a lathe when he gets down to Vauxhall.
>
> Let us spend the time in the school on education – teaching the child to be a good citizen, to learn how to appreciate the arts and good music.

1954 – Widening Horizons

The Technical School continued to be 'fodder for industry' and it was becoming obvious that changes were needed. 1954 was a very significant year in this context because a decision was made to prepare children for the General Certificate of Education O-level examinations. Pitman's examinations were introduced for commercial students.

> Although the old School Certificate was taken by pupils in the past, it was always after they had left School, and as a result of further study. Last year, however, a group of 15 pupils remained at School to their ninth term, and so became eligible to sit the new GCE examinations, which allowed them an extra qualification over and above the fact they that they were well up to the SE apprenticeship standard of the National Certificate course. Of 56 subject entries taken by boys, 34 were obtained; a noteworthy achievement for pupils who had followed a short three year course. We congratulate them, and think they have set both a precedent and a standard. Others are advised to follow their example.

Mrs Clarke and her class of 1950–52. (*June Culleton*)

Further, we have returned to external examinations for pupils on the commercial side; and, since the beginning of the year, out of 131 subject entries, 102 were obtained. Again a precedent for present and later pupils; and congratulations must go to the pioneer candidates of the Commercial side.

Subjects taken at GCE level included English Literature, Mathematics, Physics with Chemistry, Technical Drawing and French. It appears that these were all taken by boys! The next year English Language, Geography, Physics, Chemistry, Technical Drawing and Metalwork were added while two girls did Commercial Subjects. The following year, most of the entrants were boys but seven girls took Commercial Subjects and one Religious Knowledge.

The importance of this milestone cannot be over-rated. Students from the School were able to look on wider horizons and, as time went by, many took up careers which had not been considered when the School had a totally technical and commercial bias. Two years later, A-levels were being offered which put the School on a parity with the two Grammar Schools in the town.

In 1954 Governors discussed plans to change the name of the School. Suggestions included: the Duke of Bedford School, The Wardens, Bradgers Lea, Kingsdown and Rosslyn, but the 'Tech' had sentimental value and could not be abandoned.

1958 – New Building

The year, 1958, was one of the most significant in the life of the School for it was able to move into purpose-built accommodation. The Luton Technical School had been the only one of its kind in the County and 'youngsters had been prepared to travel up to 50 miles a day to attend'. By 1958, other technical schools had been opened, notably Kingsbury in Dunstable, but the Luton school was still taking large numbers of pupils from the north of the county and as far away as St Neots.

Life in the School 1938–1958

Several school magazines from the 1950s have been made available and, from these, it has been possible to build up an idea of the lively and varied life in the Technical School. The impression gleaned is of a school where everyone worked hard and played hard, a school which was happy with itself. The picture of life in the School which is presented here is far from being a complete one. For one thing, it is sometimes difficult to be accurate about specific dates and the ones which are given are often the publication dates of the relevant *Shell* magazine. It is also regrettable that it has not been possible to do justice to all the pupils and members of staff who worked so hard and in so many ways. Those who are named are *examples* of the kind of dedication and enthusiasm which was demonstrated by so many over the years. Apologies are offered to all the rest.

> When I first arrived in the hall, my first impression of the school was that I felt rather lonely; then some older boys came up and spoke to me and made friends with me. It was then that I thought of the friendliness of the boys.
>
> I, and some more first term friends of mine, asked a prefect where room seven was. He didn't just give us a rough idea, but he actually took the trouble to take us up to the room, and that is what I call real courtesy. I also noticed the tidiness of the school, which, I think, makes a good impression.
>
> The school rules are very fair, and are not too strict, and it is up to us to keep them. If we break them, it is entirely our own fault, and we deserve to go into detention. [T.W. Coppen 1954–55]

Sport

Athletics

On Sports Days, which were held on Wardown Sports Field, the School was divided into Upper Senior, Middle Senior and Lower Senior. There were flat races, hurdles, high jump, long jump and discus competitions. In 1953–54 egg and spoon, sack, three-legged and relay races were added.

The Technical School was at a disadvantage when it came to inter-school sports:

Cricket team, winners of 'Emery' Cricket Cup played at Wardown against Beech Hill School, probably 1952. *Left to right: Back:* R.Fincham (scorer), P. Harlow, I. Harry, P. Spall, A. Allen, R. Millard, R.D. Whalley, *Front:* P. Clarke, R. West, M. Jordan (capt.) J. Boyles, C. Millson. Jordan went on to play cricket for the County. Harry for Luton School football team. (*LN*)

We had no competitors in the age groups 11–13. In addition, we were a mixed school of about 550 pupils, competing against single-sex schools of around 800, for example, Luton High, Luton Grammar, Challney Boys and Challney Girls. The one year when we almost won the shield (we lost by 1 point in the final relay) our chief rivals were on their knees in prayer and our team were on their knees eating grass with anxiety. My hair turned grey. I managed the training of school teams, and the school sports from around 1951 until I took over as Head. We always had pupils competing in the County championships, and often had one or more boys or girls competing at National level.   [R. Ellis]

Cricket

There was a strong cricket team, 'mainly due to the fact that so many boys came from the country districts where they played for the village teams'. The enthusiasm was exemplary: most matches were played after school and did not finish until 8.30 to 9.00pm after which the out-of-town boys had to catch trains or buses (sometimes both) and be ready to leave for school the following morning soon after 6 o'clock.

Matches were played between the boys and the staff and also against Challney, Denbigh, the Harpur Schools in Bedford, Old Bedford Road, Northfields in Dunstable and Surrey Street. The 'Tech' regularly won the local cricket trophy and boasted one former pupil who played for Surrey. He was Tom Clarke, one of the first intake of students.

> Members of the School will have watched with pleasure and admiration the career of Tom Clarke, the Surrey opening batsman, who is an old boy – in fact, one of the first boys to wear the maroon blazer and hope to build up the good reputation of the Tech in Luton and the County.
>
> Following a successful winter's coaching engagement in South America, Tom Clarke has made consistently good scores for the champion county, and has been honoured by being invited to play for the MCC against the West Indies touring team. According to newspaper comment, he was unfortunate in not becoming England's opening batsman. [1956–57 *Shell*]

Football

Many members of staff gave up their time after school and on Saturday mornings to referee house and inter-school matches.

The football team was successful and, in the 1951–52 season, won the Luton Schools League Championship for the fourth year in succession and the Wix Shield for the first time. It was reported that there had been 'an excellent team spirit throughout the season, and boys have played the game cleanly and unselfishly for the honour of their school'. Some talented boys went on to play for Luton Town Schoolboys and Bedfordshire Schoolboys.

Hockey

Hockey was played but does not receive a lot of attention in the *Shell*. In 1953, it was reported that the weather was not good enough for classes to play in their games lessons and, as a result, no house matches could be held at the end of term. There was a lot of interest, however, and groups of girls, together with girls from the High School, regularly took trips to Wembley to watch international matches.

'Who said hockey is dangerous?' (1954-55 *Shell*)

Mr Froud and the Technical School Rugby team 1954. (*LN*)

Netball

Netball was at a disadvantage because of the problems posed by building work on and around the school playground. In 1952, the School played in the Luton Schools Netball League for the first time for some years and came sixth. In 1954–55 the *Shell* noted that

> netball facilities have been severely curtailed this term owing to the building activities of the College. We have not had the use of the playground and our only games have been on a grass court at Wardown when the weather permitted … consequently we have had to withdraw from the Luton Schools Netball League and our only match has been a friendly one with Denbigh Road. The 1955–56 season again had its difficulties.

At the end of the Spring Term, a team was selected to enter the Netball Rally held at Challney School. The team finished last out of seven, 'which was not surprising'. However, 'they took their defeats in good part and thoroughly enjoyed the afternoon'.

Rugby

1951–52 was the first real season. A number of boys consistently turned up for Saturday morning practices at Stockwood Park, many of them travelling for considerable distances. The team played against Beech Hill, Bedford, Cedars, Cheshunt, Harpur School, Luton Grammar and Old Bedford Road. During the

1956 Boxing team, taken at the back of the School. Mr Froud is on the left. (*LN*)

1953–54 season, a course of six lectures was held at the Grammar School, at the end of which the boys listened to a talk given by 'one of the game's great personalities – Mr Gadney – the uncrowned king of referees'. The following season proved to be a successful one. 'The games were not only won on the field … but by the blackboard talks which preceded every game, and by the advice and encouragement which came in the form of 'dainty whispers' from the touch-line'.

Swimming

Swimming was organized and coached by Mr W. Davies and Mr R. Ellis. Outdoor swimming was limited by the weather but there were good results from the practices in the indoor pool at Waller Street. At the School Galas, beginners, elementary, intermediate and advanced certificates were given out. There was training for intermediate life-saving awards and, in 1953–54, 14 bronze medallions were gained. Two years later, a boy became the first to win the RLSS Award of Merit. In 1954–55, the School won the Victory Shield at the Luton Schools Annual Gala. There were successes at county level and boys went on to swim at the English Schools National Gala at Lancaster. In 1955–56, the Dillingham Shield, 'after gracing our hall for a number of years, was won from us by the Grammar School team, but by such a narrow margin, that we have high hopes of regaining it soon'.

Boxing Club

In 1950, a few enthusiasts wanted to 'place the school in the foreground of the boxing world'; the outcome was the formation of the Boxing Club which became very successful. It was based at Waller St and was supervised by Mr Froud, a well-known amateur boxer.

> Training is not all drudgery; we are often invited to take a chance of hitting our instructor on the nose, but we invariably run up against what appears to be a thousand elbows, and so far none of the class has succeeded in making yet another kink in that classical proboscis!

J. Bygrave represented the School in the County Championships and was runner up in the Great Britain championships in 1951–52. The following year was very successful 'We can now boast six County champions in the club, and a finalist and a semi-finalist, and, as a reward for their showing, we are holding the county Shield awarded annually to the school obtaining the most points in the county championships'. In 1955–56, the School held the County Shield for the third time in succession. The newly-formed boxing team from Icknield School 'put up a good show in finishing second on points to us, we asked them to display the trophy for a term in appreciation of their effort'. In 1956–57, the club was invited to take part in the Open Tournament run by Vauxhall Motors.

Social Life

The 1946–47 *Shell* notes that 'two terms ago' it was decided that on Friday afternoon there would be a free period for social activities. This side of school life was obviously considered to be important and a former pupil who moved to a school in Nottingham wrote to say that 'socially, the school is a long way behind Luton, a condition which at first affected my happiness quite a lot … I am sure you are very fortunate at Luton in this respect'. The general impression is that most of these societies were for either boys or girls, not both.

Chess Club

There was a Chess Club in the 1940s but it seems to have been revived in 1951, Mr Tolley being one of the guiding lights. Thirty regular members and occasional visitors met in the dinner hour. That same year a team of six boys came second in the first year of the Luton Schools' Chess League.

Dancing Club

When two Friday afternoon periods were first set apart for social activities, a Country Dancing and Advanced Physical Training group was set up by Miss Thomas and Miss Lyus. In the 1950s, there was a very successful Dancing Club which provided enormous happiness and entertainment, not to mention social accomplishments, over the years. There were three sessions a week, one for lessons at the Mayfair School of Dancing, a practice at the Waller Street Youth Headquarters in a lunch hour and a third for 'pure enjoyment'. Dances learnt included American Swing, Samba, Rumba, Charleston and the Tango. Collections were taken and the money used to buy gramophone records. Mr R. Whalley and Mr C. Baggaley, deputy registrar in the College Office, actively supported the Dancing Club.

In 1953, free fortnightly dances were inaugurated and there were also Easter dances and Leavers' dances.

> For the great success of the dances we must thank Dr Charlesworth and his helpers, who have put in so much hard work, in giving up their evenings for our benefit … we dance to records at the normal Saturday evening dances, but at the Grand Leavers' Dance, at the end of each term, we enjoy the company and the music of Don Cleaver and his band … Mr Whalley and Mr Richardson organize the dancing club which is held on Tuesdays and Fridays. On alternate Fridays, a new dance is attempted under the guidance of Mr Whalley.

Design

In their Friday afternoon session, students made leather goods, book marks, brooches, letter racks, candlesticks and trinket boxes. '*Music while you work* was provided by Mr Abbott and his orchestra in Room 4 and by the Country Dancing group in the hall'.

Dramatic Society

This Society was formed at the beginning of the Winter Term 1946 and was led by Miss Griffiths and Mr Bowen. Two plays were produced that term: *Elizabeth Refuses* and *The Grand Cham's Diamond*.

Engineering Society

The inaugural meeting was held in September 1946 and the aim of the society was to 'encourage members to take an active part in the proceedings by entering into the discussion and preparing papers themselves'. There were talks, for example, on railway locomotives, printing processes, the production of petroleum and coal mining.

The Geographical Society

This was run by Mr Anderson. There were visits to local industries and films were shown. A number of pupils were introduced to pen-friends in Holland.

The School Orchestra, probably 1947. Dr Abbott, standing on the left with baton.

Literary Society

After 'recent extension of literary studies' (presumably the introduction of the General Certificate of Education) trips were undertaken to London theatres. The *Shell* magazine gives accounts of visits to see *Macbeth*, *As You Like It* and *Richard II*.

Music Society

There was a thriving music department in the School under Mr K.J.D. Abbott (later Dr Abbott) who was the organist and choirmaster at the neighbouring St Mary's Parish Church. The School boasted large choirs and an orchestra. The Musical Society frequently combined with Stopsley School and the choristers of the Church to give concerts. There was a musical input into Speech Days and annual Carol Services were held. In 1951, there was a concert to celebrate the Festival of Britain. Lunch hour concerts were begun in 1952. They started at 12.30 p.m. and lasted for 45 minutes.

Former students, notably John Underwood and Doreen (or Noreen) Hudson who had studied at the Royal College of Music in London, came back to give performances.

Model Engineering Club

By 1946, the Aero-Modelling group was constructing models which were capable of taking part in competitions. The School provided drawings and materials and jigs were set up to facilitate accuracy.

The Model Engineering Group was inaugurated in February 1950 for boys who wanted facilities greater than those offered by the average home for 'making things'. Mr Duell was in charge but Mr Hepburn came 'because he delighted in the thought of seeing chaps make other than mathematical hashes'. The club was held once a week, after school. Boys could make whatever they liked: angler's gaffs, angle-poise reading lamps, model water cranes, diesel aero-engines, woodworker's lathe, chessmen turned in mild steel. One project was designing an O gauge railway. In 1951–52, it was reported that 'machines have turned, the anvil has rung, and metal has been cast into sand, the results being wholly satisfying in the respect that most of the work which has been started has been followed to its successful conclusion'. Finished products were on show at a stand on Speech Day.

Trips to centres of industry were organized. These included Swindon Railway yard, Messrs. Allen at Bedford, Derby locomotive works and the Ford factory at Dagenham.

Automation

I come from haunts of iron and steel,
I make a sudden whirring,
For, in my brain of wires and valves,
Electronic thoughts are stirring.

I go to shop and factory;
My uses are abundant;
But, as I do the work of ten
The workers go redundant.

I don't need rest, or food or drink,
My parts all work together,
For men may work and then retire,
But I go on for ever.

[Michael Raynham]

Pantomime

Mr Charles Baggaley produced successful pantomimes. The first, *Cinderella*, was held in 1954. All the costumes and properties were made by the players. To say that *Aladdin* (1955) 'went with a 'bang' is almost to put it literally! A judicious admixture of magnesium flash-powder and an electric current produced some excellent effects for the entry of the Genie'. Later productions were *Little Red Riding Hood* and *Dick Whittington and His Cat*.

Perspex Club

The club started with modelling simple articles such as bracelets, rings and brooches and worked up to paper knives, cigarette cases and serviette rings.

Science Club

This group also seems to have concentrated on visits to local industry and boys were encouraged to give talks on subjects which interested them.

Social Evenings

The 1953–54 edition of the *Shell* notes that there were free fortnightly socials, held between 6.30 and 9.30 p.m. on alternate Saturday evenings during the Christmas and Easter terms. Upwards of 200 pupils came, some with friends, to the School Hall for old time and modern dancing.

Stamp Club

The stamp club met every Friday for swaps and 'much talking'. Mr Tolley had exhibited the penny black and the two-penny blue, the first stamps.

Table Tennis Club

Table tennis seems to have been the most widely played game in the School. Boys and girls practised in the dinner hours but, after school, when the College took over the building, the Warden of the Youth Headquarters in Waller Street allowed the club to use their hall and tables. There was a House League and games were played against Denbigh Road, the Grammar School, Stopsley and Surrey Street. In 1951–52, only one match was lost out of 14 played with the Grammar School. By 1954–55, the School had a team of 34.

Visits and Holidays

Britain, a land of valleys and rivers; a river on an early summer morn, with a light mist resting on the grass and on the water; the calling of the moorhen in the rushes and the rooks in the high trees; this is the scene I would remember as a fisherman.

My impression of the industrial towns of Britain would bring quite a different picture: a valley of roof tops and tall chimneys, with a smoky blue haze hanging over all; early in the morning, throngs of people winding their ways through the dark streets on their way to work; the high-pitched note of a works hooter heard in the distance.

I would always remember the sight of the South Bank Exhibition, when I first saw it from Charing Cross Bridge: the sun shining on the huge Dome of Discovery; the Skylon under the deep blue sky, still with the network of scaffolding reaching almost to its peak; the workmen busy inserting the hundreds of lamps, which at night would make it a huge pillar of fire.

These scenes of Britain, together with the friendship of its people, I should always remember if I ever left the mother country. [R Walters]

The Staff were very generous with their time and organized a variety of day trips, camps, field trips, and holidays in this country and abroad. One regular holiday venue was St Mary's Bay Holiday Camp, New Romney. In 1950, the party consisted of seventy-three boys, thirty-two girls and five members of staff. The beach was always popular and there were excursions, for example to Canterbury Cathedral, Dungeness Lighthouse and the Railway Works at Ashford. There were dances, a worst dance championship and a knobbly-knee competition. By 1953, this holiday had become an institution and there were 212 boys and girls, including some from the Grammar and Stopsley Schools, and 12 staff. The diary could not note all the activities but did mention party visits, personal trips, ice-cream in the Palm Grove Café, water-pistol battles in bathing trunks, a thrice-postponed fishing trip, sun-tan,

Visit to Kew Gardens, between 1950 and 1952. (*June Culleton*)

Parents' Association visit to Battle, 1955. *(Patricia Morgan)*

and clear, starlit nights.

Other camps were organized by the Hertfordshire and Bedfordshire Youth Camping Club. In 1954, a group went on a long camping trip to Ireland with Mr Froud. Apparently he was a good choice of leader because he spoke 'Irish in terms understood by both Irish and English'. While in Ireland, the children went walking in the countryside and visited different castles.

> Last July a party from this school spent two weeks at Skerries at a camp eighteen miles north of Dublin. Two other schools joined us, one being Stopsley Boys and the other Langley St Girls … When we arrived at the camp site we were all rather tired and hungry and were very thankful to hear that breakfast was ready. Mr Gent greeted us and explained the working of the camp and then took us to our sleeping quarters. The girls were housed in two chalets and the boys in tents.

There were regular field trips.

> A principal object of the field work was to make a close acquaintance with an area quite different [from Bedfordshire]. The party stayed at the Youth Hostel Grindleford, Derbyshire. This provided easy access to the Millstone Grit Moorlands of the Peak District, and to the Limestone of Castleton … Grindleford was an excellent centre from which to visit a Steel works, a Cutlery Works and a Coal Mine in Sheffield, and the Tube Works and the Potteries in Chesterfield …

the seven days were therefore very full, and this type of programme is a valuable contribution to the knowledge of industrial and physical geography. The practical opportunity of studying the processes of erosion in situ, and of linking particular structure with particular scenery may be compared in usefulness with the practical study which is so necessary in other subjects. (1954)

In 1955, a trip was made to the Peak District where visits were made to the Blue John caverns. There was another excursion to Cheshire. Among other things, the students saw silk and nylon being processed in Brough, studied the buildings in Leek and visited the Royal Doulton factory. The 1956 field trip was to the Bath and Bristol area. The group studied aspects of the two towns, took walks over the Mendips, explored the Cheddar Caves and toured the port of Avonmouth.

Group of pupils, probably taken in the mid-1950s and possibly prior to a School holiday trip. Waller Street is in the background. *(From material collected by Mr Barry Dymock for the Old Students' Association, now held at Luton University.)*

Mr Ellis recalls that one residential trip to study the Liverpool area was based in the Wirral. Another year the base was at Rudyard Lake in the Lancashire Pennines. These areas gave access to the silk and nylon industries of Lee, Royal Doulton Pottery, Manchester Ship Canal and the Lancashire cotton Industry. Another year, a visit was paid to Wenlock Edge and the Welsh Marches.

Day trips added another dimension to the normal curriculum. In 1952, there was a visit to London Docks.

Behind the banks of the river could be seen the masts and funnels of some large ships, which were in such docks as The London and St Catherine, The India and Millwall etc. Besides the ships, towering cranes could be seen … we passed many famous historic buildings and sites. The site of the old Execution Dock, where pirates and criminals were executed, the Prospect of Whitby, where contraband was once stowed, the Limehouse Docks, where lime was once burned, were some of them … The ships we saw had brought sugar, meat, cotton and other goods from all over the globe.

The *Shell* magazine has reports of a trip to the Kensington Museums, Stewart and Lloyd's steel works in Corby, the K & L Factories at Letchworth which produced 'the largest number of mobile cranes in Great Britain', a flying display at Farnborough and a trip to the Old Vic to see *Antony and Cleopatra*.

Visits to the Continent became a regular feature of school life and Switzerland, in particular, seems to have been a regular favourite. Some of the groups involved pupils from other Luton schools as well. Mr W. E. Davies, the head of languages, arranged an annual visit to France for boys, staying for one week in different locations, often in Normandy. During the Easter breaks, 1950–1960, Mr Ellis, with Mr and Mrs Clarke arranged two week coach visits for mixed parties comprising girls from the Technical School and boys from the Grammar School, usually to Switzerland, but also to Austria, Belgium and the Rhine.

From our hotel at Wilderswil, we made some enjoyable trips on Lakes Brienz and Thun, with bathing at Spiez and Brienz. The Giessbach Falls were very impressive … after the luxury of Wilderswil we were lodged in a primitive mountain hotel – no running water and only calor gas lighting, but we were in the heart of the Alps and enjoyed our hours of trudging.   [Holiday in Switzerland 1952]

All of the boys agreed that it had been a very interesting and enjoyable holiday. Members of Staff have counted up and found that the boys have talked, at the youth hostel, in trains, in cafes and in the hotel with young people from no less than eight countries: France, Switzerland, Italy, Holland, Denmark, Belgium, USA and Germany.   [Holiday in Switzerland and Italy 1955]

The boys soon settled in the Hostel at Courseuelles which is run as a colonie de vacances by a group of Norman teachers. The Hostel is a converted sixteenth century farmhouse, which, because of its dominating situation, was the Headquarters of the German Kommandant during the Occupation, and the Headquarters of the Canadian Commander after the Liberation of 6th June 1944 … After Arromanches, the party went on to Bayeux and saw the famous tapestry, which was made under the direction of Queen Matilda to depict the Norman Conquest of England.   [Holiday in Normandy 1956]

A Personal Observation on the Character of the School

This could not have been written fifty years ago. It would have been a completely different assemblage and of a very different flavour if our English master had required us to write, as I have been requested, *a few words to capture the character of the school.* Distilled memories mellow and become more flavoursome over the years; sheer weight of evidence will compel us to acknowledge that yes, it perhaps did rain once or twice during those blissful summer holidays, but in fifty summers nobody has suggested to me that they regarded the *Tech* as any other than one of life's better experiences.

I am aware of one person from Biggleswade that might not have agreed in his first week at the school. Years after leaving, he told a story that had a lot to say about expectations and attitudes. He said that within a group of boys he had used a shortened form of a master's name. The master he was referring to was within earshot and challenged him. Unknown to the new boy, the name he used was a shortened form of a nickname and not the master's real name. A quick and genuine apology was not appreciated when he said 'Sorry, Mr (Full Nickname)'. His punishment was detention – that evening! Biggleswade students came to school by special coach. The only alternative was public transport which meant that he arrived home many hours late. Few homes had telephones in those days and we can only imagine the reception many would receive from anxious parents, with the threat of greater penalties if they ever had detention again. Detention remained the first bastion in an effective and yet relaxed disciplinary procedure, with the added advantage of a stark lesson in resourcefulness and self-reliance for one particular young boy.

The next punitive level was to be avoided at all cost. It was to stand outside Dr Charlesworth's office. He would emerge with a gentle enquiry about the nature of the misdemeanour; stern, yet there often seemed to be a hidden smile lurking somewhere; fair, even lenient, and looking beyond the offence to a lesson in personal responsibility; a nice friendly chat that everybody would do their utmost to avoid. Perhaps, as we feared, there were some who could bear witness to a latent capacity for anger but is was better that we didn't know.

All the teaching staff made their individual contribution to the ethos of the school although their selection and their approach seemed to be a reflection of how the boss would have it. Many had not spent all their lives in cloistered places of learning but brought considerable experience of the world into our classrooms. We sailed with His Majesty's Navy, went on missionary work to India, peeped into the laboratories of a research chemist and were taken into the hearts and minds of industry. We had an economist who ran a contracting company and taught geography and electrical subjects. For building studies we had a structural engineer who could actually lay bricks. Later in our schooling we went to see full size furnaces blasting, *Bessemers* converting and steel mills rolling. We also saw how effectively engineers and metallurgists were combining their skills in some of the numerous and very highly regarded more local companies.

Sometimes the whole school went away together. The teaching staff were more than prepared to lay on events that were rather special. On one of these trips a chartered train conveyed us, with wheels squealing round the tight, rusty curves of forgotten sidings, over secluded junctions and right through the backyard of the great metropolis; from Luton station direct to the docks at Southampton.

We went on holidays together. One major location was in Kent and others were across the English Channel. There had been no opportunities for us to travel in our early childhood and it seemed to be a matter of policy to create situations that would expand our world as well as helping our language studies. We travelled from a homeland still coping with food rationing, through countries recovering from the most destructive war in European history, to emerge into the pristine beauty of Switzerland. Most of our generation would have to wait many years to have similar experiences.

About seventy-five new pupils joined the school at a time and we were divided into three forms: two technical (boys only) and one commercial (mostly girls). Students were not separated into building and engineering groups by the time that I joined but the two parallel technical forms studied both subjects. Boys and girls were thus mostly separated by their different areas of study, but a natural and beneficial mixing developed over time which would be very evident to any visitor. As we were scattered quite thinly over the county, most of us lived some distance from friends. The school itself was our special meeting point and social activities were an important part of school life. Encouraged by the teaching staff and well organised, they contributed enormously to the well being and the character of the school. Dances were not formal but they were an age away from the discos of today. Classes were available for those wishing to acquire the necessary skills, with plenty of opportunity for practice. We had lunch-time hops, Saturday evening functions and, on special occasions, we even had a live dance band.

Another feature of the School was that we were surrounded by older College students. The Art School was on the top balcony at the same level as the room that we used for physics. The old College buildings were on the same site with a constant flow of people through the School. We were under scrutiny by the general public as well. Our front door opened into Park Square and the large side gate opened directly onto Church Street. Park Square in those days had special items of interest. Beer was still made there as it had been for countless generations and, on Mondays, the area was transformed by the cattle market which, we were told, had been held there for about a thousand years. We were not inconvenienced by the livestock or farm vehicles but what we did notice was the fragrance. I say *fragrance* because *smell* would be the wrong word. To this day, I find the scent of brewing and cattle to be mildly pleasing.

On a daily basis, the local townsfolk became entangled with maroon-blazered crocodiles leaving the confines of the main building and wending their various ways to its numerous outposts. The old Higher Grade School in Waller Street was used for physical education. The Chapel Basement on the corner of Cheapside was the very large and well-equipped practical engineering facility that we shared with the College. Many contented hours of learning were spent there with patterns, moulding boxes, lathes and milling machines. There was excitement when white-hot molten metal was poured into greensand moulds. The precautionary but gruesome stories we were told about the things that could go wrong with the process only added to this. The school tuck shop was too far away to use when we were there but, in the close and narrow seclusion of Barbers Lane, there was a baker's shop that baked our warm teacakes to order.

Our swimming pool was the indoor facility in Waller Street. Our sports fields were Pope's Meadow and Bell's Close (a part of People's Park). For Rugby, we used

Mr N. Garside and his Class of 1951–53. Left to right: Back: Peter Goodwin, Bob Paterson, Derek Goodwin, Roy Martin, Derek Margerison, Richard Kilby, Anthony Taylor, Brian Roberts, *Middle:* Colin Poulton, Michael Norcross, ? Tuffnell, Donald Quick, Tony Warehand, Bob Anderson, Peter Tompkins, David Gadsden, *Front:* Richard Tomkins, Michael Quinn, William Cooper, Michael Northwood, Mr Garside, John Willett, Donald Blanking, David Higgs, Alister Jeffs. *(Peter Goodwin)*

the Luton Rugby Club pitches overlooked by the Georgian elegance of Stockwood House which sadly, like all but one of the many buildings we used, is now destroyed. On Sports Days and for Cricket matches, we walked to the first class facilities at Wardown. Is it possible that all the exercise we had in a normal school day provided the extra degree of fitness that allowed the School to excel at most sports? The Methodist School in Chapel Street, on the site of what became the Industrial Mission and later Wesley House, was a major enclave. We spent a whole school day there, one day a week, joining for Assembly at the start of the day instead of going to the main school Assembly.

Assembly at both locations reflected society as it was and, to a degree, each member of staff that took it. To see the Headmaster and Canon Davison together always conveyed the impression that they had a common view of the world. The Parish Church next to the school remains as one of the largest in the country and it could accommodate us all. Canon Davison usually took the end of term services and I recall two words from one of them that have stayed with me and maybe many more that were there at the time. The address, mainly to school leavers, was about taking responsibility. We must have been showing signs of losing our concentration a little because, after a pause, he suddenly shouted at the top of his voice, 'BY YOURSELF!'. It reverberated around the old stone building like the thirty-two foot base pipe of the organ, then died away to the silence that only seemed to happen in Church. The headmaster was out of view but you could imagine him still nodding in agreement.

[Peter Goodwin (1951–53)]

Ethos and Expectations

Our Motto

Mente et Manibus!

This is the motto

That led us to fame.

Writing our shorthand;

Sawing school wood:

They kept us all going

To do what is good!

Winter and Summer

We strove to maintain,

In class and on sports field,

Our very good name.

Some of us weakened,

Some of us fought

To solve those darned problems,

That Mrs Clarke taught.

But now in our glory –
Forgetting defeat –
We say to all England,
'Luton Tech you can't beat!'
[Marion Guerin]

There was no similar school in the area, so the Luton Technical School very soon became a highly sought-after establishment. In 1950 Dr Charlesworth wrote about the war years when 'the Technical School grew with such vitality, and to such proportions, to become a local problem, in that there are now over 2,100 candidates a year for 234 places. For, because of the quality of the past pupils, parents hope to place their children here and employers are looking for our finished products in numbers that cannot be satisfied.'

As well as children from towns and the country there was a healthy mix of 'immigrants' from Wales, Scotland and Northern England. The School also benefited from close co-operation with the parents, local firms, head teachers of local schools and the Parish Church.

Those who were fortunate enough to gain a place at the 'Tech' enjoyed a first class school spirit. There are many stories of employers (factories, offices, banks etc.) who tentatively employed former pupils but who were so impressed that they always

Speech Day 14th March 1955. Coronation Shield awarded for Citizenship.
Jacqueline Matthews and Derrick McLeod. (*LN*)

asked for Technical students afterwards. In fact, there were more jobs available than there were pupils to fill them. One of the town's biggest firms was 'amazed at the loyalty, standards and enthusiasm of the boys'. Apparently it was much easier for pupils from the Technical School to be taken on as apprentices in local firms than it was for children from any other Luton school. One reason for their excellent attitude was that they were nearing the school leaving age and were focused on their immediate future. Normal expectations were that former pupils would continue to study for further qualifications in part-time courses at the College.

The School was, without doubt, a happy one but one of the regrets of the earliest pupils was that there were no external examinations and prospects were constrained by the demands of local industry. However, there are many heartening success stories, for example one about a country boy whose original ambition was to become a lift operator but who eventually became a Ph.D. and a lecturer in education. Girls from the earlier generations of pupils did not look for a career but for 'a good job'. One former student said that, in hindsight, she would probably have preferred to do something different, 'maybe nursing or something artistic, with flowers maybe' but these were not realistic options at the time. This, of course, was not unique to the Technical School; it was a part of the spirit of the age.

Speech Days

During the 1950s the Hall in the main building was a thoroughfare in the evenings for the students of further education classes and the school needed to arrange a prizegiving elsewhere. It was normal practice for Luton Corporation to close the Waller Street Swimming Baths for the winter season, to board over the pool, and to make it available for public dances and other events, until it re-opened at Easter. It became the nearest available hall to Park Square for the School Speech Day.

> A suspended floor was put over the bath area and screens put up round the sides and all the chairs from the classrooms carried across to give seating in the main area. A stage was constructed at one end for the VIPs and a display of work set up at the other end. This took all of one day to set up and half a day to dismantle after the evening's activities.
>
> They were formal occasions with a very important guest speaker and a long report by the Headmaster on the past year's successes and problems, usually containing guarded comments on the difficulties of running the school on a shoestring budget. Additionally there were items of entertainment from the school orchestra and choir, presentations of certificates and colours to successful pupils, presentations of articles made in the school workshops and bouquets of flowers to the wife of the speaker who had graciously presented the awards …
>
> [R.D. Whalley]

ABOVE Dr Abbott and the Choir at the Winter Assembly Hall. Probably Speech Day n.d. (*LN*)
BELOW Speech Day 4th March 1954. Mayor H.C. Janes, Canon William Davison (*LN*)

Technical School Speech Day in the Winter Assembly Hall, 27th April 1956.
Mrs William Gowland, Mr Reg Blacker and the Cook twins. (*LN*)

One expects to hear gems of wisdom from speakers on Speech Days but how many former pupils remember this piece of advice from Commander P.W. Kent RN Chairman and Managing Director of George Kent Ltd?

> I think a job depends entirely upon one's approach to it. If you approach the job with zest, and friendship for your fellow workers, you will find that it has a very different aspect; but in no circumstances should you approach it in the negative way … Now, about approaching a job with imagination. When I was a very small boy, I did not like eating Brussels sprouts and by imagining myself as a giant eating giant cabbages, I got through them quite easily.

Lists of prizes given out on Speech Days give an indication of the value placed on different aspects of school life. In 1951–52, there were prizes for general excellence, English, Science, vocational subjects, Commercial subjects and Music. By 1953, Citizenship, athletic prowess and musical ability were being acknowledged. The list for 1955–56 notes Office Arts, Shorthand and Typing and, by 1956–57, there were awards for outstanding ability in sport and crafts and prizes for the best contributors to the school magazine in writing skills, art and photography.

Barnfield

A Home at Last

On 7th November 1955 the Chairman of the Luton Education Committee, Councillor L. Bowles, cut the first turf on the 28-acre field where the new School was to be built. The cost of the project was £163,000. The School moved to the new building in March 1958 and was officially opened on 21st November 1958 by Dr Horace King BA MP. The site was in the north of the town, at the junction of New Bedford Road and Barnfield Road. The field sloped down towards the River Lea and the School was built on the lower ground where the water did not drain away properly. Consequently, after the first heavy rain, the 'storage space under the main hall and all the underground channels for the pipes and cables rapidly filled with water'.

There were other problems which meant that the promised 'paradise' was somewhat less than perfect. The estimated number on roll was based on figures supplied when the School was being planned but numbers had increased meanwhile and the problem of overcrowding remained. 'Perambulations' and 'tribal wanderings' continued. Until hutted accommodation could be supplied, spare classrooms in

Cutting the first turf on the Barnfield site, 7th November 1955. (*LN*)

The School at Barnfield, August 1957. (*LN*)

OPPOSITE BELOW The Official Opening of the School at Barnfield, 21st November 1958. Alderman F.G. Simms, Chairman of the Bedfordshire Education Committee, Dr Horace King BA, MP, later speaker of the House of Commons (speaking), Alderman Mrs F.M. Brash, Mayor, Revd. Canon Davison MA. (LN) ABOVE Official Opening of the School at Barnfield, 21st November 1958. The School Choir with Mr B. Lane. (LN)

Icknield School, a quarter of a mile away and on the opposite side of the busy New Bedford Road, were used. One former member of staff recalls an occasion when he took a class across the main New Bedford Road to Icknield School for a lesson only to be told that no rooms were being allocated that term. There was no room at Barnfield and it occurred to him that it would be a good idea to sit the class down on the central reservation of the A6. But, since the School had just vacated a school with five different teaching centres, the pupils took these problems literally in their stride.

Other teething problems included delays in the provision of a prefects' room, junior library and sports pavilion, but the move from an Edwardian red-brick building 'with scattered bases and a lack of fields, to a light, airy purpose-built post-war school was greeted with an enthusiastic uplift of spirits'. There was a four-storey main building and a separate workshop block connected by a covered way, known as Pneumonia Walk. In this workshop block, there were five practical rooms for woodwork, metalwork and craft and a machine shop. Rooms were added for the teaching of housecraft and typing.

BEDFORDSHIRE EDUCATION COMMITTEE
LUTON COMMITTEE FOR EDUCATION

OFFICIAL OPENING
OF
THE SECONDARY TECHNICAL SCHOOL
BY
DR. HORACE KING, B.A., M.P.

FRIDAY, 21st NOVEMBER, 1958

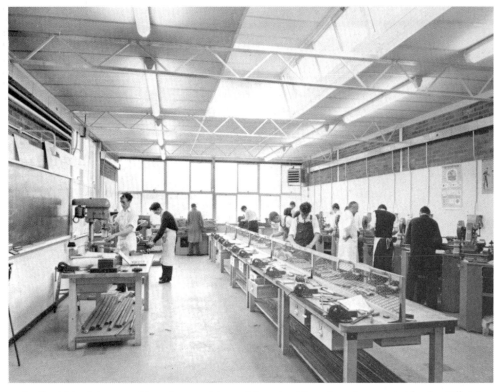

Bedfordshire Education Committee and Luton Education Committee Programme for the Official Opening of the Secondary Technical School, Pictures of the Gymnasium, Workshop, Typing Class and Library.

The School opened with 591 pupils and a staff of 33. Instead of a termly intake, children now entered the School at the beginning of the academic year. The age range became 11–18 and admission was dictated by the results of the Eleven-plus examination. This obviously caused considerable problems for the staff, some of whom were used to quite a different age range. Another negative consequence of the changes was the appearance of the 'middle school apathy' that was common in other schools. In earlier days, the courses had been shorter and the demands of the outside world ever present. Now that school life stretched over several years, this middle school lack of motivation made itself evident.

Why did I choose to study at Luton Tech? I think at the time it was my belief that all girls who went to the High School were 'posh' which was something I certainly wasn't. I didn't really know what career I wanted to pursue but as was common at that time, I decided on a secretarial route, so didn't have much of a choice of institutions to join. The fact the Luton Tech was co-ed never entered my head! I also started my working career in a drawing office which kicked the secretarial theory out of the window as well!

I could have taken the very easy option and gone to the High School – I lived at the back of it and only had to fall out of bed to get there. However, I opted for the hard life and chose walking what seemed like miles, in all weathers, to get my education.

I made lots of friends. Had some great times, have stored some great memories and, looking back, the years spent there really were some of the best. Most of the teachers were very friendly and helpful and I remember all of them vividly. Some were crazy, some quirky, but this all added to the overall experience.

I passed a few O levels eventually and it's strange that 'what comes around goes around' as, at the time of writing, I have been working at the 'parent' site of the original Tech, the University of Luton, for 13 years.

The highlight of my academic career at the Tech was becoming a prefect. The most gruelling was conducting Assembly one Friday morning with another prefect, Rob Irons.

My most worrying experience was as a first year, losing my beret in the ditch one very stormy evening whilst walking home during winter. I was so scared that Jane Clarke would exercise her wrath on me (she was obsessive about us wearing berets) that I made my dad go back and forth from home three times that night to find it. He was not best pleased, bless him, and ended up very muddy.

[Georgina Sharnock (Trotter)]

Barnfield School was set up as a Secondary Technical School but, became a Technical Grammar School and then a mixed Grammar School, the first such school Luton had seen since 1919. However, the official name of the School remained Barnfield

Secondary Technical School. The 1959–60 *Shell* included a message from Dr Charlesworth in which he said, 'I would remind those newer members of School that they are now more favoured than previous members, in that not only do they have extra facilities for sport, games and social life, but also they all come from the Luton area, and so are free to stay on after school hours and, on Saturdays, can more easily reach School and the playing fields than could their predecessors'. The School continued to be held in high esteem.

It was not that we agreed about everything but there was no falling out. People had a good sense of humour and a sense of proportion about things, bred, no doubt, from the very difficult circumstances under which they had worked in earlier years. It undoubtedly flowed from the Head downwards. Dr Sidney Charlesworth was the best Headmaster I ever worked for. He was a much respected and well-loved figure in the town.

There were daily assemblies at which the Staff would sit on the platform facing the pupils and we would all stand when the Head came into sight at the back of the Hall and walked along a raised walkway to join us on the platform. There would be a reading, a hymn and a prayer followed by announcements by anyone who wanted to make one. Like all heads, Dr Charlesworth had his pet themes and certain phrases that he often repeated, were the very stuff of wits who wanted to impersonate him. School uniform was one of his favourites and anything that anyone wore which deviated from this was usually referred to as 'beach wear' and was not allowed. 'Work when you work, and play when you play' was another oft-repeated (and very worthwhile) exhortation. There was a lot of grass and playing field around the School and not really enough asphalt so that in wet weather the Head was frequently heard urging the children to 'control your mud and litter'.

Even in Assemblies the irrepressible spirit of fun that always lurked in the School would sometimes surface. Occasionally the Head would announce with the Hymn number that verse 2 would be 'girls only', verse 3 'boys only' and verse 4 'Staff only'. We dreaded this. From his position at the grand piano on the floor of the Hall, just below the platform where we were standing in our serried rows, Brian Lane's face would light up with a look of fiendish glee! When it got to verse 4 he would deliberately delay beginning his accompaniment until some poor souls had felt obliged to start up revealing just how awful Staff singing was! Afterwards of course he would plead innocence. It was only a split second delay but it was obviously deliberate and the pupils knew it too! Such things contributed much to the atmosphere in the School between Staff and pupils.

The respect and co-operation that we received from the students was generally excellent and again I feel it was a spirit born of the adversities faced in earlier years in the Park Square days … it is the characters of the individuals interacting with each other that really matters.

[I. Jones]

Technical School Staff at Barnfield c.1963 *Left to right: Back:* J.S. Sanson, R. Blacker, A.S. Froud, G. Richmond, A. Cundick, —, R. Ellis, R. Whalley, J. Gudgeon, ? Morse, P. Taylor, *Middle:* V. Needham (sec.), I. Jones, F. Maggs, ? Wainright, ? Firman, R. Sinfield, D. Cole, J. Leovold, ? Miller, x, W. Davies, T. Hewitt, T. Collins, —, E. Bowen *Front:* —, —, L.Britain, —, —, G. Harding, D. Hopkins, Dr Charlesworth, E. Clarke, N. Garside, —, —, R. Seymour, M. Griffiths, M. Knape *(Patricia Morgan)*

Industry now laid down academic standards for entry and this changing attitude was partly responsible for the different focus within the school. The syllabus was the normal Grammar School one leading to O-levels after five years and A-levels at 18. In the fourth year, pupils opted, according to ability and interest, for an academic, commercial or general engineering course, but all sat O-level subjects in the fifth year. By 1963, commercial specialization took place only after O-levels. The Sixth Form offered Science, Arts, Commercial and Professional courses. This last, the first of its kind to be offered in Luton, covered the British Constitution, Economics and Accounts and was set up at the request of local professional bodies. The focus of History in the School was broadened to include British Social and Economic History and a General Studies programme was set up in the VI Form.

It is pleasing to welcome the children of earlier past pupils. We, of the Staff, hope that they will apply themselves to work and games with the same zeal as their parents, who, twenty years or so ago, felt a school unity and a missionary urge to succeed and put the School on the academic map, and themselves in successful careers. The facilities and amenities of School are better now than ever before, and so, members of School should be much more successful than those of the past.

[S. Charlesworth 1961]

Examinations

In the early 1960s, Barnfield School was in transition. (It has been remarked that it was always in transition!) It was set on a par with the other Grammar Schools in the town but Barnfield had an advantage in that it was co-educational. As will be seen, this was to have a positive influence on education in Luton when re-organization took place.

Examination results were published in the *Shell*. For example, in 1960, a considerable number of pupils were successful in their O-level examinations while the A-level eight boys and five girls gained A-levels. At the Speech Day on 23rd November 1961, the awards given demonstrate that there were still strong links with industry.

> To mark our long standing with Industry and Commerce, various firms have very generously donated prizes and trophies to encourage pupils within the School, which gesture and co-operation the Governors and School greatly appreciate.

Bayliss Wright	Geometrical and Machine Drawing
Gibbs and Dandy Ltd	3rd year woodwork, 3rd year metalwork
George Kent Ltd	Outstanding merit in engineering course
D. Napier and Sons Ltd	Most outstanding technical pupil in 5th year
Messrs Terry-More Ltd	VI Form – Economic and Public Affairs
	V Form – Principles of Accounts, Shorthand and Typewriting
	Economic and Public Affairs
	IV Form – Principles of Accounts, Shorthand and Typewriting
Vauxhall Motors Ltd	Cup and Prize at A level
	Prizes for work at O level
	Technical Subjects

Social Life

The 1961 edition of the *Shell* is the only one available for these years. However, there was much continuity and a happy social life was obviously still being enjoyed. In those days, there was no question of a teacher just being employed to teach. They all 'willingly gave up hours of unpaid time to extra-curricular, out-of-hours work because [they] believed it was an important part of the job and had many beneficial 'spin-offs' in the classroom and in the School as a whole'.

> It is clear that the Staff of the Technical School enjoyed one another's company and acknowledge that this was a very happy school.
>
> The highlight of the year, certainly into the early 1960s, was the Annual Staff Christmas Dance, often held at the George Hotel in George Street ... Dr and Mrs Charlesworth would lead off and everyone danced with everyone, no doubt assisted by the bar and the buffet. There was a real party atmosphere which many places of work could not support so convincingly I feel. It was just another sign of the civilized family nature of the Tech. [I. Jones]

Dr and Mrs Charlesworth, Mr and Mrs Froud n.d. *(C.W. Parrott)*

Debating Society

Mr I. Jones ran the Debating Society and insisted on very formal rules in the belief that these would stand the students in good stead when they had to make their way in the world. Debates were always run in the same way, using the same words, which in the end became 'ingrained and much loved'. Similarly, mock elections were held which followed exactly the laws of the land.

> Good traditions were beginning to emerge … In my opinion to stand up in public and face an audience with all eyes on you requires as much courage as a rugby tackle and is a lot more useful. It is essential for many careers and is what Central and Local Government depends on. For meetings to be successful you need procedure and rules. A degree of formality allows everyone to have their say and they can say more or less anything without a brawl ensuing! It is a game that can really be enjoyed once a few simple rules are appreciated. What fun it is! …
>
> The audience was allowed to interrupt speakers by rising to their feet on 'points of information' or 'points of order' which had to be addressed to the Chairman and not to the speakers directly. A point of information had to be in the form of a question e.g. asking for further information or for clarification … When all fixed speeches had been concluded the Debate was opened to the floor. Speakers had to stand, give their names to the minutes Secretary and address their remarks to the Chair (not to individual speakers or to one another.)   [I. Jones]

Mr Ivan Jones and the Committee of the Debating Society, probably 1963–64. *(LN)*

After some time, the Society began to hold Annual Dinners which were attended by both Staff and students, and sometimes guests from the Governors of the Education Office. These events involved other departments: Home Economics students cooked, served the food and waited at table. Art classes designed and produced the menus. These also received the attention of the French Department which named dishes after members of the Committee.

The light-hearted humour of the School was demonstrated by the scheming which went on behind the scenes when a debate was planned on the motion THBT *Flying Saucers have landed.* Mr Jones explains.

On the morning I announced it in Assembly I had arranged for a … lad to dress up in green with suitable antennae attached to his head. At the end of my announcement he appeared in full view outside the windows of the Hall and scuttled and leapt the full length of the building in a most convincing imitation of everyone's idea of an alien! At the end of the week, with the Debate due the following Thursday I arranged with the groundsmen to burn some mysterious circles in the grass at the top of the School field over the weekend and to erect barriers around them made from striped rugby posts. On the Monday morning with a perfectly straight face Dr Charlesworth announced that some strange marks had appeared on the field and that on no account was anyone to go near them. We then watched from top floor windows at break as practically the whole school trooped all the way across the field to see what it was all about! …

And this wasn't the end of the story either because the following Monday morning the Caretaker, Sammy Lunn, was full of the story of how, on Sunday morning, a limousine had turned up at his house and a number of men in grey suits had demanded to see the said marks! In those days, men from the ministry were sent to investigate all reports of unidentified flying objects! I'm not sure I ever got to the bottom of this. I suspect that we, the hoaxers, were the victims of an even more elaborate hoax!

[Mr Jones would like to hear from these hoaxers, if they exist.]

Other motions debated introduced:
School: *That this House believes that we, in Britain, are out of date.* Carried
Staff: *That this House believes that this country should be governed by Scientists rather than Politicians.* Defeated
That this House believes that any woman would be far better off in a home. Defeated

Dramatic Society

The Society's first production, in February 1961, was *The Winslow Boy*. Most of the cast was from the Senior School but leading roles were taken by two members of staff. The Report stated that it was hoped that the Society would soon have enough members to take responsibility for productions without any extra help. The performances, however, were always first class and remembered with great affection. Large numbers of pupils were involved and all, staff and students, appreciated and benefited from being involved with others in a teamwork situation.

In the early 1960s Brian Foreman was appointed to the English Department with a keen interest in Drama and in one memorable year organized two productions! One was for students and the other involved a cast drawn entirely from the Staff. In the Summer Term therefore the Staff put on J.B. Priestley's *An Inspector Calls* with Ray Ellis as Inspector Goule. I'm sure we didn't reach the standard set on the West End stage in recent years, but it was a good effort. Imagine any teachers nowadays having the time or energy to learn and act in a 3 Act play at the end of the academic year! It played to a packed house for 3 consecutive nights! Mr Whalley built the set and I helped him paint it. [I. Jones]

Music

Under Brian Lane, the School put on a most spectacular production of Benjamin Britten's *Noyes Fludde* in the Church. Mr Jones recalls that 'the work had only recently had its first performance and we hired many of the original costumes and props. Other organisations, including the Salvation Army Brass Band, also took part and came under Brian's masterful baton. It really was a most ambitious and prestigious production and along with a number of other Staff I enjoyed being an animal in the Ark'.

Another spectacular was *Carmina Burana.* In this performance, Brian Lane combined two school choirs, a staff choir, a parents' choir, the Parish Church choir and an orchestra, and needed the Drill Hall with 5-level tiered staging. Space for the audience became restricted.

The annual Summer Concert, which was held in June 1960, received a commendation in the *Times Educational Supplement.* It was remarked that Mr Brian Lane 'turned round to warn the audience that they were in for a pretty thin time if they did not like modern music … in the event, the audience were agreeably surprised'. The report concluded that the concert was a 'major triumph'.

A new school song was introduced with words by W.E. Bowen and music by B.M. Lane. It was entitled *Fifty Years On* and may have looked back to the building of the School on Park Square in 1908. On the other hand, it may have reflected a sense of hope for the future as the School settled at last into its promised home. If so, that would be ironic for, unbeknown to everyone, the days of the 'Tech' were numbered.

As we stand up and sing of the days that are now
    And we think of the years that are fled,
We remember the girls and the boys who have laughed
    And have sung in this hall in our stead.

        So rejoice with a cheer
        For the spirit that here
            We inherit from times that are gone;
        And we know that, one day,
        We shall wander this way,
        And dream
            When it's fifty years on.

And the field will be green and the pitches we love
    Will still be resounding with play;
And the bat and the ball and the hockey stick – all
    Will re-echo the words that we say.

        So rejoice with a cheer
        For the spirit that here
            We inherit from times that are gone;
        And we know that, one day,
        We shall wander this way

> And dream
>> When it's fifty years on.

> So let us sing loudly, united and gay,
>> Delighting that still we are here
> By the fervour of youth, to enliven our way
>> With a rousing Technical Cheer!

> So rejoice with a cheer
> For the spirit that here
>> We inherit from times that are gone;
> And we know that, one day,
> We shall wander this way
> And dream
>> When it's fifty years on.

Model Railway Club

At a general meeting (1961), it was decided to include a Locomotive Spotters Section in the Club.

Natural History Society

FACT

A well-known member of the Model Club has for some time now been looking for a bucket of vacuum dust. He will probably find it in the blue steam cupboard near the tin of striped paint.

Pupils took part in rambles, mainly in the Barton and Offley direction. There were several films and contact was made with a university organisation for animal welfare.

In 1961, 24 pupils from the School were able to take part in the South Bedfordshire Archaeology Society's excavations at Galley Hill with James Dyer. They were shown the quadrant method by which the barrow had to be dug. 'Finds' included a sheep's jaw, two Stone Age skeletons, more bones, six Roman coins, nails, a horse's head and some 14th century pottery.

Sport

Now that the School had its own playing field, sporting activities received a new lease of life. As ever, Association and Rugby Football, Swimming, Netball, Table Tennis, Boxing and Cricket were played and new events were included at the annual Sports Days. Teams took part in the Bedfordshire Championships, Bedfordshire Schools Championships and Luton Schools Championships. Inter-house cross-country championships took place on Barnfield's own course.

Technical School Athletics Team, 1960. (*LN*)

Technical School Sports, 1961. (*LN*)

Technical School team, Wardown Town Sports, 1961. (*LN*)

Technical School Sports, 1964. (*LN*)

Under 13s Football Team, 1963 with Mr Ivan Jones (left), Mr John Leovold (right). (*LN*)

Ross (St Gregory) v David Pacey (right), December 1961. (*LN*)

Expectations

We may, we feel, justifiably delight in the emergence of the first university graduates whose names head so splendidly our new honours board in the library corridor … we feel that we should register our delight at the flavour and quality of these fine vintage products of our own vineyards. Let us hope that much larger sixth forms, blessed as they are with greater library, laboratory and field facilities, attain at least those high standards of the splendid pioneers. Reader, the future is yours.

[Editorial in the *Shell* (1961)]

Pupils still left to take up posts in industry or commerce but those who stayed on into the VI Form were able to move to universities and colleges. In 1960, one boy went to University while another boy and five girls went to Teacher Training Colleges. One boy went to a College of Technology and seven took up senior student apprenticeships in Cable and Wireless, ICI, Scientific and Industrial Research, the Civil Service, Surveying and Accounting.

Examinationitis

Written examinations are, and probably always will be, to nearly all people, whether they are brilliant, average or just ignorant, absolutely awful … an interview is usually looked upon as fairly easy, the reason being, I believe, that one can more easily adjust oneself to the immediate surroundings, and that the sound of one's own voice generally inspires a confidence which increases when the interviewer generally nods his head in almost complete agreement after hearing one's answer to a question …

The average person will start at the beginning and methodically work through his papers, doing as much as he can, and, gradually, the feeling of being over-wrought will overcome him, and he will momentarily lapse into utter despair. The plainly ignorant will work out parts of some problems, omit others altogether, and he, too, will eventually succumb to that same feeling, the only difference being that mentally he will never live to fight again in an examination … To whichever class you belong, you should realise that the only way to pass any examination is to work hard, and study well in advance of the all-important day!

[Derek E. Sharman]

Comprehensive Education 1965

In 1964, Luton became a County Borough and was given the freedom to control all the education in the area. The Luton Education Committee decided to implement the 'Corbett plan' which proposed to reduce the number of children who were admitted to Grammar Schools and, at the same time, set up O-level classes in every

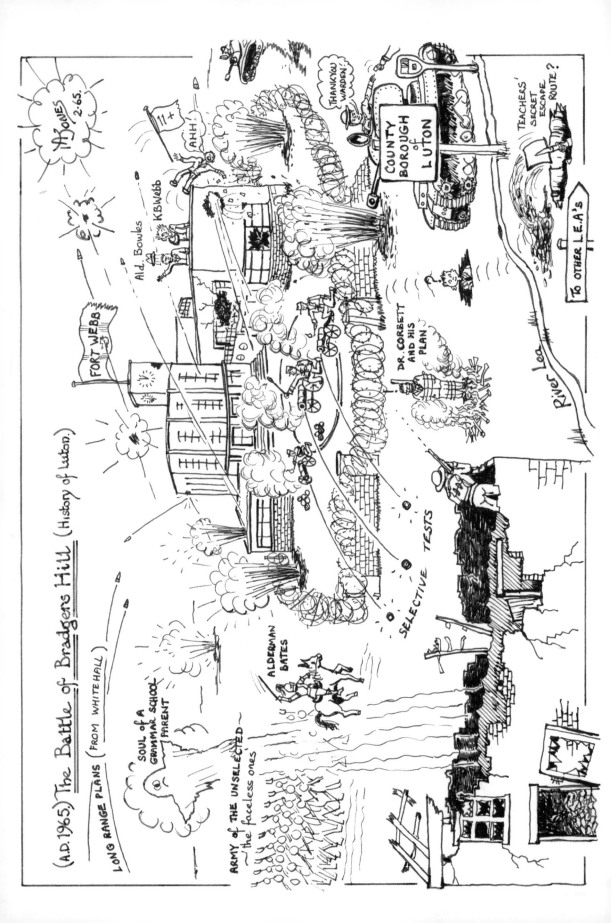

Secondary Modern School. This would mean that every child had the opportunity to take GCE examinations and could continue to study A-levels at one of the Sixth Forms in the Grammar Schools.

This scheme was well received but the government of the day was determined to introduce comprehensive education. The Corbett plan had had no time to become established before Luton Education Committee declared that, from 1965, selection would be discontinued. Secondary Modern Schools were to become High Schools and all A-level work would be concentrated on one Sixth Form College – a new concept in education. The plan was delayed for a year but, in September 1967, Luton schools became fully comprehensive. More details about these changes are included in other sections of this book.

It was claimed that this new kind of college would concentrate well-qualified staff, specialist equipment and a mature body of students on one site. As all the students would be studying for A-level examinations, they would be able to motivate one another and good relationships could be built up with colleges and universities. On the other hand, it was feared that a change of school at the age of 16 could be detrimental and that two years was too short a time for students to bond together into a loyal group.

The transition could not be completed immediately because there were different year groups of children who had passed the Eleven-plus examination and who needed to finish their courses. Special arrangements had to be made for these children until the changeover had been finalized.

A decision had to be made about which building was the most suitable base for the new Sixth Form College. Barnfield School was the most modern; it already had facilities for boys and girls and also had better workshops and laboratories. Not surprisingly it was considered by many to be the best choice. However, the Boys' Grammar School at Bradgers Hill had an established tradition and was considered by some influential people to be a centre of excellence. So, for whatever reason, the former Grammar School was nominated as the new Sixth Form College and Barnfield Technical School became Barnfield High School. The following figures, taken from a Report published by the Luton Education Committee, demonstrate the changing roles of Barnfield School.

	1964	1965	1966	1967	1968
Barnfield Secondary Technical	623	590	587		
Barnfield High (Mixed)				594	441

Provision had to be made for the children who were already at the Grammar Schools. Girls from the High School stayed there until they were 16. Second and third year

LEFT A.D. 1965 The Battle of Bradgers Hill. (Ivan Jones)

Dr Charlesworth's retirement 1967, Dr and Mrs Charlesworth and Mr Birchmore from the Old Students' Association. (*LN*) Dr Charlesworth's retirement 1967, Dr and Mrs Charlesworth and Mr Davis. The cake was shaped like a greenhouse to represent the practical greenhouse which was a retirement gift. (*LN*)

boys from the Grammar School transferred to Barnfield, leaving those in the fourth and fifth years to complete their course at Bradgers Hill. Pupils doing O-level courses at the new Barnfield High School stayed until they were completed. Numbers on roll at Barnfield High School fell until July 1970 when the building was taken over by the College of Further Education.

> The deputy heads of the three schools, who were responsible for timetabling, held a series of meetings. They had the difficult and unenviable task of producing the 1967 timetable which permitted the Sixth Form staff of the High and Barnfield to travel to Bradgers Hill to teach in the new VI Form College. Dovetailing the three timetables was the proverbial nightmare …
>
> Timetabling became increasingly difficult and constricted since in 1968 the Technical College took over the top floor as hairdressing and dressmaking departments. There were certain perks, since pupils who offered their services as models after school could obtain free hair cuts, and boys who were prepared to be shaved could earn 2s 6d! The following year, 1969, the school lost half of the laboratories and two further classrooms on the first floor.   [R. Ellis]

A major difficulty was the allocation of responsibility. Each School had its own head of department and there was considerable upheaval involved in re-organizing these posts. The headmistress of the High School had, apparently, been promised the post of Vice-Principal of the Sixth Form College at her interview in 1965 so she transferred there in 1967. The long-serving heads of Luton Grammar School, Mr K.B. Webb, and the Technical School, Dr S. Charlesworth, retired, their places being taken by Mr B.D. Dance and Mr R.H. Ellis.

Mr Roy H. Ellis

Mr Ellis was educated at Varndean Grammar School for Boys in Brighton (1934–1941) and then joined the Royal Navy (1942–1946). He studied at the University of Sheffield (1946–1950) where he gained a BA (Hons) in Geography and a Diploma in Education.

He joined the Technical School in 1950 and became a much-respected member of staff and spent many hours encouraging and coaching sports teams. In 1964, he became Deputy Head and, from 1967 until January 1970, he was Headmaster. His recollections have been invaluable in the preparation of this book.

Mr R. Ellis.

Mr N. Garside.

Mr Norman Garside

Norman Garside came to Luton in 1943 from Ilkley, Yorkshire, where he had his own plumbing business. He joined the staff of the College Building Department and when, in 1948, the Luton Junior Technical School separated from the College, he moved on to the school staff with responsibility for engineering and building subjects.

Norman was an 'all round' sportsman. He played cricket and, I believe hockey, for the Town teams. He was an excellent tennis and badminton player and he also played football. When I joined the staff, he was on their panel of referees. I know that many past pupils remember him with gratitude for the encouragement and coaching he gave them in these sports.

Norman was also an outstanding teacher and organiser. He had a personality that enabled him to get on so well with pupils and staff. In the 45+ years I knew him we only had one disagreement which simmered one afternoon at school. Just before the end of the afternoon, he came into my room and said 'What are you doing after school?' 'Nothing', I replied. 'Come and have a game of golf' was his answer. Our tiff was forgotten – he was not a person to leave matters unresolved or to hold a grudge.

When Dr Charlesworth retired in 1967, Roy Ellis was appointed headmaster and Norman was appointed Deputy-Headmaster. He held this post until January 1970 when Roy Ellis left to take up the Headship of Lealands High School. Norman then took over as Headmaster for the two remaining terms until the school ceased to exist in July 1970. Norman then moved as Joint Headmaster with Mr A. Milner to Halyard High School until the new Headmaster was appointed and then served as Deputy Head in that school until his retirement.

[R.D. Whalley]

It was not easy for the staffs of the three schools to bond as a group. There were female members who had never taught boys and male teachers who had never taught girls. In this respect, the staff from the old Technical School had the advantage for they had been used to co-education.

It was like mixing chalk and cheese … our down to earth humour and sense of fun were a complete eye-opener to both of the other groups … However, even the hallowed ground of the old Grammar School staff room was too much for us and so we, along with the ex-High School staff, took over the new Lecture Theatre staff room. We soon had the ice broken and they were laughing and joking with us. Gradually, some of the younger members of the Grammar School staff moved over

… and we soon became integrated with new staff joining us to take the place of those who had retired. They never knew the divisions that had existed in those early days.

[R.D. Whalley]

Old Students' Association

Due to the extensive social side of the School one soon cultivates many friends, but after two years one is sent into the wide world to fend for oneself and consequently many former friendships are broken and the social life curtailed.

In order to obviate these hardships, the Old Students' Association was formed and through the medium of this Association one can relive one's 'cherished memories' of life at the Junior Technical School in the company of former friends and fellow 'sufferers'. The Association Gazette is issued periodically and gives details of the activities of the sections and branches together with news of 'Old Techites' and the Staff …

The Association has flourishing football and table tennis sections and it is hoped that, in the very near future, it will be possible to form a tennis section …

Socials and dances are organised throughout the year by the parent Association and the Ampthill Branch …

Old Students' Social Evening at *The George* n.d. but before 1950. *Seated centre:* Mrs Charlesworth, Mr and Mrs Parks, Mr and Mrs Burgoyne, Dr Charlesworth. (*C.W. Parrott*)

Members of the Old Students Association played cricket and tennis, danced at the George and the Winter Assembly Hall, dined at the Leicester Arms and went on outings. Their table tennis team competed in the County League. There were social occasions such as Christmas parties. Several reunions were organized by Barry Dymock over the years and CVs and photographs which he collected have been saved for posterity.

And Afterwards ...

It has not been possible to list all the names and careers of pupils who have passed through the Technical School. Some successes have been noted and they are included as representative of the achievements of many. As in the case of the Grammar and the High School sections of these books, apologies are offered to those whose names have been omitted.

A favoured line of employment, especially for boys, was an apprenticeship with a local firm, most notably Vauxhall Motors, but also W.H. Allen in Bedford, the Gas Board, Kent's and Skefko. Many former pupils succeeded in gaining important posts in engineering or technology.

It is worth pointing out that, at least in the early life of the School, girls were expected to be primarily domestic as one girl who went between 1951 and 1953 has observed. 'Careers as such were not much sought after ... a 'good job' being the main ambition'. Later on, a number of girl students were able to resume their studies and follow a chosen career. The ethos of the School seems to have encouraged further education for boys as well and many CVs include an impressive list of professional qualifications and notable promotions.

Old students can be found in countries as far away as Australia, Canada, New Zealand and the United States. Throughout the world, students have taken up employment in a variety of fields: administration, the armed services, aviation, beauty therapy, caring professions, the Church, commerce, communication, construction, design, education, engineering, finance, insurance, leisure, local government, local industry, management, the media, performing arts, police, the post office, research and the utilities. Many have set up and run their own businesses.

Jeane Bailey (Bligh) is an example of the way in which women in the twentieth century frequently changed the direction of their careers and took up further study. When she left school, she started work in a junior capacity in the offices of Vauxhall Motors. She progressed to the post of Secretary to the General Sales Manager, then the Production Engineering Manager and, finally became a Director's Secretary, working for four Directors over the years. She took voluntary redundancy and began training as a nurse at the Luton and Dunstable Hospital where she qualified in 1978. Again she made progress and became a Senior Ward Sister.

Jean Godfrey became a secretary and then went on to train as a teacher.

Owen Ballard trained as an aeronautical engineer.

Derek Birchmore (1940–42) had a variety of careers. He was a draughtsman and went on to be a training officer. He also served as a magistrate.

Charles Brewer left school to become an apprentice at George Kent's. He became a chartered engineer and a member of several prestigious professional bodies.

Ken Cooper (b.1927) is well known for his regular contributions to *The Luton News* which resulted in the production of his book of photographs: *Luton Scene Again*.

Rex Cooper became a member of the Magic Circle.

Christopher Gillespie worked for a Ph.D. degree and became a consultant psychologist.

Barrie Holland took up a successful career as a professional actor, photographer's model and fashion mode.

David Lowe (1956–59) studied theology. He took up several posts within the Church and also became a chaplain to the Territorial Army.

David Matthews worked at Luton Water Company and, later, worked in Australia as an expert in storm water, drainage, sewage and water reticulation.

Sir William Penney was an atomic scientist.

Charles Shotbolt won a scholarship from General Motors in the USA. He succeeded in gaining several qualifications, FIEE, MIMechE, MIQA, and became a senior lecturer in the department of engineering technology at the College on Park Square. He was awarded the OBE.

John Theodorson (40–42) was a radio design engineer at Murphy Radio. During his further studies at Luton Technical College he gained an ONC and HNC in electrical engineering and an ONC in mechanical engineering. He trained as a teacher and returned to Luton in 1955 as a lecturer. He remained there until his retirement.

James Vass (38–40) also acquired a long string of professional qualifications: AMIMechE, MInstMC, CEng, MIMechE and FIMechE. He was also awarded a Ph.D. by Surrey University. His career went from student apprentice, to research engineer and then lecturer in engineering. He may hold the record as having attended the Park Square College site (as student or lecturer) in every academic year from April 1938 to August 1986.

An Appreciation

The former staff and pupils who have so generously helped by contributing to the production of this book have, without exception, spoken affectionately of the happy school which was the Luton 'Tech'. Due credit must be given to Dr Charlesworth who was the driving force behind the success of this very special place. It has been a pleasure to be able to pay tribute to all those who were involved and to place on record the life of this much-loved school.

Appendix
Staff and Head Prefects

This list is far from complete; names have been found in various places but there are sure to be gaps. There is also the problem of ladies who married being mentioned under two different names. Staff who joined before 1948 were members of the College Staff. In 1948, they had the choice of staying with the College or joining the Junior Technical School staff.

Nicknames are in brackets.

The dates given usually refer to the edition of the *Shell* which gives the information.

No dates have been found for these members of staff.

Mr Bateson	(Basher)	
Miss Belsher	(Miss)	
Miss Baster	(Miss)	
Mr Boothman	(Nelly Moran)	
Mr Goodwin	(Whispers)	
Mr Gates		
Mr Gray		Mathematics
Mr Hanson		
Mr McIntyre		
Mr Templeton		
Mr Williams		
Mr Westwood		

These members of staff moved to the School when it became independent from the College.

Dr S. Charlesworth	(Charlie)	
K.J.D. Abbott (later Dr)		Music
W.E. Barnett	(Wilf)	
T.E. Collins	(Titmus)	RI
W.E. Davies	(Bill)	French
J. Dawe	(Jack)	
A.L. Hepburn		Mathematics
T.H. Hewitt	(Zeke)	
W.G. Tolley		
E. Wolf	(Dagwood)	English

These members of staff remained on the staff of the College.

Mr Banner
Mr Crofton
Registrar Mr Jeffs
Secretary Lesley Jackson

Dr Charlesworth had his own secretarial staff:
    Pam Seward (Mrs Pam Allen) to 1947
    Audrey Cole (Mrs Audrey Whalley) 1947–51

1946–47 NB the page of autographs from the Shell magazine.

J.E. Cule	(Mouth Almighty)	Commerce
Left 51–52		
A.F. Bourlet	(Alf)	
Appointed 1939		
Miss Hartley		
Mrs Talbot		
Mr Barnett		
Mr Birch		
Miss Harley		
Miss Cahill		
Mr Bardsley	(Gaffer)	
Mr Hewittt		Electrical Science
Mr Talbot	(Frank/Mr Piano)	Woodwork
Miss Bootham		Chemistry
Mr Anderson	(Dismal Desmond)	Mathematics or Geography
Mr McGregor		Drawing
Mr Evans		PT
Miss Lowe		English
Miss Brown	(Mary)	Student English
Mrs Anderson		Geography
Mr Tate	(Kosher)	Mathematics
Mr Skinner		Art
Mr D.A.R. Clark	(Clacker)	Head of engineering
Mr Gudgeon	(Omo)	
Mr Marlowe	(Muscles)	
Mrs Booker		

From *Technique Old Students Association January 1950*

Mr Tonkin	Mathematics and Geometry
Mr Barmer	Mathematics
Mr Crofter	Practical Instructor
Mr Banner	
Mr Barnett	
Mr Talbot	
Mr Cule	
Mr Birch	
Miss Hartley	Commercial

Miss Cahill	Commercial
Mr Brooks	
Mr P Hill	
Mr Price	
Miss Burns	Commercial
Miss Coar	
Mrs Talbot	
Mr Brooks	
Mr Smith	

1950–51 (County Secondary Technical School)

Mr K.J. D. Abbott B Mus, FRCO, ARCM	Music
Mr W.E. Barnett B.Sc.	Science
Mr R.G. Blacker B.Sc.	Science
Mr W.E. Bowen BA	English Subjects
Mrs E.C. Clarke	Mathematics
Later Senior mistress	
Mr W.H. Coe	Art
Mr T.E.Collins B.Com	Commercial Subjects
Mr W.E. Davies BA	French
Mr J.T. Duell	Workshop and Technology
Mr R.H. Ellis BA	Geography
Mr B.D. Eveleigh B.Sc.	Science
Mr A.S. Froud (Froggy)	English and Workshop
Mr N. Garside MRSI, M.InstB.E.	Building Subjects
Miss M.C. Griffiths BA	English
Mr I. Harrison FLPS, ACI	Commercial Subjects
Mr P.B. Henderson	Mathematics and Science
Mr A.L. Hepburn B.Sc.	Mathematics
Mr T.H. Hewitt AMIEE	Technical Drawing
Mr D.E. Hopkins BA	Commercial Subjects
Deputy Head	
Mr H.R. Jenkins ACIS	Commercial Subjects
Miss Z.E. Lyus BA	Geography
Miss C.M. Petteford BA	French
Mr L. Richardson ABICC	Workshop and Technology
Mr W.G. Tolley AMIStrE	Building Subjects
Mr R.D. Whalley (Pop)	PE and Woodwork

Part-time members of College staff (building) 1951–1971

Mr E. Wolf B.Sc.	Geography
Left during the year	

Mrs F.C. Dolbe BA	English Subjects
Mr R.E. Button	English and Games
Mr B.J.B. Hazel (Jock)	Geography/Sports/History
Miss Z.E. Lyus BA	Geography
(Mrs Evans)	

51–52

Mrs M. Kinsella BA	English Subjects
Mrs C.M. Kenigsman BA	French and English
Mr N. Suggett B.Sc.	Mathematics
Mrs M. Whitaker	Needlework and Games
Mrs M.H. Knape BA	French
Left Dec 52	
Mr W.E. Barnett B.Sc.	Science
Mr N. Suggett B.Sc.	Mathematics

1953

Mr J.E. Blacklocks BA	English subjects
Mr C. Mellow (Part-time)	PE

53–54

Mr C.W. Baggaley	Commercial subjects and PE
Mrs A. Kitching BA	English subjects
Mr J.F. Sanson B.Sc.	Science
Mr H.F. Shaw B.Sc.	Mathematics
Left	
Mr J.E. Blacklocks BA	English subjects
Mr I. Harrison ACIS FIPS	Commercial subjects
Mrs M. Kinsella BA	English subjects
Mrs M.H. Knape BA	French

1954–55

Mrs M. Winters BA	French
Left	
Mrs C. Kenigsman	French

55–56

Mr C.L. Deavin B.Sc.	Mathematics
Mr J. Wainwright	Commercial subjects
Mrs M. Walker	Cookery
Left	
Mr H.R. Jenkins	Commercial subjects
Mr H.F. Shaw	Mathematics

56–57

Mr Gudgin	Eng Workshop and Technology
Mrs E. Harding BA AKC	French (part-time)
Mrs G. Herbert	Domestic Science
Mr B.M. Lane BA ARCO ABSM	Music
Mrs B. Metcalfe BA	French (part-time)
Mr J.D. Plumb	Science
Mr F. Slim BA	English subjects
Mr H. Staszewski MA	Mathematics

Left

Mr K.J. D. Abbott	Music
Mr J.T. Duell	Eng Workshop and Technology
Mr P.B. Henderson	Mathematics and Science
Mr J. Wainwright	Commercial Subjects
Mrs B. Winters	French

Members of Staff at the time of the opening of the new school in New Bedford Road

* already noted

Dr C.W. Charlesworth MA

Mr M.J. Beadle

Mr R.G. Blacker B.Sc.*

Mr W.E. Bowen BA*

Mrs E.C. Clarke*

Mr T.E. Collins B.Com.*

Miss J.Crombie
  (Mrs Shaddock)

Mr A.G. Cundick B.Sc.

Mr W.E.Davies BA*

Mr C.L.Deavin B.Sc.*

Mr R.H. Ellis BA*

Mr B.D. Everleigh B.Sc.

Mr A.S. Froud*

Mr N.Garside*

Miss M.C. Griffiths BA*

Mr E.J. Gudgin*

Mrs G.Herbert*

Mr T.H. Hewitt AMIEE*

Mr D.E. Hopkins BA*

Mr B.M. Lane BA*

Mr F.H.C. Maggs BA

Mr J.D. Plumb*

Mr J.F. Sanson B.Sc.*

Mr R. Sinfield B.Sc.*

Mr S. Thornton B.Sc.
Mr R.G. Tolley*
Mr R.D. Whalley*
Mrs E. Harding BA*
Mrs J. Rae
Mrs M. Knape BA*
Miss J. Verdcourt
   (Mrs Lawrence)
Mrs E.M. Read

1959–60

Miss A. Higginbotham	English
(Mrs Ord)	
Mr R.H. Barter B.Sc.	Biology
Mr J.A. Davies	Mathematics
Left	
Mr C.W. Baggaley	
Mr J.W. Plumb	
Mrs Herbert	
Mrs Lawrence	
Mrs Shaddock	
Mr S. Thornton	

1961

Mr M. Beadle PE Dip.	PE
Mrs E. Burrows BA	English subjects
Mr A G Cundick B.Sc	Science
Mr K. Dickens	Mathematics and Science
Mrs P.A. Lavis B.Sc.	Science
Mr F.H.C. Maggs BA	History
Miss S. Payling	PE Diploma
Mrs J.J.L. Rae (Sorbonne)	French (part-time)
Mr R.C. Sinfield B.Sc.	Economics, History, Geography
Mrs L. Palmer B.Sc.	
(Teacher exchange – Melbourne)	
W.G. Tolley (on staff from 1943)	
C.L. Deavin	
Mr Pounder B.Sc.	

1962 Shell

Mr D. E. Hopkins BA	Deputy Headmaster
Mr R.H.Barter ARCS	Biology
Mr M. Beadle P.E. Dip.	Physical Education

Mr R.G. Blacker B.Sc. ARIC	Mathematics and Science
Mr W. E. Bowen BA	English
Mrs E. Burrows CGLI	Needlework (part-time)
Mrs E.C. Clarke	Senior Mistress
Mr T.E. Collins B.Com.	Professional Studies
Mr A.G. Cundick B.Sc.	Science
Mr J.A. Davies BA	General subjects
Mr W.E. Davies BA	French
Mr K. Dickens	Mathematics and Science
Mr R.H. Ellis	Geography
Mr B.D. Eveleigh B.Sc	Science
Mr A.S. Froud	English
Nr N. Garside MRSanI AMInstBE	Engineering and Workshop Technology
Miss M.C. Griffiths	English
Mr J.E. Gudgin	Engineering and Workshop Technology
Mrs G.A. Harding BA AKC	French (part-time)
Mr T.H. Hewitt AMIEE	Technical Drawing
Mr I.A. Jones BA	History
Mr J. Kerr BA (Exchange from Melbourne)	English
Mrs M. Knape BA AKC	French (part-time)
Mr B. Lane MA ARCO ABSM	Music
Mrs P. Lavis B.Sc	Science
Mr F.H.C. Maggs BA	History
Mr W. Mecready	Mathematics and Physics
Mr E.J. Morse	Woodwork (part-time)
Miss S. Payling P.E.Dip.	Physical Education
Mr S.J. Poulten	English
Miss J.J.L. Rae (Sorbonne)	French (part-time)
Mr J.F. Sanson B.Sc.	Science
Mr R.C. Sinfield B.Sc.	Economics, Geography, History
Mr C.J.T. Thamotheram B.Sc	Mathematics
Mrs Walker CGLI	Domestic Science (part-time)
Mr R.H. Whalley ACP	Woodwork
Mr C.L. Deavin B.Sc	Mathematics
Mrs Ord BA ALCM	English
Mr W.G. Tolley AMIStructE MRSanI	Religious Instruction and Woodwork

Also mentioned

Miss R.M. Seymour BA	English
Mr A.J. Miller B.Sc.	Science
Mrs Lovelock Dip.Housecraft	Domestic Science

Miss A. Marlow Dip.P.E.	Physical Education
Mr R.W. Rust B.Sc.	Biology
Mr B.J. Foreman BA	
Mr J.M. Leavold Dip.P.E.	Physical Education
Mr K. Dickens	
Mrs Walker	
Miss S. Payling	
Mr R.J. Barter B.Sc.	
Mr J. Davies	
Mr M.J. Beadle	
Mrs Burrows	

Head Boys and Girls

This list is also incomplete.

1947		Lois Counter
1950–51	Donald Sinfield	Alma Eaves
	Keith Nicols	Jane Clark
	John Fountain	Audrey Jeeves
1951–52	Edward Clements	June Lucas
	Michael Wharton	Margaret McKean
		Pat Willey
1953	Frank Griffin	Christine Bullard
	Gordon Mills	Pamela White
		Mary Cheshire
1953–4	G. Mills	Mary Cheshire
	M. Eells	Jennifer Carter
	R. Seabrook	Vivienne Burr
1954–55	Seabrook	Jacqueline Matthews
	McLeod	Ann White
	Hucklesby	Janet Gambriel
1955–56	David Stamford	Janet Gambriel
	Waller	
	Hucklesby	
1956–57	John Brown	Judith Veal
	D. Stamford	Janet Gambriel
1958–59	John Brown	Janet Marsden
1959–60	Philip Holmes	Janet Marsden
1960–1	Robert Squires	Linda Stent
1961–62	Graham Robinson	Marianne Fishenden

Bibliography

Published books

Aldrich R.A. ed. *A Century of Education* Routledge/Falmer (2002)

Barnard H.C. *History of English Education from 1760* University of London Press (1969)

Bryant M. *The Unexpected Revolution* University of London Institute of Education (1979)

Bunker S. Holgate R. and Nichols M. *The Changing Face of Luton* The Book Castle (1993)

Dony J. *A History of Education in Luton* Luton Museum and Art Gallery (1970)

Dyer J. Stygall F. and Dony J. *The Story of Luton* White Crescent Press Ltd (1966)

Dyhouse C. *Girls Growing up in late Victorian and Edwardian England* RKP (1981)

Essays: *North London Collegiate School* Oxford University Press (1950)

Evans K. *The Development and Structure of the English Educational System* Hodder and Stoughton (1975)

The Luton News *Luton at War* Home Counties Newspapers Ltd (1947)

Maclure J.S. *Educational Documents* Methuen (1979)

Simon B. *Studies in the History of Education: 1780–1870 The Two Nations and the Educational Structure*

  1870 – 1920 Education and the Labour Movement (1965)

  1920 – 1940 The Politics of Educational Reform (1978)

Vowles G. *A Century of Achievement: A History of Local Education Authorities in Bedfordshire 1903 – 2003* Bedfordshire County Council (2003)

Wood T. & Bunker S. *A Hatful of Talent* University of Luton Press (1994)

Miscellaneous

Archive material from Denbigh High School, Luton

Articles in local newspapers

Background material from the Library of the London Institute of Education

Dissertations: the late Mrs Iris Bond, Mrs Clarke, the late Mrs Peggy Taylor and Mr R.D. Whalley

Drawings, illustrations and photographs

HMI Reports

Information sent by the North London Collegiate School

Luton Year Books and *Almanacs*

Maps

Material collected by Mr Barry Dymock (Old Students' Association) now held at Luton University

Material collected by Mrs Kathy Green for a Reunion at Denbigh High School (2000)

Papers found at Luton Museum and Art Gallery and at the Bedford and Luton Archive and Record Service including Admission Registers, Education Committee Minutes and Visitors' Books

Reminiscences: I. Jones, W. Rainbow

School Magazines: *The Blue Jacket, The Sheaf, The Shell* and *Technique*

The Bedfordshire Magazine

Luton Technical School

Sheila Allen (née Thripp)
Jeane Bailey (née Bligh)
Mrs Gillian Barham (née Woods)
Moyra Barker (née Skinner)
John Barton
Richard Barton
Donald Clifford Bennett
Barbara Blackburn (née Glenister)
Eileen D. Bonner (née Brandham)
Cynthia Booth (née Charlesworth)
Elizabeth Briggs (née Hey)
Roy & Hilary Brown
    (née Whitham)
Jean Bullimore (née Clemitson)
Marilyn Burrows (née Jones)
Gulielma Butcher (née Lawrence)
Madge Cheesbrough
    (née Brightman)
Daphne Cheveralls (née Little)
Alan & Enid Clifton
    (née Coleman)
Mavis (Mimi) Coe
Elizabeth Collins (née Christie)
Ann Crooke (née Waugh)
Ann Cruttenden (née Rymell)
Margaret Currie (née Lodge)
Judy Darby
Mary H. Dawson (née Nicholas)
Jose Dobing (née Denton)
Joan Don (née Middleton)
Mary Eddy (née Baker)
Philip Eden
Rita Farr (née Durrant)
Mary Fearn (née Walters)
Paddie Fleet (née Tregaskiss)
Margaret Folkes (née Field)
Wendy Foster (née Houlston)
Gillian Gain (née Odam)
Patricia D. Gillespie (née Evans)
Enid B. Godwin
Gina Gosling (née Watson)
Rosemary Grant (née Godfrey)
Catherine Gravelle (née Irons)
Thelma Gregory (née Murden)
Gwendoline D. Gribble
Gillian E. Harris
Mary Kirk Harrison
Priscilla Hart (née Ireland)
Julie Hawes (née Bray)
Audrey E. Hawkins
    (née Sare-Soar)
Shirley Hawkins (née Grubb)

Sheila Dawn Hawtin
    (née Baynham)
Maureen Hillman (née Cook)
Patricia Hinds
Shirley Hobbs (née Thompson)
Ann Holes (née Evans)
Christine Holland (née Sanderson)
Pauline Holmes (née Wilkinson)
Lila Horne (née Horn)
Betty Summerfield Horniblew
    (née Holland)
Colin Humphreys
Margaret Inns (née Grubb)
Peter Isherwood
Beryl Jarvis (née Horton)
Anne Jenkins
Vi Jennings (née Wrycroft)
Jean M. Johns (née Godfrey)
Ivan Jones (staff)
Professor Shirley R. Jones
    (née Phillips)
Jan Joyner (née Saunders)
Shirley Joyner (née Stringer)
Pauline Keen (née Moore)
Janet C. Kempson (née Patrick)
David Kennett
Monica Lacey (née Tofield)
Christine Lesniak (née Robinson)
Agnes Lewin (née Murchie)
Rita Lewis (née Jeakings)
Janet Lowden (McKenzie)
Sheila Marsden (née Willmott)
Mary M. McDonald (née Childs)
Betty McKean (née Hickman)
Pauline McKenzie (née Wilson)
Judith Merrick (née Vass)
Jennifer Moody, MBE
    (née Southgate)
Guy Jeffrey Morgan
Peter & Patricia Morgan
    (née Charlesworth)
Zena Louise Morgan
Joy Munnerley (née Birdsall)
Gillian Newns (née Anslow)
Frances Norman (née Robson)
Margaret Nye (née McKean)
Stan & Sylvia O'Flynn (née Hyde)
Rhoda Patterson (née Kingham)
Julie Pearce (née Kempson)
Christine Pell (née Reed)
Katherine Piper (née Moore)
Joyce Barbara Potter (née Smart)

Maureen Powell (née Indge)
Mrs Moyra Preece
Beryl Prentice (née Coe)
Marilyn Price (née Short)
Wally Rainbow
Margaret Randall (née Lewis)
Janet Richardson (née Aynsley)
Phyllis Ride
Edna Rippengale (née Waller)
Sylvia Robinson (née Bowker)
Margaret Rowley (née Marsom)
Julie Rushton (née Tiplady)
Mollie Russell (née Tullett)
Ethel Sarrington (née Roe)
Dora Scott (née Offer)
Sally Siddons (née Overhill)
Elizabeth Sieling (née Vass)
Anne Simkins
    (née Kathleen Thursby)
Christine Dyer Simpson
    (née Lewis)
June E. Sinfield (née Gladman)
Joy Singer (née Tear)
Pat Skeggs (née Marsom)
Don & Margaret Smith
    (née Heddon)
Gail Smith (née Parsons)
Joan Smith (née Kidd) (staff)
Stella M. Smith (née Mills)
Janet Stevens
Janet M.J. Stow (née Sewell)
Mora Sutherland
Sheena Thomasson (née Mann)
Diana Thomson
Brenda Tiley (née Owen)
Betty P. Tompkins (née Brandon)
Joy Tompkins (née Simms)
Janet Troisvallets (née Sterling)
Christine Turner
Alan Tweedie
Claudia Ward (née Davies)
David Webb, RADA. Dip
A. D. Whalley (née Cole)
Margaret Wild (née Wilkins)
Catherine Windle (née McFarlane)
Mary Woods
Josephine Wrighton (née Figgins)
Gillian P. Yuill (née Chapple)

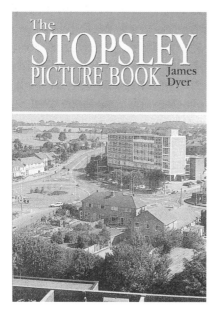

THE STOPSLEY BOOK
THE STOPSLEY PICTURE BOOK

James Dyer

The hamlet of Stopsley, two miles from Luton in Bedfordshire, has a history that stretches back some 300,000 years. Situated in a region initially dependent on agriculture, straw plaiting and brick making, it can be seen as a microcosm of life in almost any village on the northern edge of the Chiltern Hills.

The Stopsley Book tells the story of 20 farms, 16 schools and 4 churches within the civil parish which stretched from Someries Castle in the south to Galley Hill and the Icknield Way in the north. It looks in detail at almost every aspect of village life, particularly in the 19th and 20th centuries, and includes the work of the Parish Council, the weather, water and gas supplies, health care, policing, farm work, brick making and a wide variety of leisure pursuits. Based on thirty years of extensive search and interviews with local people, many now deceased; it is an exhaustive account of a community that still prides itself on its village spirit and individuality.

It includes a collection of 146 photographs, many of which have not been published before.

The Stopsley Book aroused such a great deal of interest in Britain and abroad that a number of readers submitted archive photographs of Stopsley and its surrounding area to the author. These are included in *The Stopsley Picture Book*, which contains 150 photographs and carefully researched captions, to supplement the original work.

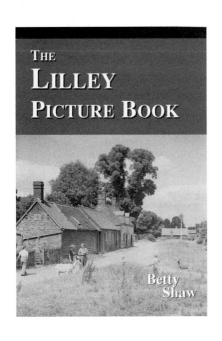

THE LILLEY PICTURE BOOK

Betty Shaw

For some years pictures of the old village of Lilley in Hertfordshire have formed a popular feature at the Flower Festivals held each May in St.Peter's Church. Though some photos date back to the late nineteenth century, this book mainly focuses on activities in the village during the twentieth century. During that time the Church, and the Sowerby family as Lords of the manor, largely dominated village life and most of the populace were engaged in agriculture-related activities. By the latter half of the century, with little new housing development and rising property prices, many of the younger people moved away, leading indirectly to the closure of the village school and numerous small shops. New financially enhanced families moved into some of the cottages, renovating and improving them. In the closing years of the century the Sowerby family sold the Manor and left Lilley. Today, whilst many of the children are bussed to nearby schools, the adult population make their living by commuting to neighbouring towns or travelling to London and the wider world beyond. Farming, once the mainstay of the village life, is now highly mechanised and depends largely on occasional contract labour. At the beginning of the new century, whilst to the eyes of visitors it remains an attractive rural haven, frequented by ramblers and sightseers, it is still a living village with a church, two popular public houses and many activities in its recently modernised village hall.

The author, Betty Shaw, was educated at Luton High School for Girls.

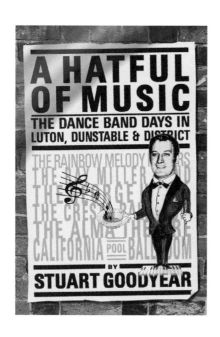

A HATFUL OF MUSIC
The Dance Band Days in Luton, Dunstable & District

Stuart Goodyear

In 1939 Lutonian Stuart Goodyear was born into a musical household, whose father, also Stuart, encouraged him to embrace his love of music.

As a millennium project, Stuart was asked by the Luton Historical Society to write a page or two about the local "dance band days" of the last century, and drawing on his own involvement as novice pianist through to bandleader, was happy to undertake the challenge.

Starting in a modest way in the 1950s with fellow airport apprentices, his first band The Rainbow Melody Makers, rapidly became a larger and more polished dance band, and was subsequently renamed The Ray Miller Band. Remaining as leader of the band through to the 1980s, he became well connected with the local musical establishment, and has comprehensively collated his experiences during that time, although it soon became apparent that the finished article would be a book, rather than a dossier.

In a most fascinating personal and wider-ranging survey of musical days gone by in Luton, Dunstable and the surrounding area, Stuart has compiled a detailed impression of how he remembered the busy dance scene, and the many brilliant musicians who contributed to a period of live musical entertainment that will never return.

Deliberating over a title, he shortlisted "Batons and Bows" and "You've gotta lot to learn my boy", but thinks that a "Hatful of Music" just about strikes the right chord. The book contains over 300 photos of events covered over the years. People born and bred in Luton will be pouring over the nostalgia for weeks to come.

WERE YOU BEING SERVED?
Remembering 50 Luton Shops of Yesteryear

Bob Norman

The "nation of shopkeepers" has entered a new era. Our high streets have become impersonal, filled with efficient but bland chain-stores. Gone are the days of the privately-owned stores and shops, when personal service was paramount. Gone but, as far as Luton is concerned, and thanks to this book, not forgotten.

Bob Norman one of their number himself, knew many of those retailers personally. In retirement, he has supplemented his own memories by talking to past employees and family descendants of the original entrepreneurs.

So here are the stories of the traditional chemist, barber, baker, butcher, tobacconist, garage, clothier, jeweller and dozens of other specialists who really knew their trade inside out … and their customers too. A tribute to 50 of Luton's best businesses of yesteryear, profusely illustrated with private and archive photographs, almost all previously unpublished.

The author, Bob Norman was educated at Luton Grammar School.

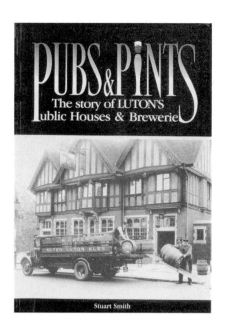

PUBS AND PINTS
The story of Luton's Public Houses and Breweries

Stuart Smith

Whilst the town of Luton is well documented in other ways, this book is the first comprehensive history of its important brewing industry and retail beer outlets – linked, staple trades in the area for over five hundred years.

The development of the modern public house from the early taverns and coaching inns closely followed that of the breweries, with the final decades of the last century seen as the high point in the number of houses licensed to sell beers for consumption on or off the premises. Since then the total has declined with the loss of around 40% during the last one hundred years, most of these losses occurring in the period from 1950 to 1970.

Although documentation dealing with the early breweries and public houses is extremely sparse, it is the intention of this book to try and record the history of each brewery and public house that has had its bearing on the social and drinking pastimes of Lutonians over the last one hundred and fifty years. A special feature of this book is the vast range of three hundred photographs – many old, rare and unusual.

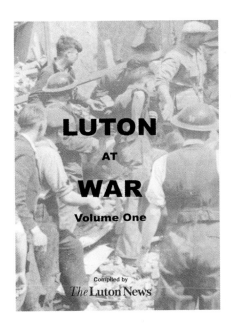

LUTON AT WAR
Volume One & Volume Two

Initially published by the Luton News in 1947, the story of how the people of Luton withstood the dark years of war between 1939 and 1945.

Luton and its population have changed so dramatically in the years since the war that now only a few will recall how the town stood up to the trauma of those war years.

Because of strict war-time censorship much of what occurred during those years was not mentioned in The Luton News. Once the war was over however, The Luton News set about the mammoth task of presenting a complete and vivid picture of war-time life. It tells of the long anxious nights, the joy and the sorrow that made even the most terrifying moments bearable thanks to the tremendous way in which the people joined to help each other.

Written and compiled by the staff of The Luton News at the time, it contains the most comprehensive and fascinating pictorial record. As well as being a moving personal account it is also a unique historical document.

This large format paperback is published in two parts.

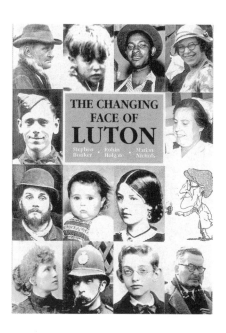

THE CHANGING FACE OF LUTON

Stephen Bunker, Robin Holgate & Marian Nichols

The Changing Face of Luton traces the fortunes of the settlement and economy of the town from the earliest recorded arrival of people in the area to the present day. It looks at different aspects of Luton and its development rather than giving a straight chronological account of its history.

Luton's roots go back a very long way, yet in less than 200 years it has changed from a small market town to today's busy industrial and commercial centre. This transformation is described, helped by a range of excellent photographs, thereby answering many of the questions frequently asked, and perhaps raising more, about this intriguing town.

The three authors from Luton Museum are all experts in local history, archaeology and industry.

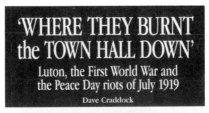

"WHERE THEY BURNT THE TOWN HALL DOWN"
Luton, The First World War and the Peace Day riots of July 1919

Dave Craddock

The weekend of 19/20th July 1919 was arguably the most momentous in the history of Luton. What began as an afternoon of peace celebrations marking the end of the Great War turned into riots that had by the Sunday morning left the Town hall a smouldering, gutted ruin with the military in control of the town. Yet over the years, the story of the riots has been largely neglected.

Drawing broadly on contemporary documents, witness statements and newspaper reports, the book gives a blow-by-blow account of the riots, their aftermath and subsequent trials. The hostility between the Town Council and ex-servicemen's organisations in the preceding months is also covered extensively, as is the impact of the First World War on Luton.

Features of this book include informative appendices containing a wealth of information and over 50 illustrations.

LEGACIES
Tales and Legends of Luton and the North Chilterns

Vic Lea

Vic Lea spent most of his lifetime researching and collecting famous and infamous historical tales of Bedfordshire and Hertfordshire. Following his best selling book, Echoes, here is a further choice of fascinating gleanings from his archives.

Recounted compulsively as only he could, Legacies offers twenty-five gripping sagas of yesteryear... bravery, murder, sport, riot, achievement, disaster, superstition, crime, devilry, transport, danger, intrigue... and many more such dramatic ingredients in an irresistible anthology of legacies from the past.

BARKING MAD

Danae Johnston

Every dog lover between nine and ninety will enjoy following the exploits of Tom and Gill, two delinquent poodles. On their retirement, despite the risk to their prize-winning garden and resident cats, Danae and David rashly take on these canine comedians, their first dogs!

So naïve that they did not know how big the puppies would get, or even that they would need to be clipped at six weekly intervals, the pensioners were to learn everything the hard way – how to deal with scrape after scrape. When Tom jumped the garden fence and returned with one of the neighbours' chickens, for instance! When the dogs herded a flock of sheep into a pond on Christmas Day, or paid an unscheduled visit to a retirement home, or stole the cream from the Jersey milk as it cooled in a bucket on the farmer's kitchen floor, or chased a wallaby at Whipsnade Wild Animal Park – the mischievious adventures go on and on.

Author Danae is a Lutonian, and many of the dogs' exploits are in and around Bedfordshire. Her humorous cartoons and original pithy style make this book a must for all dog lovers. She is also a talented gardener and her garden "Seal Point" has appeared in magazines and on T.V. many times, the most notable being in 1999 when she won the title "B.B.C. Gardener of the Year for the East and South East of England." Many famous gardeners have been to her garden. Geoff Hamilton, back in 1986, Gay Search in 1998, and of course during the recent competition Adam Pasco, Nigel Colborn and Ali Ward as the judges, plus Charlie Dimmock and Alan Titchmarsh, who masterminded the whole show, were around. At certain times her garden is also open to the public to view for charity. And throughout Tom and Gill were never far away!

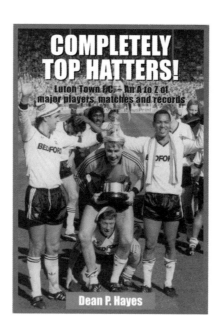

COMPLETELY TOP HATTERS
Luton Town F.C. – An A to Z of major players, matches and records

Dean P. Hayes

Packed full of information on players, managers, outstanding games, glorious and inglorious times, this is the essential guide for all Hatters fans.

Dean Hayes has compiled this encyclopaedia of Luton Town Football Club for all to enjoy. From abandoned matches to the Zenith Data Cup, from the biggest victory to the worst defeat, everything is included. Players' profiles include Joe Payne, Syd Owen, Bob Morton, Billy Bingham, Allan Brown, Bruce Rioch, Malcolm MacDonald, Ricky Hill and Brian Stein to name only a few.

The book includes statistics of major honours, championships, FA Cup performances, greatest number of appearances in a Luton shirt and much, much more.

"Completely Top Hatters – Luton Town F.C. – An A to Z" is a book for every Hatters fan and with its easy alphabetical system, a wealth of Luton Town facts are available in an instant.

The
Book
Castle

DUNSTABLE SCHOOL
1888-1971

F.M. Bancroft

" It was not one of the leading schools in the country…But it was a grammar school, a good grammar school, and it gave a sound all round education aligned with sporting activities of note. It taught courtesy, politeness and the home truths of life. And because of the masters over the years and a lot of the boys who went there it was a character school, with a happy atmosphere."

So, for all these reasons along with their own personal memories, though the school was superseded over a generation ago thousands of Old Boys still remember it with deep affection and gratitude.

THE HISTORY OF

The 1887 story of the town

W.H. Derbyshire M.A.

This is the third in the Book Castle series of reprints of fascinating old books about Dunstable, all published as collector's editions in handsome bindings, with a new preface by John Buckledee, the present editor of The Dunstable Gazette.

This book was first published in 1872 with an expanded volume in 1882. The formidable William Derbyshire was the editor of the town's first newspaper and became the borough's Mayor in 1879. His book has the authority of a man who was at the heart of town affairs for more than 50 years during a time of considerable expansion and change.

The other two books in reprinted as facsimiles are Dunno's Originals and Dunstaplelogia.

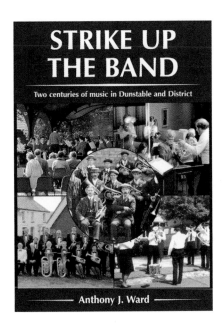

STRIKE UP THE BAND
Two centuries of music in Dunstable and District

Anthony J. Ward

In 'Strike Up The Band', the author traces the history of music-making in Dunstable and District from the earliest times where information is available, up to the present day. It is derived from a wider ongoing project by the author.

The book particularly emphasises the history and development of Brass Bands, Orchestras and other groups, recording their contributions to the changing life of the Town and District, and highlighting the various celebrations that have taken place over so many years. The book closes with a series of chapters on the three local Senior Schools in Dunstable with their bands, orchestras and music.

The design of the book is largely based on a collection of photographs and memorabilia, derived from the wide number of contributors having connections with the organisations featured in the book, featuring their recollections of events and personalities. The story of music-making in Dunstable and its surrounding villages is shown in the context of the history of the area and its citizens.

CHANGES IN OUR LANDSCAPE
Aspects of Bedfordshire, Buckinghamshire and the Chilterns 1947–1992

Eric Meadows

In the post-War years, this once quiet rural backwater between Oxford and Cambridge has undergone growth and change – and the expert camera of Eric Meadows has captured it all . . .

An enormous variety of landscape, natural and man-made, from yesteryear and today – open downs and rolling farmland, woods and commons, ancient earthworks, lakes and moats, vanished elms. Quarries, nature reserves and landscape gardens. Many building styles – churches of all periods, stately homes and town dwellings, rural pubs, gatehouses and bridges. Secluded villages contrast their timeless lifestyle with the bustle of modern developing towns and their industries.

Distilled from a huge collection of 25,000 photographs, this book offers the author's personal selection of over 350 that best display the area's most attractive features and its notable changes over 50 years. The author's detailed captions and notes complete a valuable local history. The original hardback edition was in print for only 4 weeks in 1992. By popular demand now in a large format paperback.

JOURNEYS INTO BEDFORDSHIRE

JOURNEYS INTO HERTFORDSHIRE

Anthony Mackay

These two books of ink drawings reveal an intriguing historic heritage and capture the spirit of England's rural heartland, ranging widely over cottages and stately homes, over bridges, churches and mills, over sandy woods, chalk downs and watery river valleys.

Every corner of Bedfordshire and Hertfordshire has been explored in the search for material, and, although the choice of subjects is essentially a personal one, the resulting collection represents a unique record of the environment today.

The notes and maps, which accompany the drawings, lend depth to the books, and will assist others on their own journeys around the counties.

Anthony Mackay's pen-and-ink drawings are of outstanding quality. An architectural graduate, he is equally at home depicting landscapes and buildings. The medium he uses is better able to show both depth and detail than any photograph.

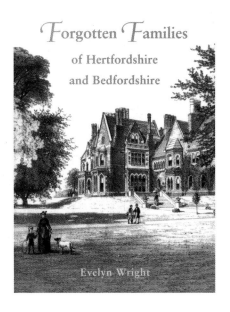

FORGOTTEN FAMILIES
of Hertfordshire and Bedfordshire

Evelyn Wright

This book tells the story of families once famous but whose fame is now mainly forgotten. They all lived in Hertfordshire and Bedfordshire in the 16th and 17th centuries, and include the Bechers of Renhold (of Becher's Brook fame), the Mordaunts of Turvey Abbey, Lady Cathcart of Tewin, the Bull family of Hertford, the Nodes family of Stevenage, the Docuras of Lilley and the Wicked Lady of Markyate Cell. All the families were related to each other, forming an intricate network over two counties: Hertfordshire and Bedfordshire. The author is one of their 20th century descendants. The book includes pedigrees showing the relationship between various families, and illustrations of many of the manor houses and mansions in which they lived.

Evelyn Wright was born in the village of Wingfield in Suffolk, and moved to Bedfordshire soon after her marriage in 1952. During a busy life bringing up five children, running a Nursery School and looking after elderly parents, she has always found time for writing. Evelyn is married to John Wright, a Chartered Surveyor, and they live in Aspley Heath in Bedfordshire.

EXPLORING HISTORY ALL AROUND

Vivienne Evans

A handbook of local history, arranged as a series of routes to cover Bedfordshire and adjoining parts of Hertfordshire and Buckinghamshire. It is organised as two books in one. There are seven thematic sections full of fascinating historical detail and anecdotes for armchair reading. Also it is a perfect source of family days out as the book is organised as circular motoring/cycling explorations, highlighting attractions and landmarks. Also included is a background history to all the major towns in the area, plus dozens of villages, which will enhance your appreciation and understanding of the history that is all around you!

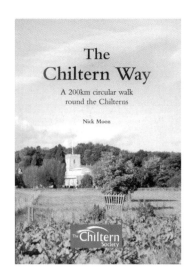

THE CHILTERN WAY
A 200km circular walk round the Chilterns

Nick Moon

This book is a guide to the original circular long distance path through Bedfordshire, Buckinghamshire, Hertfordshire & Oxfordshire.

The Chiltern Way was established by the Chiltern Society to mark the Millennium by providing walkers in the twenty-first century with a new way of exploring the diverse, beautiful countryside which all four Chiltern counties have to offer. Based on the idea of the late Jimmy Parson's Chiltern Hundred but expanded to cover the whole Chilterns, the route has been designed by the author and has been signposted, waymarked and improved by the Society's Rights of Way Group.

In addition to a description of the route and points of interest along the way, this guide includes 29 specially drawn maps of the route indicating local pubs, car parks, railway stations and a skeleton road network and details are provided of the Ordnance Survey and Chiltern Society maps covering the route.

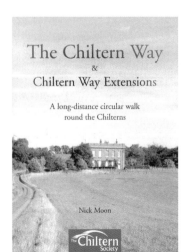

THE CHILTERN WAY
& CHILTERN WAY EXTENSIONS
A long-distance circular walk
round the Chilterns

Nick Moon

This is the new complete official guide to the now extended circular long-distance path through Bedfordshire, Buckinghamshire, Hertfordshire and Oxfordshire, whereby the society has responded to demand by incorporating further mileage both to the north and to the south of the original route.

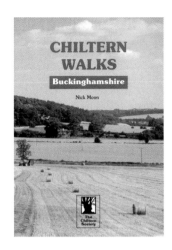 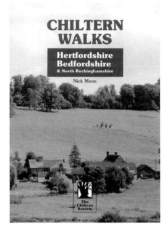 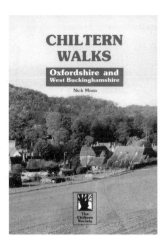

CHILTERN WALKS
Hertfordshire, Bedfordshire and North Buckinghamshire

CHILTERN WALKS
Buckinghamshire

CHILTERN WALKS
Oxfordshire and West Buckinghamshire

Nick Moon

A series of three books providing a comprehensive coverage of walks throughout the whole of the Chiltern area (as defined by the Chiltern Society). The walks included vary in length from 3.0 to 10.9 miles, but are mainly in the 5–7 mile range popular for half-day walks, although suggestions of possible combinations of walks are given for those preferring a full day's walk.

Each walk gives details of nearby places of interest and is accompanied by a specially drawn map of the route which also indicates local pubs and a skeleton road network.

THE CHILTERN AREA'S LEADING SERIES OF MAPS FOR WALKERS
by Nick Moon

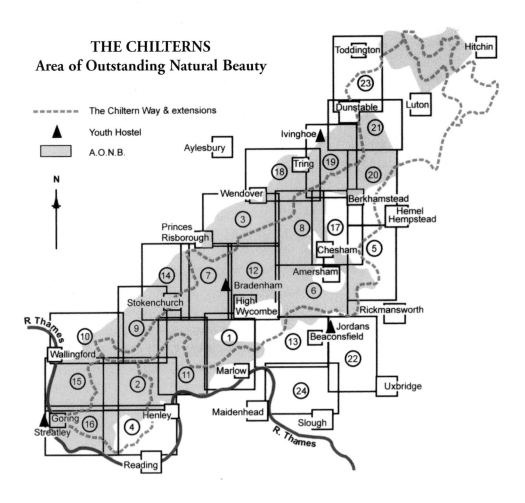

This expanding series of currently 24 maps at a scale of 2½ inches to the mile depicts footpaths, bridleways and other routes available to walkers, riders and cyclists across the Chilterns, as well as pubs, railway stations, car parking facilities and other features of interest. Several suggested walks also appear on the back of each map. New titles appear regularly and will soon extend coverage from the Thames in the south to Hitchin in the north.

COMPLETE LIST OF CHILTERN SOCIETY FOOTPATH MAPS

1. High Wycombe & Marlow
2. Henley & Nettlebed
3. Wendover & Princes Risborough
4. Henley & Caversham
5. Sarratt & Chipperfield
6. Amersham & Penn Country
7. West Wycombe & Princes Risborough
8. Chartridge & Cholesbury
9. The Oxfordshire Escarpment
10. Wallingford & Watlington
11. The Hambleden Valley
12. Hughenden Valley & Gt.Missenden
13. Beaconsfield & District

14. Stokenchurch & Chinnor
15. Crowmarsh & Nuffield
16. Goring & Mapledurham
17. Chesham & Berkhamsted
18. Tring & Wendover
19. Ivinghoe & Ashridge
20. Hemel Hempstead & the Gade Valley
21. Dunstable Downs & Caddington
22. Gerrards Cross & Chalfont St.Peter
23. Toddington & Houghton Regis
24. Burnham Beeches and Stoke Poges

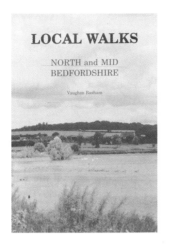
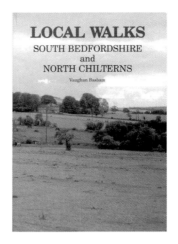

LOCAL WALKS NORTH AND MID-BEDFORDSHIRE

LOCAL WALKS SOUTH BEDFORDSHIRE AND NORTH CHILTERNS

Vaughan Basham

A series of two comprehensive books of circular walks in this lovely rural area.

Walking in the countryside is always enjoyable, but, with these books as his companion, the rambler will also be led to many interesting discoveries. An appropriate theme has been selected for every walk, and a stimulating introductory article sets the scene.

Full practical route information and comments are also provided, plus specially drawn maps.

An appendix of further walking areas includes the author's suggestions for two new long-distance circular walks.

The author, Vaughan Basham, lived in and explored the area all his life. His keen interest in social history led to a continuing involvement in heritage affairs, conservation projects, local organisations and charities. Scouting and the Outward Bound schools were influential in his love of the countryside and, together with his wife Una, he had always been an enthusiastic rambler.